THE *Maciste* FILMS

OF ITALIAN SILENT CINEMA

With an appendix by

CLAUDIA GIANETTO (Head of Film Archive)
&
STELLA DAGNA (Film Archivist)

Museo Nazionale del Cinema, Turin, Italy

INDIANA UNIVERSITY PRESS

Bloomington & Indianapolis

THE *Maciste* FILMS

OF ITALIAN SILENT CINEMA

JACQUELINE REICH

This book is a publication of

INDIANA UNIVERSITY PRESS
Office of Scholarly Publishing
Herman B Wells Library 350
1320 East 10th Street
Bloomington, Indiana 47405 USA

iupress.indiana.edu

The paper used in this publication
meets the minimum requirements of
the American National Standard for
Information Sciences – Permanence of
Paper for Printed Library Materials,
ANSI Z39.48–1992.

*Manufactured in the
United States of America*

*Library of Congress
Cataloging-in-Publication Data*

Reich, Jacqueline, 1965–
  The Maciste films of Italian silent
cinema / Jacqueline Reich ; with an
appendix by Claudia Gianetto (head
of film archive) and Stella Dagna
(film archivist), Cineteca del Museo
Nazionale del Cinema, Turin, Italy.
  pages cm
  Includes bibliographical
references and index.
  ISBN 978-0-253-01745-1 (pb : alk.
paper) – ISBN 978-0-253-01740-6 (cl : alk.
paper) – ISBN 978-0-253-01748-2 (eb)
1. Motion pictures – Italy – History – 20th
century. 2. Masculinity in motion
pictures. 3. Motion pictures – Political
aspects – Italy. 4. Pagano,
Bartolomeo, 1878–1947 – Criticism
and interpretation. I. Title.
  PN1993.5.I88R435 2015
  791.430945'0904 – dc23

                                  2015005278

1 2 3 4 5   20 19 18 17 16 15

To

SEAN DE GANON *&* TIMOTHY DE GANON

my gentle giants

Contents

*Appendix by Claudia Gianetto and Stella
Dagna, translated by Maria Elena D'Amelio*

Illustrations follow page 224.

Acknowledgments

IN FEDERICO FELLINI'S *LA CITTÀ DELLE DONNE* (CITY OF WOMEN, 1980), a group of young boys lie in an enormous bed with billowing white sheets, watching images flicker on a large movie screen above them. The click of the movie projector mixes with the ominous soundtrack accompanying the black-and-white image of a silent film. The first image on screen is an image of hell, with flames shooting up from the ground and scantily clad women guarding their queen on the throne. The queen, whose piercing, heavily lined eyes and naked thighs appear in close-up, stares directly into the camera as the boys in bed return the gaze, open-mouthed, with their hands strategically placed under the covers. The shot is the first in a montage of imaginary yet vaguely familiar female actresses, from Greta Garbo to Mae West to Marlene Dietrich, all subjects of the boys', and by proxy Fellini's, sexual imagination. In the screenplay published upon the film's release, the director attributed that initial image to his first memory of film, *Maciste all'inferno* (Maciste in Hell, Guido Brignone, FERT-Pittaluga, 1925, released in 1926), a film that Fellini repeatedly cited as one of the strongest influences on his directorial oeuvre.

Little did I know when I was writing my first book that Marcello Mastroianni and Fellini would lead me to the Italian strongman Maciste and the brand-new world, for me at least, of stardom and silent film. Once I began that research, however, I found myself in uncharted waters, and many colleagues, institutions, friends, and family members provided me with the support, guidance, and courage to brave and ultimately complete the journey.

I have received financial support from several institutions over this project's long gestation. The FAHSS Research and Interdisciplinary Initiatives Fund at Stony Brook University provided the initial seed money for archival research and travel to conferences, and the generous publication subvention I received from the dean of the College of Arts and Sciences, Dr. Nancy Squires, went a long way to help bring Maciste to life in color in these pages. A mid-career fellowship from the George A. and Eliza Gardner Howard Foundation, combined with a sabbatical from Stony Brook, gave me time off to put words on the page. The Office of Research at Fordham University provided additional monetary support for translations and bibliographic help as well as indexing. Dean John Harrington and Dean Eva Badowska also deserve special mention for guiding me through the bureaucratic maze of research funding at Fordham.

This project never would have been possible without my collaboration with the Museo Nazionale del Cinema in Turin, Italy, an institution that has embraced me and my work in ways I never imagined. Their restoration and promotion of Italian silent film culture, and encouraging public access to it, is a model to which all similar institutions should aspire. Alberto Barbera and Donata Pesenti Campagnoni generously granted me the status of official collaborator, allowing me access to a wealth of material of which a scholar can usually only dream. At the museum's library, archive and cinématèque, I owe an enormous amount of gratitude to Claudia Gianetto, Antonella Angelini, Carla Ceresa, Silvio Alovisio, Stella Dagna, Marco Grifo, Mauro Genovese, Andreina Sarale, Stefania Carta, Anna Sperone, Roberta Cocon, and Fabio Prezzetti-Tognon. Nicoletta Pacini and Roberta Basano efficiently coordinated and fulfilled my multiple image requests. I hope this book can do justice to the incredible work that they, along with the Cineteca di Bologna and the L'Immagine Ritrovata laboratory in Bologna, have done in beautifully restoring these films and bringing them to an increasingly appreciative public. I wish to thank Gian Luca Farinelli, from the Fondazione Cineteca di Bologna, and Davide Pozzi, director of the L'Immagine Ritrovata laboratory, for their tremendous work.

Other colleagues and institutions in Italy offered their collections to me as well as their expertise: the Mediateca Regionale Toscana, the

Biblioteca Civica Centrale di Torino, and the Archivio Storico della Città di Torino are just a few. At the Cineteca di Bologna, Luigi Virgolin and Alessandra Bani of the Fondo Martinelli gave me access to the late Vittorio Martinelli's copious collection of extra-cinematic materials. Giulia Carluccio and Silvio Alovisio of the Università di Torino welcomed me with open arms whenever I was in town, and Giaime Alonge guided me through the morass of Italian cinema and World War I on both sides of the Atlantic. I would also like to thank Monica Dall'Asta, Cristina Jandelli, Francesco Pitassio, Mariagrazia Franchi, Silvia Margaria, Giuliana Muscio, Peppino Ortoleva, and the late Alberto Friedemann for their help and their inspiration. Denis Lotti generously shared his research on Maciste with me, and this book owes a great deal to what he has uncovered and discovered, as it does to Pierluigi Ercole, who provided unique materials on the Maciste films as they circulated in Great Britain.

This book is more than just my labor of love; it belongs in many ways to the greatest Maciste fans of all, Claudia Gianetto and Stella Dagna of the Museo Nazionale del Cinema. I first met them in late June 2007, and we have since become single-minded in our mission to do justice to the Maciste series as a cultural artifact and product of the modern restoration process. While they have contributed the appendix materials to this volume, their imprint and impact is felt throughout the book, and I am exceedingly grateful for their help, their generosity, and their friendship. A special thanks to their families, Margherita and Francesca Elia and Enrico Tomasini, for their warmth and hospitality during my stays in Turin and Milan.

In the United States I have done research at the New York Library for the Performing Arts and the university libraries of the University of Michigan–Ann Arbor, Columbia University, Stony Brook, and Fordham. The interlibrary loan departments of the latter two deserve extra thanks for their search for sources and their patience in my often late returns. A very special thanks goes to Giorgio Bertellini and the "Fondo Bertellini," one of the few resource facilities that comes with its own personal barista. Beyond the citation of his personal collection of books, articles, and primary sources, this book bears his influence and imprint on almost every page, and I owe him a tremendous debt of gratitude for helping me successfully achieve this goal and many others in my life.

Other colleagues to whom I am indebted include Richard Abel, Aaron Baker, Jennifer Bean, Ivo Blom, Peter Bondanella, Steven Botterill, the late Peter Brunette, David Forgacs, Stephen Gundle, Barbara Hodgdon, Elizabeth Leake, William Luhr, Ernest Ialongo, Gaylyn Studlar, Matthew Solomon, and John P. Welle.

Giancarlo Lombardi, Ruth Ben-Ghiat, and especially Ellen Nerenberg, my writing partners in crime, were the ideal sounding board and drinking partners at all stages of this manuscript. First Jane Behnken and now Raina Polivka of Indiana University Press have been the ideal acquisition editors, and we still have great things to accomplish together. Outside readers and manuscript reviewers shaped this project only for the better; the copyeditor, Jill R. Hughes, my indexer Silvia Benvenuto, and all of the production staff at Indiana, especially David Miller, deserve incredible thanks for making this book what it is. Many of the primary sources on the Maciste films appeared in other languages, and I thank Helène Volat and Myriam Galli for their assistance on French and Maria Elena D'Amelio, Giorgio Bertellini, and Giancarlo Lombardi for their expertise in their own *madre lingua,* although ultimately I take full responsibility for any mistranslations that might have occurred. Elena D'Amelio provided the translations for the appendix, filmography, and "In Focus" sections at the end of the manuscript (as well as the bibliography), and working with her has been one of the great pleasures I have had along this voyage. My four undergraduate researcher assistants at Stony Brook – Emily Fedele, Alex Mignone, Jeremy Schara, and especially Elizabeth Yoo – contributed scholarly rigor to the manuscript. Nicholas Lowry of Swann Auction Galleries in New York was a tremendous help in poster identification.

My ideas have been shaped by the many exciting opportunities I had to present my research in Italy and the United States, and I'd like to thank the organizers and participants of the 2007 and 2010 Society for Cinema and Media Studies conferences, the Dante Seminar in Manhattan College (Rocco Marinaccio in particular) in March 2009, and Texas A&M University's symposium on European cinema in April 2009; the graduate students in my 2010 research seminar; the Stony Brook departmental colloquia; the Italian Studies department at the University of California, Berkeley, my alma mater; the 2010 and 2012 American Association for Italian Studies; and the 2007 Cult of Mussolini workshop at the University of Reading/Royal Holloway; the 2013 Interdisciplinary Italy seminar at New York University; and the 2014 Columbia University Seminar on Modern Italian Studies. Three published works have appeared based on preliminary research on this topic: "Slave to Master: The Racial Metamorphosis of Maciste in Italian Silent Cinema," *Film History* 25, no. 3 (2013): 32–56; "Italian Cinema of the 1920s," in *Italian Silent Cinema,* ed. Giorgio Bertellini (John Libbey, 2013), 135–142; and "Slave to Fashion: Masculinity, Suits, and the Maciste Films of Italian Silent Cinema," in *Fashion in Film,* ed. Adrienne Munich (Indiana University Press, 2011), 236–259.

This project's final year saw me transition from Stony Brook to Fordham University, and people at both institutions played fundamental roles in various stages of the project. At Stony Brook I'd like to extend my personal gratitude to Adrienne Munich, E. Ann Kaplan, Patrice Nganang, Raiford Guins, E. K. Tan, Izabela Kalinowska-Blackwood, Michael Kimmel, Lori Repetti, Sandy Petrey, and Jeremy Marchese. As chair of the Department of Comparative Literary and Cultural Studies and then the Department of Cultural Analysis and Theory, Robert Harvey deserves special mention for all his support over the years. Alinda Askew provided much clerical support and great female solidarity; Mary-Moran Luba offered countless hours of labor and laughter. The irrepressible Krin Gabbard was more than just a colleague: he has read almost everything I have written almost all the way through, to paraphrase Martin Short's character in *The Big Picture,* and has been a mentor inside and outside academia. I am blessed to have him and his wife, Paula, my shopping partner in crime in Pordenone, in my life. My graduate students, who probably know way more about Maciste than they had ever dreamed, were excellent sounding boards, and I am very proud of their success. I extend a special thank-you to Maria Elena D'Amelio, Michael High, Lunpeng Ma, Hans Staats, Beth Tsai, Laine Nooney, and Sean Springer.

At Fordham my new colleagues in the Department of Communication and Media Studies have welcomed me and embraced me. I thank them for taking the last steps of this journey with me and look forward to our many future accomplishments together. Outside the department I'd like to thank the university provost, Stephen Freedman; Associate Vice President Jonathan Crystal; J. Patrick Hornbeck; Glenn Hendler; Kirsten Swinth; and deans John Harrington, Eva Badowska, Michael

Latham, Isabelle Frank, and Robert Grimes for their unending support and for having my back as a new chair in a new university. An extra-special dose of gratitude goes to my administrative assistants, Michelle O'Dwyer and Claudia Rivera.

The friends and family who have stood by me over the (many) years that it took to bring Maciste to life are numerous, and all of them deserve credit: Lindsay, Jason, Eleanor, and Elizabeth Jerutis; Alexandra Reich; Elaine and Larry Glickman; Allison, Greg, Julia, and Samantha Sundel; and my late grandparents, Sylvia and Solomon Kopman and Sydney and Harriette Reich, who provided me with the means and the love to allow me to believe that I could accomplish anything. My gratitude extends to my extended family: Pamela Metzger, Cole and Phoebe Metzger-Leavitt; my "wife" Sandra MacSweeney, for her countless meals and priceless council, and Laura Denobrega, for her angelic gluten-free desserts; Brian Downey; Lori Nasrallah; Lorene A. Cervini, for loving my boys as her own; Noah Zipper and Zachary Zipper, for keeping me up to date with the latest series and serials; and Matthew de Ganon, who deserves a special shout-out as co-parent and friend. Last but far from least, Michael Zipper, who returned to my life from what seems a far and distant time and place, is my light in the rabbit hole, the ultimate beacon ever ready to generously bestow love, wisdom, and wine in true Gotham splendor.

Extra-special thanks, love, and gratitude goes to my parents, Barbara Gardiner, Robert Reich, Dale Reich, and our newest, very welcome addition, David Mack, each of whom deserve way more than their own paragraph to describe the support, as well as the many babysitting hours logged, they have given me over the years. To consider myself fortunate to have them in my life is the understatement of the year.

Lastly, I dedicate this book to my sons, Sean de Ganon and Timmy de Ganon, who despite their age are among the strongest of men. Their love, humor, and intelligence are the joys of my life, and I look forward to viewing their own narratives as they become gentle giants of warmth, kindness, and strength.

All images are from the Collection of the Museo Nazionale del Cinema in Turin unless otherwise specified.

THE *Maciste* FILMS

OF ITALIAN SILENT CINEMA

Introduction

IN 1914 THE ITALA FILM COMPANY OF TURIN, ITALY, RELEASED the historical epic *Cabiria,* a film that was to alter the landscape of early Italian cinema. With intertitles by the renowned poet Gabriele D'Annunzio and directed by Giovanni Pastrone, a frequent contributor on many fronts to Turin's thriving film industry, *Cabiria* told the story of the kidnapping and liberation of a noble Roman girl during the Punic Wars in the third century BC. The film's enormous impact sprang from its many cinematic innovations: the historical accuracy of its elaborate sets, its highbrow literary aspirations, its pioneering tracking and dolly shots, and the extraordinary popularity of its unexpected hero, Maciste – a muscular African slave who, on behalf of his Roman commander, rescues the incarcerated heroine in enemy territory.

The Italian actor playing Maciste, Bartolomeo Pagano, was new to national screens. He had been a dock loader employed at the Genoa ports when discovered by Itala Film to play the role of Maciste. The strongman, however, was a familiar character in Italian cinema's early years. Historical films set in Ancient Rome such as *Quo Vadis?* (Cines, 1913) and *Spartaco* (*Spartacus,* Pasquali e C., 1913), among others, had featured muscled heroes performing feats of athletic daring.[1] The strongman in these extremely popular historical epics, for which Italian cinema was world renowned at the time, evolved from various cultural practices: the circus, specifically the clown and the strongman's acts of strength; a new widespread interest in physical culture and the emergence of gymnasiums in cities such as Turin, Bologna, and Milan, where the nascent

1

film industry flourished; and variety theater (*il teatro di varietà*) and its comic tradition, based on regional theatrical practices in local dialects.

Upon *Cabiria's* release the popular press and national and international audiences hailed Maciste as an Italian hero, admired for his bravery and strength, as well as his kindness and gentleness, quickly dubbing him "The Gentle Giant" (*il gigante buono*). Following the film's and the character's phenomenal international success, Itala Film decided to produce a series of adventure films with Maciste as protagonist, beginning with the 1915 *Maciste,* directed by Vincenzo Dénizot and Romano Luigi Borgnetto and supervised by Pastrone. Pagano subsequently starred as Maciste in nine films produced by Itala Film between the mid-1910s and the early 1920s. These productions included *Maciste alpino* (*The Warrior,* 1916); *Maciste innamorato* (Maciste in Love, 1919); *La trilogia di Maciste* (The Maciste Trilogy, 1920), an American-style serial of three films – *Maciste contro la morte* (Maciste Conquers Death), *Il viaggio di Maciste* (Maciste's Voyage), and *Il testamento di Maciste* (Maciste's Last Will and Testament); and *Maciste in vacanza* (Maciste on Vacation, 1921). In the 1920s, as the Italian film industry began to collapse due to intense competition, lack of innovation, and overtaxation (among other reasons), Pagano, like many other performers, found work in Germany, where he made three films akin to the popular German *Sensationfilm,* a genre that integrated high doses of spectacle and action. He ultimately returned to Italy to make some of his most successful blockbuster films for the distributor/producer Stefano Pittaluga and Turin's FERT film studio: *Maciste imperatore* (Maciste the Emperor, 1924); *Maciste contro lo sceicco* (Maciste against the Sheik, 1926); *Maciste nella gabbia dei leoni* (*The Hero of the Circus,* 1926); *Maciste all'inferno* (*Maciste in Hell,* 1926); and *Il gigante delle Dolomiti* (The Giant of the Dolomites, 1926).[2]

Drawing on both previous research and new archival sources, this study argues that Maciste and his muscular body played a crucial role in Italian cinema's narrativization of a unified national identity before, during, and after World War I for both a national and international audience.[3] The period from Italian unification (1870) to the beginning of World War I was characterized by political instability, disharmony between church and state, and major economic changes. In the eyes of many prominent and vocal citizens, it represented a failure to "invent

I.1. Publicity photo of Maciste.

the nation" and was indicative of shortcomings in the nature of Italian character, plagued by indolence (*ozio*), excessive individualism, and effeminacy.[4] Italy was, in short, "a state in search of a nation."[5]

In his passage from supporting character in *Cabiria* to the series' leading man, Maciste underwent several radical alterations: he moved from Ancient Rome to modern-day Italy, and he changed from a black-skinned African slave to a white northern Italian. His metamorphosis from African to Italian and from black to white solidified his status as national hero and a racially acceptable patriotic strongman.[6] Classical ideals of masculine beauty – as they had come to be represented in Ancient Greek and Roman sculpture, Renaissance art, eighteenth-century neoclassicism, nineteenth-century photography, and eventually film – informed these contemporary nationalist ideas of the male body.

The Maciste films are simultaneously reactionary and progressive; as he glanced backward, Maciste embodied the future – modernity fed on the past in order to become more modern than the present. The transposition of his heroic narratives to contemporary Italy aligned him with pressing national and political imperatives, including Italy's intervention in World War I, modernization, and the birth of Fascism and its colonial aspirations. Thus, class and ideology eventually superseded racialization as the cultural intertexts that engage with the Maciste films. Maciste gradually transformed from colonized slave to bourgeois citizen to heroic soldier to colonizing agent, particularly as Italy's government passed from liberal democracy to totalitarian regime in the 1920s. At the same time, as Italian national cinema began its precipitous decline after World War I, his charismatic appeal and associations with strength and bravery maintained his heroic national status. His films were big-budget extravaganzas in a period when domestic production was disastrously scarce, and Pagano became the highest-paid Italian male star. Maciste effectively bridged Italy's past and present, and, in a convergence of Italian politics and popular entertainment, his fame anticipated the political stardom of Benito Mussolini.

A central question of this project is why this particular type of film – a genre that inscribed nationalism on the muscular male physique and, by extension, the feats of strength and bravery that the body performed – flourished at this particular time in Italy and thrived as the industry neared total collapse. The Maciste films were, in essence, a genre in and of themselves, sealed in a pleasant, comedic popular package. Vibrant discussions about nationalism, the body, and masculinity found popular expression in Italy not in the epic film, not even in the strongman film, but rather in the Maciste films. Borrowing from early cinema's repertoire of comic shorts, historical epics, and detective serials, they became a means through which Italian cinema constructed a narrative of national identity. They capitalized on other genres' narrative and visual routines and added elements of stardom and seriality. Maciste's weapons were not just his classically structured muscles; the irony and humor present in narrative and character served not only to distinguish him from other series' protagonists but also to create a vibrant, charismatic star who captivated the Italian film-going public. As such, they were in direct dialogue with international film culture, particularly Hollywood.

In this study I argue that the social, cultural, and political conditions that gave rise to film stardom in Italy allowed Maciste/Pagano to surface as its *primary* male agent. Along these lines, I see and read film not as a reflection of reality but as one of the many discourses that engage in a dialogue with the national, social, economic, political, cultural, and ideological context in which it thrives, including why certain types of films flourish at particular times, and how the figure of the star – as sign, as commodity, as discourse itself – participates in these various convergences and divergences across national platforms.[7] Drawing on archival research, gender studies, film theory, and cultural history, I show that the message the Maciste films conveyed to audiences was that by playing an extraordinary character, an ordinary actor plucked from obscurity could become an exceptional Italian citizen. Cinema, in the form of the Maciste films, met and served the cogent ideological needs of a young nation in formation: Italy had begun the process of unification only thirty years before the birth of cinema, and the confluence between these two vectors begs further investigation.

NATIONALISM, ITALY, AND THE MUSCLED MALE BODY

The first two decades of the twentieth century had witnessed the emergence of radical nationalism in Italy as well as the call for its broad popularization. After the Risorgimento, the nineteenth-century movement toward Italian political unity, the newly formed Italian nation was faced with the question of national identity, specifically what it meant to be an Italian in a nation marked by stark regional differences, most evident in language, customs, and striking economic disparities. The constitution of a nation as a political and geographic unit does not necessarily instill a sense of patriotism and national pride. While not mutually exclusive, nationalism and nation formation consist of diverse discourses that shaped their development, especially during the nineteenth century, when the young governments in search of legitimizing power turned to the ideal of the nation as a centralizing force.[8] Here I adopt Emilio Gentile's distinction between national formation and nationalism, whereby the myth of nation is a symbolic construction, mainly the creation of intellectuals, and nationalism is the cultural and political movement that proclaims the superiority of a particular nation.[9]

Nationalism, as George L. Mosse observes, had much to do with the formation of modern masculinity (and vice versa) in conjunction with the emergence of racially defined nationalist ideals; the rise of nationalism as a political movement relied on the male as a symbol of a new national consciousness. At the beginning of the nineteenth century, the stereotype of modern masculinity in Western Europe had begun to take shape, and greater attention was placed on the athletic male body, which, after the French Revolution and the need for professional armies, had come to symbolize both physical and moral virtue.[10] Nationalism coincides with this search for strength. For Mosse, it was a movement that "began and evolved parallel to modern masculinity," and the body, both male and female, became a public symbol of the nation. Modern masculinity "was to define itself through an ideal of manly beauty that symbolized virtue."[11] Similarly, respectability defined the middle class and normalized its values of moderation; subsumed in the masculine was sexual control and restraint. Such normality and decency incorporated the Greek ideal of manliness as a nationalist and national self-representation. Women, on the other hand, as guardians of morality, were represented not by classical iconography but by medieval iconography – the holy mother: virtuous, passive, and maternal.[12]

Increasingly, with both this greater national(ist) attention to the body as well as the development of international competitions, the athletic body became a revered secular symbol of the nation.[13] Richard Dyer notes how the bodybuilder constitutes an ideal who achieves his status as a perfect man through contest, display, and performance – the planned, hairless body is one that is meant to be seen. Rather than vulnerability, the naked muscular body signifies both white mental and physical power: the white man is not born with the hard, muscular body – it takes both brains and brawn to achieve it. In terms of representational strategies, physical culture, and bodybuilding in particular, articulates white masculinity in popular culture by referencing Ancient Greek and Roman art.[14] Contemporary displays of bodybuilding were "bound up in classical rhetoric," according to Maria Wyke. Bodybuilders would adopt names of classical heroes in their displays of strength. Animalesque elements "helped provide a supposedly natural and traditional (and, therefore, seemingly unproblematic) context for circus exhibitions of muscled men."[15]

Furthermore, bodybuilding not only displayed muscles but also projected the ideal of good, male citizenship. Classical athleticism integrated the aesthetic of the male body (*kalos*) with the moral and political ideal of citizenship, proving his literal fitness for self-government (*agathos*).[16] Developments central to modernity – in particular, civilization, industrialization, and technology – both reinforced and destabilized gender roles, especially masculinity. In the twentieth century the popularity of physical culture and muscularity served to affirm masculinity in light of the growing public presence of women in and out of the workplace; to counter the feminizing and degenerate discourse of modern society; and to embody older, classical ideals of proportion, balance, and grace. Physical fitness was thus an "index of the vitality of the nation." [17]

In Italy after unification, both Italian schools and the Italian army institutionalized gymnastics as a means of creating manly men: the notion of *mens sana in corpore sano* – a healthy mind in a healthy body – began in the nineteenth-century project of educational and military reform. The northern Italian region of Piedmont was one of the centers of this new athletic movement under the influence of Swiss teacher Rudolph

I.2. Publicity photo of Maciste.

Obermann. The march toward industrialization, for people like Obermann and Emilio Baumann in Bologna, another exponent of physical culture, led to an unhealthy way of life, and physical education was a way of preserving workers' sanity and filling their leisure time. Obermann founded the first society for sport in 1844 in Turin, the eventual home of the Maciste series, which broke from traditional societies of this type by concentrating its attention on civilians and workers rather than soldiers. It focused on the tie between physical and intellectual life, an ideological premise that the Fascist regime would later exploit for its own political advantages.[18]

This muscular body, in addition to being nationalized, was also racialized. In the case of late nineteenth- and early twentieth-century Italy, "race" was a popular term in the scientific (or pseudoscientific) community that, often with incompatible meanings, derived from intense discussions and visual practices associated with national, geographic, and color classifications pervading Western scientific and popular culture.[19] The anthropological treatises of Cesare Lombroso, also from Turin, and Sergio Niceforo regularly influenced the popular press, advocating the superiority of the lighter-skinned north over the darker south, and found pseudoscientific justifications for these conclusions. For Lombroso, the southern Italian was the criminal incarnate, physically and racially inferior to his (and especially her) northern counterpart. For the Sicilian nationalist Niceforo, as John Dickie has argued, the south's inferiority, its "Mediteranneanness," was distinct from the northern "Aryans," and Niceforo based his conclusions on anthropologist Giuseppe Sergi's work on cranial morphology. This difference, however, was always in greater service to the national, at a time when the Italian nationalist movement was gaining in popularity. Despite their integral racially and biologically determined discrepancies, both southerners and northerners, according to Niceforo, were at their core Italians.[20]

This equation between physical, moral, political, and racial superiority was at the heart of contemporary theories on the superman, and its key proponent on Italian soil was not Friedrich Nietzsche, but rather Gabriele D'Annunzio, who created the character of Maciste in *Cabiria* and is a recurring player in the cast of characters that make up this study.[21] D'Annunzio, who did and would play many roles in contemporary Italian culture – novelist, poet, literary dandy, nationalist, and war hero (he enlisted in World War I and received a total of eight medals) – proposed an ideal of the *superuomo* (superman) that manifested itself in some of his more important works that circulated at the turn of these centuries: *Il trionfo della morte* (The Triumph of Death, 1894), *Le vergini delle rocce* (The Maidens of the Rocks, 1895), and *Il fuoco* (The Fire, 1900), among others. Beyond interpreting (and to some critics misinterpreting) Nietzsche's theories, for the *Vate* (Prophet), as D'Annunzio was known, the superuomo was a much more egocentric and self-glorifying concept than Nietzsche's moral one, one that meshed with his own agenda of self-promotion, pleasure, and self-aggrandizement.[22] As a public master manipulator of the people and his own image, D'Annunzio proposed a "pastiche heroism" that privileged theatricality over action itself and culminated in the 1919 fifteen-month irredentist occupation of the city of Fiume. Adept at creating spectacle that featured himself as protagonist and star, D'Annunzio publicly projected an image of masculinity that both grew out of and contradicted the heroes of the Risorgimento, and one that drew on the myths and symbols of the superuomo.[23]

Among other public intellectuals and the ruling elite, there was also a marked turn to a masculine political rhetoric, one that at first privileged, like D'Annunzio, its ties to the Risorgimento and later, with the successful war on Libya and participation in World War I, assumed more direct references to the myths of imperial Rome as a legitimizing discourse.[24] This re-virilization of a seemingly effeminate preunification Italy was both mental and physical.[25] The futurists, led by Filippo Tommaso Marinetti, embraced much of Nietzsche's aggressive vitalism, incorporating their own brand of dynamic, active, and avant-garde virility into their poetry, prose, artwork, and political writings. In the 1920s, Fascism, while it had an ambivalent and troubled relationship with futurism, appropriated many of its tenets of *superuomismo* as a "national and collective model that best suited the plan of socializing and standardizing the Italians," especially the cult of strength, youth, dynamism, war, and virility.[26] The writers of the Florentine literary journal *La voce* (the *vociani*) and other twentieth-century avant-garde movements, regardless of their ideological positions, stressed the active importance of the new modern, Italian man who would fill the void created by both the rise of the nation-state and a crisis in traditional religion.[27]

Giovanni Papini's *Maschilità*, a 1915 collection of essays the *vociano* author had written for important literary journals and newspapers, also epitomized this literary engagement with a gender discourse.[28] Concerned with Italy's cultural heritage and its regeneration, and influenced by Otto Weininger's *Sex and Character* (published in Germany in 1903 and translated into Italian in 1912), Papini and other vociani advocated for a "new spiritual virility" through a cultivation of masculine and heroic virtues.[29] Papini writes that Italy "lacked courage" (38) because it lacked genius (*genio*), greatness, and originality. In two essays in particular, "Two Literary Traditions" and "Honey and Rock," he discusses two "dynasties" of literature. First there is the masculine, representing everything "unyielding, sturdy, hard, atrocious, solid, concrete and plebian" in Italian literature and best epitomized by Dante, Machiavelli, Ugo Foscolo, Vittorio Alfieri, and Giosuè Carducci, among others. On the other side there is the feminine, Petrarchan tradition, or everything "gentle, elegant, musical, harmonious, decorative, conventional, literary, and empty" (84–85), represented by the Petrarchisti of the fifteenth, sixteenth, and seventeenth centuries, the Romantics, and the *decadenti* of the late nineteenth century, including most of D'Annunzio's literary production. Papini even employs the term "*razze,*" or "races," to describe these dynasties. He goes on to further clarify how he signifies these gender constructs: "There are not only biological but also spiritual sexes. When I say male I intend, now, strength, energy, toughness, and pride; when I speak of female I intend feebleness, sweetness, bland voluptuousness, modesty, easy tears, silly gossip and a faint and wearisome musicality" (95).

The words Papini employs to elucidate Italy's two literary tendencies, particularly the more masculine literature that he clearly favors, could easily describe Maciste himself: solid, unyielding, hardness, energy (clearly a reference to futurism as well), and pride. The metaphor of the rock (concreteness, solidity) aligns it with classical notions of strength and virility, as does his description of the "good, masculine" D'Annunzio, extolling the virtues of his superuomo. No cinematic figure would better epitomize this convergence of Italian vigor, virility, and vitality and racial and national superiority than Maciste, and no better genre could capitalize on the various discursive intersections among nationalism, masculinity, and stardom than the Maciste films.

CINEMA, MUSCLES, AND MACISTE

The muscled male body on screen was not a new concept. Pre-cinema's fascination with capturing movement often focused on muscularity in motion, in some cases drawing on contemporary photographic representations of the male body that began to circulate as commodities, via postcards and reproductions, in the late nineteenth century. The male nude photography of Thomas Eakins as well as early experiments by Eadweard Muybridge and Étienne-Jules Marey had featured copiously the male body in stasis and action.[30] Cinema's early experimental years, with its reliance on popular forms of entertainment for inspiration, turned to the circus and the strongman as a type of attraction that perfectly fit the new medium; the brief acts of lifting, holding, breaking, and posing were ideal representations to showcase the new technology's ability to capture movement. Early films by Thomas Edison, such as *Sandow* (1894), *Athlete with Wand* (1894), *Louis Martinetti* (1894), *High Diving Scene* (1901), and *Trapeze Disrobing Act* (1902), all displayed feats of strength and agility that featured the body, both female and male, in motion. The first sporting events brought to the screen were boxing matches, which showcased live and scantily clad bodies using their muscles.[31] The medium, particularly the early viewing practice of the Kinetoscope, lent itself well to pornographic voyeurism of the naked body by predominantly, but not exclusively, male spectators.

The Italian strongman's body, particularly that of Maciste, functioned as the on-screen embodiment of modern Italian masculinity in motion through its association both with the classical tradition and the most modern of media: the cinema, and stardom in particular. The phenomenon of *divismo,* the Italian word for stardom, emerged in Italy in the 1910s, predominantly with the female stars who came to epitomize much of Italian silent cinema. As films themselves are national products, so too are stars. Stars are about the production and fabrication of the public self; they in turn create a star persona, a hybrid of the characters he or she plays on screen and their off-screen reality. They are highly intertextual, constructed not only through their cinematic roles but also through publicity materials, often referred to as the extra-cinematic discourse, where off-screen images circulate. Representing more than just a physical body, they exist not in isolation but in dialogue with the political, social, cultural, and sexual issues of the time. The star is a product, deliberately marketed, distributed, and sold in the greater economy, promoting both the film and his or her intertextual persona. Although a studio system can promote a star ad nauseam, he or she becomes a star only by public acclamation. Historically, in the 1910s, stars emerged as fundamental

I.3. Postcard of Maciste.

From the author's personal collection.

to the marketing and selling of film commodities and the focal point for vertical integration (in the United States), where the discursively constituted separation of character, actor, and star began to take form.

Although this study focuses on Maciste's relation to Italian cinema as a national cinema, most of the action takes place in one place: Turin. The northern city was Italy's most industrialized, as well as the Italian nation's first capital in its modern state. While many Italian cities had thriving film industries, in particular Milan, Naples, and Rome, Turin was the country's most vibrant center of film production. As a 1914 article in the magazine *Secolo XX* phrased it, Italy's former capital was the nation's *filmopolis,* a "cinema city," where modes of film production and exhibition pervaded all walks of life.[32] Film periodicals thrived, including the very influential *La Vita Cinematografica* (founded in 1910); artists flocked to participate in set and costume design; and the Italian star system was born. As Italy itself became more urbanized, with Turin leading the way through its rapid industrialization, film became a force of mass integration into modern life (it was also the birthplace of the Italian automobile industry).[33] As the home of the world's exposition in 1911, commemorating the fiftieth anniversary of a united Italy (and the site of an international film festival), film featured prominently among the many exhibits, showcasing Turin as the most modern and cosmopolitan of Italian cities.[34]

Turin's fairs, popular variety theater, and public performances in piazzas featured acts whose short vignettes and feats of strength, comedy, and agility fit perfectly with the exigencies and the limitations of early film production and provided the first attractions that found their way onto the screen. This type of popular entertainment was part of the daily fabric of nineteenth-century Turinese life. At the Porta Palazzo, one of Italy's largest markets, clowns, acrobats, illusionists, and strongmen mingled with the shoppers. Emerging in the late nineteenth century the Politeama was a large multipurpose theatrical space, one unique to urban Italy, with a flexible stage and a large audience capacity in order to accommodate the widest possible social swath.

Even before Arturo Ambrosio, who would go on to found Ambrosio Film, one of Turin's early major film studios, and the pioneering Turinese nonfiction filmmaker Roberto Omegna began making their first films in 1904, early Edison and Lumière brothers films had made their way to the city, exhibited first as scientific-didactic practices, organized by the photographer Vittorio Calcina, and then moving to a larger public venues. By 1904, when Ambrosio and Omegna began showing their own documentaries, Turin had nine more theaters dedicated to showing films. Soon thereafter Ambrosio established the first film studio in Turin's periphery, to be joined later by Pasquali & Company, Aquila Films, Gloria Film, and Itala Film, where Maciste was born.[35]

MACISTE UP CLOSE

This book is a comprehensive study of the available Italian-produced Maciste films; unfortunately, prints of many of the films no longer exist or are in poor condition and thus unavailable for viewing. Here the scholar is at the mercy of the archive and the restorer, who also have strong voices in this project. I have also chosen to focus on the films Pagano made in Italy and neglect those in Germany, examining instead the few sources that exist on the exhibition of the German films in Italy at the time. In addition, the book's six chapters following the introduction are organized chronologically, focusing on individual films and the cultural, social, historical, and political intertexts with which they interacted.[36] The rationale behind this structuring is to reinforce how films, particularly popular, ideologically loaded ones like the Maciste series, consistently interacted with forces beyond the screen's parameters. In short, this study is only a beginning, and many avenues remain to be discovered and explored.

Chapter 1, "The Birth of the Strongman: Italian Silent Cinema, Stardom, and Genre," provides an overview of the cinematic and cultural panorama that set the stage for the emergence of the Maciste films. I examine the birth of the character of Maciste against the backdrop of the nascent Italian film industry and its fledgling star system through the lens of early film genres, in particular short comic films, detective serials, and historical epics that culminated in the advent of the strongman films. What emerges is a portrait of a film industry without a single centralized site of production for the manufacturing of both films and stars. Distinctions also materialized between male and female stardom, with the former, in particular that of Bartolomeo Pagano, being interconnected first with the historical epic and then with the strongman film. Moreover, from the outset those genres linked Pagano's stardom not only to screen character but also to national character as a symbolic screen icon of national masculinity. His fame materialized at a time when the classical male body came to signify new symbolic myths for the newly unified and newly secular Italian nation. Moreover, with his strength, kindness, and, above all, comedic character, Maciste appealed to a wide swath of the Italian public, adding the crucial element of populism that distinguished him from his female counterparts on screen and integrated a broader, American sensibility to his on-screen persona.

In chapter 2, "From Slave to Master: *Cabiria* (1914) and *Maciste* (1915)," the focus is on Pagano's first two incarnations as Maciste. In *Cabiria*, Maciste's on- and off-screen configuration as national icon trumps his foreign provenance and skin color. The film's unique combination of high art and popular appeal launched Pagano's career and the birth of the series. *Maciste* establishes the patterns of subsequent films, conflating the identities of actor and character: Maciste is now a real-life actor, played on screen by Pagano but known only as Maciste. The film broadcasts the notion that Maciste is both ordinary, as a typical member of Italy's urban bourgeoisie, and extraordinary, as an exceptionally powerful strongman. The fact that the first Maciste film was shot on location and set in a contemporary Italy; employed realistic photographic effects; and regularly exhibited such daily deeds as eating, washing up, and dressing reinforced the charming normality of Maciste's life, a fact stressed throughout many of the films he was to make with Itala Film. At the same time, however, his associations with classical, statuesque strength and bravery amplified his heroic and extraordinary status, and his charismatic appeal and comic gentleness further broadened his audience. Through its narrative and popular success, the film ultimately cements the very codes and conventions that would go on to characterize and popularize the series.

Chapter 3, "Maciste Goes to War: *Maciste alpino* (1916)," turns to the series' incarnation of the war film, in which Maciste the actor is filming on the Italian-Austrian border as Italy enters World War I. During the war years, in which Italian cinema began the decline that increased to monumental proportions during the 1920s, both fiction and nonfiction films relating to the war populated Italian screens. This chapter examines *Maciste alpino* in light of several factors: the growing nationalist movement, which saw intervention in World War I as the means of creating political consensus; the sophistication and development of narrative, character, and attractions in the Maciste series; and its iconographic importance in relation to the nonfiction newsreels produced during the war, as well as other fiction films. Moreover, Maciste functioned as a weapon in and of himself, a futurist mechanized man whose muscled body constituted its own fighting machine but one with a jocular heart of gold, whose humorous antics delighted critics and audiences on multiple continents. As a hybrid genre the film lent itself to flexible marketing strategies; it was both popular entertainment and an "instructional" manual for soldiers at the front.

Chapter 4, "Over There: The Maciste Series, World War I, and American Film Culture," follows the distribution and exhibition of these first three films *Cabiria*, *Maciste*, and *Maciste alpino* to the United States, where Maciste/Pagano came to be billed as the Douglas Fairbanks of Italian cinema. By placing the Maciste films in a wider international context, I follow the lead of silent film scholars who have addressed the issue of transnational stardom – that is, how a particular star's appeal – for example, Rudolph Valentino and Sessue Hayakawa – changes meaning as it crosses national borders.[37] Maciste's transatlantic passage is relevant for two reasons: first, the United States was, at the time, the world's largest film market, and, second, the films, exhibited during the exact years of Italian and American intervention into World War I, reveal how feature films were marketed to support national policies. *Maciste* and *Maciste alpino*, released in the United States respectively as *Marvelous Maciste* (1916) and *The Warrior* (1917), were major successes from coast to coast, as attested to by the blanket coverage the films received in the press. They celebrated the wartime alliance between Italy and the United States for both American and Italian immigrant spectators as they interacted with the popularity of both the American serial and the war film.

Chapter 5, "Love, Labor, and Leadership: The Modernity of the Maciste Series, 1919–1922," returns to Italy to interrogate the continued popularity of the Maciste films after World War I, when Italian cinema entered its most serious commercial crisis and during a period of political and economic instability known as the Red Biennium (*Biennio rosso*). *Maciste innamorato*, *La trilogia di Maciste*, and *Maciste in vacanza* survived the catastrophe of the national film industry by relying and expanding upon a proven formula – Maciste. The Red Biennium Maciste films engaged with the increasing importance of work, labor, and industrialization against the backdrop of Italy's most industrialized city, Turin; the relationship between labor and capital, work and leisure; and the increasing presence of the mechanical in Italians' everyday lives. From a political standpoint, there is little agenda of subversion here; the strongman and his muscles are in service to the ruling class and its preservation, be it in a factory setting (*Maciste innamorato*) or in government (*La trilogia di Maciste*). In the films' march toward modernization, Maciste's consistent modus operandi is to liberate society from the parasites – from all classes – that infest it and threaten its sovereignty.[38] If the first film and the three American-style serial films that compose *La trilogia di Maciste* repeated the athletic heroics of earlier productions, *Maciste in vacanza* incorporated technological modernization, specifically Italy's growing automobile culture. The car was not a stranger to Italian cinema; many comic films from the 1910s featuring the reoccurring characters Cretinetti and Robinet alternatively marveled in and feared this new technology. The dense correspondence archived at the Museo Nazionale del Cinema in Turin (National Film Museum, or the MNC) reveals the extent to which the Diatto auto company, FIAT's main rival, went to accommodate its product placement in the film and proves Maciste's lasting brand appeal. What unites all three films is their reliance on comedy and irony in its various forms: Maciste soothes the wounds of the war's aftermath and leads the way into the age of modernity with his wide smile and broad, popular appeal.

Chapter 6, "Muscling the Nation: Mussolini and the Maciste Films of the 1920s," turns its attention to the last Maciste films made in Italy, all released after Benito Mussolini's 1922 rise to power. Mussolini was a figure whose emergence as a political force shadowed the development of the Maciste series. The same year that *Cabiria* burst onto the cinematic scene (1914), Mussolini was expelled from the Socialist Party for his support of intervention in World War I and founded the proto-Fascist newspaper *Il Popolo d'Italia* and the group Fasci Rivoluzionari d'Azione Internazionalista, the proto-Fascist political party. The increasing nationalist bent of the series, and the convergence of various themes central to the development of Fascism in Italy – modernization, traditionalism, and leadership – parallel shifts in Italian politics, culture, and society.[39] While I am not arguing for a direct correspondence between the fictional and the real, it is undeniable that much of the iconography that was central to the imagery of Mussolini as a virile leader was in dialogue with the Maciste films. Mussolini's interaction with Maciste's character goes beyond their physical resemblance. The dictator positioned himself in his many on-screen appearances in photographs and documentary films, like Maciste, as a political "strongman," with frequent iconic references to his own strength and virility and, at least initially, his connection to the masses, yet without Maciste's characteristic comedic charm.

Likewise, Maciste's films preceding and following the Fascist consolidation of power engage with Mussolini's growing popularity in the 1920s. In these films, Maciste, as both political and national symbol, shed his realistic milieu in favor of costume dramas and high adventure. In *Maciste imperatore* (1924), the protagonist defeats a cruel dictator and arises as a leader chosen by the masses to lead the fictitious nation of Sirdagna, but not without a lesson in rightful rule. Similarly, *Maciste all'inferno* (1926), as an allegorical tale of good and evil, features a hell in political chaos begging for the forceful restitution of order. In *Maciste nella gabbia dei leoni* (1926), in which he plays a lion tamer, the circus, with its connotations of difference and otherness, becomes a stand-in for Italy's colonial territories; as the good, gentle "animal tamer," Maciste is more than able and willing to crack the whip, literally and figuratively, to keep the natives in line. *Maciste contro lo sceicco* (1926) likewise plays on fears of miscegenation as Italy embarked on its own colonial mission. The last film Pagano made as Maciste, *Il gigante delle Dolomiti* (1926), constitutes this book's conclusion, as it returns to the Alps as both *locus amenus* and national symbol. The last five films are notable for an additional factor: much of the irony and comedic tone of the previous films disappears in favor of a more solid, stately representation of masculinity, more akin to that of Il Duce than the character's previous roles.

Despite their long chronological trajectory, multiple directors, and studios, the films that comprise the Maciste series share consistent commonalities. They were distributed both nationally and internationally, albeit not always successfully, and interacted with other cinematic traditions, especially in the United States and Germany. They engaged with issues of class, gender, and race in a period when those issues were at the fore of public and political rhetoric. And they all to some extent used costume and fashion as a means of engaging with those very discourses. Maciste's racial transformation from slave in *Cabiria* to bourgeois citizen in *Maciste* necessitated a costume change from toga to dapper suit. The uniform he wears when he goes to war (*Maciste alpino*) and assumes the role of emperor (*Maciste imperatore*) are markers, just like his muscles, of his nationalized virility. Equally important are the clothes he does not adorn; his naked torso, so frequently featured in all the films, reveals that no matter what role he plays, Maciste is all man and all Italian.

While this analysis situates the Maciste films in a specific historical context, through recourse to the archival documentation of periodicals, production notes, scripts, and publicity materials, I am nonetheless viewing these films in the twenty-first century. The ability to have access to these texts, many of which were believed lost for decades, is the result of the careful reconstruction and restoration of multiple prints conducted by the MNC and the Cineteca di Bologna (also known as the Fondazione Cineteca di Bologna). Without such dedication to film preservation, projects like this one would not be possible. The study of silent film brings with it a set of imperatives – from conservation, documentation, authentication, and reconstruction – and my approach combines a traditional preparation in film theory and criticism with a strong archival grounding.[40]

To that effect, the book includes three sections in which the two supervisors of the Maciste restoration project, Claudia Gianetto and Stella Dagna of the MNC, detail their painstaking work in reconstructing and restoring the original films. What the three of us share, beyond a passion for all things Maciste, is the discovery of the richness of the films and the archival material. The appendix consists of three parts: an essay that describes the processes involved in locating, analyzing, and restoring the Maciste films; an "In Focus" section that explores, from the restorer's point of view, selected scenes and topics analyzed in detail in previous chapters; and a detailed critical filmography reconstructed from recently discovered archival sources. The decision to include these contributions is not solely for bibliographic or filmographic purposes. Rather, it is a manifesto of a methodology central to this book: that our work as cultural studies/film scholars relies intrinsically on the conservation of cultural artifacts and the work of librarians and preservationists whose dedication to safeguarding and cataloguing the past is consistently threatened by financial concerns. As film historians and film scholars, we are all engaged in projects of restoration and recuperation – of the films themselves, the various contexts in which they circulated, and the extra-cinematic discourses that accompanied their circulation – and too often our work remains separate rather than united on the printed page. As we give voice to Maciste, we hope to bring to the forefront the struggles involved in the process of film preservation.

*   *   *

It is difficult to underplay Maciste's influence, as well as the novelty of his films, despite his many imitators and followers and their varying degrees of box-office and critical success. *Maciste* inaugurated the characteristics of what would become the most consistent and successful serial based on a recurring character in Italian silent cinema, not only by creating a consistency of character, plot, and setting, as most genre films do, but also by establishing the soon-to-be-consistent interpenetration of the fictional and actual identities of Pagano/Maciste: his on- and off-screen persona merged into one, creating the star. Advertisements post-*Cabiria* omitted Pagano from the film's publicity; either the character's name was explicitly stated or was given as "Signor Maciste." Many advertisements for his subsequent non-Maciste roles in *Il vetturale di Montecisio* (The Carter from Montecisio, Pittaluga, 1927) and *Gli ultimi zar* (The Last Czars, Pittaluga, 1928) billed him as Maciste, or at least had the character's name in parenthesis next to the actor's. So strong was the identification of body with character that the actor himself would almost completely disappear.

Maciste constitutes a unique figure in the history of silent cinema: he was the first of many strongmen who would come to populate Italian and other national cinemas even after the advent of sound, from Tarzan to Hercules to Conan the Barbarian. His cinematic reach was extraordinary for the times, even in comparison to the better-known *dive*, or divas, of early Italian screens. The word "Maciste" entered the Italian vocabulary as a general term for a colossus or giant; one would say that a person "is a real Maciste."[41] His films had incredible legs, as we might say today, in terms of exhibition; they continued to play in second-run cinemas many years after their initial release, and some, in the case of *Cabiria* and *Maciste contro lo sceicco,* were exhibited in sound versions in the 1930s once the technology permitted (*Maciste all'inferno* appeared in sound version in 1941). His popularity was such that even in the 1940s and in his retirement, as Pagano, in poor health, had retreated to his Villa Maciste outside Genoa, he was approached to reincarnate the series. That revitalization would have to wait until the 1960s, well after Pagano's death, with the popularity of the sword-and-sandal peplum films that bore Maciste's name.[42] None other than Federico Fellini eloquently said, "So many times I say jokingly that I am always trying to remake that film, that all the films I make are the repetition of *Maciste in Hell*."[43]

ONE

The Birth of the Strongman

ITALIAN SILENT CINEMA, STARDOM, AND GENRE

ACCORDING TO OFFICIAL STATE RECORDS, BARTOLOMEO Pagano, the actor who was to gain national and international fame as Maciste, was born on 27 September 1878, at Via dei Marsano 9 in Sant'Ilario Ligure in the province of Genoa, Italy.[1] The town, about ten miles to the east of the port city, was where he lived most of his life and where he died on 24 June 1947 at the age of sixty-nine in his home, the Villa Maciste. Little else is known about Pagano's life. The generally accepted story was that he was discovered by Itala Film while working as a stevedore at the Genoa port. He married Camilla Balduzzi, had one son, Oreste, in 1916, and suffered from sleepwalking after a severe fall (a fact that excused him from military service before and during World War I). He eventually retired from filmmaking not, as was often the case, due to the advent of sound, but because of a severe case of diabetes and arteriosclerosis. The salary he received for his work on *Cabiria* was 20 Italian lire per day; by 1921 he was making close to 17,000 lire per month, an extraordinary fee for a male actor at that time.[2]

While verifiable biographical information on Pagano is sparse, publicity materials are copious. What emerges from the first moment his name appears in print is a complete and total (con)fusion between character and actor. Mostly it is the character, Maciste, and not the actor, Pagano, who is front and center. Only one printed interview with Pagano exists, and it appeared identically in two different periodicals in 1924, under two different titles: "Un'intervista con Maciste" (An Interview with Maciste) and "'Maciste, il gigante buono.' Intervista con Bartolomeo Pagano" (Maciste, the Gentle Giant: An Interview with

Bartolomeo Pagano).[3] In both texts the same anonymous interviewers consistently refer to Pagano as Maciste. Even when the journalist notes how, at the Villa Maciste, Maciste returns to "becoming" Pagano, he essentially remains "in character," "with an elastic gait" and described as an "eminent man of action," reinforcing his classical physique. The writer stresses Maciste's attachment to his castle, which he bought from "the fruits of his labor" and built with his "Herculean" strength; the work that takes three days is done in one (clearly Rome was built in a day here). The writer also reinforces Maciste's tie to the earth and, by extension, Italy, symbolized by his great love for gardening. The fact that Liguria, the region in which Genoa resides, is "in his body and courses through his veins" signals a possible reference to the city's most famous denizen, Christopher Columbus, and his status as world traveler who longed for the motherland.[4]

This fusion of character and actor had legal ramifications. Twice Pagano found himself in the courtroom over legal disputes pertaining to the ownership of Maciste's brand name, prompted first by the Maciste series' move to Germany in 1922 and then its subsequent return to Italy and Turin's FERT Studio in 1923. The first legal action, dated February 1923, was brought by Itala Film against Karol Film, the producers of the German films, in an attempt to prevent the German company from using the name Maciste in their productions. On 20 July 1923 a Berlin court ruled in Itala Film's favor, forcing Pagano to return to Italy or face grave economic penalty.[5] Once back in Italy, Pagano sued Itala Film in return for the rights to the character Maciste, a battle he won in the courts twice in 1923 on both initial judgment and appeal.

Itala Film's original case against Pagano was personal and brutal. Their argument was that Pagano no longer had the physique to represent Maciste's "type," and that he was "neither Othello or Cyrano or even Charles Chaplin. . . . Maciste is always Maciste, and with the contract expired we can always find another one."[6] What both of these court cases reveal is the economic importance of the brand as well as the fusion of character and actor, even in the minds of the court. It ultimately ruled that Pagano and "Maciste" were indistinguishable; that Itala Film had exploited that connection in the production, advertising, and marketing of the film and series; and that, ironically, its lawsuit against Karol Film had discounted its own legal standing. The court concluded that Maciste was an individual, not a type, and that Pagano was the only actor who could portray him on screen, much like, as the tribunal argued, only Chaplin could play the Little Tramp.[7] Pagano and Maciste were ruled inseparable, and their stardom was consistently rising throughout the 1920s.

Other press pieces stressed the issue of his national significance. The interviews cited above claim that while working in Berlin, Pagano insisted on being paid in Italian lire, not German marks. The 1926 biographical publicity booklet *Maciste (Bartolomeo Pagano)* affirms (or rather exaggerates) his regional and national prestige, referring to him as someone with a face that was "characteristic of the good, Ligurian race" and as a "Modern Hercules" (4).[8] "No Italian is more famous abroad than he is: as an exceptional artist, with natural gifts, and for the love of art, Maciste honors our Cinema and our country in Italy and beyond" (2). The writer continues, citing a previous observation in the periodical *Al Cinemà:* "Bartolomeo Pagano . . . was born an artist: coming into this world he was already destined to become the high priest of the Tenth Muse, a representative of Cinema on the Olympus of the Arts" (4).

This chapter examines the interplay of cinema, stardom, genre, and the national in the Italian film industry's first two decades in order to contextualize this Maciste/Pagano trajectory.[9] I argue that the Maciste films, in coming into their own as a unique and highly successful genre, did not emerge out of nowhere; instead they borrowed heavily from the previous generic codes and conventions of Italian and French early cinema. The comic film and the historical film in particular are the two main sources of inspiration for the fusion of nationalism, heroism, and humor that characterized this distinctive series. On the one hand, the Maciste films drew on their comic predecessors in a variety of ways: with their reoccurring motif of the chase; their use of humor and irony, especially in the intertitles; and the interplay between character and star. On the other hand, the muscled male star of the historical epics and later the strongman films came to the fore as the modern-day Herculean national icon, a secular rather than sacred hero.

Early Italian cinema's male heroes were markedly worldly and markedly nationalized. As I discussed in the introduction, the rise of nationalism affected the positioning of the male body in the emerging mass media of early twentieth-century Italy, and the Italian strongman's muscles, particularly those of Maciste, functioned as the visual personification of modern Italian masculine citizenship. As Maurizia Boscagli has argued, the male body in the twentieth century was "also a hegemonic medium of mass interpellation" that "must always be assessed within the historical conditions of its production."[10] What sustained the projection of nationalist ideas onto the male body were classical ideals of masculine beauty that Italian cinema furthered and popularized to an unprecedented extent. The Italian film industry had relied on classical mythology since its inception, epitomized in the historical epics for which it was world-renowned: for its collective cultural symbols, for its narrative inspiration and structure (particularly in the hero's screen representation), and for the construction of stardom.[11]

We know from Roland Barthes that myths have an ideological function: they serve to naturalize and normalize what is cultural and constructed. [12] In the case of Maciste, his diegetic association with the Ancient Roman Empire (he is an African slave in *Cabiria*) and his subsequent metamorphosis into modern hero drew on the classical myths of the heroic Roman soldier, the new turn-of-the-century parables of patriotic heroism, and a popular charismatic appeal through his athletic ability and his comedic geniality. The highest-paid female stars of the day projected a celestial otherworldliness highlighting their detachment from the everyday world. Conversely, Italian cinema firmly grounded its male counterparts in everyday life, no matter how great their physical gifts or mental acumen. The Maciste series fused classical genealogy and modern nationalism into popular iconic Italian stardom, one that would produce a unique hybrid genre that resonated within the Italian peninsula and beyond its borders.

ITALIAN STARDOM AND *DIVISMO*

The second decade of the twentieth century marked fundamental shifts and radical changes in modern Italian politics, culture, and society. Its first years signaled the beginning of Italy's renewed colonialist expansion, this time into Libya; the initiation of reforms that would bring about universal male suffrage; and its increasing economic progress and presence on an international political scene despite internal strife and large waves of emigration. Intellectually and artistically, it witnessed the national and international prominence of the avant-garde futurist movement and the continued expansion of its domestic film industry, particularly with forays into multi-reel and soon feature-length productions, represented by the pioneering epics *La caduta di Troia* (*The Fall of Troy,* Itala Film, 1910) and *L'inferno* (*Dante's Inferno,* Milano Films, 1911). The year 1911 marked the commemoration of the nation's first jubilee, which provided an opportunity to exalt and consecrate the national myths of the Third Italy, fusing the glories of Ancient Rome, humanism, and the Renaissance with the adoration of the heroes and heroics of the Risorgimento in light of Italy's march toward freedom, monarchic democracy, and modernization. It was an opportunity for those across a wide political spectrum to celebrate the economic, social, and political progress made during the Italian nation's first fifty years as well as the promise of future glories and conquests.[13]

One highlight of these celebrations was the inauguration of a national monument in Rome, the Altare della Patria (the Altar of the Fatherland), in honor of Vittorio Emanuele II, the first king of the united Italy (fig. 1.1). Commissioned in 1878 after the king's death, and designed by Giuseppe Sacconi, an architect who would not live to see his work completed, the monument was meant to constitute a lay, symbolic space that would be capable of conveying the Italian state formation and, simultaneously, secularize Papal Rome into an appropriate capital for the Liberal state. Construction began in 1885; its official completion, following the addition of the country's tomb of the unknown soldier, came only in 1921. Its impending construction forced alterations to the city's geography, taking the phrase "all roads lead to Rome" literally; city planners rerouted streets away from the Vatican to lead to the Piazza Venezia, where the monument would stand. With its beaux arts style, the monument, representing both the classical (the Dea Romana) and the pagan (King Vittorio Emanuele II), fused "ancient unity of Italy and the reborn Italian nation," a fact reinforced by its deliberate proximity to the Roman Forum and other ancient ruins. Moreover, as the embodiment of the new state religion, the Altare della Patria communicated a national spirit and

1.1. The Altare della Patria.

From the author's personal collection.

identity, most visible in its classically posed and chiseled muscular male bodies.[14]

The Altare della Patria serves as an objective correlative for many of the variant discourses that converge in and around the Maciste films: the fusion of and transition from antiquity to modernity; the rise of nationalism; and the importance of the heroic male body, both sculpted and sepulchered, for the construction of the ideal Italian citizen. Throughout this chapter references to the Maciste series and Pagano's stardom serve as examples of these convergences. Italian cinema's first years coincided and coexisted with these cultural forces, with which it also engaged both on screen in the types of films that populated early cinematic exhibition, and off screen, in what was being written about the new medium, especially in relation to stardom.

The early twentieth-century Italian political landscape revealed various attempts to construct a civic religion, what the historian Emilio Gentile defines as "a system of beliefs, values, myths, rituals, and symbols that confer an aura of sanctity . . . [on] a political entity, and on the country's institutions, history, and destiny in the world."[15] During the profoundly anticlerical disposition of post-unification Italy, moves to popularize patriotic religion through rituals and celebrations of the new nation-state sought to find ways to "make Italians." Nationalism was the most powerful and effective concretization of this sacralization of politics. It conferred "a sacred aura on their political institutions, to exalt the fundamental principles and values of the national community, and to cultivate a collective identity among its citizens, which required them to feel a sense of duty, loyalty, and devotion toward both state and nation," culminating in the Fascist regime's institutionalized celebration of its various constitutional symbols, beliefs and rituals.[16]

At the same time, film emerges as its own civic religion, a new, secular place of worship that is tied to the national from its inception. Cinema became a sacred site of popular culture and created its own rituals (filmgoing), sites of worship (theaters), and gods (stars, or *divas* and *divos*) as objects of worship and devotion.[17] And just as the extra-cinematic discourse can mythologize actors into divine creatures, "myths and rituals can also be the spontaneous expression of the masses" as audiences play a fundamental role in creating stars.[18] Spectators consume the stars, whom they worship and who, in turn, particularly during the silent era, allow themselves to be worshipped. Sociologist Edgar Morin, one of the first to theorize stardom in the 1950s (and thus one of the first observers of the phenomenon before the multiplications of mass media), writes:

> The star is like a patron saint to whom the faithful dedicate themselves, but who must also to a certain degree dedicate himself to the faithful. Furthermore, the worshipper always desires to *consume* his god. From the cannibal repasts in which the ancestor was eaten, and the totemic feasts in which the sacred animal was devoured, down to our own religious communion and receiving of the Eucharist, every god is created to be eaten – that is, incorporated, assimilated.[19]

Cinema thus assumes an essentially polytheistic pagan form; theaters are the new modern temples and places of worship, and stars are the new gods, both human and immortal idols of worship.[20]

Similarly, the Italian words adopted for stars – *diva* and *divo*, literally translated as "goddess" and "god" – betray this religious imprint, proposing an otherworldliness, a separation from mortal individuals' average and everyday existence.[21] The Italian word *divismo* appeared as a general term in reference to Italian stardom in both Italian contemporary periodicals and film histories of the period.[22] Divismo and the female divas had their antecedents in lyric opera and the dramatic theater that filled Europe's major theaters in the nineteenth century. The most important theatrical actresses of the day – Sarah Bernhardt and Eleonora Duse – became the models, both for their onstage performances and off-stage popularity, for the screen divas. The case of Lyda Borelli, who was a popular stage actress before she made her film debut, further reveals the continuities between stage and film stardom.[23]

In Italy what materializes is a portrait of a national film production that lacks an institutional structure that could consistently discover and manufacture stars, as did most national cinemas in the 1910s. Nevertheless, it produces some of the most significant star phenomena of the silent period in Europe and abroad. In the early 1910s these stars' potential gross at the box office as attractions for the public made them valuable commodities. Rival studios, both national and international, would bid and attempt to woo such stars in order to bolster their own respective productions and profits. Early cinema's cross-cultural and international distributional exchanges, while at first involving early film production – generally one-reel films – eventually came to include actors, such as the Danish Asta Nielsen, who established their popularity simultaneously in their native countries and abroad. The major turning point for film stardom in Italy was not a homegrown entity, but rather Nielsen herself. Her 1910 film *Afgrunden,* directed by Urban Gad and released as *L'abisso* (The Abyss) in Italy and *Woman Always Pays* in the United States, featured the wild-haired and wide-eyed actress performing a highly erotic dance and made her an international sensation. In many ways Nielsen became the model for the diva and her on-/off-screen persona.[24] The rise of stardom in Italian silent cinema also benefited from significant industrial developments that occurred between 1910 and 1913: the standardization of film stock; the movement toward full-length feature films; better-structured distribution and exhibition networks; and the emergence of effective promotion strategies and critical discourses pervading the trade press, film magazines, and daily newspapers.[25]

At a time when studios were more actively marketing their products through promotional publicity campaigns, Italian spectators learned to appreciate and inquire about various participants in the nascent production, from actors, directors, and screenwriters to technical and artistic directors. Although initially reluctant to recognize certain individuals for fear they might realize their popularity and seek additional monetary compensation, in 1909 Italian film studios began to credit the names of actors and use them to publicize their films. By 1910 new periodicals devoted to the film industry soon published biographical profiles and photographs of popular actors. Subsequently the actor started to replace the studio as the primary commodity used to sell the film in the greater marketplace.[26] Periodicals advertised film series featuring a popular actor or actress, and in the years immediately preceding Italy's intervention into World War I, studios created vehicles for their stars, including Lyda Borelli and Francesca Bertini, as well as, on the men's side, Emilio Ghione and Bartolomeo Pagano.

Yet the characteristics and attributes ascribed to male and female stars were fundamentally different, as were the genres in which they flourished. The diva's film stardom was born not out of a commonality between the spectator and what he or she saw on screen, but rather out of a lack of reference to everyday life, to the untouchability of its characters placed in a world – indeed, an otherworldliness – of forbidden passions paired with a growing desire among the middle class for social mobility.[27] The "diva film" refers to a genre of films made in Italy from 1913 to the mid-1920s with distinct characteristics in terms of character, plot, and setting. These films featured the most popular actresses of the day – Borelli, Bertini, and Pina Menichelli, among others – and took place in high society, consigning the actresses to eloquent parlors and high fashion and removing them from the travails of everyday life.[28] Their plots often revolved around torrid love affairs, sacrificing mothers, or femmes fatales, who were either victims of circumstance or architects of their own ruin. For Angela Dalle Vacche, they exemplified the tension between the new woman of modernity and the Catholic *mater dolorosa*. As divine creatures, stars were more akin to Greek and Roman mythology, as they lived out the contradictions between being human and otherworldly, specifically the relationship of the sacred to the self. This conflict between the sacred and the profane, and of on-screen and off-screen identities, was a continuous process, with constant shifts as the performers assumed different roles on screen and interacted with the changing landscape of gender roles in the first decades of twentieth-century Italy. [29]

Female performers, in articles devoted to them in film magazines, appeared noble, aristocratic, and godlike. They were statues in motion, whose pantomimic gestures articulated their primordial status.[30] In describing the actress Adriana Costamagna, an early star working for Itala Film, *La Vita Cinematografica* wrote in 1911:

> A Greek form that designs her supple body; two large eyes that scrutinize the depths of one's soul, whose profound pupils reflect in their entirety a poem of sweetness and a hymn of persuasive gentleness; culminating in an exquisite intelligence, a supremely noble instinct that wants to consistently elevate itself, in order to soar into a sky that does not know the melancholy of sunsets: all these elements of perfection form Adriana Costamagna into an exceptional, superior woman.[31]

The fact that the above-cited metaphors make recourse to other arts – poetry and dance in particular – elevates the description to a lofty, artistic level while reinforcing the intermediality of cinema's first years. Lacking is any reference to her daily personal life in favor of her professional abilities and an aristocratic agenda, reinforcing a class distinction that the divas and the diva films actively cultivated. Moreover, the female stars did not seem functional to a national ideology, but rather to a sacred, celestial ideal, one in Italy's case that is more sexualized than others. For Cristina Jandelli, their bodies were "vehicles of spirituality," whose mystic, sublime bodies appeared as priestesses of pagan love rights.[32]

The divas had to play off a male counterpart, but these actors, such as Alberto Capozzi, Mario Bonnard, Febo Mari, Tullio Carminati, and Alberto Collo, never achieved the equivalent level of stardom. The two most popular Italian actors – Pagano (Maciste) and Ghione (Za La Mort) – belonged instead to the more populist genres of the strongman and serial dramas. These were films that, unlike the diva film, appealed predominantly to the lower- and middle-class spectator, family films filled with suspense, action, and, in the case of the Maciste series, ironic humor. One important difference between the two stars is that while

Ghione played a variety of roles (even in some notable diva films opposite Bertini in Baldassarre Negroni's *Histoire d'un Pierrot* (*Pierrot the Prodigal,* Celio Film, 1914), Pagano remained associated with only one character, Maciste, from the 1914 release of *Cabiria* until the series had run its course in 1926 (and even thereafter, when the series ended). Ghione was also a prominent figure behind the camera, directing more than fifty films throughout his career.[33]

If the divas were sacred, divine creatures, their male counterparts were profoundly secular. As Morin also observed generally about the first decades of stars and cinema, "The personality of the male star is much more closely related to qualities that are actually heroic: the masculine hero does battle not only for his love but against wickedness, destiny, injustice, death."[34] Male stars, with their physical, iconographic, and historical ties to the nation, were clearly of this world. The emphasis on their physicality, whether muscular or not, and their connection to the more lowbrow genres, such as comedies, serials, and detective series, further grounded their stardom in the everyday world. Their magic came from their ability to perform tricks on screen, an aspect that was especially relevant for early cinema and its recourse to magic for attraction and spectacle, and later for Maciste for his feats of strength, provoking the question: "How does he do that?"[35] Maciste was the secularized symbol of the sacred nation, and, as such, sexuality had no place or space within diegetic and extradiegetic imperatives. Instead, the strongman emerged as the genres' moral compass. In his exhibitions (and exhibitionism), the strongman commanded being a nationalist rather than a sexual spectacle.[36] The national narration of Italian male stardom, to paraphrase Elena dell'Agnese, finds the perfect instrument in the on- and off-screen body of Maciste as his character merges with nation to create the country's iconic masculine ideal.[37]

The primacy of stardom in relation to the film industry continued as the divas' popularity soared, as did, to some extent, that of the divos as well, much to the chagrin of many intellectuals and industry players. A September 1918 editorial in *La Vita Cinematografica* bemoaned the power that stars held over the creative process: "No one thinks about, writes, or creates a beautiful and original work anymore, but instead throws together the usual mess to allow a more or less authentic actress, or a pseudo-actor, to sentimentalize verbosely on screen."[38] A similar piece, written five months earlier, equally lamented this tendency: "Italian film studios, rather than make films, have for the last several years made celebrities.... Celebrity walks hand in hand with the stupidity of our studio heads, along with discord, disorder and disorganization."[39] Although more of an exhortation to the film industry to consolidate and unionize, as much of it would with the formation of the Unione Cinematografica Italiana (UCI) in the following year, the latter editorial's use of the word "celebrity" conveniently historicized the term. *La Vita Cinematografica* lamented the power that stars held as commodities that dictated artistic production, and both the UCI and the journal employ the word "celebrity" in a pejorative way: the first as an admonition to what would happen if the industry relied too much on star power over good scripts and direction, the second as the potential result of a failure of the Italian film industry to consolidate in the face of imminently increasing international competition from abroad at the war's end.

What becomes apparent is that in Italian silent cinema, stardom was inseparable from film form. Each genre had its own means of signification that were intrinsically linked to how it narratively and visually constructed its protagonists. Relevant for this discussion is the broader notion of "type": the types of films (genres) in which each actor/character/star was featured, the types of social and cultural constructions to which they spoke, and the types of shots employed to configure their protagonists on screen. The types of shots used created distinct configurations of time and space: close-ups and static camera in the diva films, and long and tracking shots privileging action in the strongman film, as well as quicker-paced editing in the latter. Certain genres also played to particular audiences: comedies, serials, and action-adventure films constituted more popular forms of entertainment, while the melodramas, historical epics, and literary adaptations betrayed attempts to artistically elevate the cinematic medium to a greater artistic level. Rather than being types themselves, it was the types of films that aided in determining stardom.[40]

COMEDIES, HISTORICAL EPICS, AND THE MACISTE SERIES

Despite early cinema's widely acknowledged and inherent international nature, each national industry presented significant features that were more typical of local rather than national or international dynamics.[41] Early Italian cinema was locally centered, with much of the production concentrated in the cosmopolitan centers of Rome, Milan, Turin, and Naples and exhibition more of a traveling urban and rural phenomenon as non-native-produced films arrived in Italy's various regions.[42] Fairs, both urban and rural, were also early sites of display for these traveling film displays (known as *cinema ambulante,* or mobile cinema). And while cinema was more an urban than a rural phenomenon and still concentrated in the northern half of the peninsula, the new medium became more dispersed through exhibitions during provincial carnivals, fairs, and local celebrations, already the homes to early pre-cinematic forms of entertainment such as the magic lantern and its more recent incarnations.[43]

It was not until 1905, with, among other developments and innovations, the success of what is considered the first Italian film, *La presa di Roma (20 settembre 1870)* (The Capture of Rome, 20 September 1870; Alberini and Santoni), that the industry began establishing, defining, and articulating a national cinematic production.[44] Filoteo Alberini and Dante Santoni inaugurated the first Italian film studio, later to become the renowned Cines. With the institution of additional film studios in major cities, films' increasing length (up through one reel), and the proliferation of permanent venues devoted exclusively to their exhibition, cinema began its rapid takeoff in Italy after 1905, first with an emphasis solely on production and then on the expansion of points of distribution.[45] The development and international distribution of genre production – in particular the comic series and historical epics – spoke to Italian cinema's global ambitions. Their phenomenal success was an indication, to Italian studios, that Italian cinema would conquer the world, just as Italy itself had begun and should continue to do as a nation.[46]

Early Italian film genres ranged from elaborate costume films, historical dramas, and literary adaptations; *actualités* (topical nonfiction films based on current events); scientific and educational films; and comic films, which in Italy constituted the first film series.[47] Comics and historical epics, although seemingly radically different in their tone, style, and narrative composition, were the most influential for the strongman film in general and the Maciste series in particular, with their vivid popular appeal, comedy and comic relief, and physicality, whether in service to humor or history. Comic films especially possessed a self-awareness and featured an ironic self-referentiality that would become a characteristic of the Maciste films.[48]

Early comic films in Europe, initially 15–17 meters in length (approximately one minute in screen time), were mostly farcical sketches centered on one character with recognizable traits and features along with one principle action or sight gag. The first known Italian comic film was *Il finto storpio del castello* (The Fake Cripple of the Castle, 1896) by Italo Pacchioni, in which a man posing as a beggar is ultimately revealed to be a charlatan and chased away. Leopoldo Fregoli, a theatrical *transformiste* (a performer known for his rapid change of costume and character), soon followed, creating a series of short films that were some of the first to feature the performer's name in the title, among them *Fregoli trasformista* (Fregoli the Transformist), *Fregoli donna* (Lady Fregoli), and *Fregoli al ristorante* (Fregoli at a Restaurant), all from 1898. In the years between 1908 and 1911, Italy experienced the birth and establishment of its own homegrown comic series (the *comica a serie*), which would appear regularly on screen (about once per month) and feature a consistency of character but a variable in situation.[49] With relatively few intertitles, the flow from one situation into another produced the comic rhythm. The main goal of such films was entertainment at any cost, often through the blatant plagiarism of other films (particularly in the case of Italian cinema "borrowing" from French comics such as Max Linder) and the repetition of proven formulas rather than any kind of innovative strategies.

According to Gian Piero Brunetta, precisely what made these comic films unique, as opposed to mere copies of their French counterparts and what the Maciste series would later borrow, was their immersion in the everyday life of turn-of-the-century Italy: they appealed to both popular and bourgeois spectators and at the same time recorded, in an almost diary-like fashion, the lower middle-class and middle-class caught between a traditional and a modernizing Italy. Filmed more often in urban settings rather than rural ones, these films were parodies of emerging bourgeois rituals and cultures, although, unlike many early American comics working under Mack Sennett, they had a less problematic connection to modernization in terms of the characters' relationship to and

1.2. Publicity photo of André Deed.

interaction with mechanical objects, such as cars and machines. Authority, particularly law enforcement, was not the target of their jokes and gags. Instead, political institutions and public assistance, such as the Red Cross, anti-drinking societies, and feminists and suffragettes, bore the brunt of their humor.[50]

In many ways these comic short films, and the rise to prominence of the comedians featured therein, revealed the economic, commercial, and psychological mechanisms at the base of what would become the Italian star system; the actors and actresses who commanded the highest salaries and achieved the greatest recognition were inextricably linked to particular generic forms and modes of expression. One of the

most successful comic series was that of Cretinetti, known in English as
Foolshead, featuring André Deed (fig. 1.2). Deed had already established
himself as a successful French screen actor as the character Boireau.[51]
Recognizing the monetary potential behind these French comic serials,
Giovanni Pastrone, Itala Film's creative director (and the subsequent
creative force behind the Maciste series), chose Deed over Max Linder,
believing Deed to be better known and more popular in Italy.[52] What
made Deed's films different from other comic characters' cinematic
sketches was that they featured a narrative arc and did not focus solely
on the gag – an important, highly imitable diegetic characteristic that
later genres, including the Maciste series, could and would successfully
adapt. Similarly, select Deed films featured surreal special effects, such as
the use of visual tricks and the acceleration of the hectic rhythm typical
of chase comedies, all later borrowed by Maciste through the genius of
the renowned special effects wizard Segundo de Chomón.[53]

Other popular comic series, in addition to Cretinetti, included those
featuring Fricot (Ernesto Vaser), Kri Kri (Raymond Frau, under the
pseudonym Raymond Dandy), Robinet (Marcelo Fernández Peréz,
under the pseudonym Marcel Fabre), Tontolini (known in the United
States as Jenkins) and Polidor (both played by Ferdinand Guillaume).
The comic series, however, did not prove to be a viable form as the industry shifted to multi-reel production in the mid-1910s, and these films
were among the first to suffer during the post–World War I crisis that
affected the Italian film industry. It did not move as successfully to the
feature-length film as the selected American few did, such as the films
of Charlie Chaplin, Buster Keaton, and Harold Lloyd. In addition, the
relatively underdeveloped avenue of the sophisticated comedy exemplified in the late 1910s and early 1920s by the films of Lucio D'Ambra, with
their refined sentimentalism and social sarcasm and cynicism (the opposite of Maciste), yielded few lasting results.[54]

Following closely on the heels of the comics was the detective or
crime series, which, instead of featuring a recognizable performer, such
as Guillaume or Deed, focused on reoccurring characters. Once again

1.3. (*facing*) Publicity photo of Emilio Ghione.

the blueprint here is French cinema, which was the locus of most of this type of early serial production and the home of the literary serial, the *roman-feuilleton*. Although many of these performers were recognizably French – Arséne Lupin, Zigomar, and, the most popular of all, Fantô-mas – others possessed Anglo-Saxon names, such as Nick Carter and Sherlock Holmes. Essential to these more dramatically oriented series was the idea of transformation; not only were actors interchangeable, but the characters themselves could morph into other creatures.[55]

The Italian film industry's best attempt to adapt these successful formulas to feature-length productions was a series of Za La Mort films, starring, actor-director Emilio Ghione, who played the eponymous thief (fig. 1.3). Ghione acted in and directed *Za La Mort* (Tiber-Film, 1915), *Topi grigi* in eight episodes (The Grey Mice, Tiber-Film, 1918), and *Dollari e fraks* (Dollars and Tuxedos, Itala Film, 1919, four episodes). In a blatant attempt to co-opt the French Fantômas series, Za La Mort continued his crime spree from one film to the other, constantly evading capture. Although most serial films featured Italian characters in the service of appropriate social goals and as embodiments of the status quo, for Brunetta, the Za La Mort serial, with its popular settings and nefarious underworld, revealed a poor and socially arrested Italy unseen in other films of the era. Yet the series firmly established, as Monica Dall'Asta has argued, the fusion between character and actor that would become characteristic to Italian serial and episodic films, especially the Maciste/Pagano synthesis.[56]

Unlike comic films, detective and crime one-reelers began to mutate successfully into longer multi-reel films, as would the Maciste films.[57] Eventually, overarching narratives that carried from one film to the next gave birth to what came to be known as the serial, which added the concept of continuity of narrative to the continuity of character. One story would be told over several episodes, or the plot would leave the viewer hanging – the cliffhanger – until he or she was able to go to the theater to see the next episode. Also known as episodic films (*film a episodi*), they had varying viewing practices: sometimes shown one per week (as in the Pathé-produced *The Perils of Pauline* series or the Kalem Company's *Hazards of Helen*), or several episodes would be shown all at once, making up, in a sense, a feature-length film. For the nascent film industries in the United States and Europe, serials were the perfect model to invigorate the marketplace in that they standardized production, recycled materials and ideas, were easily publicized from one film to the next, and guaranteed an audience. The Maciste films had several serial incarnations: the now lost 1918 films *Maciste poliziotto* (Maciste the Policeman), *Maciste atleta* (Maciste the Athlete), and *Maciste medium* (Maciste the Medium); the twenty-four-reel, twelve-part American serial *The Liberator* (1919), released only in the United States; and *La trilogia di Maciste* (The Maciste Trilogy), a serial of three full-length feature films with a continuing story arc, cliffhangers between each film, and exhibited in consecutive order within a tight chronological timeline.[58]

The historical epic, the most popular and profitable product of early Italian cinema as well as the cinematic birthplace of the strongman and Maciste, was a genre that, like the comic films and detective serials, borrowed from existing tropes, owing part of its success (again) to early French films and early Italian cinema's emphasis on the national. Film d'Art (1908), a French production company whose films were distributed by Pathé-Frères, specialized in theatrical, literary, and historical adaptations for the screen. The Rome-based Film d'Arte Italiana (1909) was one of Pathé-Frères' attempts to enter into production in another country rather than solely distribution on foreign soil. Like Film d'Art, the company focused on transcultural literary adaptations, including the Italian versions of Shakespeare's *Othello* (1909) and *The Merchant of Venice* (1910), both directed by Gerolamo Lo Savio.[59] Italy's picturesque and relatively unchanged landscape, not to mention the preservation of Ancient Roman monuments and ruins, made location shooting easy, even though most films constructed their own sets. Low-cost labor made large crowd scenes, an Italian hallmark of these types of films, both possible and affordable.[60]

What distinguished Italian films from these and other national epic productions was an authenticity of settings, costumes, and mise-en-scène that exuded a genuine nationalist sentiment, including the prominently featured strongman character as a national symbol.[61] Contemporary periodicals echoed this nationalist tone; articles abounded about the patriotic potential of cinema and cinema's own capacity to bring artistic glory to the nation, consistently comparing Italian production to that of other nations (at first France and then in the late 1910s and 1920s the United States). Articles with titles such as the 1912 "Dai trionfi del palcoscenico agli splendori della cinematografia: glorie italiane" (From Stage Triumph to Screen Splendor: Italian Glory) appeared in *L'Illustrazione Cinematografica*, one of the many new periodicals devoted to the new medium.[62] Even an Art Nouveau–styled magazine like *Il Maggese Cinematografico* couched its 1913 mission statement in nationalistic terms:

> We begin the publication of a new and elegant journal, dedicated entirely to the artistic life. England, America, Germany and France have had a similar journal for a long time. Italy, one of the first nations of the world, had had nothing similar. "Il Maggese Cinematografico" is the most beautiful journal of its kind.[63]

Similarly, in the 30 December 1911 issue of *La Vita Cinematografica*, the editors lamented the French company Pathè-Frères' Film d'Arte Italiana, the Italian branch office modeled on its Film D'Art, and their "illogical" and poorly shot adaptations of Italian classics like *Françoise de Rimini* (1910) and praised Italian efforts to correct the situation:

> When, as we do, one suffers from that malady one calls patriotism, nothing is more painful than to see our great and beautiful nation, that was always the cradle of all the beautiful arts, lag behind in a manifestation of ingenuity and progress. Cinema is now surging to be a real and true art form, and as such Italy must not be second to anyone. . . .
> Films of Italian Art!
> This time, yes. Actors, directors, setting, manufacturing: all Italian and all absolutely good. Success is assured!
> And may the warm approval of *La Vita Cinematografia* accompany them to this victory.[64]

Many Italian historical epics were in fact adaptations of successful national literary works; others expanded upon a contemporary theatrical trend whose major exponent was Pietro Cossa (1830–1881), and whose works based on historical events – including *Nerone* (1872), *Messalina* (1876), *Giuliano l'Apostata* (Giuliano the Apostate, 1877), and *Cleopatra* (1877) – imbued historical characters with human dimensions. The historical epic's stock characters were the bold and loyal young man who falls in love with a helpless young woman because she is a slave or a hostage; the shifty rival; the young girl snared by individuals without scruples; the faithful nurse or slave; an old man unable to understand the young people's love; and the good giant with superhuman force who can solve any problem. Common dramatic tropes and spectacles included an explosion of natural elements and a violent encounter of opposing forces (Christians vs. Pagans, Romans vs. Jews, liberty vs. slavery) serving as backdrops for the story of the individual characters.[65]

This popular dimension of nationalism expressed itself in the historical epic's vibrant spectacles and their widespread appeal.[66] With their literary origins and their recourse to the historical past, as well as their spectacularity and attractiveness, these films brought together both bourgeois and popular audiences in an attempt to educate, elevate, and enlighten Italian and international viewers. For Brunetta, they were a way of turning film, as it developed in its early years, into an effective, new instrument of cultural hegemony while at the same time promoting an agenda of class mobility that allowed for slaves to fall in love with their masters and, in the case of the strongmen to whom this genre gave birth – Ursus, Spartacus, and Maciste – to be celebrated as heroes.[67] Those heroes, moreover, represent and satisfy the desire for redemption of the socially inferior class but always in service to a greater power, be it Christianity in *Quo Vadis?* (Cines, 1913) or the glory of the nation, in *Spartaco* (*Spartacus,* Pasquali, 1913), and, as we will see, in *Cabiria.*

The first historical epic dates to 1908 and the first of two eventual adaptations of *The Last Days of Pompeii* produced by Ambrosio Film.[68] Based on the 1834 novel by Edward Bulwer-Lytton (translated and published in Italian in 1865), the film spurred other epic productions, such as *Nerone* (*Nero; or, The Burning of Rome,* Ambrosio, 1909), *Giulio Cesare* (*Julius Caesar,* Itala Film, 1909), and *La caduta di Troia.*[69] The major turning point in the genre's evolution was Enrico Guazzoni's *Quo Vadis?* which, like many of the films under discussion, continued to circulate well after its release in early 1913 (it was shot and edited in 1912). The rhetorical references to Ancient Rome, particularly the notion of the myth of an imperial nation based on a collective of strongmen – a theme that

1.4. The coliseum scene in *Spartaco* (1913).

would play itself out particularly well in *Spartacus* – contributed to the film's success (fig.1.4). Its use of depth of field and the crowd, a hallmark of the early Italian historical films, increased in sophistication; for example, the scene at the Roman forum as the slaves are fed to the lions, while not particularly complex in terms of its editing, created realistic suspense through the use of reaction shots of the on-screen spectators and actual lions prowling in the frame's foreground. The Roman forum scene in *Quo Vadis?* is noteworthy as well for the heroic exploits of Ursus the slave, who saves a woman strapped to the back of a bull and then kills the bull with his bare hands, providing one of the first of Maciste's models. Heavily promoted in film magazines (it received a four-page spread announcing its imminent arrival in the January 1913 issue of *La Vita Cinematografica*), *Quo Vadis?* cemented the industry's reliance on the full-length feature film and was exported all over the world to great acclaim.[70] Similarly, the publicity for *Spartacus* in the 30 September issue of the same publication touted its forty free-roaming lions and the gladiators' battles against them, horse races, and athletic competitions, all part of the "greatest cinematic spectacle yet," only to inspire and ultimately to be surpassed a little over a year later by *Cabiria*.[71]

Ironically, the success of the historical epics was one of the many causes of the crisis that plagued the Italian film industry after the First World War. Their soaring costs, the industry's inability to innovate the formula, and its stubborn reliance on the genre in a misguided attempt to improve its grave fortune proved fatal. But the genre would not disappear before the making of Italy's most groundbreaking silent film, *Cabiria*, and introducing the character who would spawn the most successful character to populate a film series and the most successful male actor of the day: Maciste. What would ultimately distinguish the historical epic from the Maciste series, and the later strongman films as well, was not only the temporal shift to contemporary Italy and the centrality of the muscled hero but also the strategic and essential place of humor in the characters' exploits and the films' narrative strategies.

THE STRONGMAN FILM

Historical films valorized the muscular spectacles of Ancient Rome: exhibitions of strength, gymnastics, and athletic displays. The strongman therein was a leader, albeit one who was circumscribed by the limits of slavery. Once freed from those bounds as the protagonist of his own series, however, the strongman passed from slave to autonomous subject, from supporting actor to protagonist, who brought a unique genre to Italian screens at a time when Italy was itself in search of its own national identity. After World War I his whole, hard image contrasted the mangled and dismembered male body that was so prevalent in the public eye. It is no coincidence that the years following the war, between 1919 and 1922, are what Alberto Farassino considers the golden age of the strongman film, when 118 strongman films were produced by a variety of studios, mostly centered, as might be expected at this point, in northern Italy.[72] With the immense popularity of the Maciste series in the mid-1910s, they preceded their American counterparts – Elmo Lincoln's Tarzan, Eddie Polo, and Jack Dempsey, to name a few – by several years.[73] The muscular genre also intersected with various ideologies and movements of the day, from nationalism and *arditismo,* the political movement spurred by the power and renown of specially trained shock troops employed during World War I; the philosophical tenets on strength and action of D'Annunzio's *superuomo;* Darwin's survival of the fittest; the futurist writer Aldo Palazzeschi's *saltimbanco* (acrobat); and futurism's embodiment of movement and dynamism.[74]

The phenomenal popularity of the first Maciste films, *Maciste* (see chapter 2) and *Maciste alpino* (see chapter 3), while not the first films to feature strongmen, did prove that there was an audience for this type of film. In addition to Ursus and Spartacus, an important transitional character was Domenico Gambino as Saltarelli, whose 1909–1910 series for Itala Film fused the comic genre with his acrobatic prowess. Gambino would later gain greater fame as Saetta, star of his own strongman series in the late 1910s into the 1920s (and co-star in *Maciste imperatore*) (fig. 1.5).[75] While films with circus or adventure themes began to appear on screen with such titles as *L'acrobata mascherato* (The Masked Acrobat, Cines, 1915), *Il jockey della morte* (The Jockey of Death, Vay Film, 1915), *Il principino saltimbanco* (The Acrobat Prince, Società Italiana Eclair, 1914), and *Il romanzo di un atleta* (The Story of an Athlete, Gloria Films, 1915), it was not until after the end of World War I, and after the success of *Maciste,* that the genre flourished. As one 1919 article in *La Vita Cinematografica* observed: "Who can keep track of these giants, these male phenomena, who spilled out onto film screens? But if these men are numerous, very few of them are interesting or have any value. There was and exists nevertheless a real *macistismo.*"[76]

Its major protagonists, aside from Maciste and Saetta, included Sansone or Sansonia (Luciano Albertini), Ausonia (Mario Guaita Ausonia), Aiax (Carlo Aldini), and even several women: Astrea (the Countess Barbieri) and Sansonetta (Albertini's wife) were two of the most celebrated.[77] Some, such as Albertini, founded their own film studios and produced their own movies. Although the strongman proved popular as the Italian film industry itself began its rapid decline in the 1920s, the genre too suffered due to critical pressure; the shift in the public's more sophisticated taste for American, German, and French films; and the collapse of Italy's finances and the financial disarray of the industry

1.5. Domenico Gambino as Saetta in *Saetta e la ghigliottina* (1923).

itself. Several important stars, like Pagano, left for Germany to populate its Sensationfilm. Ironically, upon his return from Germany, Pagano would go on to make some of the Maciste series' most celebrated films with FERT and the producer/film mogul Stefano Pittaluga, whose focus on big-budget tent-pole films revived the Maciste series to the original glories of *Cabiria* in the guise of the exotic adventure film.

Alberto Farassino has isolated several characteristics that were common to the strongman films, which continued the tradition of mining the porous boundaries of other contemporary film genres that would require action: detective films, spy films, adventure films, and war films, with the strongman as the added pivotal element. While there are some exceptions, the strongman does not kill his (or her) enemy, but rather uses his strength to subdue and deliver him to the proper law-enforcement authorities. Many of the characters' names recalled mythological characters, such as Sansone, Maciste, Aiax, and Galaor. Not a uniquely urban phenomenon (many take place in the open countryside as opposed to closed urban environments), these films regaled in the modern world, as many featured cars, trains, factories and other signs of Italy's progressive march toward further industrialization and modernization, including an ironic modernist sensibility in their intertitles that provided much of the films' humor. Further signs of this ironic tone lie in their recourse to the "film within the film motif," which became the premise of many a Maciste film as well others, such as *Sansone acrobata del Kolossal* (Sansone, Blockbuster Acrobat, Albertini Film, 1920). With a strategic balance between action and narrative, these were films made with a good heart and good sense for the entire family.[78]

The strongman films fit somewhere between the realist and decadent/expressionist tendencies of Italian cinema's early years. On the one hand, such films required a suspension of disbelief with respect to their plot twists, the main character's incredible feats of strength, and their often ludicrous inciting incidents. On the other hand, they were filmed on location all over Italy, although mostly in the north, in both urban and rural settings, thus designed to appeal to the widest possible audience. Their characters' familiarity via popular theatrical traditions, their naturalistic acting, even with incredible and incredulous feats of strength, ran counter to the overwrought acting style of their female counterparts, the divas.[79] Moreover, as opposed to the divas, the strongmen were desexualized heroes representing a realistic fusion between the extraordinary and the everyday, a characteristic that was essential to Italian male stardom of the silent period.[80] These were lay and pagan spectacles that valorized the body over the spirit, infused with popular good sense and good humor.

Firmly cemented in that pagan, modern ground is our hero, Bartolomeo Pagano. Pagano is the prime example of an actor whose star persona merged with and subsumed his off-screen existence. The relationship between character and actor was at the heart of early Italian series production and is fundamental for comprehending the Maciste/Pagano collapse as well as the dawn of his stardom. As his biographical booklet *Maciste (Bartolomeo Pagano)* explicitly stated: "Now, the Maciste we see on screen is the same in private life; he is the same man for his goodness, for his strength, and for his unending triumphs" (2). His stardom also articulated multiple significations of early twentieth-century Italian masculinity, reinforcing his status as a pagan yet sacred national screen icon. For the strongman, despite his extraordinary physique and astonishing abilities, he was basically an ordinary man and a national role model for a struggling nation. Much of his terrestrial appeal, and that of other strongmen as well, grew out of the genres to which they turned for inspiration: the comic and serial film.

*   *   *

The increasing secularization of everyday life, the integration of new technologies and forms of narrative, and the rise of cinema as both popular culture and legitimate art form radically altered the Italian cultural scene. Political changes, culminating in Italy's entry into the First World War, paved the way for the emergence of the strongman film out of the ruins, so to speak, of the historical epic genre to develop into the ideal and serialized muscular citizen of the young Italian nation. In evoking old myths and forms of representation, the film star, in this case in the guise of the strongman, created new ones that were more akin to and in line with a rapidly changing but still lagging twentieth-century Italy: the myth of the efficient mechanized man who, through humor and goodwill, leads the nation by example. Maciste embodied on screen the powerful male body as national screen symbol and pagan idol as he made the transition from the ancient world to twentieth-century Turin, from the historical epic *Cabiria* to the first of what would be Italy's most successful and most original film series, *Maciste.*

TWO

From Slave to Master

CABIRIA (1914) AND MACISTE (1915)

IN OCTOBER 1914, AS ITALY DEBATED INTERVENTION INTO World War I, a young Benito Mussolini wrote in the socialist newspaper *Avanti:* "Reality is moving at an accelerated pace. We have had the very singular privilege of living during the most tragic period in world history. Do we want to be – as men and as socialists – inert spectators to this grandiose drama? Or don't we want to be – in some way and in some sense – protagonists?"[1] The deliberate use of theatrical or cinematic terminology – "spectators" and "protagonists" – within the context of Mussolini's eventual rejection of socialism due to his support for intervention into the war echoes significant political and cultural developments that would reverberate throughout the coming years: what would Italy's role as a nation be in the larger international context, and what role would individual Italians play therein? It also indicates the increasing importance that theatricality and performativity played in Italian culture, society, and politics. This transformation occurred during a crucial transitional phase in Italian cinema as films became more ideologically marked in support of nationalist policies and as the film series (and subsequently the film serial) passed from short one- to two-reel films to a feature-length format, both episodic and self-contained.

The year 1914 also witnessed the release of Itala Film's historical epic *Cabiria,* the most expensive and ambitious to date of the many historical epics. Directed by Giovanni Pastrone, Itala Film's primary creative force, the film bases its story on Livy's account of the history of the Roman Republic; other literary influences include Petrarch's *Africa* and Gustave Flaubert's *Salammbô* (1862).[2] In its intended historical accuracy, the plot of *Cabiria* features strategic appearances by the Roman military leader Scipio Africanus and the Carthaginian commander Hannibal showcased in elaborately staged battle scenes and a stunning desert-crossing sequence. Pastrone oversaw all aspects of the film's production, from its intricate sets and elegant costume design to complex shooting and editing. The director employed four cameras to shoot more than twenty thousand meters of film on location in Rome, Sicily, and Tunisia. *Cabiria*'s final cost was equal to approximately twenty less extravagant films of the day.[3]

In addition to its groundbreaking role in early film history, *Cabiria* is remembered as the birthplace of the character Maciste, who, as the loveable "Gentle Giant," stole the show. This chapter examines Maciste's passage from supporting character in *Cabiria* (1914) to leading man in the first film in the series, *Maciste* (1915), directed by Vincenzo Dénizot. From one film to the other, the character of Maciste underwent several radical alterations; most dramatically, he changed from a black-bodied African slave to a white Italian. Through a close examination of both films, as well as contemporary periodicals and archival documents, I show that Maciste, already embraced as a national icon, had to be white, and the first Maciste film takes pains to reinforce his whiteness through a complete collapse of the dichotomy between character and actor and, in a kind of intertextual backward reading, by revealing Maciste's previous blackness on screen in *Cabiria* as a masquerade. Italian audiences had already been rooting for the slave in the 1913 historical epics *Quo Vadis?* (Ursus) and *Spartacus,* in which virility trumped class and, by extension, race. The racial discourses at work in Maciste's metamorphosis popularized current anthropological tenets of northern Italian and white superiority through the classic cinematic devices of heroic sacrifice, spectacular feats, and moral righteousness, all embodied in his muscled, hypermasculine, white physique.

Maciste's transformation from slave to master invites interpretation on multiple levels. First, it represents one of the first "spin-off" series in Italian cinema, a practice that would become the trademark of such popular and unique post–World War II Italian genres as the peplum and the spaghetti western, while simultaneously establishing the conventions that would characterize not only the Maciste series but also the strongman films overall. Second, the 1915 *Maciste* narrativizes the character's transformation by referencing self-consciously the cultural mechanisms at work in film stardom as elucidated in chapter 1, which were already quite familiar to producers and critics both in Italy and abroad. Off screen, Itala Film and the popular press propagated a star persona that firmly cemented the identity of Bartolomeo Pagano within a racial and national discourse that privileged the north over the south.

This chapter unpacks Maciste's racial repositioning from black to white within the context of rising Italian nationalism of the 1910s. The serialized character constituted a national hero as he exuded a white muscular ideal, safely affixed as racially and nationally Italian, at the crux of the country's intervention into World War I. On a broader scale it shows how in the second half of the 1910s the character's stardom would pave the way for Maciste to become a symbol of wartime heroism and patriotism as well as an emblem of the alliance between the United States and Italy in that conflict while simultaneously establishing Pagano as an autonomous star of his own highly successful series of films.

CABIRIA

Subtitled "Historical Vision of the Third Century BC," *Cabiria* recounts the kidnapping of a young Roman girl after the eruption of Mount Etna in Catania and her imprisonment and intended sacrifice at Carthage's Temple of Moloch.[4] Fulvio Axilla (played by Umberto Mozzato), a Roman patrician living secretly in Carthage as a spy, and his faithful African slave Maciste (Pagano) undertake the daring task of rescuing Cabiria from her doom, persuaded by Croessa, Cabiria's nurse. They bravely and successfully accomplish their goal, fending off multiple Carthaginians (Croessa does not survive). Later, when the group attempts to leave Carthage in order to save Rome from Hannibal's imminent attack, they are ambushed. Fulvio Axilla escapes, but Maciste, after having passed Cabiria off to Sofonisba, the daughter of King Hasdrubal, becomes a tortured prisoner and is chained to a millstone for a life of hard labor; Cabiria, renamed Elissa, becomes Sofonisba's slave. Ten years later Fulvio Axilla returns to Carthage and rescues Maciste, who in a famous scene liberates himself from the chains that bind him. After almost starving to death during their escape, Fulvio Axilla and Maciste are captured by the Carthaginians once again. This time Cabiria/Elissa comes to their rescue, bringing them water and kindness. Eventually Maciste breaks out of the jail by bending the prison's iron bars, but ultimately he and Fulvio Axilla are forced to take refuge and hold siege, this time in a conveniently well-stocked wine and food cellar. Sofonisba persuades Massinissa, the Numidian king now ruling Carthage, to spare their lives, and before she sacrifices her own life for the greater good of Rome, she frees Cabiria. Fulvio Axilla and Cabiria fall in love as Maciste accompanies them on their victorious voyage back to Rome.

The film premiered simultaneously on 18 April 1914 in Turin at the Teatro Vittorio Emanuele (fig. 2.1), and at Milan's Teatro Lirico.[5] It subsequently replicated these elaborate, high-class premieres in major Italian cities and, following its immediate success, in more popular venues for many years. Musical accompaniment featured a live orchestra playing an original score by Manlio Mazza and included an eleven-minute interlude titled *The Symphony of Fire* by the renowned composer Ildebrando Pizzetti, Mazza's teacher.[6] More than a mere film exhibition, the premieres and showings of *Cabiria* around Italy and later around the world were major and unique events, highly promoted and publicized by Itala Film with elaborately designed posters, brochures, and programs. In Rome, for instance, the noted pilot Giovanni Widmer distributed flyers from the air on the day of the film's premiere in that city (21 April).[7]

Pastrone was arguably, at that time, the most influential figure in the nascent years of the Italian film industry. In 1905 he began his career working as an accountant for the film studio Carlo Rossi and Company, and, because of his facility with technology and his ability to speak several foreign languages, quickly rose in the ranks to become the studio's administrative director. Upon Rossi's liquidation of the company and departure for the Cines studio in Rome, Pastrone and his collaborator Carlo Sciamengo formed Itala Film in 1908; at only twenty-six years of age, Pastrone became its artistic director and the film studio's creative epicenter, while Sciamengo concerned himself with the business side of the operation. That is not to say, however, that Pastrone saw himself as an artist in a sea of industrialists, although his perfectionist nature revealed itself on the sets of some of Itala Film's most noteworthy productions,

2.1. Publicity for *Cabiria*'s exhibition at the Teatro
Vittorio Emanuele in Turin (1914).

such as the previously mentioned comedies of Cretinetti, as well as one of the early historical epics, *La caduta di Troia* (1910), and the feuilleton/ detective hybrid *Tigris* (1913), directed by Vincenzo Dénizot, one of the many Frenchmen who contributed to the explosion of early Italian cinema.[8] On the contrary, Pastrone recognized film's role as a highly profitable industry from the outset. *Cabiria* constituted both an artistic and commercial experiment, one that simultaneously attempted to create a work of art and a money-making endeavor.[9]

In addition to its elaborate set design and groundbreaking moving camera,[10] *Cabiria's* other technical innovations included strategic use of artificial lighting, ornate costume design, and a complexity in plot previously unseen in Italian cinema. Scenes of volcano eruptions, the human sacrifice at the Temple of Moloch, and Hannibal crossing the Alps reveal the unique range of special effects and inventive use of color that the film achieved thanks to well-known Catalán film director/cinematographer/ special effects man Segundo de Chomón, whom Pastrone had wooed to Itala Film in 1912.[11] At the same time, it borrowed from previous historical epics: Ursus and Spartacus were the models for Maciste, a volcanic eruption had already been seen in both versions of *Gli ultimi giorni di Pompeii* (Ambrosio Film, 1908 and 1913), and Pastrone had featured massive crowd scenes in *La caduta di Troia*.

The film was a resounding critical and popular success, a fact that was well documented in newspaper reviews all across the world.[12] The day after its premiere an anonymous reviewer writing for the Milan newspaper *Corriere della Sera* noted the potential implications of its landmark achievement for film criticism:

> Are we perhaps at the point to see the formation of a new type of critic: the film critic? . . . Only, instead of speaking about acting, voice, accent, actors, dialogue, and style, the new critic will have to talk about feature films, well-developed positive prints, lighting effects, still or even projection – Heaven bless it – and about a few other things that until now had not been in the critic's purview, but rather had to do with the apparatus of photography.[13]

Others discussed its impact on the audience:

> As I have already said, warm applause greeted the end of each episode, as well as several marvelous scenes, all of which show that the film's success was not and will not be solely due to the Poet [D'Annunzio] who designed

this historical reenactment for the cinema, but also due to the film studio that actually arranged the production with such stylishness and fine artistic understanding.[14]

Central to *Cabiria*'s appeal, as well as its marketing strategy, was the literary star Gabriele D'Annunzio, whom Pastrone recruited to pen the film's intertitles.[15] As previously discussed, D'Annunzio's significance as a prominent public literary and political figure was central to the development and articulation of Italian nationalism. He was far from the first contemporary writer to engage with cinema, and his participation was rather unreliable and reluctant. In 1909 the filmmaker Luca Comerio and his company, S.A.F.F.I.–Comerio, contracted and paid D'Annunzio to adapt several of his works for the screen, a contract that the author did not honor. He was later forced to pay back the advance (plus legal expenses). Eventually he sold the rights to several of his works, including the play *La figlia di Iorio* (Iorio's Daughter, 1904) to Ambrosio to help pay off his debts, the same reason why he would undertake the task of writing the intertitles for *Cabiria*.[16]

Because of his international popularity and recognition, D'Annunzio was the primary commodity used to sell the film, a promotional strategy that Pastrone actively pursued. The author's above-the-title billing in the film's publicity materials – posters, booklets, and programs – attested to the recognition and respect that he commanded at the time, as well as Itala Film's positioning of the film as a production of high quality and pedigree (plate 1). At the same time, promotional material, including the highly stylized posters by the celebrated Leopoldo Metlicovitz, featured not only the film's namesake but also Maciste himself, indicating a promotional awareness of the character's popular appeal and an indication of the character's future box-office potential.[17]

Although Pastrone created the character of Maciste, D'Annunzio invented his name. In a note collected in the archives of the Museo Nazionale del Cinema in Turin, D'Annunzio wrote: "The name of the story's Roman hero is Fulvio Axilla. His most powerful companion is a freedman, from the proud country of the Marsi, named Maciste, which is a very ancient nickname for the semi-God Hercules."[18] Earlier drafts of the script in fact refer to the character as Ercole, Italian for Hercules. The exact reason for the change remains unknown, but the name

Maciste, in addition to referencing the Greek *mékistos,* superlative of *makròs,* meaning "large," arguably plays with the Italian word *macigno,* for "huge rock."[19]

The actors appearing in *Cabiria* consisted of a mix of well-known stage and screen performers and newcomers to the screen. The actress who played the adult Cabiria, Lydia Quaranta, had been a frequent Itala Film star, appearing in such films as *Tigris* and *Addio giovinezza!* (Goodbye, Youth!, Itala Film, 1913), as well as part of an acting dynasty; her sister Letizia Quaranta would later appear in *La trilogia di Maciste* (see chapter 5). Italia Almirante Manzini, in the role of the femme fatale Sofonisba, had also been working in films for quite some time, as had Umberto Mozzato (Fulvio Axilla), who had starred in the 1908 Italian version of *Gli ultimi giorni di Pompeii.* Unlike the casting of these actors, who had strong roots in the business, the process for choosing who would play Maciste was fairly unorthodox. In March 1912 Pastrone sent two representatives, one of whom was Andrea Cesare Cassiano, an acrobat and gymnastics trainer and one of his closest collaborators, to look for an appropriate person who could embody the character's physical strength and at the same time project a sympathetic sense of kindness and decency that would be essential to his success in the role.[20] After finding Bartolomeo Pagano, they brought him back to Turin, where he underwent both physical training with Cassiano and acting lessons under the direction of Mozzato, the actor who would play his master on screen.

While D'Annunzio thought of the name Maciste, it was Pastrone who made him black. As he wrote to D'Annunzio in an undated letter (most likely from 1913, during the film's preproduction): "Most ingenious the name of Maciste, for whom we must find another country of origin: I made him a mulatto."[21] In turn-of-the-century Italy the term "mulatto" intended, as it does today, a person of mixed race, with one parent white and the other of black skin. Mulattos were a common presence in third-century BC Carthage, [22] and they populated Italian literature of the late nineteenth and early twentieth centuries. Emilio Salgari, an extremely popular writer of adventure and children's literature (also from Turin), often featured racialized characters in his works.[23] In his novel *La capitana del Yucatan* (*The Captain of the Yucatan,* 1899), for instance, he describes one minor character, Dal Monte, as "muscular" and "sturdy" with very brown skin, much like Maciste. At the same time, with Italian colonial expansion, the mulatto became an object of contemporary policy debates. As Italian males in the African colonies such as Eritrea, Somalia, and Ethiopia began to take on native women as concubines and produce offspring (and Italian white women entered into relationships with African males), the civic status of mixed-race children began to enter into public discourse as debates surfaced regarding not only the moral position of these unions but the legal position as well.[24]

Why Pastrone chose to refer to the character as "mulatto" as opposed to Numidian or African remains a mystery, specifically since the film never explicitly addresses the issue of his mixed race in the diegesis; he is referred to only as an African slave. On the one hand, Pastrone and his collaborators were fervid researchers and avid readers of ancient historical texts. Given the chronological accuracies that preoccupied the director during the film's realization, the most likely casting scenario would have been to find an Italian and blacken him, thus making him a mulatto out of necessity. In fact makeup artists darkened Pagano's skin, although he is not the only character to appear that way in *Cabiria*. That a mulatto is not completely black signals an otherness that is not completely "other," one who embodies both a Romanness and an Africanness and is a much more ambiguous figure than his predecessor Ursus.[25] This ambiguity both rescues Maciste in terms of the narrative – he remains central as opposed to marginal – and allows for greater audience identification and appreciation, not to mention a quicker segue into whiteness, as occurs in his subsequent films.[26]

While only a supporting player in the complicated drama, Maciste's role is central to the narrative and crosses various emotional and dramatic registers as it draws on the historical epic and the comic genre for inspiration. His first appearance on screen follows an intertitle that reads: "With his slave Maciste the Roman Patrician Fulvio Axilla lives incognito in Carthage, secretly watching the moves of Rome's rival republic." Although Fulvio Axilla is the subject of the intertitle, Maciste is the subject of the shot. He is in the foreground on the rocky seashore, assuming a variety of static, muscular poses as he stands guard while his master obtains directions from a bystander.[27] The toga he wears in

2.2. Maciste's first appearance in *Cabiria* (1914).

this and subsequent scenes highlights both his size and, in contrast, the darkness of his skin and muscles (fig. 2.2). Throughout the film he always appears bare-chested, often only in a leopard-print loincloth or cloth draped around his waist, with the most coverage at any time being the white toga casually draped over his shoulders or his head. In this scene and in many others in the film, he crosses his arms, a gesture that not only highlights his sculpted biceps but also prefigures Mussolini (see chapter 6). Maciste's poses here evoke classical statuesque lines (Hercules/Ercole) against a rocky seaside backdrop (Maciste/macigno).

2.3. A rendering of the "*Cavalletto Maciste.*"

Maciste himself represents one of the film's many innovations, as the camera reinforces the spectacularity of his muscles and his actions with its movements on the horizontal and depth-of-field axes. Pastrone even named a design for one of his particularly large camera stands the Maciste tripod (*cavalletto Maciste*). Operated by a smaller mechanism and a cameraman on a special platform and intended to be three to five meters high, it created a more spectacular camera setup that prefigures in some way the crane shot (fig. 2.3). This use of depth of field was one of *Cabiria's* many technical novelties, whereby the characters become part of a "socially structured landscape."[28] In Cabiria's rescue from the Temple of Moloch, for instance, the camera moves slightly to the right but then stays fixed as Maciste approaches the gaping mouth in which Cabiria is to be sacrificed. The film then cuts, in an axis match, to a closer view of the rescue itself as Maciste plucks Cabiria from the priest's hands. Once outside the temple, the camera pans to follow Maciste and Fulvio Axilla as they exit screen right. Maciste's body, here and elsewhere, consistently dominates Fulvio Axilla, and almost everyone else, in the film's mise-en-scène. His size, however, is threatening only to those who challenge his kind and gentle nature.[29] Fulvio Axilla is also a man of action, but one of agility and daring rather than brute strength; for instance, he jumps off a staggeringly high cliff into the sea to escape after Cabiria's initial rescue, and he scales the Carthaginian city walls pyramid-style with other Roman soldiers.[30]

Although fully integrated into the narrative, Maciste's feats of strength, such as when he breaks the millstone's chains, highlight his classically proportioned, sculpted athletic body. It is a desexualized muscularity that signifies, beyond individual force and valor, the national might of Ancient Rome. After an intertitle invoking Maciste's will and power – "In the joy of unexpected liberation strength is multiplied" – the camera cuts to a medium long shot as he struggles to free himself, his veins bulging and muscles ripping with Herculean might. The loincloth he wears in this scene, although appropriately modest, further showcases his strength of character. Similarly, in a scene that would later be featured in *Maciste,* he bends the window bars of the Carthaginian jail, allowing him and Fulvio Axilla to escape. The second shot, from outside the prison window looking in, showcases Maciste's bicep center screen, flexed and curled, as he works himself free. This shot borrows heavily from a similar scene in *Spartaco,* when the title character breaks through his prison bars in a similar shirtless fashion. Unlike in this earlier historical epic, however, *Cabiria's* intertitle announcing his attempt – "Maciste wiles away the boredom" – is one of many in the Maciste series to employ irony and humor to accentuate his feats of bravery.

Many of his scenes are in fact quite humorous, such as the one that immediately follows Maciste's first appearance as he and Fulvio Axilla

2.4. Fulvio Axilla and Maciste in the wine cellar in *Cabiria* (1914).

take refuge in the innkeeper Bodastoret's tavern. Because of his size, Maciste has trouble sitting at the table, and he attracts the flirtatious attention of the female server, much to his embarrassment. This is the only time in the film when Maciste – and more specifically Maciste's muscles – becomes the object of the desiring gaze: Maciste is purely a man's man, here to serve and facilitate the creating of the couple at the film's end, as well as to provide the film's moral compass. Bodastoret provides comic relief in the film and is often Maciste's foil. When Maciste is chained to the millstone, Bodastoret, having informed on Maciste and Cabiria to the Carthaginian authorities, taunts him, but in the end

Maciste gets the better of the innkeeper as he humorously chases him in circles. In a subsequent scene, Maciste and Fulvio Axilla become inebriated as they take refuge in a wine cellar (fig. 2.4), preceded by a humorously ironic intertitle: "Fulvio and Maciste continue their prodigious resistance, wiling away the tedium of the siege with wine and dreams." Here the camera pulls back to reveal multiple lines of ceramic flasks of wine of all shapes and sizes and dried meats hanging from the ceiling. The depth-of-field effect of the camera movement is both efficient, allowing us to experience "close up" the prisoners in their drunken stupor, and comic, as the reverse dolly exposes numerous toppled and now empty vats of wine and the characters' inebriated state. Maciste also has moments of tenderness on screen; for instance, he plays with the young Cabiria on his lap and tends to her in an almost maternal fashion, sewing her a dress and caressing her affectionately in much the same way Croessa had, revealing the acts of kindness and gentleness that both humanized and popularized him.

Film reviews from all over Italy were quick to single out the character of Maciste and Pagano's performance with classical rhetoric, calling him "a superb athletic champion" and "a magnificent colossus, who never having been a dramatic actor, knows how to sell himself through his body and his artistically sympathetic good will."[31] At the same time, many cited his comic gifts, as well as the warm reception of his on-screen achievements: "The appearance of the Roman patrician Fulvio Axilla and his giant slave Maciste . . . was greeted with particular sympathy. Both will become popular very soon: Fulvio for his heroic devotion to Roman ideals, and Maciste for his Herculean musculature that overwhelms everything."[32]

Historical films in general, and *Cabiria* in particular, constituted more than just spectacular displays of production design; they exerted a unique and remarkable political resonance for contemporary audiences, evoking Roman victories in the name of current nationalist and colonialist enterprises.[33] One critic, referring to *Cabiria's* reception, described this fusion of past and present:

> The thunderous applause of the audience, which reemerged purified by the glaring light of the Costanzi's theater after extended absorption in the darkness, seemed to me to be like a luminous reawakening after a dream, after an upsetting nightmare.

> The commotion won me over when I saw, shining on the spectators' faces and through their eyes, Italians' passionate love for how our marvelous past inspires lessons and new conquests.[34]

The intended historical connection being made is not only with past glories but also with contemporary colonial ambitions, including recent victories on the battlefield in Tripolitania (Libya). Scholars have pointed out the similarities between the plot of *Cabiria* and the 1912 Libyan war: Carthage assumes the role of the African country that opposes the rule of Rome, and *Cabiria* presents a unified Rome under the strong leadership of Scipione defeating the Carthaginians,[35] a victory that Fascism would later exploit with its own regime-sponsored filmic version of the events, *Scipione l'africano* (Scipio Africanus: The Defeat of Hannibal, Carmine Gallone, 1937).[36] Lucia Re argues that the Libyan war "sought to unify Italians by displacing racism from inside to outside the body of the nation and its people" during a period when racism, colonialism, and imperialism became fundamental components of Italian national identity. The concept of race is essential to the formation of "imaginary yet essential identity" and finds its way into the literature of the day, with none other than D'Annunzio being its primary intellectual spokesperson.[37]

As early as the 1890s D'Annunzio began to incorporate words like *razza* (race) and *stirpe* (stock) into his literary and journalistic pieces to define the Latin spirit against the barbarous other through struggle and war. The origins of racial stereotyping lie in the proliferation of social Darwinism in Europe (and the United States), as well as in writings that circulated internationally at the time by contemporary Italian anthropologists and scientists. The notion of type was a prominent and functional feature of racial discourses, since it guided attempts to characterize individuals according to broader racial and geopolitical narratives. Types required semiotic recognition and as such relied on physical components, mostly focusing on individuals' cranial and facial characteristics (phrenology and physiognomy). Italian and American cinema found racial types quite valuable, since they translated the stereotypes originally articulated in written form into visual ones.[38] As was common in Italy (and in the West) at the time, the word "race" often intended the idea of the nation, hence Pastrone's conflation of Maciste's change of national origin with a change in skin color. In a 1914 proto-theoretical essay on film, excerpted from an interview he gave to the *Corriere della Sera* on 28 February of that year, D'Annunzio talked about *Cabiria*, saying:

> And what tremendous effort of culture and creation it took to finally repre-
> sent this story, set in the third century BC, about the most tragic spectacle
> that war of the races [*stirpi*] has ever staged for the world! . . . Here the
> supreme conflict of two adversarial races [*stirpi*], which are both led by the
> Genius of the Flame "that tames and devours everything; powerful sire of
> everything; the eternal craftsman." . . . Here is the vision of the ardent isle
> that the Herculean hand of the Dorian people seems to have fashioned into
> a model of greatness fulfilled.[39]

Also an avid advocate for colonialism, D'Annunzio believed the Italian race derived its greatness from the heritage of Ancient Rome and
that through war and imperial conquest twentieth-century Italy would
achieve its rightful place as superpower of supermen. Works such as the
fourth book of his *Laudi* (1912), the "Songs of the Deeds from Beyond
the Sea," written after Italy's victory in Libya, celebrated the myth of the
supernation and Italy's destiny as a great imperial power. His subsequent
1919 occupation and attempt at annexation of the city of Fiume (now
Rijeka, Croatia) was the practical application of his irredentist position.
As Italy's premiere public intellectual of the day, whose views on race,
nation, and ideology circulated widely in print, both in journalistic and
book form in Italy and abroad, D'Annunzio and his views on race and
imperialism could not help but pervade a cinematic text like *Cabiria*,
regardless of questions of authorship. His notion of a civilized Italy (here
Ancient Rome) versus a Barbarian other (the Carthaginians) found its
cinematic articulation in *Cabiria* and the historical epic's "us versus
them" ethos, along with the superhuman strength of Maciste (fig. 2.5).[40]

Racialized characterizations pervaded the popular press as well.
One anonymous reviewer of *Cabiria* noted how "[the audience] also
showed warm demonstrations of compassion for the slave Maciste, who,
besides being a very beautiful specimen of man, is also a fine humor-
ist."[41] The original Italian word for specimen, *tipo*, had racial and, specifically, social anthropological connotations related to the practice of
classification. This triumph of the national over the racial partly explains
Maciste's appeal: Maciste's moral character, aligned with the glories of
Ancient Rome as well as the Italian nationalism in the 1910s, supplanted
the ambiguous racial status of his on-screen character.[42] In this regard,

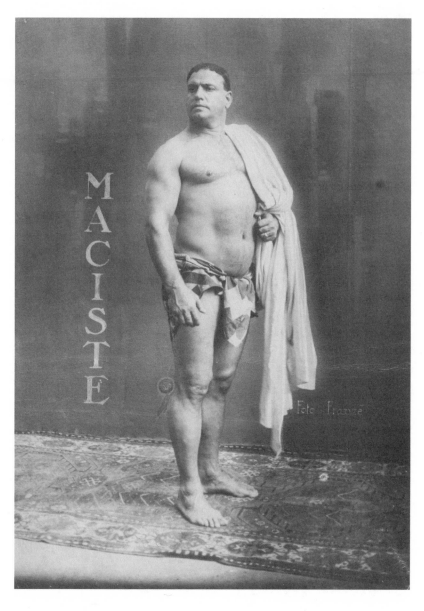

2.5. Publicity photo of Maciste for *Cabiria* (1914).

one of the most explicit sources of evidence of his national superiority is a newspaper review that appeared in the 9 May 1914 edition of *Corriere della Sera*:

> Whether young or old, the audience befriends Maciste; they admire the superb beauty of his Herculean form which makes him a rare champion of *our race* (he was discovered in Genoa, where he practiced the humble and noble profession of dockworker), they applaud him, feel the agony of his imprisonment, rejoice in his liberation, smile with him, detach his black figure from the screen and turn that into a friendly companion, always accessible in their imagination, in order to tell stories about his deeds and glorify the natural beauty of his actions.[43]

In this appreciation the exigencies of the national, as personified by the figure of Maciste, superseded his temporary, and divisive, darkness.[44] Also telling from this description is the positioning of Maciste as both ordinary (the humble dockworker) and extraordinary (Herculean), as well as the audience's instantaneous appropriation of both his heroic greatness and social modesty.

This appeal literally jumped out from the screen as Pagano routinely made live appearances at several screenings of *Cabiria*, often in blackface makeup but wearing modern Italian dress. According to an anonymous 1931 biography of Giovanni Pastrone, Pagano wore a checkered jacket to these appearances, typical of the costumes that American (and African American) blackfaced actors would wear on screen and on stage.[45] The conflation of the character Maciste with the actor, and this rupture of the divide between screen and public life, allowed for his appropriation as a symbol of the national ("our race"). Subsequently, in the first Maciste spin-off film, the racial masquerading in the guise of blackface further heightened the self-reflexive theatricality of his racial positioning.

MACISTE

As early as December 1914, advertisements began to appear in such prominent film trade publications as *La Vita Cinematografica* announcing an imminent Maciste series.[46] Notices of the film *Maciste* itself materialized in July 1915, accompanied by the tag line "with the Gentle Giant of *Cabiria* as Protagonist," and there was a spike in distribution of *Cabiria*'s publicity materials right around the time of Maciste's release.[47]

The idea for the series most likely came from Pastrone, who, as Itala Film's primary creative force, recognized the popular potential of a serial based on Maciste's wide appeal.[48] Although the film is credited to the Itala filmmakers Vincenzo Dénizot and Romano Luigi Borgnetto as directors, Pastrone personally supervised the production and relied on his frequent collaborator de Chomón for special effects.

However, it is one thing to have a supporting character as an African slave and another to have him as the star of his own series of films; as such, Maciste, as strongman and national hero, underwent the far-reaching modification into white subject. As if to reinforce the elements stressed in the *Corriere* article – his immediacy, his greatness, and his ordinariness – he moved from Ancient Rome to modern-day Italy; he changed from an African slave to a white, northern Italian (*Maciste* is unambiguously set in Turin); and he passed from slave to a well-dressed member of the *borghesia*. Yet there remains continuity of character in his feats of strength and bravery, as well as his good nature, infectious smile, the humorous tone of many of the scenes, and his muscles. The new film appropriates the positive elements of his racial difference, looted for the new white Italian, and maintains the strong populist appeal of his humble origins, transposed to contemporary Italy.[49]

Maciste the film signals a shift from the lofty artistic aspirations of *Cabiria* toward a populism, soon to be typical of the strongman films, whereby the hero, in this case Maciste, would be both ordinary and extraordinary and would appeal to the common man as national hero. That is not to say there was no populist vein to *Cabiria*. On the contrary, as Giovanni Calendoli has astutely observed, *Cabiria* translated a young country's desire to locate a historical justification in the glories of its Ancient Roman past while simultaneously finding ways to relate on a micro-historical level with the contemporary spectator. The figure of Maciste, with the kindness and goodness of his character and the warm popular reception he received, became that conduit.[50] Pastrone's own comments concur:

> The exaggerated gestures, and a silent ranting, are the principle defects that one finds in *Cabiria*. But you have to remember the times – it was the era of Sarah Bernhardt, with her excessive makeup and her magniloquent gesticulations. If I hadn't, with other actors, paid tribute to Bernhardt's style, my film would have never been judged a work of art. Once this concession

to the elite audience was accomplished, I concerned myself with other
actors in an atmosphere of simplicity and modesty. Take the example of
Maciste, who alone, or almost all alone, made the film a success.[51]

Maciste's opening scenes neatly explain this transition to the audience with a meta-cinematic pretense, not uncommon in the comic films
of the era, that further plays on the dialectic between character and actor. The film begins with a damsel in distress (the unnamed female lead,
played by Clementina Gay) on the run from a cohort of bandits who have
also imprisoned her mother at the behest of her evil uncle, who desires
to take over the family fortune. The unnamed woman takes refuge from
her pursuers in a crowded beaux arts theater, where *Cabiria* is showing,
complete with full orchestra and posters featuring Pagano as Maciste
in an exterior shot (they are, in fact, some of the film's original publicity
materials). The intertitle that presents the scene functions as a product
placement for Itala Film (as well as protection against copyright infringe-
ment) and its premiere attraction: "That night again, after infinite showings, the film 'Cabiria' filled the room."[52] This statement is not false;
Cabiria continued to play throughout 1915 and beyond at both first- and
second-run urban and rural theaters. One issue of the periodical *La Cine-
Fono* featured separate announcements advertising the distribution of
both *Cabiria* and *Maciste,* indicating the simultaneity, in certain locales,
of their exhibition.[53] Moreover, the theater's neoclassical interior recalls
the nationalistic fervor that late nineteenth and early twentieth-century
architecture sought to imbue in its monuments and structures, such as
the Altare della Patria, examined in chapter 1: heroism and muscular
beauty are expressed on and around the stage.[54]

Once inside the theater, the shot presents the packed house watching
the film, with the special effect of *Cabiria* superimposed on the stage's
small screen. The title card on the theater's screen reads, "CABIRIA – GA-
BRIELE D'ANNUNZIO/ITALA-FILM TORINO," followed by a singular
intertitle, "MACISTE," representing an elliptic compression of the earlier film (plate 7). The first image presented of Maciste features him in
the same toga he wears in *Cabiria* and assumes a classical, statuesque
pose. When the heroine enters the theater, she sees Maciste on screen
in the scene from *Cabiria* where he bends the prison bars in order to free

himself and Fulvio Axilla from the Carthaginian prison. She collapses the distance between spectator and screen as she physically approaches the proscenium while watching the scene.[55] The film self-consciously reinforces this collapse: the special effect of "a screen within the screen" disappears as *Maciste*'s diegetic and actual spectators are viewing in full screen Maciste as he contorts the metal bars of his prison window. This scene concludes with further self-publicity (and copyright protection) for Itala Film; the last title card on the smaller screen reads, "Itala Film, Torino."

The woman decides to seek out Maciste for aid in resolving her predicament, and the actor receives her plea for help in the form of a letter. The location shifts to the actual Itala Film studio, which is bustling with activity, and a panorama shot reveals the studio's glass-paneled exterior as well as its interior, featuring the classically inspired sets for which Itala Film was famous. A worker delivers the letter to our protagonist, whom the spectator first sees in "real life" as he exercises, his torso naked, in the studio's gymnasium (fig. 2.6).[56] His appearance in bare chest is significant for several reasons. First, and perhaps foremost, it reveals the character's whiteness, in comparison to the darkness of his on-screen *Cabiria* counterpart. The contrast between the lightness of his bare, muscular, yet hairy chest and the darkness of his pants (as opposed to the slave Maciste's dark chest and white toga) highlights his newly revealed light skin. The shot that immediately follows, as he towels off to read the letter requesting his help, has spotlighting directed toward his torso, creating a slight halo effect that later would be perfected in silent cinema to signify purity and holiness. This use of lighting was Pastrone's signature; he was one of the few directors at the time who employed a mix of both natural and artificial light sources.[57] Maciste is seen in a gymnasium performing feats of strength as the extraordinary strongman who lifts not only the barbell but also several men attached to it. Here Maciste's muscled body in well-choreographed action participates in the impressive exhibition of the well-oiled film manufacturing machine (fig. 2.7).

The contemporary references in *Maciste*'s first six minutes – the Itala Film studio, the screening of *Cabiria*, the young woman's letter carefully dated October 1915 – all reinforce the temporal shift from Ancient Rome

2.6. Maciste flexing his muscles in *Maciste* (1915).

to present-day Italy. Itala Film would rely and even further elaborate on this formula throughout the Maciste series; subsequent films would begin with Maciste at work on a particular film set, and the action would depart from there. Whether he goes off to war (*Maciste alpino*) or vacation (*Maciste in vacanza*), Maciste-the-character displaces Pagano-the-actor. The meta-cinematic reconfiguration of the character of Maciste as an actor at Itala Film identified only by his character's name neatly bridges the gaps between past and present and between spectacle and audience. Moreover, the film's self-conscious play on the character's

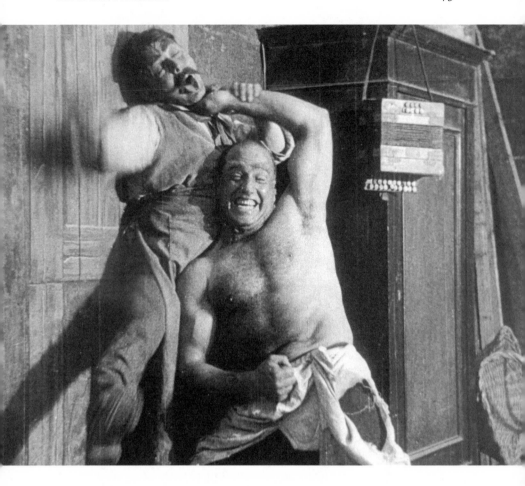

2.7. Maciste battles his enemies in *Maciste* (1915).

extra-cinematic popularity resolves the race question: Pagano as contemporary actor is safely and visibly white.

Costume and fashion were other tools through which the film accomplishes Maciste's successful metamorphosis as it refashions his body
along different racial, national, and class lines.[58] In many instances Maciste presents himself as a master of disguise in order to rescue the female
protagonist. This spectacle of vested transformation has a precursor both
on stage and on screen in Italy in the vaudeville performer Leopoldo
Fregoli (see chapter 1). Known as the "wizard of disguise," Fregoli was

2.8. Maciste and his suit in *Maciste* (1915).

famous for his ability to change costumes in a matter of seconds on the stage (the quick-change artist) and, later, on screen. He quickly saw the potential of film to increase his creative capacity by allowing greater velocity in the costume changes and to widen his audience beyond that of the stage. Maciste's costume changes and multiple disguises clearly draw on this tradition of popular *transformistes* and further reinforce his performative profession as "actor."[59]

In his first fully clothed appearance on screen, Maciste wears a classic double-breasted suit (fig. 2.8). The suit is impeccable and typical of bourgeois fashion at the time. According to Farid Chenoune, two kinds of suits were popular in Europe in the 1910s: the double-breasted model, with the long jacket with wide lapels, tapered waist, and slight flaring, as perfectly adorned by Maciste; and the single-breasted, with nipped waist and sloping shoulders. Both came to epitomize the classic bourgeois suit that the futurists railed against in their contemporary fashion manifestos.[60] In proposing his "anti-neutral" suit in 1914, the futurist painter and theorist Giacomo Balla lambasted the traditional suit's "neutral shades and colors, degraded by black, stifled by belts, and imprisoned by folds of fabric," as well as its "symmetrical cut and static lines that tire, depress, sadden and bind the muscles; the uniformity of ill-fitting lapels and all wrinkles; useless buttons and starched collars and cuffs."[61] Although Maciste's suit almost exactly matches both Chenoune's and Balla's descriptions, the sheer size of it (and Maciste himself) cannot hide, mask, or restrict his muscles. In fact, during the film Maciste performs most of his feats of bravery and strength fully and impeccably clothed, rarely restricted by his size or his suit except for one gratuitous scene with his shirt off, showcasing his sculpted chest and his newly whitened muscles. The importance of costume for fashioning a nationalized masculinity successively would become essential for another Italian of humble origins – Benito Mussolini, the blacksmith's son.

In addition to its contemporary setting, its self-consciousness, and its play with costume and masquerade, *Maciste* also elaborates on its cinematic precursor in how it films the protagonist's feats of strength. *Cabiria* showcased Maciste's muscles, particularly in his escape from the millstone; *Maciste,* as would subsequent installments in the series, turns them into more spectacular events, displays of attractions more common to early cinema and its origins in the circus and the piazza. Maciste's fight sequences are longer in duration, and it takes him more time to escape from situations in which he finds himself in peril. The films often integrate humor, not just through ironic intertitles (a continuation from *Cabiria*) but also via the reactions of the victims of Maciste's power and the character's own delight in his strength. More sophisticated camera work – alternate scenes (the contemporary term for crosscutting), tilts and pans, and transitions via cut-ins and position matches – adds to the suspense. In one lengthy sequence Maciste manages to incapacitate his captor, break through a ceiling, and untie the young heroine, all with his hands and legs bound. This shift aligns the films with its American and

French serial counterparts, especially those featuring female protagonists such as Helen and Pauline, and sets the tone for future films, such
as the American-serial-like *La trilogia di Maciste* (see chapter 5).

Similarly, the film establishes what will be the solid if not always consistent conventions of the Maciste series as a genre: the meta-cinematic
premise; his might and strength in defeating his opponents as opposed
to weapons (in *Maciste* only the young woman brandishes a gun); and
the fact that the size of Maciste's appetite is equivalent to that of his
muscles. Although settings can be both urban and rural, they feature
symbols of modernity, especially modes of transportation; train travel
and automobiles, including elaborate car chases, abound in the films.[62]
Unlike other films in the series, however, in *Maciste* the hero gets the girl
in the end. They walk off arm in arm after he has liberated her mother
from the clutches of Duke Alexis and the duke's malicious collaborator,
Dr. Krauss, the psychiatrist, referred to in the intertitles as an "alienist,"
one of many contemporary terms used to describe a doctor working in
a mental institution.

Dr. Krauss is an enigmatic character who, although he appears only
briefly in the film, displaces Maciste's previous otherness onto another
marginal group: the foreigner. Italian intellectuals had a difficult time
accepting psychoanalysis as a scientific mode of inquiry, a victim of the
firm hold that Catholicism, Marxism, and idealism had on the their way
of thinking. The cosmopolitan city of Turin was one of the major early
centers where psychology was able to enter into official channels. In 1906
the University of Turin established one of the first professorships in the
field, held by Friedrich Kiesow, a student of Wilhelm Wundt, one of the
early founders of experimental psychology and a mentor to the contemporary psychologist and film theorist Hugo Münsterberg. Dr. Krauss
bears a marked resemblance to Wundt, and it is no surprise that the figure of the evil or troubled psychiatrist, soon to be a trope or stereotype
in films, would emerge here as well.[63] In the end, Dr. Krauss's highbrow
intellectualism is no match for the populist strength of our hero.

If at the end of the film there existed any doubt of Maciste's new racial positioning, the film erases it when Maciste dons black facial makeup
and masquerades undercover as a servant at the duke's party as he at-

2.9. Maciste in blackface in *Maciste* (1915).

tempts to rescue the mother of the film's damsel in distress. Maciste was far from the first character to masquerade racially in Italian cinema.[64] Blackface characters appeared in early comic films, such as Cretinetti, in *Cretinetti alcoolista* (Cretinetti the Alcoholic, Itala Film, 1909), who appears wearing a billboard advertisement for a brand of rum. In *Maciste*, however, Maciste's cane, long jacket, checkered pants, and top hat evoke instead the image of the black dandy (fig. 2.9), popularized by American minstrel shows as well as their European incarnations, particularly through Victorian theatrical productions, contemporary British popular culture, and the transnational circulation with Africans and Europeans via the slave trade.[65] On screens, Italian audiences would have been exposed, for the most part, to African American characters being played by white actors in blackface in American-made films.[66]

Once a servant, the referent of Maciste's masquerade shifts to include that of the commedia dell'arte's acrobatic servant Arlecchino (the name means "harlequin," also a master of disguise and transformation), with the agile yet gluttonous Maciste evoking the stock character.[67] The desired effect in this scene is clearly comic, given the exaggerated physicality involved when Maciste towers over all the party guests and secretly eats their food, but there is also self-conscious play with racial overtones. Clearly the spectator knows (and the film itself takes pains to stress) that Maciste/Pagano's blackness is theater, like the mask that Arlecchino himself wears; there are shots showing Maciste putting on and removing his blackface makeup, as if to contradict those personal appearances Pagano made in character at screenings of *Cabiria*. His performative blackness self-consciously reinforces an authentic whiteness underneath by revealing the blackness exhibited in both this film and *Cabiria* to be a disguise, comparable to the many others Pagano wears in *Maciste*. In terms of race, the film fully constitutes the character's whiteness by establishing an "eradication of ambiguity," in Jane Gaines's words, much as the American cinema of the analogous period does with respect to race.[68] Darkness or otherness becomes a masquerade, something Maciste can take on and off, very much like the dandified suit that he wears or the commedia dell'arte mask he references. Blackface and dandyism are the prerogative of the white male star, whose racial identity is confirmed in the film's final images.[69] When asked for his identity by the policemen who have come to arrest Dr. Krauss and Duke Alexis, the film responds with an intertitle of his calling card – "Maciste, Itala Film–Torino" – firmly cementing his identity as film character and star.

*　　*　　*

Contemporary reviewers, often to their surprise and dismay, delighted in Maciste's transformation from supporting actor to star, and from historical epic to the more plebian strongman film. Their reaction was typical of the general critical response to this genre; as one critic stated, "I confess that I enjoy myself immensely at these type of films, much more than when I view certain films made for artistic purposes."[70] Another reviewer in *La Cine-Fono,* in describing the scene at Turin's Cinema Ghersi, observed, "*Maciste* . . . has brought thousands and thousands of people to the elegant theater, and not without reason. *Maciste* is one of those works that never grows tired. It maintains its consistent hilarity. . . . Itala Film unquestionably knows well what it is doing and what kind of product it launches into the marketplace."[71] The well-regarded Turinese critic known as Il Rondone (literally, the aerial bird known as the swift) accepted the protagonist's racial and epochal metamorphosis as a necessity of cinematic exigencies, writing:

> We find ourselves in the face of a very special phenomenon.
> While the adventurous events that make the plot's action incredibly lively still have a tragic essence, this film is presented to us as the arouser of the most genuine and wholesome joy, of the most cheerful enjoyment. And in this sense the vast audiences that have given *Maciste* its most favorable judgment have for many days rushed to admire the film.
> But is this phenomenon really new? We don't think so.
> Itala Film, with this series that it has recently begun to create, has attempted to exhibit, on the silent screen, the extraordinary strength, the most beautiful figure and the very unique skills that made *Cabiria's* gentle giant famous, and of whom spectators from around the world grew immediately and lastingly fond. . . .
> Certainly we need to take this spectacle as it is offered to us, without the haughtiness of recognizing art, without looking too much at the subtleties but by arming ourselves with logic and good sense. The whole sequence of adventures was created only to showcase Maciste, without concerning itself with anything else.
> And we must confess that even we found ourselves drawn to him heartily, and that we laughed from beginning to end: in short, we enjoyed

ourselves immensely. And given the scope of this film, that seems to us to
be enough, if not everything. . . .

And we, like the audience, are pleased with this film, and we hope soon
to be able to admire the continuation of the series.[72]

What is unique about this contribution is that the critic, who writes in
the first-person plural, takes pains to distinguish syntactically between
his opinion and that of the public, but ultimately concludes that they
are one and the same. Although seemingly contradictory – the article
highlights the film's originality as well as the continuity of the essence
of Maciste's character from *Cabiria* to this film – the critic, like the audience, revels in Maciste's humor, his energy, and, most significantly,
his popular appeal. At a time when most periodicals and critics were
concerned with establishing cinema as an art form, *Maciste* served as
an elegant example of its general power to entertain, a feature the series
would continue to exploit through the 1910s and 1920s.

In this first Maciste spin-off and throughout the series, Maciste
proved himself more than just physically fit. He came to serve as the
paradigm for the strongman's metamorphosis from serious icon of ancient glories of the classical film epics, so celebrated in the early years of
Italian cinema, to exemplary symbol of modern and entertaining Italian
heroism. The initial *Maciste* film accomplished this transformation in
four distinct ways: (1) it changed his race from African to Italian; (2) it
set his films in contemporary Italy; (3) it altered his skin color from black
to white through a self-conscious referencing of the blackface tradition;
and (4) it shifted the tone of the films from serious and academic to consistently lighthearted in order to appeal to a wider film-going public. In
righting wrongs first in Ancient Rome and then in contemporary Turin,
Maciste also broadened cinema's reach: by expanding the audience to appeal to the bourgeoisie in *Cabiria* and by taking that audience with him,
sometimes kicking and screaming, to the successful and ever more populist series and (later) serial formula. In this convergence of D'Annunzian
rhetoric, historical actuality, and film spectacle, *Maciste* paved the way
for the character to become the model Italian to lead and accompany
the relatively young Italian nation by example through important historical developments such as Italy's participation in World War I, which
was mostly fought by lower-class Italians – those who favored Maciste's
populist humor and feats.

THREE

Maciste Goes to War

MACISTE ALPINO (1916)

ALTHOUGH BY FAR NOT THE FIRST WAR TO BE FILMED – THAT distinction belongs to the Anglo-Boer War of 1899–1902 – World War I was the first that used both fiction and nonfiction to recount its story on screen.[1] With Britain, Russia, and Germany leading the way, the governments of the Triple Alliance and the Allies all moved at various speeds to mobilize the film industry for war propaganda. Film soon became the most effective medium for promoting various national political agendas, another modern weapon, along with airplanes, tanks, and mustard gas, to combat the enemy.[2] For Gian Piero Brunetta, cinema also functioned as an instantaneous site of the war's monumentalization, celebration, and canonization of heroism on the battlefield, even before movie cameras were allowed at the front or monuments themselves could be erected to memorialize the cause.[3]

At the same time, cinema was undergoing its own form of modernization as narratives and editing became more sophisticated and camera mobility improved, resulting in new technologies of storytelling on screens. Film spectatorship consistently increased during the early 1910s across the Continent, and the medium became part of everyday life and entered the vocabulary of contemporary culture. Modris Eksteins notes how many times references to films and moviegoing appear in the diaries and letters of British and German soldiers, evidence not only of the infiltration of the new medium in popular consciousness but also of the idea that the war experience, simultaneously real and surreal, seemed to belong more on screen than in real life.[4] What eventually did emerge on screen during the war, however, was far from a mirror image of what was

3.1. Maciste as alpine soldier in *Maciste alpino* (1916).

happening on various fronts. Through heavy censorship, propaganda, and manipulation of both fiction and documentary film, what the average spectator saw in theaters was an imaginary war, "represented as the sum of heroic actions carried out by a handful of individuals,"[5] a description that could easily fit *Maciste alpino*.

Maciste alpino (*The Warrior*, 1916), along with *Maciste all'inferno*, is the best-known and critically praised film of the Maciste series. References to its exhibition include an "uproarious success" in Rome, its monthlong run in Turin "annihilating the competition," and its sold-out stay in Genoa.[6] As the bravest of soldiers, Maciste was the symbolic hero of the interventionist cause, despite the fact that Pagano himself was excused from military service because of his rarely publicized somnambulism.[7] Far from the only fiction film made about the war during wartime, *Maciste alpino,* closely supervised by Itala Film's primary visionary, Giovanni Pastrone, transposed the racially tinged and nationalist discourse of *Maciste* onto the Italian war front and exalted the protagonist as civilian hero, soldier, and popular leader.

This chapter explores *Maciste alpino* in light of other Italian fiction and documentary films about the war, as well as the unique features of the Maciste series and Pagano's stardom. Although film was the most modern of media at the time, many Italian war films relied on the tropes of nineteenth-century theatrical and literary melodramas to ideologically situate the conflict as one between good and evil.[8] Tensions between the old and the new, truth and fiction, and military realism and the exigencies of entertainment manifest themselves in the film's diegesis as well as its aesthetic realization.[9] Here the sacrality of stardom serves the nation's military agenda.

But *Maciste alpino* is more than just a war film. Like most of the films in the series, its hybrid nature as wartime drama, comedy, and serial-like adventure film explained to a certain extent its phenomenal success and its wide appeal. The film combines Maciste's masculinity and muscularity, the backdrop of the rugged alpine landscape, and his characteristic humor as his character continues his development from morally just citizen to leader of the masses on a sacred mission to vanquish the enemy and save the homeland. The film invests the Italian Alps with dramatic and heroic meanings as Maciste masters the majestic yet savage terrain. His unflinching patriotism solidifies his standing as national hero, perfect specimen of the Italian race, and popular film star, combining political and cinematic imperatives into a consistently appealing, admired package.

ITALY'S MARCH TO WAR

Although films like *Cabiria* and other historical epics had already been mobilized toward the nationalist cause, Italian cinema did not immediately engage with any of the passionate political cries for intervention when Austria declared war on Serbia on 28 July 1914. Italy, which had previously been part of the Triple Alliance (with Germany and the Austro-Hungarian Empire), immediately declared its neutrality.[10] During the nine months before its decision to enter the war on the side of the Allies on 23 May 1915 and against the Austro-Hungarian Empire (and then one year later against Germany), intense political negotiations, public debates, and popular rallies ensued both for and against intervention. At the heart of the interventionists' concerns was territory: on which side would Italy have the most to gain if it won? The principal backers of the war in the government, besides Antonio Salandra, were the foreign minister Sidney Sonnino and King Vittorio Emanuele III, who, although possessing little actual power, lent his cachet to the movement.[11] The government, led by the right-leaning authoritarian Salandra, denounced the Triple Alliance in favor of forming ties to the Allies (Britain, France, and Russia) and secretly signed the Treaty of London on 26 April 1915 after a month of clandestine negotiations.[12] This temporal gap allowed four weeks to build support for what was, at the time, weak interventionist backing. Italy's status as a relatively young nation, as well as the strong regional ties of its people, did not lend itself well to fervid nationalist sentiment, except on the screen.

Salandra's case to the Italian people rested on the notions that the war would be brief and profitable; it would invigorate Italian industrial production; it would stimulate its lagging economy; and it would help unify the fractured nation. But he was not capable of articulating that argument alone. The interventionist cause needed a prominent spokesperson, one with both the political and cultural capital to rally the masses and create a groundswell of support and a spectacular setting to promote it. Fulfilling that exigency was none other Gabriele D'Annunzio, already well known to the Maciste series as the scribe of *Cabiria's* intertitles. Even before Salandra had signed the Treaty of London, plans were under way to bring D'Annunzio from Paris, where he had been living for the previous five years, to give a series of public speeches in order to turn the tide toward intervention and rally the Italian populace.

The *maggio radioso* (Glorious May) was the two-week period in May 1915 when the Salandra administration used spectacle, rhetoric, and even violence to build popular consensus for the war, "starring" the literary prophet D'Annunzio. From 4 May to 20 May 1915, D'Annunzio roused the masses through carefully choreographed public appearances in Genoa and Rome. He exalted Italy's past glories, Ancient Rome and the Risorgimento in particular, in an attempt to mobilize all forces, rational and irrational, in the name of war. It was a "showy/gaudy example of the interrelationship between the individual use of a great occasion and the political use of the demands and the suggestive, aggressive and mystic rapture of violence and sacrifice" that gradually assumed nastier invective tones against Parliament and the Italian prime minister, Giovanni Giolitti, ultimately assisting in turning the tide toward intervention.[13]

It is no coincidence that the first speech D'Annunzio recited, on 5 May 1915 in Genoa, was given on the occasion of the unveiling of the monument commemorating the fiftieth anniversary of Giuseppe Garibaldi's Expedition of a Thousand, when Garibaldi had spearheaded the departure of thousands of volunteers to invade Sicily during the Risorgimento. Eugenio Baroni's sculpture *Monumento ai Mille* features a muscular, half-naked Garibaldi surrounded by eleven men and a winged female figure with her arms outstretched over Garibaldi in a halo-like quasi-embrace (fig. 3.2). Born in Taranto, Baroni, who worked predominantly in Genoa and won the 1910 competition to create the monument, was known for his expressionist, nontraditional sculptures and memorials that, according to Amy Boylan, "emphasized the consequences rather than the triumphs" of war. This particular monument, in fact, lacks the traditional icons and symbols associated with Garibaldian patriotism – lions, eagles, red shirts, and the tricolor flag – opting instead for a more subdued and "abstract idea of heroism."[14]

D'Annunzio's speech, on the other hand, was a rousing, patriotic rhetorical reawakening.[15] The poet employs the metaphor of the sculpture being cast in the oven and of the kiln's fire burning with ardor ready to explode in order to rouse the flame inside the Italian people. The speech aimed to resurrect Italians' innate call to battle as it reifies and masculinizes the statue itself: the cast contains the Italian spirit waiting to erupt. Emblematic of classical D'Annunzian rhetoric, filled with repetition (*furnace*/furnace), hard alliteration (in Italian the sound "f" dominates with the words *fossa fusoria*/metallurgic ditch, *fratelli*/brothers,

3.2. Eugenio Baroni's *Monumento ai Mille.*
From the author's personal collection.

and *fuoco*/fire), the passage is nothing less than a call to arms for Italians to fan the fire within and cast themselves as bronze statues in battle.

While the sculpture's inauguration was the oration's pretext, D'Annunzio was clearly its star.[16] Set against a maritime backdrop festooned with ships, flags, and exploding cannons firing, the massive crowds clearly responded to the oration. As one contemporary observer wrote, the crowd "shuddered and stopped, and in certain moments extended their applause with a fervor with which one might make a vow, aware that they were constituting not only a muscular force but also a spiritual one, able to obtain miracles with the passion of unanimous desire."[17] D'Annunzio's rhetorical fervor, full of spiritual invectives inviting the masses to embrace Italy's sacred mission, had its desired effect, as his speeches throughout the maggio radioso significantly contributed to the shifting of public opinion toward intervention into the war.[18]

ITALIAN CINEMA GOES TO WAR

Like Italy itself, Italian cinema's industrial and narrative state was unprepared for the exigencies of war. Although the relatively young medium was in synch with new ways of thinking and expression in the age of modernity, most national cinemas, particularly in the United States and Italy, represented the new mass conflict in archaic forms through paradigms taken from traditional nineteenth-century literature and artistic war representations. Even though the war itself inspired breaks from old artistic and visual forms (Surrealism and German Expressionism are two dramatic examples of the new aesthetic season), Italian films about the war relied primarily on melodrama, the historical novel, and battle painting to give expression to the conflict.[19]

The war film as an Italian genre began with World War I and, like the Maciste films, borrowed explicitly from other genres. The first Italian fiction film set during the conflict was in theaters barely one month after Italy's entrance into the war: Carmine Gallone's *Sempre nel cor la Patria!* (The Fatherland Always in My Heart, Cines, 1915).[20] Extremely successful at the box office, it spurred a spate of films with war themes, especially between the second half of 1915 and early 1916, including *Patria!* (The Fatherland!, Itala Film, 1915), *Patria mia!* (My Country!, Etna Film,

1915), *La patria redime* (The Fatherland Redeems, Fulgor Film, 1915), and *Viva la Patria!* (Long Live the Fatherland!, Savoia Film, 1915), often accompanied with military music at their exhibitions.[21] Even comic series jumped on the war bandwagon, showing how war, for the most part, remained safe and distant from everyday life. *La paura degli aereomobili nemici* (The Fear of Enemy Aircraft, Itala Film, 1915), featuring André Deed's Cretinetti, recounts the protagonist's hysterical fear of air warfare and his outlandish preparations against it, ultimately ending with his being sent to war to fight the very enemy aircraft he feared. In Gennaro Righelli's *Il sogno patriottico di Cinessino* (Cinessino's Patriotic Dream, Cines, 1915), the title character dreams of fighting to glorious victory in Libya only to wake up in his mother's arms.[22] As the conflict deepened and the effects on the Italian peninsula worsened between 1916 and 1917, films presented an even more sanitized view of the war, with heavy oversight. Additional comic films, such as *Kri Kri contro i gas asfissianti* (Kri Kri versus Asphyxiating Gases, Cines, 1916) and *Farulli si arruola* (Farulli Enlists, Alberto Traversa, Latina-Ars, 1916), were films based on actual events, as were the more serious fare: Amleto Palermi's *Come morì Ms. Cavell* (How Ms. Cavell Died, Augusta Film, 1916), the story of an English nurse captured by Germans and shot to death, and Oreste Gherardini's *Turbine rosso* (Red Storm, Volsca Films, 1916), about Serbian resistance and inspired by the Luca Comerio documentary *Prodigiosa opera della marina italiana in aiuto dell'esercito serbo* (The Italian Navy's Prodigious Operation in Helping the Serbian Army, Comerio, 1916).[23] Other films featured the exaltation of Risorgimento heroes recast in the light of the present conflict. Prominent among them was the Triestine Guglielmo Oberdan, the irredentist pioneer who was executed in 1882 after his assassination attempt on the Austrian emperor and the protagonist of *Oberdan* (Tiber-Film, 1915). Like Edmondo De Amicis's Sardinian drummer boy (*Il tamburino sardo* [The Sardinian Drummer Boy], Film Artistica Gloria, 1915) and the imprisoned, anti-Austrian nineteenth-century writer Silvio Pellico (*Silvio Pellico*, Alba Film, 1915), Oberdan was a symbolic figures, capable of representing a national ideal, a sense of country, and the common values of the populace.[24] Also popular were religious-themed films about the life of Christ. Although certainly not new to Italian screens (about fifty films had already been made worldwide on the subject, according to Riccardo Redi), films such as *Christus* (Cines, 1916), one of the highly promoted, big-budget productions of the war years, fused the religious with the patriotic. The film was based on the religious "sacred rhapsody" by the poet and librettist Fausto Salvatori and filmed on location in Egypt with spectacular desert sequences, fused with realistic mise-en-scène and special effect – laden representations of Jesus's miracles. The film's narrative carried both a religious and political message as it juxtaposed the moral and just Jesus against the evil and barbaric excesses of Caesar and Herod and their "slaughter of the innocents."[25]

As a whole, however, the war did not have a positive financial effect on the Italian film industry as it did, for instance, in the United States. Instead it initiated a period of decline that would continue throughout the 1920s. The war effort forced the closing of some studios as their personnel enlisted, as was the case with Milano-Film.[26] Film periodicals such as *La Vita Cinematografica* and *La Cine-Fono* decried such moves, fearing a takeover by the all too eager American industry and prompting published reassurances that the Italian film industry was alive and well.[27] Other filmmakers were called upon to serve in the Sezione Cinematografica del Ministero della Guerra, the war ministry's film division.[28] Equally dramatic was the impact of the war on distribution, domestically and, especially, abroad. The number of films being exported plummeted during the period of neutrality while imports increased, especially American films. In 1917, for instance, both D. W. Griffith's *Intolerance* (1916) and Cecil B. DeMille's *The Cheat* (1915) appeared on Italian screens, as well as films by Thomas Ince, Mack Sennett, Roscoe "Fatty" Arbuckle, and Charlie Chaplin. National production fell as well; in 1916 Italian films numbered 446, which was 117 fewer than the previous year, and by 1918 the domestic output had fallen to 359. The news was not all terrible, however; Rome, being located far from the front, saw its film industry flourish, and films starring the extravagantly elegant divas prospered.[29] The gradual emergence of the strongman genre, particularly after the success of *Maciste alpino,* inspired such war films as *La spirale della morte* (The Spiral of Death, Società Anonima Ambrosio, 1917), directed by Filippo Costamagna and Domenico Gambino and starring Luciano Albertini. Augusto Genina's *Il siluramento dell'*Oceania

(The Torpedoing of the *Oceania,* Società Anonima Ambrosio, 1917), starring the former circus performer Alfredo Boccolini (later the strongman
Galaor), was based on Boccolini's actual experiences as a sailor when he
was miraculously rescued after the Germans torpedoed his steamship as
it crossed the Atlantic.[30] The experience at the front and its popularization reinforced the importance of sports training for the combat mission,
with Maciste, Sansone, and Galaor as models of the heroic soldier.[31]

Nonfiction films, although heavily censored and controlled, told
a much different story, providing a more direct means of propaganda
than their fictitional counterparts. An important fixture in Italian cinema from its earliest days, nonfiction films had both national and international importance: they celebrated Italian art and landscape (tourist films), the nation's slowly increasing march toward modernization
(industrial films), and the heroes and institutions of the young nation-
state. War newsreels, already established with the Italo-Turkish War
(1911–1912), became an important source of information about World
War I before and after Italy's engagement in the conflict, exhibited alone
and on the same program with feature films as part of the war film-
going experience. Foremost among the filmmakers was Luca Comerio,
whose films included *La grande giornata storica italiana: 20 Maggio 1915*
(The Important Historical Day: 20 May 1915, Comerio, 1915), about the
parliamentary sessions debating intervention; *La guerra d'Italia a 3000
metri sull'Adamello* (Italy's War at 3,000 Meters above the Adamello,
Comerio, 1916), about waging war in the Alps; and *Dentro la trincea* (In
the Trenches, Sezione Cinematografica dell'Esercito, 1917). Heavily censored, in the same way as the war photography that sanitized, mythologized, and romanticized the war experience for those far from the front,
these films showcased, at least initially, picturesque and heroic images of
war highlighting the Italians' supposed readiness and prowess in combat, with little actual fighting portrayed.[32] As the war progressed, they
became more graphic in their details, representing the devastation of war
on cities like Gorizia (for example, *Paesi devastati dalla guerra* [Towns
Devastated by the War], Reparto Cinematografico Esercito Italiano,
1917), but still eliminating most of the gruesome scenes of death so chill-
ingly described in many of the diaries left behind after the war.[33]

3.3. Maciste on the set in *Maciste alpino* (1916).

MACISTE ALPINO

It is against this cinematic and historical backdrop that Itala Film re-leased *Maciste alpino* in late 1916.[34] The series once again borrows from previously established generic traditions to create the most nationally and internationally successful Italian war film of its time. Its initial inter-title is a dedication that firmly cements the film in both the war genre and as anti-enemy propaganda: "We offer this commemoration, as homage, to the generous people, to the children of civilization who are fighting against German barbarity."[35] Yet the film quickly anchors itself within the meta-cinematic context of Itala Film's Maciste productions. On 23 May 1915, Maciste and "Italia Film" are filming near the Austrian border, under the watchful eye of the suspicious Austrians, when they receive a telegram informing them to suspend work on the film and depart immediately (fig. 3.3). Assuming Italy has entered the war, Maciste exclaims "*Viva l'Italia!*" The Austrians subsequently arrest and imprison the company at a labor camp with several other (presumably) Italians from the contested region. After a torturous day of famished marching, Maciste engineers their escape by luring and then capturing the guards who had tortured him the previous day. The refugees take shelter at the large estate of the count of Pratolungo, where his niece Giulietta is preparing her fiancé, Giorgio Lanfranchi, for departure to the front. When Austrian soldiers descend on the villa, Maciste serves as a decoy and gives chase on horseback, while the count leads the masses to safety over the Italian border. Ultimately Maciste is captured despite a noble effort to fight off at least ten Austrian soldiers in the river. He is tied up and led away, but then is quickly able to break off on horseback, even jumping over a bridge into the river while evading the Austrians' bullets. Eventually Maciste comes upon an Italian soldier and quickly enrolls as an *alpino* (Italian alpine soldier), donning the uniform of Italy's most elite corps of fighters at the time. He takes it upon himself to fight the enemy in gun and hand-to-hand combat, taking personal revenge against one of the guards who had imprisoned him (the character Fritz Pluffer) and then leading the entire regiment over treacherous mountain passes and dangerously high cliffs to conquer the Austrians' position. When Maciste chances upon Giorgio at an encampment, he informs him that the count and Giulietta have become Austrian prisoners at the villa. Seeking permission from their commander, they lead a large troop of men to rescue the heavily fortified villa, just in time to save Giulietta from certain rape. The film concludes with Maciste hoisting the happy couple onto his shoulders as he toasts victory with a bottle of red wine and a large grin.

Maciste alpino constituted an unusual hybrid at the time, a fusion of the emerging strongman film, comedy, and the war film. The Austrians here function as Maciste's standard enemy, clearly the nefarious foil to his kindness and moral goodness. Their cruelty toward women and children as well as their drunken escapades at the castle and threat to Giulietta's chastity were typical of representations of "hate the Hun" sentiment on screen throughout the Allied countries.[36] Its anti-Austrian position in the extant print is in fact highly pronounced: Maciste draws a caricature of the emperor Franz Joseph next to the two soldiers he has bound, gagged, and hung up on hooks; and he refers to the Austrian soldiers approaching the villa as *"quei quattro mangiasego"* (literally, those four "fat eaters"), referencing the wax the Austrians would use to tame their very long mustaches. The violence against Pluffer, for whom Maciste reserves unusual wrath, is highly torturous, involving being dragged in the snow by his hair, used as human sled, and being shaken down from a tree.

Although the plot itself is far from realistic, the film evoked the realities of war on the Italian front, with its on-location filming and evocative panning shots of the alpine landscape.[37] The off-screen effect of trench and gas warfare was horrific destruction, resulting in scores of dead and wounded soldiers and civilians. The brutal living conditions on the front and the long periods of boredom made the actual experience far more wretched than the imported images from the front belied. On screen the scenes of combat once Maciste enlists are sanitized yet still evocative of the everyday war experience; the uniforms, encampments, weaponry, and even trench warfare, complete with sandbags and barbed wire, all form the backdrop of the story. Maciste sets off nitroglycerine explosives, carries cannons on his shoulders (the task of four men, the intertitles tell us), and even complains that the weapons echo too loudly in the cavernous mountains to surprise the enemy. He also laments the boredom of trench warfare: "But Maciste is not made for sedentary life," proclaims the intertitle, prompting his self-motivated encroaching on enemy lines. Maciste's charismatic and committed personality dominates these military exploits; his larger-than-life body and actions overwhelm even the most potentially detrimental and depressing of situations.

Comedic, ironic, and adventurous elements characteristic of the Maciste series infuse the military "realism" with a lightheartedness that is essential for its entertainment value. When the army tailor attempts to fit Maciste with the "glorious uniform" of the alpine soldier, the jackets keep ripping at the seam, with the tailor throwing up his arms in despair (fig. 3.4). And of course Maciste's uniform itself is a site to behold: perfectly tailored, pressed, and complete with an extraordinarily large feather attached to its characteristic hat.[38] Jokes about Maciste's voracious appetite abound, set up from the film's first scenes as he grabs a

3.4. Maciste being fitted for his "glorious uniform" in *Maciste alpino* (1916).

roast from the table when he is about to be interned (*"Voi arrestate me, io arresto l'arrosto!* [You arrest me, I'll arrest the roast!]") and later as he bemoans his hunger while imprisoned in the concentration camp, eventually opening a sealed tin of food with his bare hands.[39] Even in the trenches he quickly downs the rations of food that were meant to feed three soldiers, not one. His preoccupation with nourishment is not just self-centered; in the concentration camp he distracts the soldiers, steals food for the refugees, and procures them safety and sustenance at the count's villa.

The contrast between the seriousness of most war films (other than the comic shorts) and the lighthearted elements of the Maciste series speaks to the dialectic between the traditional and the modern that is at the heart of many representations of World War I appearing on Italian screens. The film's traditionalism lies in the melodramatic love story that enables Maciste to save Giulietta from disaster and reunite the betrothed, a topos that would become standard in the Maciste series, where he enables rather than belongs to the couple.[40] The setting itself, the castle of

Pratolungo, described in an intertitle as "a beautiful construction from the 1700s," evokes the past in its four separate establishing exterior shots, as does its neoclassical interior and denizen's aristocratic pedigree. Even contemporary critics acknowledged the film's debt to previous literary traditions: "*Maciste alpino* is like an adventure novel based on a historical foundation of great interest," wrote one reviewer.[41] The intertitles, while maintaining some of the humor and irony of *Maciste,* also lean toward the melodramatic, especially when extolling patriotic virtues. As Giulietta sews a flag for Giorgio to take with him to the front, the intertitles exclaim, "Let the tricolor flag that my hands have sewn be your shield in this dangerous endeavor!" When Maciste has planted the Italian flag on the peak after vanquishing the enemy, the film exclaims: "And the ardor of those courageous foot soldiers was the triggering spark of the burst of flame that swept away the centuries-old oppressor from our mountains. And the tricolor flag flew from the highest peaks" (fig. 3.5).

On the other hand, realism and technology converge in the film's representation of war as the ultimate expression of the modern. Brunetta sees the modernity of *Maciste alpino* not only in its use of film technology and special effects by Segundo de Chomón, the Itala Film specialist whose magic informed *Cabiria,* but also because it presented the greatest "impression of truth" within the conventions of contemporary cinema.[42] The extensive panoramic shots across the majestic Alps and the extreme tilting shots reinforced their vast beauty and their vertical stature. Superimposition technology here serves the exigencies of realism, in particular the scenes in which the alpine soldiers move their regiment into position by scaling mountains, hauling equipment via rope up steep cliffs, and cabling in between the peaks. Point-of-view shots through binoculars as Maciste spies on the enemy and vice versa bring visual cues to the perspective of warfare.[43]

Maciste alpino was not the only film about the war to which de Chomón contributed his special effects wizardry. *La guerra e il sogno di Momi* (*The Hand of the Hun,* Segundo de Chomón, Itala Film, 1917) fused fantasy and reality as well as modern and traditional modes of representation as an early known example of Italian animation and stop-motion cinematography. The story revolves around a young boy – another common topos of Italian war films – who receives a letter from his father describing life at the front, which the spectator then witnesses through reenactment. While taking a nap, Momi dreams of his toy soldiers Trik and Trak waging war on the battlefront. The film is not without accurate historical references; letters were often the most truthful reporting of the war, and the war saw a rise in children's consumption of realistic tin soldiers and other war toys with which, through play, children could accurately recreate and engage in the battles in which many of their male relatives were fighting.[44] The father's anachronistic story, like the *Maciste alpino* subplot, involves a damsel in distress under sexual threat. The battle between Trik and Trak, ironically, is the most evocative of the modern war experience, including air combat, sophisticated weaponry, bombs, missiles, and gas warfare, despite being marketed as a family film. One tagline in *La Vita Cinematografica* read: "A curiosity for the old, a delight for the young."[45] The vision of the toy soldiers wearing gas masks reinforces the war's disjunction from the real.[46] The animated depiction of mass weaponry and warfare, as a safe way of showing the unshowable, reveals the Momi film's ambiguous position toward the conflict. It addresses the horrors of war, albeit through the dreams and fantasies of a child, as it solemnly narrates a more intimate interpretation of the conflict.

Maciste alpino's patriotism, on the other hand, is much more direct than that of *La guerra e il sogno di Momi,* and the film clearly frames it along the lines of what George L. Mosse has termed the "Myth of the War Experience." For Mosse, "the reality of the war experience came to be transformed into what one might call the Myth of the War Experience, which looked back upon the war as a meaningful and even sacred event." Images of sacrifice and martyrdom, often making recourse to the pietà-like motif of the fallen soldier in the arms of Christ, "projected the traditional belief in martyrdom and resurrection onto the nation as an all-encompassing civic religion."[47] In Italy the conservative prime minister Antonio Salandra's concept of sacred self-interest (*sacro egoismo*) conceived the interventionist cause as a holy, nationalist mission. The cult of the fallen soldier became a centerpiece of the religion of nationalism during and after the war. The symbolic victory of personal and national regeneration over wounded virility culminated, particularly in visual culture related to the conflict, in a fusion of the sacred and the profane.

3.5. Maciste and the tricolor flag in *Maciste alpino* (1916).

Italian war monuments constructed in the conflict's aftermath (and even before Fascism's fetishization of the naked male body) often showcased the naked or semi-naked male body, turning to its direct classical lineage as symbols of the regenerative myth and its power to transcend death.[48]

In *Maciste alpino* the notion of war as a sacred and meaningful event promulgated through symbols does not yet reach the heights of the postwar exaltation of the dead and the cult of martyrdom and sacrifice. Instead the film focuses on tangible expressions of nationalism that are designed to rally the audience to the cause. The *tricolore* flag, the shield that protects Giorgio from harm, is a symbol of both what the film calls "*amor di patria*" (love of the fatherland) and Italian irredentism, as evidenced in the extreme panorama shots of Maciste on top of an alpine peak, in full uniform with gun in hand, next to the flag waving in the wind (fig. 3.5).[49] It becomes the unifying element of a regionally fragmented populace, which the film acknowledges and even embraces. When Giorgio leads the troops to storm the castle, he exclaims, "Young men – for the colors of Italy – Go forward – Avenge me – Onward Savoia! Follow Maciste." Thus Maciste and the flag are symbols of a newly, and finally, united Italian nation.[50]

Although *Maciste alpino* is one of the few films in the series in which Maciste bears firearms, he prefers to use his own strength to subdue the enemy; lamenting the ambush's difficulty with modern warfare, he instead launches a fierce snowball at Pluffer, hitting him so hard as to knock him off his perch. In many ways Maciste anticipates the squadrons of *arditi* (literally "the bold and courageous ones" but translated as "shock troops") who were brought into combat in 1917 and became the symbol, in the Italian popular consciousness, of the war hero, ready to sacrifice himself for devotion to the fatherland. The use of Maciste's body as a weapon also connects him to the Italian futurist movement and the equation of the body to a machine; his is a non-mechanized body in an increasingly mechanized world, both within and outside of the war context.[51]

The masculine body in motion was a subject of fervent interest in Italian culture during the war, brought to the forefront by the vocal, interventionist, avant-garde futurist movement, spearheaded by Filippo Tommaso Marinetti.[52] What attracted the generation of 1914 – as the young, European men who enlisted in World War I came to be known – were patriotism, the search for purpose in life, love of adventure, and the ideals of masculinity that the myth of the war experience appeared to embody. As such, it became a stimulus to the imagination, spurring an outpouring of creative activity during its build-up and duration. For intellectuals such as the futurists, war epitomized the modern condition, with its new technological inventions – the car, telephone, telegraph, and cinema – that "seemed to revolutionize time itself" as "signs of a modernity to be accepted or rejected."[53] Futurism's antitraditional celebration of speed, technology, violence, and ultimately war embraced interventionism as it exalted the regenerative myth of war for virility: "The Great War," wrote Marinetti in 1917, "which represents the fusion of fervid patriotism, militarism, Garibaldian impulsiveness, revolutionary power, imperialism and the democratic spirit, renounces all political parties, ridicules all pacifistic diplomatic machinations, crushes and smashes every kind of traditionalism, and revitalizes the world."[54]

The idea that war was an ideal space for initiation into a modern, vital virility did not solely belong to the futurists, but they were some of its principal proponents.[55] From the 1909 "Foundation and Manifesto of Futurism," the movement extolled the link between man, machine, and motion. In position five of the manifesto's eleven points, Marinetti wrote, "We wish to sing the praises of the man behind the steering wheel, whose sleek shaft traverses the Earth, which itself is hurtling at breakneck speed along the racetrack of its orbit."[56] In the subsequent work "Extended Man and the Kingdom of the Machine" (1910), the love of the machine substitutes for the love of the woman, completely foreign to futurism's taxonomy: she functions only in her reproductive capacity. Arousal emanates from the machine: "We have therefore to prepare for the imminent, inevitable identification of man with his motorcar, so as to facilitate and perfect an unending exchange of intuitions, rhythms, instincts, and metallic discipline," resulting in the proliferation of a "nonhuman, mechanical species, built for constant speed . . . cruel, omniscient, and warlike."[57]

Maciste as warrior aptly fits the description of the mechanized man, not only in what Marinetti called a "beautiful steel-tone frame of mind" (and body) but also in the way he moves with machinelike precision in his pursuit of the enemy. Yet with Maciste, bodies are dehumanized tools that serve the film's spectacularized slapstick purposes, using corporeal humor to address even such a serious and dramatic subject as war. His muscular mechanized body is a modern weapon in and of itself, hence his preference for corporeal combat rather than armed warfare.[58] His ability to quickly subdue the Austrian enemy with his bare hands comes to the forefront in the film's initial scenes: Maciste is to be punished for throwing his boot at the general in charge of his initial internment, but instead of receiving fifty lashes himself, winds up doling them out to

3.6. Maciste uses the enemy as a weapon in *Maciste alpino* (1916).

the four Austrians who failed to subdue him. Smiling as his stature and strength dominate the aggressors, he even begins to beat them using one of their own men as a weapon (fig. 3.6).[59]

After Maciste has captured Pluffer, he tortures him – or as the intertitle ironically reads, *"Maciste negotiates with Pluffer"* – by shaking him (he grabs and drags him by his hair several times throughout the scene) and sits atop him while Pluffer is facedown in the deep snow. At one point he even carries three prisoners up the pass only to later throw them down a steeper incline as they tumble violently through the snow. Thus Maciste, like the film itself, represents a fusion of the modern and the traditional; his classically sculptured, muscular body is simultaneously a national symbol of strength as well as a highly efficient weapon with a firmly anchored sense of duty and determination in his sacred mission.

The mountainous alpine landscape that forms the film's beautifully scenic backdrop functions as a symbol of Italian national, virile potency and its consecrated charge of irredentism. Marco Armiero contends that as one of the most mountainous countries in Europe (35 percent of its territory is covered by the Alps and the Apennines and 42 percent by hills), Italy has nationalized Italian nature in service to its cultural, political, and social aims throughout its history. During World War I the Alps were the "natural bastions of the nation, the ultimate borders of the Italian community, and, at the same time, their inhabitants became the prototypical true patriots standing guard over the nation." Later, in the postwar era the mountains hosted memorials and pilgrimages, especially by those who had lost relatives on the front.[60] Writers at the front, such as Piero Jahier and Ardengo Soffici, extolled their beauty and celebrated the populist spirit of their inhabitants.[61] Moreover, the Alps were a sacred and idealized space – *Maciste alpino* in fact refers to the region as being "*Tra cielo e nieve* [*sic*]," literally between the sky and the snow but figuratively implying heaven and earth. The mountains are locus amenus for the idealized man: "patriotic, hard, simple, and beautiful."[62] The film consistently frames Maciste against a mountain backdrop, whether he is scaling cliffs or hiking in the deep snow, and his stature – he towers over everyone around him – evokes the dominance of the snowcapped peaks over the rest of the landscape. The phallic equation is not lost here, nor is it subtle in the film's cinematography, with its ample tilt shots, uncomplicated mise-en-scène, and visual and verbal references to Maciste's "rigid hat with grand feather" as he climbs the rocks and scales the "unsurmountable" mountain peaks (fig. 3.1).

The film efficaciously showcases Maciste's muscularity in a spectacular scene of display against the mountainous landscape.[63] With the intertitle "A washroom at 2000 meter elevation," the camera tilts down in an extreme long shot of a beautiful cascading waterfall surrounded by snow to reveal a bare-chested Maciste lifting rocks to hone his physique. After this feat of strength he approaches the water and, in a medium long shot highlighting his shimmering muscles and ear-to-ear grin, bathes himself in the cold snow against the backdrop of the majestic waterfall (fig. 3.7). His muscles glisten with the water and the sunlight, and in a cut to a reverse angle, the audience even gets a look at his muscular back when he is delivered a taunting letter from Pluffer. The bare-chested shot is, and will continue to be, part and parcel of the Maciste series: the non-mechanized body, as a symbol of traditional masculine and muscularized strength, survives and prevails in an increasingly modernized

3.7. Maciste bathing bare-chested in the snow in *Maciste alpino*.

3.8. Benito Mussolini skiing bare-chested in the snow, 1937.

Courtesy of the Istituto Luce.

world. What makes this scene so interesting is the way Maciste's muscles incorporate the national ideals of the alpine and the phallic majesty of the landscape, as well as, perhaps, how it inspired Benito Mussolini to frame his own virile image in much the same way (fig. 3.8).

While the connection between Maciste and Mussolini is explored in further detail in the final chapter of this book, what emerges at this point in the Maciste series is that the film positions him as a mass leader, here both military and civilian, a topos that emerges with increasing frequency as the series progresses.[64] His military leadership, however, respects the very well established hierarchical chain of command; Maciste knows when to lead and when to seek permission to do so. From his cry of "*Viva l'Italia!*" upon hearing of Italy's entry into the war, to taking it upon himself to guide the refugees to safety, to the final fight to seize the castle, "Follow Maciste" is the emblematic battle cry, whether uttered or not, throughout the film. Personal affront, however, remains his major motivator; when first imprisoned with the refugees, Maciste is angered most when the guards kick his hat, and that incites his plan to entrap them. Similarly, while at the first internment camp, Maciste steals food as he laments his own hunger but is not shown sharing it with the masses. There exists a tension, at least initially, between individual needs versus the collective good, but one that is quickly overcome. For instance, he waits for his furlough from the front to seek personal revenge on Pluffer; when Maciste informs Giorgio, his military superior, about his fiancée's imprisonment and the castle's occupation, both request official authorization to engage the enemy in battle. Thus Maciste as leader, particularly within the military context, reinforces the political status quo, a position that takes on further ideological weight as the series moves into the highly politically charged climate of the late 1910s and early 1920s.

Maciste as leader of the masses, however, tells a different story; it is framed within a moral and secular-religious discourse of Italy's sacred mission to reclaim its land and reconstitute the nation. While he is in prison, Maciste's insubordination is clearly justified; his rebellious antics serve to portray the Austrians as bumbling and inept soldiers who are easily foiled by his cunning and strength. But the brutality of the enemy takes on a more serious tone when several hundred desperate refugees arrive at the internment camp. Most of the prisoners are women, children, the elderly, and the disabled; several men have lost limbs and appear on crutches, a possible acknowledgment of the increasing numbers of war wounded returning from the front. The long shots (and long takes) of the "unhappy" multitudes on the "torturous" march toward the concentration camp play on the notion of the displaced innocents looking to return to the promised land. The fact that the soldiers violently manhandle the prisoners emphasizes the suffering of the innocent. When Maciste leads them to the castle after their escape, class differences dissolve as the refugees literally pour into the extravagant abode. The camera pulls back to create depth of field as the downtrodden overtake the room, and the intertitles frame the count's acceptance of his compatriots in religious terms by paraphrasing Matthew 25: 34–35: "You who are blessed by my Father . . . for I was hungry and you gave me something to eat; I was thirsty and you gave me something to drink; I was a stranger and you invited me in."[65] A shot of a cow being slaughtered follows the quotation, and the implication of sacrifice is not lost as the group then rejoices in their salvation with an abundant feast. Maciste furthers the notion of rescue by empowering Giorgio and the count to "bring these wretched to salvation." As the count later leads them to safety through the woods, the film once again highlights the masses on the move as they ultimately arrive, with cries of joy, in "the beautiful homeland." Sacred egoism has become the national sacred mission of saving innocent Italians who have been exploited by a brutal enemy, with Maciste as supreme defender of the powerless and the weak.

MACISTE ALPINO VIEWED AND REVIEWED

Before *Maciste alpino* reached the theaters, however, it had to pass through the wartime censorship office, which had become increasingly more stringent as the war progressed. In Italy, according to Vittorio Martinelli, foreign films were the first to broach the subject of war and thus among the first film productions that were subject to political interference. Louis Feuillade's comic *Bout-de-zan va-t-en guerre* (Bout-de-zan Goes to War, 1915), for instance, had to change an intertitle reference to the German enemy from "*barbaro*" (barbarian) to "*nemico*" (enemy).[66] With the politically ambivalent *La guerra e il sogno di Momi*, censors in fact required that its final title card, intended to read only the indistinct "*Pax*" (peace), be changed to "*Pax gloriosa*" (glorious peace), invoking a militaristic and spiritual rather than pacifist finale to the conflict.

In the case of *Maciste alpino*, censors were concerned about excessive violence and asked for the elimination of several scenes involving exaggerated cruelty toward the enemy, including when Maciste grabs and shakes Pluffer by his hair and later uses him as a sled in the snow.[67] Several months after the film's release, however, and despite its incredibly successful box-office run, the Ministry of Public Security pulled the film from theaters once again, claiming that the filmmakers had not removed the censored scenes. Itala Film's studio head, Carlo Sciamengo, and the film's distributor, Stefano Pittaluga, successfully argued that they had indeed followed the censors' original requests, which while specifying the omission of specific scenes nevertheless approved the script with reference to those scenes and the intertitles intact.[68] The fact that the film was pulled after its initial approval became a cause célèbre in the specialized press, with several publications, including *La Vita Cinematografica* and *La Cine-Fono,* decrying the overreaching authority of the public security ministry and the censorship board.[69] The film returned to theaters in May 1917, including at the Salone Ghersi in Turin, where it had had its premiere, "and was received by the public with the same favor as several months prior."[70]

Publicity materials, including posters, advertisements, articles, and brochures, all reinforced the nationalistic rhetoric that is abundant in the film while at the same time drawing on Maciste's appeal as popular reoccurring series character. Official publicity began simply with an attempt to build notice via print advertising in June 1916, with the simple two-page spread reading, in large type, "ITALA FILM–Torino" and "MACISTE?" In late October ads appeared with the tagline "Coming soon: Itala Film's *Maciste alpino.* The season's most magnificent achievement and most resounding success," followed by "*Maciste alpino* has reached the highest cinematic peak."[71] This superlative-laden campaign (certainly not unusual for the time) continued as *La Vita Cinematografica* announced its imminent showing in November 1916, having finally cleared the censorship hurdles. It assured its readers that this "most awaited" film would be an unprecedented success.[72]

The program accompanying the film's run in Bologna, dated 29 January 1917, departed from the generic advertising campaign, instead reinforcing the film's connection to the war as well as Maciste's status as a popular film character. It billed the protagonist as "The gentle and generous giant" and summed up the film as follows: "*Cabiria*'s sweet and sympathetic hero, who today serves as alpine soldier and fights the enemy with noble, courageous sentiment, accomplishes, with the sacred love of an Italian, even greater heroic deeds, and triumphs through strength, valor, and his genial trickery."[73] The program drew on the continuity of character by invoking Pastrone's epic, his Italianness, and the sacredness of his mission as well his ever present geniality and sense of goodness. It was illustrated with copious film stills and a plot summary that stressed Maciste's patriotic devotion and moral decency.

Film stills published in newspapers were not the only visual material used to promote the film. Graphic art was one of the major modes of mass communication in Italy until the advent of cinema, and it played a vital role in war iconography, crossing a variety of registers – humor, satire, duty, sacrifice – to transmit films' propagandistic messages.[74] Wartime poster art drew on much of the familiar painterly and photographic culture that helped create consensus for the war, suppress dissent, and maintain support on a popular level.[75] Posters by the graphic artist Leopoldo Metlicovitz and others used figurative rather than literal language to visualize the conflict. Metlicovitz, whose iconic images for the alcoholic *digestif* Fernet and other products were well known, was no stranger to cinema and the Maciste series, having designed the original posters for *Cabiria* (plate 1). His posters for *Maciste alpino*'s release in both Italy and France are much more violent and direct than his war art, playing on Maciste's larger-than-life presence, his magnificent splendor in his glorious uniform, and his direct menace to the enemy (plate 3). They also reinforce the dominance of Maciste's corporeal strength as powerful armament against the enemy seen and unseen; even the weapon he bears in the Italian poster appears as a menacing extension of his body.[76] Yet the French version also plays off the film's comic nature, choosing to illustrate one of the more humorous (and also violent) of the film's scenes.

Reviewers quickly picked up on the film's patriotic spirit and its potential for instilling popular consensus for the war. Citing the influence

of Pastrone on Maciste's formation – Pastrone often went by the pseudonym Piero Fosco – *La Vita Cinematografica*'s Fabrizio Romano wrote
in his January 1917 review of the film how even the previously released
Maciste films *Cabiria* and *Maciste* could be mobilized for the war effort:

> Under Piero Fosco's guidance, Maciste has shed little by little the mentality
> and form of the savage, and has become distinctly modern, so much so to
> be touched by the tears and pain of an unknown girl. And now his master
> has infused his own patriotic ardor in him, so that the heroic athlete has
> risen to be the symbol of national aspirations and of the sacrifices that
> every Italian must perform for the attainment of sacred ideals that guide
> and animate our great war.[77]

As Maciste passed from "savage" to "modern," his athletic body conveyed
nationalism, patriotism, and sacrifice for the good of the war. He appeared as a model of behavior for the Italian everyman in trying times
of difficult loss as well as tremendous possibilities for the glory of the
fatherland.

A review by the French film critic Roland de Beaumont, whose
French-language reviews also appeared in *La Vita Cinematografica,* spent
four pages extolling the virtues of the series, Itala Film, and the character
Maciste. His praise for *Maciste alpino* above all rested in its realism, calling it "a documentary film, a true page of history," and "entirely made of
images that are startling with truth," a sentiment echoed by his colleague
Angelo Menini at the periodical *Film,* who described *Maciste alpino* as a
"revocation of Italian achievements (*gesta italiche*), in which the superb
champion of strength, the good-natured and giant *alpino,* finds himself
not in a fictitious, ephemeral or false world, but rather in one that real,
powerful, and abundant in truth."[78] De Beaumont concluded the article
with a quasi-liturgical rapture:

> It is not a film.
> It is a glorious feat; and a work of high patriotism.
> It is also a service to all mankind, which must understand the reasons
> why those who fight in a long, fierce war, almost beyond human strength,
> for civilization and right . . . also want a glorious peace which ensures the
> future and independence of all people.
> *Maciste alpino* represents the most accurate and lively depiction of the
> most astonishing feats of the great European conflict.

> Which is why this time we must say that instead of a film, Itala-Film has given us bronze pages on which war has forever engraved its heroes.
> Therefore, *Maciste alpino* is not just entertainment. It is also a lesson. A teaching that warms the hearts and raises the souls![79]

From its opening alliteration (in French "*C'est, ce n'est pas*"), this critical exaltation stresses not only the film's main patriotic themes but also their universality: its service to "mankind" in helping achieve a "glorious peace . . . for all people" as well as its "accurate and lively depiction" of the great "European" conflict. At the same time, it notes how the film becomes in and of itself a memorial to the war, cast in "bronze" as it immortalizes its heroics and the Myth of the War Experience (another review reported that a bronze statue of Maciste by the young sculptor Giovanni Riva adorned the outside of the Salone Ghersi in Turin).[80] It concludes with praise for the film's potential pedagogical function, one that could, and would, be carried over to civilian and military spectators alike.

A notice in the January 1917 issue of *La Vita Cinematografica* confirmed that in fact *Maciste alpino* was screened for soldiers at these venues:

> At the *casa del soldato* Itala's marvelous film was projected for the soldiers who attended the screening as ordered by the superior authorities, having said authorities determined that the most enlivening tonic to infuse enthusiastic courage in those departing for the front would be the heroic gestures of the immense Maciste.
> Itala Film could never have imagined having a more splendid success and a more authentic triumph.[81]

The *case del soldato,* founded in August 1916 by the military chaplain Giovanni Minozzi, were places where soldiers could enjoy "safe" recreational forms at the Italian front; oftentimes they showed films.[82] Maciste's patriotic mission thus jumped from the text to the training ground; the fictional character served as a model soldier both on screen and off, supported by civilian and military audiences alike. The use of the word "tonic" reinforced the prevailing sentiment of war as a cure for what ailed Italy. In Italy the myth of the Great War, as Mario Isenghi has classically termed the relationship between World War I and the contemporary intellectuals who wrote about it, was viewed as an opportunity for regeneration of the individual and society, a vehicle of protest, and an antidote for class struggles and differences. The idea that war as a drug or cure (*farmaco*) for the constitutional ills plaguing the nation emerged as a common thread among intellectuals up through the period of neutrality.[83]

Maciste is thus an "authentic" hero, anointed as such by the highest military authorities. The above-quoted notice's many references to greatness – "superior authorities," "immense Maciste," and "splendid success" – linked the character, the film, and the war effort by conferring upon them an aura of supreme grandiosity and enormous gravity. De Beaumont, in a subsequent article defending himself against what many readers felt was his over-the-top praise for the film, reported that the soldiers in the *case del soldato* "create quite a ruckus when the Austrians appear on the screen. But when Maciste tricks them, beats them, routs them . . . they scream with encouragement, they support him with their approval."[84]

Fabrizio Romano, the critic who wrote the notice for *La Vita Cinematografica*, also confirmed that the film was being screened for soldiers departing for the front. He contextualized his assessment of the film's patriotic and nationalist potential in much the same way as the notice above, as a strong tonic for the least stable temperaments:

> This show is a vigorous restorative [*tonificante*] for even the most steadfast temperaments. And if the show continues normally among the loudest laughter, this is a case – more unique than rare – in which one can affirm with certainty that "laughter is good medicine." The blood of heroes and avengers; the blood of liberators of the fatherland's sacred soil, unjustly oppressed for centuries and contaminated by crude, filthy and atrocious barbarians.[85]

Romano's vivid language frames the film within the nation's sacred mission of vindication against past oppression and the liberation from the barbarian enemy. He concluded the article by invoking the film's international appeal, not in terms of its box-office cachet but rather as a product that would further glorify national pride and honor: "The document of Italian valor is at the same time an act of faith and hope, a superb and proud affirmation of the real and present merit of our race [*stirpe nostra*]."[86] Race, specifically the idea of Italy as embodiment of the superior, virile Latin race (against the barbarian Germans), was an idea that circulated widely during the years of the conflict in journalism and propaganda, with D'Annunzio and Mussolini being two of its major exponents.[87] *Maciste alpino,* and the character himself, firmly whitened and nationalized as hypermasculine hero and leader of the masses, continued to function during the war as the "affirmation" of "our race" and as symbol of Italy's valor in its sacred mission of hope and faith.

What is noticeably missing from the film and from the extra-cinematic discourse surrounding it is any emphasis on sacrifice or martyrdom. There was no place for death in our hero's popular lighthearted escapades, even against the backdrop of war. Here the exigencies of film genre and the nature of film stardom trump the imperatives of the Myth of the War Experience. National film industries mobilized stars for the war effort on both sides: Henny Porten (in the Austro-Hungarian Empire) incarnated the idea of the motherland to inflame hearts and inspire young men to enlist in the German army, just as Douglas Fairbanks, Mary Pickford, Charlie Chaplin, and many others famously pitched American war bonds.[88] A May 1917 notice about the film's successful run in Sassari (on the island of Sardinia) states, "Maciste is popular and perhaps even more so than Cadorna," referring to the commander in chief of the Italian army, Luigi Cadorna.[89] Maciste, like the general, was a symbol of invulnerability rather than death, whereby his self-defense stood in for the self-defense of the nation.[90] The lightheartedness of the strongman film could not call for the ultimate sacrifice for the good of the fatherland. Maciste had to survive so that both the genre and the nation could live on, regaling in the joyful exuberance of the patriotic spirit.

* * *

Maciste alpino's representation of the war mythologized and spectacularized the heroic endeavors of the Italian soldier by having recourse to the motifs that rallied the country to the interventionist cause. The reality on the ground, however, was a different story. Italy had entered war wildly unprepared – without popular support, industrial or financial organization, adequate military preparation, or autonomy of raw materials needed for the war effort.[91] War on the Italian front, far from the brief encounter Salandra had envisioned, was a slow, exasperating process marked less by victories than by defeats and setbacks. The Italian campaign was an extremely difficult one from the beginning. Most soldiers were inexperienced on the mountainous terrain, which stretched 375 miles from the Tyrol in the west to the Julian Alps and the Isonzo River in the east.[92] There was more reluctance rather than exuberance on the part of the soldiers to endure the harsh mountain conditions, meager rations for food, and poor ammunition supplies.[93] At least 689,000 Italian soldiers lost their lives in combat, some dying at the hands of their own commanding officers, who took a hard line against disobedience and desertion. More than one million were wounded, and approximately 600,000 civilians died due to famine, disease, or other hardships.[94] Protests against food shortages in the countryside and strikes against difficult work conditions in factories continued throughout the war. This urban and rural opposition constituted "a moral revolt against the injustice perpetrated toward individuals, a community, or an entire nation."[95]

Despite devastation and dissent, *Maciste alpino*'s popularity was phenomenal and would spread beyond the Italian peninsula. It circulated in Holland, where Maciste was the "idol" of the Dutch, and even Mexico.[96] When the film finally reached the theaters in the Allied countries, especially Britain, France, and the United States, it was an enormous popular and critical success. The United Kingdom, for example, had long been one of the major importers of Italian films, including many of the historical epics of Italian early cinema's golden age and touristic films highlighting the country's picturesque beauty. Pierluigi Ercole has discovered that *Maciste alpino* appeared in London theaters in August 1917 and, according to the British film periodical *The Kinematograph and Lantern Weekly*, was a "truly remarkable film" and "one of the great films of 1917." It followed in the tradition of other patriotic documentaries featuring alpine soldiers and scenes, such as *La battaglia di Gorizia* (On the Way to Gorizia, 1916) and the above-mentioned *La guerra d'Italia a 3000 metri sull'Adamello* (shown in Great Britain as *The Battle of the Alps*), which had special premieres that served as patriotic events to rally behind the Allied cause. [97] In France, *Cabiria, Maciste,* and *Maciste alpino* had a similar history. *Cabiria,* which had taken almost one and a half years to arrive in British and French theaters because of concerns over its length, had been a huge success, playing continuously from 25 November 1915 to 19 March 1916 – 250 times – at the Théâtre du Vaudeville in Paris. The theatrical programs accompanying these screenings of *Cabiria* began to promote the next installment in the series with the tagline "Remember well the name of Maciste: you will be hearing a lot about him soon."[98] *Maciste* also screened at the Théâtre du Vaudeville with a successful run from 20 March to 1 May 1916, and *Maciste alpino* premiered there on 14 March 1917 with a charity benefit in the presence of the Italian ambassador, playing for 90 consecutive shows. A review from *Le Cinéma et l'Echo du cinema réunis* in March 1917 recounted: "Nothing is more curious and more surprising than this film. Maciste carries the Italian flag victoriously across enemy lines and illuminates with his gaiety and his intrepid bravery several moving scenes of war. The film can appear new in its genre. It's a good drama, a notable war film, and a beautiful love story."[99] Even the French writer Colette, writing for the French journal *Le Film,* praised both the star and the film and framed her admiration within Italy's irredentist mission:

> Maciste, Italian Alpine soldier, this time places in the service of his country his good-giant's torso, his arms that rock cannon redoubts, and his jaw muscles that can bend iron. This ogre, who wouldn't harm a fly, saves women and children, uproots trees, knocks down a horse with the flat of his hand, and ties Austrians in bunches of four or five and brings them back to camp, a little like a housewife bringing home the leeks. The day in which his heroic adventures have Carso or Trentino as their theater will make the fame of this superb Maciste complete.[100]

According to archival documentation, Itala Film attempted to alter the ending of *Maciste alpino* once the United States entered the war on Italy's side in the spring of 1917. A document dated 27 June 1917, filed with the Ministry of the Interior's Office of Public Safety and its film division and titled "Addition to the Ending of 'Maciste alpino,'" describes the addition of two shots to the conclusion: "On the ground a large German soldier with the smaller soldiers who captured him around him. Apparition of Maciste with an American soldier who waves the flag."[101] These additional scenes clearly have the intention of further demarcating enemy lines, and good versus evil, by extending the notion of ally and enemy in light of recent political and military developments. The alteration to the film's ending gives credence to the fact that Italian cinema consistently engaged with the changing war panorama, as well as the protean dimension of both this particular film's generic profile and its charismatic hero. It was added at the same time as *Maciste alpino* began its successful distribution and exhibition in the United States.

It was in the United States during the wartime years and even after that the series had its greatest and most traceable impact. *Cabiria, Maciste,* and *Maciste alpino* were all exhibited during the conflict. In addition, the three now-lost 1918 Maciste films – *Maciste poliziotto* (Maciste the Detective), *Maciste atleta* (Maciste the Athlete), and *Maciste medium* (Maciste the Psychic, Vicenzo Dénizot) – were reworked into a twelve-episode, twenty-four-reel American serial called *The Liberator* (1919). Thus we leave Italy for a brief transatlantic journey to America, ten years before Pagano made the only Italian film that had been partially shot in the United States, Eleuterio Rodolfi's *Maciste e il nipote d'America* (Maciste and His American Nephew, FERT, 1924). As the following chapter explains, thanks to the flexibility of his films' mode of address, Maciste was to become a fixture of the character-dominated American serial mania, a symbol of the wartime alliance between the two countries, and a point of pride for the Italian community living in the United States, particularly in New York City.

FOUR

Over There

THE MACISTE SERIES, WORLD WAR I,
AND AMERICAN FILM CULTURE

DURING WORLD WAR I BOTH *MACISTE* (1915) AND *MACISTE alpino* (1916) received extensive distribution across the United States. The series' first film was released in the spring of 1916 as both *Maciste* and *Marvelous Maciste,* and the second as *The Warrior* in 1917. The films were extremely well received from coast to coast as contemporary newspaper reviews, advertisements, and other published testimonials attest. Italians had clearly seen the potential of exporting their films to help create consensus for their cause. Giaime Alonge cites an undated archival document from the *Sezione cinematografica dell'esercito* titled "Propaganda in America" that sustained that film was a particularly apt tool for presenting the Italian point of view of the war in the United States.[1] The publicity surrounding the transatlantic exhibition of the Maciste films continued the mobilization effort aimed at maintaining popular support for the war while at the same time reinforcing Maciste's popular appeal as character and star. It was a balancing act that was not uncommon in the era as the American film industry attempted to reconcile its desire to use the medium to create consensus for the war effort as well as entertain the masses. The American distribution of *Maciste* and *Maciste alpino,* which I have reconstructed from newspaper articles and film trade periodicals, speaks to that exigency, to the saturated geographic diffusion of the films, and to the unique characteristics of the popular American serial form – in particular that of its heroines, heroes, and stars – that exploded in the 1910s.

As the industry shifted to the multi-reel feature film, the serial, along with comedy shorts and animated cartoons, was one of the few single-reel film forms that survived in the short format and helped studios such as Vitagraph and Universal outlast this transitional period. Originally headlined by female characters – Mary, Pauline, and Helen, to name just a few – and tied to novelizations in women's periodicals and newspapers, American serials coincided with the modernization of publicity technology, as the repetitive nature of the films practically advertised themselves. They thrived during the war, because they engaged with patriotic themes – such as Pearl White in *Pearl of the Army* (1916); Margarita Fisher in *Miss Jackie of the Navy* (1916); and the *Patria* (1917) series, produced by William Randolph Hearst and starring Irene Castle as the intrepid Patria Channing – and because their primary audience and fan base remained at home.[2] Yet these serials, beginning with G. M. Anderson's "Broncho Billy" in 1911 paved the way for the fusion of character and actor into the "picture personality" and star. They also proved the importance of print culture in the proliferation of the star persona along with the significant role stars would play in the promotion of the films across a variety of media platforms.[3]

Within the context of the serial form I see the Maciste series' success in the United States as linked to the postwar cinematic proliferation of American strongmen on screens just as the serial queens were disappearing from screen and print form.[4] Take, for example, the case of Elmo Lincoln, whose eponymous serials followed his breakout role as the title character in *Tarzan of the Apes* (1918). Newspapers publicizing *Elmo the Mighty* (1919) billed Lincoln as the "Yankee Maciste." One article publicizing the film proclaimed, "Elmo Is Said to be Stronger than Maciste."[5] Likewise, Maciste's character interacted in many ways with those played by Douglas Fairbanks, who became a ubiquitous star and public figure between the release of *Marvelous Maciste* and *The Warrior*. As I will show, the latter film's marketing strategy astutely played off the stars' potential rivalry to draw spectators to the theaters. Like Fairbanks, Maciste's physical prowess dialogued with the growing physical culture movement in the United States in the 1910s. Yet whereas scholars have shown that Fairbanks remained planted in youth culture, Maciste was all man.[6]

At the same time, however, Maciste appeared to be something entirely new and unique to American screens, not just in terms of the character's superhuman strength and enormous size – one report had him at seven feet and over three hundred pounds[7] – but also in terms of how the series fused humor and drama with the character's optimistic disposition. Its hybrid nature as both a comedy and a war film allowed for a flexible marketing strategy to promote its patriotic educational and entertainment value. The distribution and exhibition of the Maciste series in the United States during precisely this period results in a diegetic and extra-diegetic inscription of the foreigner as friend, not foe. Maciste's transatlantic journey constituted one of the first examples of an Italian film star's success in the United States, one whose popularity affected to a certain degree the American film industry's positioning of its own products.[8] From its inception cinema was internationally mobile, and stars, as increasingly important components of the industry's promotional strategies in those years, became commodities that traveled with the films as they crossed international boundaries. As Daisuke Miyao has revealed with his research on the Japanese-born silent film star Sessue Hayakawa, the ways in which non-native audiences "consumed" stars changed dramatically from one national context to the other and necessarily engaged with questions of nationalism as well as race.[9] Once the United States entered the war in the spring of 1917, both the industry and the government mobilized stars to gain and maintain consensus for the war, with their films and with their extra-cinematic activities promoting the war effort. The cases of both Hayakawa and Maciste/Pagano prove that foreign-born stars, if "allied" to the proper cause, could participate in this effort.

Maciste's journey was transatlantic and thus engages with the notion of Italianness in the United States just as the period of mass emigration from Italy was winding down and when Italians, especially in New York City, constituted a significant potential audience for the Maciste series. Interpreted in this light, Maciste's triumph prefigured that of Rudolph Valentino; the former faded from view just as the latter burst onto the cinematic scene. The theatrical exhibition and newspaper reports of the Maciste series created a "rhetorical space of modern and transnational Italianness," in particular of Italian virility.[10] Whereas Valentino's masculinity was sometimes the subject of conjecture, however, Maciste's masculinity was never called into question. His virility was literally front

and center despite his "spectacle of foreignness."[11] Moreover, publicity materials did not racialize Maciste's Italianness, even as Italian immigrants maintained a status of otherness, considered not quite white
within the American racial hierarchy. Italian characters, such as those
played by the American actor George Beban in the years preceding the
conflict, had already exposed American audiences to sympathetic por-
trayals of Italians.[12] Instead, unlike Italian coverage, the American press
was preoccupied with Maciste's racial metamorphosis. In Italy Maciste's
status as national hero supplanted his racial transformation from African
slave in *Cabiria* to white bourgeois in *Maciste*. As this chapter shows,
however, in the United States race mattered, and this change from black
to white occupied a significant space in the first film's public discourse.
In the racial hierarchy of 1910s America (and unlike Italy of the same period), whiteness and color trumped all else. What the circulation of the
Maciste films in the United States tells us above all is that, unlike many
Italian films during the war, they easily adapted to the American market;
that Maciste as a character was tailor-made for the American-style serial
and broadened its appeal; and that the star persona could travel across
the Atlantic as easily as the films themselves.

THE AMERICAN FILM INDUSTRY AND WORLD WAR I

The distribution and exhibition of the Maciste films during the years
of American intervention into the conflict necessitates their interpretation in light of America's patriotic initiatives within the film industry.
The years preceding the Great War saw the spectacular growth of the
American film industry with major shifts in production, distribution,
and exhibition, including the gradual movement toward vertical integration of those three arenas. It also embraced the full-length multi-reel
format; continuously engaged with issues of censorship; and achieved
greater connectivity between urban and rural centers through innovations in transportation, communication, and distribution. War films in
general, both native-grown and imported as well as documentary and
fiction films, were an important staple of American theaters from even
before the United States entered the conflict in April 1917. Nonfiction

films from the Spanish-American war appeared on American screens beginning in 1898, and early films of Theodore Roosevelt and his Rough Riders, as well as Thomas Edison's *Love and War* (1899), the first fictional narrative of war on screen, provided the generic template for images of the hero's masculine strength, sacrifice, and bravery.[13] The American war film itself is a hybrid genre, often involving other characteristics from the Western (in the case of the Civil War, for instance), the historical epic, or even the combat film.[14]

During World War I, films were a means by which the nation attempted to sway "neutral" Americans toward their cause. Homegrown productions liberally mixed the codes of realist and fiction filmmaking, collapsing for the first time the traditional dichotomy between documentary and narrative feature film yet stressing their dramatic and emotional potential and impact.[15] Anti-pacifist and pro-preparedness films ideologically battled it out on screens. James Stuart Blackton's *The Battle Cry of Peace* (Vitagraph, 1915), made with the support of Theodore Roosevelt about a potential foreign invasion of the United States, contrasted with neutralists ones such as Thomas Ince's religiously inflected blockbuster *Civilization* (1916) and D. W. Griffith's corresponding box-office failure *Intolerance* (1916).[16] Once the United States sided with the Allies and began fighting in the conflict, there was an uptick in the number of war films produced. According to *Motion Picture World* (and the work of Leslie DeBauche), the number of patriotic fiction films produced both by Hollywood and the government increased from eight in May 1917, to eighteen in October 1917, twenty-eight in March 1918, thirty-two in August 1918, and fifty-four by October 1918, although they still represented a small percentage of overall films produced during the nineteen months in which Americans participated in the war.

These films corresponded to a strategy of what Midkiff DeBauche has termed "practical patriotism" – namely, that it was "appropriate and reasonable to combine allegiance to country and to business." The industry fostered the development of "specials" – big-budget productions with extravagant mise-en-scènes that could command higher ticket prices, featuring important box-office-drawing stars of the day. Although war films still constituted a significant minority of total films produced, over half the specials released during 1917 and 1918 were war-related.[17] Films such as D. W. Griffith's *Hearts of the World* (1918), shot and set in Great Britain, were huge prestige pictures that received extensive play in the press and helped the industry gain the favor of both high- and low-ranking government officials.[18] *Hearts of the World* also starred the popular Griffith stars Dorothy and Lillian Gish.

Fundamental to the war effort from its earliest days were film stars, who gradually emerged, as in Italy and Europe, as fundamental to new industry models. On-screen "actors" passed from "picture personalities" – whose popularity among fans created the hunger and corresponding consumer market for photographs, magazines, and other intermedial extra-cinematic discourses – to stars in their own right. The distinction between public and private collapsed in the creation and manufacturing of the star persona, with film narratives and star discourses working together to contain the actor within certain boundaries.[19] Producers saw stars as magnets for ticket buyers, crucial to the industry's "bigger and better" film mantra that pervaded the shift to larger, first-run theaters. They helped sell block booking and were vital to attract the desired middle-class spectator in both regional and international markets.[20] After 1915 the symbiosis between on- and off-screen personae was not a question of mere reproduction. Rather, as Gaylyn Studlar has shown, "publicity was being leveraged in more complex ways to construct a coherent extrafilmic identity for the actor that would not contradict the tenor of his or her screen casting," with a shared identity but "measured distancing," making the star a more marketable commodity.[21]

In terms of the war, the government, through the Committee for Public Information (CPI), led by the journalist and former Denver police commissioner George Creel, involved the film industry in its effort to rally and sustain popular support for the conflict both in the United States and abroad. It cooperated in the creation of a war cooperation board, headed by the producer William A. Brady as its president and D. W. Griffith as its chairman. President Woodrow Wilson had appointed William A. Brady of World Film to head the National Association of the Motion Picture Industry (NAMPI), an organization allied with the government's Committee on Public Information. According to an article in the *New York Times* announcing its creation, "This board will work in co-operation with the Committee on Public Information, the various departments of the Government, the Red Cross, and the Council of National Defense in using the film to spread information regarding the plans and purposes of the Government in the war."[22]

As Suzanne W. Collins has shown, the recruitment of the film industry into the World War I propaganda campaign was "critical to the mobilization of a resistant and divided public," and film stars were essential to that mission in that they "performed and normalized a dominant mode of citizenship with which the public was to identify and adopt during a moment of intense national crisis over the government's decision to go to war."[23] The war savings stamp campaigns became another way for the public to show patriotism and loyalty to the United States, and stars such as Marguerite Clark and later Mary Pickford, Douglas Fairbanks, and Charlie Chaplin (as himself, not in costume as the Little Tramp) traveled for weeks at a time, leading parades, attending benefits and military balls, and personally adopting soldiers.[24] Fairbanks was particularly engaged in the fund-raising effort; he was among the first to actually tour, performing stunts on the road and donating large sums of his own personal fortune to various war causes and charities. As an example, the promotion of the hugely popular *Wild and Woolly* (1917) was linked with a fund-raising campaign for the Red Cross, complete with coin boxes displayed in theater lobbies to encourage donations.[25]

While under contract with the Jesse L. Lasky Feature Play Company, Sessue Hayakawa also participated in the war effort, part of a deliberate strategy of assimilation and Americanization in Lasky's efficacious construction of the actor's star persona in the United States. Hayakawa was one of many stars who made short skits/trailers encouraging the film-going public to buy Liberty Loan bonds in its fourth campaign of September 1917. The fact that the United States and Japan were allies during World War I allowed for the recuperation of the Hayakawa persona both on screen, as the sympathetic patriotic spy who sacrifices his life for woman and country in the World War I film *The Secret Game* (William C. DeMille, 1917), and off screen, with his active participation in government sponsored industry initiatives.[26] Similarly, the fact that

Italy was, like the United States, at first a neutral party in the conflict, and then its partner affected the way in which American film distributors and exhibitioners positioned and sold an Italian star such as Maciste in the marketplace.

Maciste, alternatively known as *Marvelous Maciste*, premiered in New York in March 1916 at the Park Theatre (the American copyright for the film is from 30 July 1915), and *Maciste alpino*, known as *The Warrior*, also had its theatrical premiere in New York at the Criterion Theatre on 18 July 1917, where it was accompanied by a live orchestra and played successfully for four weeks to packed houses.[27] The two films were imported by Harry R. Raver, a film impresario based in New York City. In 1913 he founded, among other various entrepreneurial efforts both within and outside the film industry, the All Star Feature Company, a production company that specialized in adaptations of popular plays featuring well-known stars and produced, among other films, the adaptation of Upton Sinclair's *The Jungle* (1914). He partnered with Exclusive Supply Corporation, a distribution company that was among the first to distribute feature films, including those of All Star. One of those films was *Cabiria*, which Raver, in his capacity since June 1912 as the American representative of Itala Film Company of America (Itala Film's distribution arm in the United States), brought over to tremendous acclaim, even screening it at the White House for President Wilson.[28] Raver had originally (and extraordinarily) tried to secure the Metropolitan Opera House for its premiere but was ultimately unsuccessful. *Cabiria* opened instead at the New York's Knickerbocker Theatre, which had been decorated with Italian and American flags, on 1 June 1914, with full orchestra accompaniment, a chorus, and many Italian and American industry players in attendance (fig. 4.1).[29] The tenor of the publicity for the film in the United States followed much the same tack as it had in Italy, highlighting its stylistic innovations, literary pedigree, and budgetary ($250,000) and decorative extravagance. Raver promoted Itala Film's other features in the United States throughout the war years. In late 1914 his advertisements highlighted the fact that "Italy was not at war" and had many pic-

4.1. Exterior photograph of the Knickerbocker Theatre's
New York exhibition of *Cabiria* (1914).

tures still to import; Itala Film's offerings still reflected "the Itala Brand,"
bore the artistic imprint of Giovanni Pastrone, and featured many of the
same players who appeared in *Cabiria*.[30]

    Cabiria was, as might be expected, a phenomenal success in the
United States, a familiar market with a ready-made thirst for Italian
historical epics. Its impact, however, expanded beyond audiences and
onto the screen. D. W. Griffith's *Intolerance* clearly bears the imprint

of *Cabiria*'s influence. The elaborate sets of *Intolerance*'s Babylonian sequence draw on the production design of Pastrone's film, in particular
its relative scale and its use of elephants. Although in a minor role in
comparison to Maciste, Elmo Lincoln's character, known as The Mighty
Man of Valor, betrays traces of the Italian genre's strongman, with his
bulging muscles and his kindness and goodness; the film, in true Griffith
fashion, humanizes him through his association with the animal world,
in his case the caressing of a pure, white dove.[31]

Maciste's distribution and exhibition, which appeared with the alternate titles of *Marvelous Maciste* and *The Perplexities of Maciste*, reflected
Harry Raver's promotional wizardry. He was no stranger to the publicity stunt, having started out in circus promotion and the traveling film
circuit hawking, among other films, Thomas Edison's *The Kiss* (1896) and
Edwin S. Porter's *The Great Train Robbery* (1903).[32] At the same time, it
appears that Raver also wanted to Americanize the film in order to expand its audience when the interest in and presence of foreign imports
began to wane. In the spring and summer of 1915, articles appeared about
Raver's intention to open a production studio for Itala Film in the United
States, although the notices were very short on specifics. They featured
evasive statements, such as that Raver "has withheld information until
operations were actually begun and definite statements could be made,"
and that "Raver . . . has been reticent about the new policy of his company, details of his operations being withheld until definite statements
could be made."[33] One notice stated that the production of *Maciste*, already partially filmed in Italy, would be completed at the studio. Raver
even held a luncheon for a special preview of *Maciste* for critics to invent
the best title for the film; the winner would receive a twenty-five-dollar
prize. An American screenwriter was also added to the mix, Agnes L.
Bain, under the supposed directive guidance of both D'Annunzio and
Pastrone. Ms. Bain (alternatively billed as Agnes Fletcher Bain), whose
sole writing credits were for Raver productions, was in fact Mrs. Harry
Raver. In addition, credits Anglicized the actors' names: Bartolomeo Pagano became "Ernest Pagano" – he had been billed as "Ernesto Pagani"
in *Cabiria*; Clementina Gay was "Arline Costello," and the Duke (Didaco
Chellini) became "Robert Ormand."[34]

Maciste the character had already established a following with the phenomenal American success of *Cabiria,* and Raver clearly and cleverly drew upon his appeal with the advertising campaign for the second film.[35] Advertisements for *Marvelous Maciste* rarely appeared without reference to "The Giant of Cabiria" and were often illustrated with an image of Maciste wearing his iconic toga, not with a scene from the new film. Once the United States entered the war (and *The Warrior* had already been released), some advertisements took a more nationalist bent: "The Giant of Cabiria" became "The Giant Warrior of Italy," and another billed him as "the Italian soldier and screen star" (fig. 4.2).[36] Depending on the venue, advertisements stressed the film's highbrow pedigree with references to the character as D'Annunzio's "great creation" or "great character," or its popular appeal, catering specifically to the serial-mad audience: "An amazing modern melodramatic comedy. Amazing acts – tantalizing thrills – stirring struggles – mystery," "a gasp and grin in every scene – a giant's game of brain and brawn," and "a great show for the children as well as the grown-ups."[37] One article placed him fully in the American context of other stars of the day:

> This time Maciste appears in modern garb in a series of adventures which show him as a blending of the characters of Charley [*sic*] Chaplin, William Farnum and Francis Bushman. . . . It is impossible to see his massive frame on the screen without a longing to see him meet Jess Willard. For a big fellow, Maciste has unusual grace and alertness and is as graceful and quick on his feet as Vernon Castle.[38]

Each of these men did, in their own way, prefigure Maciste on American soil. Farnum's characters in many Westerns and action films displayed a combative spirit (he had recently gained fame with an epic fight lasting an entire reel in the 1914 feature-length film *The Spoilers*). Bushman was a matinee idol with a muscled physique that was often used as a model by sculptors such as Daniel Chester French. Films showcased the pugilistic prowess of Jess Willard and the grace of dancer Vernon Castle, whose film *The Whirl of Life* (1915) had just been released to popular acclaim. Farnum and Bushman were top stars of their day, with Bushman in particular consistently listed in the top ten most popular actors and actresses from 1914 to 1918.[39]

BIJOU TODAY
Your Last Chance to See

The Marvelous
MACISTE

A Wonder Play made to fit the most remarkable character that has been given the amusement world in years

The Giant Warrior of Italy

Showing Continuous from 12 M. to 11 P M.

4.2. Advertisement for *Marvelous Maciste, Petersburg (VA) Daily Progress,* 27 October 1917, 7. Now that the United States had entered the war on Italy's side, Maciste was "The Giant Warrior of Italy."

From the author's personal collection.

Chaplin at first might seem an odd choice, given the actor's diminutive stature and less-than-powerful persona (although he was quite strong and nimble). American publicity, however, stressed Maciste's comic talents and the film's lightheartedness and humor, which put him in direct line with Chaplin's Little Tramp. Chaplin also became an important foreign public presence during the war effort, and *Shoulder Arms* (1918), his two-reel bittersweet but hilarious parody of life in the trenches, brought comic relief to a not so comical situation.

Film publicity for *Marvelous Maciste* also incorporated the complete fusion of character and actor, as was often the case with serial film production, as well as his comic talents and geniality. Pagano's name, when it is mentioned, appeared in various forms, if at all: as Edward Pagano, Ernest Pagano, or Ernesto Pagani. The fact that the actor's name is consistently misspelled or reworked in reviews, advertisements, and articles speaks to its inconsequentiality (as a signifier); it was Maciste and Maciste alone that mattered. "Since the sensational success of *Cabiria* three years ago," wrote the reviewer of *The Warrior* in the *New York Sun*, "Pagani has practically lost his identity in the character which he portrayed in that spectacle."[40] Moreover, Maciste as a character was so novel and unique to American screens in his combination of strength and humor that he overshadowed the actor. "Maciste cannot be compared with any other figure on the screen today because this superhuman is not equaled by any living actor," hawked an advertisement in *Moving Picture World*. "A wonder play, made to fit the most remarkable character which has been given the amusement world in years" proclaimed the *Petersburg Daily Progress*.[41] *Motion Picture News* wrote in its review, as excerpted in a newspaper advertisement, "A welcome novelty. The most entertaining of all the exploits type of production seen to this day. Radiates with what is called personality. Never before has there been such a figure as Maciste, who is always a comedian."[42]

While Italian publicity and reception of both *Cabiria* and *Maciste* showcased the character as national hero triumphing over the issue of race, Americans, on the other hand, did not shy away from the racial question. Maciste's race was a problem that had to be reconciled with the unequivocal black/white racial divide in the United States. Early American cinema teemed with representations of threatening black masculinity, either in the boxing ring (Jack Johnson) or outside (*The Birth of a Nation*).[43] Contrary to this dominant representation of black masculinity, Maciste of *Cabiria* saves and sacrifices himself for the young, virginal white girl, functioning more in a paternal role than as a sexual threat. Maciste's muscles, rather than a menace to the white man (à la

Jack Johnson), inscribed both good nature and moral goodness in service
to whiteness from the film's first images of him on screen as he protects
his master, muscles rippling on the rocky seashore.

In the United States, so heavily invested in racial hierarchies, the
extra-cinematic discourse sought to whiten Maciste's character even
before the narrative of *Marvelous Maciste* could, and would, address the
issue. With the premiere of *Cabiria* in America, the character of Maciste
emerged as a popular favorite, yet he was not the focus of the publicity. Several newspapers published feature articles about how Pagano
was discovered (in one instance by D'Annunzio, referred to as "Italy's
Shakespeare"), citing as well the audience's appreciation of his performance.[44] But very rarely did Maciste's image appear in promotional advertisements for *Cabiria,* and when it did, his racial difference figured
prominently. In the United States, Maciste's darkness materialized as
masquerade, his race a costume that ultimately revealed his whiteness:
"Maciste . . . who does most of the hand power rescuing, is a great ebony-
hued person, his piano polish finish very generously exposed," wrote
the reviewer in the *Chicago Daily Tribune.*[45] Similarly, an article in the
Trenton Evening Times reported of the large crowds going to see *Cabiria*
in both the United States and Italy, and how although the film "appeals
to all classes, races and religions alike," Italians in particular "proudly
speak of Ernesto Pagani, the Italian giant, who portrays the character of
Maciste the slave, and his wonderful Numidian make-up."[46]

When *Marvelous Maciste* was released, American spectators were
clearly interested in the character's racial metamorphosis. Titles of reviews and notices included "Black Wore Off, but He Didn't Die, Brudder
Maciste," and "He Is Not An African!"[47] Others reinforced his passage
from "negro slave" to "white gentleman,"[48] from "African" to "full-
blooded Italian."[49] In one newspaper column titled "Answers to Movie
Fans," the author addressed a female letter-writer who presumably had
inquired about Maciste's racial origins: "In 'Cabiria' the part of Maciste,
the slave, was played by Ernesto Pagani. At the time of the presentation
of the picture those promoting it declared Maciste to be a genuine black
whom Gabriel [*sic*] d'Annunzio found walking along the wharfs one day.
Recently a story has been circulating that he is white. The conflicting
stories are each based on authority."[50] Interpreted within the context

of the racial politics of American cinema, Maciste's racial recuperation further legitimizes his passage to leading strong man.

In spite of the prejudice facing southern Italians at the time, or perhaps in an appeal to Newark, New Jersey's southern Italian population, one article's dateline was Naples, Italy, and it fabricated a soon-to-be Hollywood-like breakthrough:

> Maciste is rapidly supplanting the other Italian film heroes in popular affection. He was formerly a longshoreman on the docks here. One day a film operator, taking the departure of a ship with some heroes and heroines of a film drama registering "farewells," asked the boss stevedore to help him in the action by hustling in some longshoremen. "I'll get Maciste for you," was the answer. Maciste, famous about the port for his size, strength and good humor, registered action so well that he became part of the movie company.[51]

Building on the fusion between character and actor, this discovery myth plays on cinematic fantasies of stardom – that stars are both superhuman and like everyone else – as it disregards the regional implications in positioning Pagano as southern. In this report and others like it, Maciste is only Italian.[52]

The American press's emphasis on Maciste's strength echoed the growing physical culture movement of the United States at the time, epitomized in film's earliest days with Thomas Edison's first images of Eugen Sandow's muscular poses, boxing films, and the emergence of strong men such as Charles Atlas, originally the southern Italian immigrant Angelo Siciliano.[53] The *New York Times* wrote:

> Maciste is back on Broadway again, this time in a picture called "Marvelous Maciste," which was shown for the first time here yesterday at the Park Theatre. Appreciating the publicity value of the Italian actor's magnificent physique, just as Charles Chaplin's producers were quick to capitalize his mustache and walk, the Italo [sic] Film Company has prepared a picture in which the athletic prowess of this superman is featured. For the most part it is an amusing picture, in which there are some clever touches.[54]

Another places him in the context of the classically informed American strongman: "Aside from its melodramatic surprises the picture is full of charm and beauty, and promises to create special attention as his feats are those of Samson, Sandow, and [the boxer] John L. Sullivan."[55] Similarly, "'Maciste' will be certainly admired by devotees of physical fitness and the strength of manhood. For he is seen in conflict with scores of men and tosses giants about as a giant might toss a baby, all in keeping with the title of 'superman' conferred upon him by D'Annunzio."[56] Maciste's muscularity, already essential to his racial recuperation, here plays an integral role in situating him as the ultimate masculine specimen at a time when the suffrage movement as well as increasing modernization, urbanization, and industrialization posed threats to American manliness.[57] Soon that muscularity would be mobilized in service to both the American and Italian cause in World War I with *The Warrior.*

THE WARRIOR

Just as *Marvelous Maciste* had concluded its New York run and would soon embark on nationwide distribution, articles began appearing in the American press in September 1917 reporting the death of the man who played "Maciste." Newspapers such as the *New York Times* (21 September), the *Warren Evening Times* in Pennsylvania (21 September), and California's *Oakland Tribune* (11 November) all carried notices of his death in battle; specialty publications such as *Photoplay* as late as December picked the story as well, despite the fact that Raver issued an official denial in October, two weeks after the story first broke.[58] In a report in the *New York Dramatic Mirror,* Raver is quoted as saying:

> I was very much astounded when I read of Ernesto Pagani's death in a morning New York Paper, on September 14. I cabled the same day asking for confirmation. Two weeks elapsed before a reply was received here from Turin, which reached me on the 27th, stating that "Maciste" was in good health and "enjoying his usual good appetite." Needless to say, I am pleased at the good news as Mr. Pagani's death would interfere seriously with the elaborate plans I have arranged for the future of this unique star.[59]

It does not appear, however, that Raver protested too loudly, perhaps borrowing a page from Carl Laemmle's playbook and his publicity stunts that catapulted Florence Turner to fame in 1910 with the false reports of her death. Nor did he speak the truth that Pagano was excused from military service rather unceremoniously. Instead, word of "Maciste's death" continued in newspapers through early 1918, with the idea, probably, that all publicity for *The Warrior* was good publicity, especially the kind that transformed Pagano into a war hero. "If Ernesto Pagani, otherwise Maciste of 'Cabiria' fame, survives the vicissitudes of war on the Italian front and returns to photo play with proper direction and proper vehicles, he should prove the most popular film star ever produced," wrote one reviewer in the *Cleveland Plain Dealer*.[60] Publicity for *The Warrior's* exhibition in Philadelphia first reported his death and then issued a denial only a few days later, fabricating his record of service on the Italian front: "After his service as an actor, Maciste rejoined the colors and took part in the famous Italian drive a year ago against the Austrians. He is the biggest man in the army and a great favorite with his comrades."[61] Others, unaware of his survival, used his supposed death as a draw: "Maciste at the outbreak of the war was called upon by the Italian government to join his colors, which he did with the greatest of patriotism. . . . It was on the 'Defense of Venience' [*sic*] that Austrian shell and gas got this giant hero and the odds were too much for man or superman."[62]

Regardless of its star's mortality, *The Warrior's* hybrid nature as war film, comedy, and serial-like adventure film lent itself to multiple marketing strategies and explained, to a certain extent, its wide appeal. Raver employed much of the original marketing strategy for *Marvelous Maciste* in advertising his latest product to the public. Still dominant was the connection with *Cabiria*; so unprecedented had been its blockbuster status and Maciste's presence therein that it still remained fresh in the minds of the film-going public. Maciste's novelty endured in many advertisements, stressing his unusualness in superlative terms: "Special – Extraordinary – Unusual," hawked the *Fort Wayne News and Sentinel*.[63] Its uniqueness was not lost on the public; an Indianapolis article noted, "If, in these present times, a war comedy can seem plausible, 'The Warrior,' the photo novelty being screened at the Circle all this week, attains that distinction."[64] Although war comedies existed, most of their humor, according to Michael Isenberg, was itself not related to death and devastation typical of the conflict, but rather to the gags and comical mechanisms external to that drama.[65]

After its premiere in New York City in July 1917, *The Warrior* began to tour around the country in early 1918, at the height of both the United States' and the new Italian military push after the humiliating defeat of Caporetto in October 1917.[66] It was by far the more popular of the first two Maciste films, with a wider distribution, bigger advertising campaign, more newspaper buys, and greater topicality with its war setting. It was also, as the critics agreed, a better film than *Marvelous Maciste*: "so ludicrous were the situations [in *Marvelous Maciste*] that the American public – or the small fraction of it which occasionally infests the Park Theater – refused to accept the thing as either good melodrama or good face . . . but this picture is one of the best entertainments of the year, since it is all original stuff, and well done."[67]

Reports of the film's success abound: "When this picture was shown for the first time at the Criterion Theater in New York City, it was greeted with a tumultuous cheering which reminded one of a national political convention just after the man of the hour had been nominated for president of the United States," reported *Photoplay* in September 1917.[68] It played in first-run theaters, often charging the top-billing price of two-dollar admission with full orchestra accompaniment in major cities; the Los Angeles screenings even featured a yodeler as well as a singer accompanying the film.[69] In Lowell, Massachusetts, the management of the Owl Theatre decided to admit children under sixteen free (plus the supplemental war tax) for select performances if accompanied by a parent: "Here is an opportunity for parents to bring their children to see a picture which is of great educational worth as well as entertaining."[70] It was so popular in Lowell that it returned for another engagement the next month: "No one should miss this second opportunity to see this wonderful play. It shows the humorous side of this great struggle and the sport this man makes of the enemies of democracy with his prodigious strength. There is a scream and a roar in every scene."[71]

The breadth of *The Warrior*'s charm, as well as its rating as wholesome entertainment, was a selling point in certain markets. In Kennebec, Maine, for instance, the film was promoted as an appropriate, "clean" picture that passed untouched through the National Board of Review (originally established in 1909),[72] the only agency that issued various regulatory guidelines for each picture:

> There is not the slightest suggestion of the usual nauseating sex interest which forms an important part of many film productions and every reel of the seven-part picture has a clean, wholesome atmosphere. In the wide appeal which Manager Keller feels "The Warrior" will make to his audience he wishes to emphasize above all things the cleanliness of the production, which will be a strong factor in "making picture-theatres safe for women and children." The strong strain of delightful comedy which the film contains is particularly attractive to the female sex while the virile manhood of Maciste in his daring adventures in the Alps will reach the hearts of the opposite sex.[73]

The naiveté of this assessment, in assuming that the female spectator would not be attracted to Maciste's "virile manhood," betrays the larger issue of censorship and American silent cinema, and its effect on spectatorship, particularly that of women and children. In addition to the pronouncements of the National Board of Review, rules and regulations varied from state to state (only six had their own censorship boards), but Maine's preoccupation with nefarious sexual influences on women and children were not unique to that particular geographic area. The representation of sexuality (female in particular) on American screens was both a local and national issue before, during, and after the war, because concerns about the immoral and the obscene, always present from the early days of the medium, affected the discursive formation of what would become the classical Hollywood narrative and gained speed as women made up an ever increasing portion of the film audience.[74]

In various newspapers across the country, both industry directives and regional exigencies dictated whether publicity would promote *The Warrior*'s connection to the war. Trade publications revealed a general overall ambivalence on the part of the studios about the audience's desire to engage with the war on screens, reflecting two commonly held positions by producers, distributors, and exhibitors: that movies should show escapist fare or should bring the war into the theater through a variety of cinematic signifying practices, including some of the less sensational footage produced by the Committee for Public Information and the U.S. Army Signal Corps.[75] Many theaters were hesitant to promote films that might offend a significant portion of their audiences, particularly in the Midwest, where there were large German American populations. Yet there appears to be no geographic pattern for this film's

4.3. Advertisement for *The Warrior* in the *Waterloo (IA) Evening Courier*, 29 January 1918, 8.

From the author's personal collection.

marketing strategy. Depending on the venue, advertisements for *The Warrior* either oriented the film within the war picture genre or advertised decidedly against it. In Pennsylvania one advertisement billed the film as "A Battle Drama of the Alps"; one Indianapolis paper titled its review of the film "Maciste Shows How the Italians Are Fighting"; and the *New York Sun* praised the lead character in civil terms: "Maciste is one, great, big, strong, citizen."[76] When *The Warrior* returned to Kennebec for another run in August 1918, the correspondent framed the film within patriotic terms, whereby the reviewer appropriates Maciste as an American symbol:

> Out of the background of white, blue, and the red of bloody battle stands the silhouette of Maciste of "Cabiria," prestidigitator of strength, whose every move bruises, breaks, pulverizes. . . . You will see, not only the most astounding spectacle, the prodigies accomplished by a man whose bright, clear eye and perfect form evoke the plaudits of the multitude, but you will also follow the entire Alpine warfare, the audacious manoeuvres on the summits of mountains [*sic*] heights which seem only possible for the eagle to reach.[77]

On the other hand, "not a war picture" was a common subheading that appeared in the publicity surrounding the film, focusing instead on its entertainment value as a comedy or adventure film. "Has your spine a thrill vibrator?" asked one advertisement; "It will need one to absorb the countless thrills and spectacular action throughout" (fig. 4.3). An article announcing its imminent showing at a first-run Dallas theater prevaricated: "An advance notice says, 'The Warrior' is not a war picture as some might surmise from the title. It is a comedy drama taken on the Italian frontier, and throughout the entire seven parts of the picture there is not one scene of war or battle.'"[78] One advertisement even seemingly contradicted itself, billing the film as "not a war picture," but with the tagline "You'll enjoy seeing how Maciste handles the Huns" (fig. 4.4). When it was released in the United States, *The Warrior* was in fact one of the few fiction films to portray events on the Austrian-Italian front, for most films focused on the Germans, particularly the kaiser, as the embodiments of evil.[79]

Other markets positioned the film as a biographical retelling of Pagano's "near-death experience" while fighting in the war, yet they still

4.4. Advertisement for *The Warrior* in the *Marion (OH) Daily Star,* 4 June 1918, 12. The copy contradicts itself, advertising the film as "not a war picture" but also extolling how "You'll enjoy seeing how Maciste handles the Huns."

From the author's personal collection.

varied wildly in categorizing it as a war film: "Maciste's new play is called 'The Warrior,' and, while its title indicates that it is a war drama, it has no battle scenes and neither does it show any particular atrocities on the part of the Austrians or Germans. It is, instead, more of a pictorial account of Maciste's personal history when he was caught just over the Italian boundary line in Austria at the time Italy declared war."[80] A personal report from the London premiere for the *Boston Transcript* titled "Maciste's Final Film," believing him killed in action, interpreted the film not only as a war picture but also in a documentary-like fashion: "The film is beautifully mounted, and many scenes of authentic life in the Italian army are introduced, in which we get a vivid idea of the energy and heroism demanded of troops in regions where the opposition of nature would seem to belittle that of the Austrians to sheer insignificance."[81] A story in the *Detroit News* is even more direct: "The story simply duplicates the actual experiences through which Maciste is said to have passed at the outbreak of hostilities between Italy and Austria."[82]

Evidence of the influential, abundant theatrical presence of nonfiction war films appeared in the widespread praise for the film's realist aesthetic. The *Boston Transcript* chimed: "The action, concerning as it does the exploits of Maciste in the Alpine theatre of war, often carried the actors, and now carries the spectator, straight into the mountains. The views of the peaks, chasms and cliffs of the Italian Alps are extraordinarily well done, and the feats of the Italian soldiery in scaling perpendicular heights, and in crossing vast depths hand over hand on cables, are only less amazing than the 'stunts' turned off by the principal actor himself."[83] The *New York Times* extolled the film's use of special effects for realistic effects: "Some of Maciste's feats are real exhibitions of strength, while others are tricks of the camera so cleverly done that they have every appearance of reality."[84]

The *Times* was also one of the many newspapers to draw comparisons between Maciste and Douglas Fairbanks: "Pagani, or Maciste, as he has been known since the 'Cabiria' film, is the Douglas Fairbanks of Italy. As a matter of fact, he out-Fairbanks Fairbanks, since he is almost twice as big as our own favorite athletic actor. Fairbanks has often whipped a whole township in live reels, but in 'The Warrior' Maciste makes the whole Austrian Army shake in its boots."[85] This comparison with Fairbanks is extremely indicative, because two primary changes occurred during the period between the American release of *Marvelous Maciste* and *The Warrior*: the United States entered the war, and Douglas Fairbanks achieved massive popularity as a film star and public figure. The *Times* review observed how with Maciste, like Fairbanks, everything is done with a smile: Maciste's good nature and disposition overwhelm the potential violence of his actions. Fairbanks was so popular at the time that variations on his name had become part of the American vocabulary: in praising Maciste's stunts, *Photoplay* wrote that "he engages in a dougfairbanks with the Austrian defenders of a certain castle"; the *Minneapolis Tribune,* in an article titled "Giant Maciste Does Real Fairbanks Stunts in 'The Warrior' at the New Unique," proclaimed, "Douglas Fairbanks has a rival." [86] And according to the *Los Angeles Times* review, "The Warrior: Superfairbanksereno," even the film's intertitles were altered to play off the connection between the two actors: "In 'The Warrior,' he is a film actor known as Douglaseno Fairbanksereno. Jack Lait, who wrote all the subtitles to the picture play, named him so, and named him both wisely and humorously. For Maciste does indeed resemble our Doug in body, smile and method, though, of course, he is twice as big as Doug – hence the Super. He is, as Lait says, Douglas Fairbanks grown to man's size."[87]

Fairbanks incarnated, from early on in his successful Broadway career, the all-American boy next door, full of youthful vigor, energy, and optimism. He made his theatrical debut in 1902 and consistently played, up through his transfer to films with Harry Aitken's Triangle Film company in 1915 with *The Lamb*, extremely likeable, "appealing, lighthearted persona."[88] His characters underwent radical yet most often humorous transformations from urban mollycoddle to rugged, primitive masculine citizen à la Teddy Roosevelt, whose muscularity incarnated the early twentieth-century cult of the body, which in turn was emblematic, in the muscular Christianity movement, of moral goodness.[89] Because most of the characters Fairbanks played were upper class, their unburdened and carefree lifestyle allowed for a greater focus on playfulness, reinforcing the actor's youthful image as well as his physicality. Maciste, on the other hand, had no time for play, as his heroic exploits at this point carried national, patriotic implications. His leisure-time experiences would come after the war, as he would fall in love (*Maciste innamorato*) and would take a vacation (*Maciste in vacanza*) (see chapter 5).

In addition to infectious grins and attractive physicality, Fairbanks's on-screen similarities with Maciste are many. The increasing importance of physical culture in the construction of modern masculinity, thanks in part to the publishing empire of the fitness guru Bernarr MacFadden, was a growing industry in and of itself with ties to the film world. [90] With his good friend and ghostwriter Kenneth Davenport, Fairbanks "wrote" many articles and books extolling his personal philosophy on life. The books *Laugh and Live* (1917) and *Making Life Worth While* (1918), among others, advocated taking control of one's life, the power of positive thinking, and, naturally, good health. Copiously illustrated with film stills and personal photos, they were not the fitness manuals that were growing in popularity at the time (and often written by stars such as Rudolph Valentino), but nevertheless incorporated words of wisdom on health, exuberance, and the importance of physical exercise. "Energy is the natural outpouring of a healthy body," Fairbanks writes in *Laugh and Live*. "The mere possession of energy and enthusiasm makes us feel like laughing. . . . *Get out in the air and run like a schoolboy. Jump ditches, vault fences, swing the arms! . . . Let yourself go!*"[91] In addition, the hybrid nature of many of Fairbanks's first films – comedy, Western, and action films rolled into one appealing package – resembled the Maciste product in their showcasing of the athletic spectacle. Both actors would also make the shift, in the 1920s, to elaborate, big-budget costume-adventure productions – *The Thief of Baghdad* (1924) and *Maciste contro lo sceicco* (*Maciste against the Sheik,* 1926), for instance – while maintaining their respective virile identities.

In Maciste's case, however, the displays of physicality are related to his extraordinary strength. Fairbanks's characters instead showcased their nimbleness and acrobatic prowess, although he is decidedly not a wimp in the boxing ring in *His Picture in the Papers* (1916). Also relevant is the question of size. Although both men were full of virile vigor, Pagano dwarfed the comparatively small Fairbanks, whose average height allowed him, especially when next to his diminutive wife, Mary Pickford, to still project an aura of youthfulness well into his thirties.[92] While many of Fairbanks's films reinforced the importance of masculine transformation, both mental and corporal (*The Lamb*), Maciste, on the other hand, could only be 100 percent man, one who was perfectly adaptable to the growing popularity of the male serials that gradually replaced the serial queens on American screens (a subject explored in greater detail in the following chapter).

SERIALIZED MACISTE: THE CASE OF *THE LIBERATOR*

In 1919 Harry Raver released *The Liberator,* a compilation of twelve two-reel episodes totaling five and one-half hours to be released weekly across the country. Directorial credit went to Pastrone and screenplay credit to

Raver's wife, this time billed as Agnes Fletcher Bain, attempting once again to put an American twist on a decidedly Italian film. Although billed as an original Raver production, *The Liberator* was most likely coiled from variously extant Maciste films, including the first *Maciste* and three Maciste 1918 Itala films: *Maciste poliziotto* (Maciste the Police-man), directed by Roberto Leone Roberti, and *Maciste atleta* (Maciste the Athlete) and *Maciste medium* (Maciste the Medium), both directed by Vincenzo Dénizot, with *Maciste atleta* supervised by Pastrone as well.[93] There are no existing prints of the original Italian films or *The Liberator,* limiting much of what is known about the films to archival documents and newspaper reports.[94] Davide Turconi, the first to attempt to reconstruct *The Liberator,* notes that the serial's specifications indeed corresponded to a compilation of the four films: its 8,000 meter length was more or less the equivalent of *Maciste atleta* (2,135 meters), *Maciste poliziotto* (2,520), *Maciste medium* (1,455 meters), plus the original *Maciste* (2,000 meters). It might appear odd that the original *Maciste* would reappear in the serial, given the fact that the film had been released only a few years before, but serials often recycled and reworked previously screened material into new episodes. Of the twelve episodes only seven individual titles are traceable: the first, *The Morosini Mystery,* and the sixth through the eleventh: *The Satanic Sculptress, The Spectre of the Past, Hercules and the Vampire, At Death's Door, The Hypnotic Eye,* and *Mystery of the Sanitarium.*[95]

The serial was screened in its entirety for critics in December 1918 be-fore its 1919 release, breaking the usual practice of screening only the first few episodes, because it was "so novel and unusual," like its protagonist.[96] In fact, *Moving Picture World'*s film review refers to the whole serial, com-menting on the protagonist's charismatic presence, the picturesque scen-ery of "life in the land of Garibaldi," and the excellent supporting cast, including Italia Almirante Manzini (the femme fatale Sofonisba from *Cabiria*), who appeared in all three of the above-mentioned 1918 films. Giving additional credence to the theory that the serial was a reworked compilation of extant films, the reviewer writes: "The variety of its the-atrical fare is quite astonishing. Melodrama, emotional drama, comedy, farce, comic and bewildering stunts are all introduced. In fact, it gives the impression of three stories rolled into one."[97] Other reviews praised its value as entertainment – "'The Liberator' is a constant delight" – as well as the series' adaptability to the serial format: "That Maciste's accomplishments should provide fertile material for the serial director was a foregone conclusion, and his superhuman strength as shown in 'The Liberator' form a series of high lights the true value of which will be appreciated by any audience whatsoever."[98] Gone, however, is the tone and spirit of national cooperation between the United States and Italy, with several citations touting American superiority: "'The Liberator' is good entertainment, but cannot be touted as a rival of 'Cabiria' or 'The Warrior' and in many ways is proof that the European director has much to learn from his American brother," and "Maciste is certainly an unusual personage and his presence may off-set all the foreign technique and shortcomings of the story."[99]

This broad appeal carried into the film's exhibition, which underwent a noticeable shift in the venues where it played. Gone are notices of elaborate premieres and full orchestra accompaniment. Instead, the film was shown in more popular theaters with broad appeal, ones better fitted to the serial form, or that billed themselves, as did Chicago's Marlowe Hippodrome, as a "house of varieties" "where everybody goes."[100] "Is it any wonder that 'Maciste' is a great favorite with all classes?" posited Chicago's *Suburbanite Economist*.[101]

Incorporated in the promotion were many of the same Maciste-inspired myths upon which Raver relied to promote the previous films: his heroic "service" in the war, his novelty, and his similarities to Fairbanks. A November 1918 report in *Moving Picture World* talks about the trials and tribulations in shooting the film due to three interruptions with the cast during wartime (including Maciste's service at the Italian front), D'Annunzio's intervention in obtaining proper military leaves for the cast members to shoot the film, and Raver's own Maciste-like determination in getting the film made: "Casualties among members of the cast and their relatives at the front added to the uncertainty and gloom, but Mr. Raver never gave up hope. . . . Realizing the big fellow's popularity in this country, [he] did not believe in giving up without pulling the very last wire."[102] Advertisements billed the "sensational hero idol" Maciste as "Gabriele D'Annunzio's World Famous Soldier Star."[103] A two-page spread in the 7 December 1918 *Moving Picture World* sold Maciste as "The

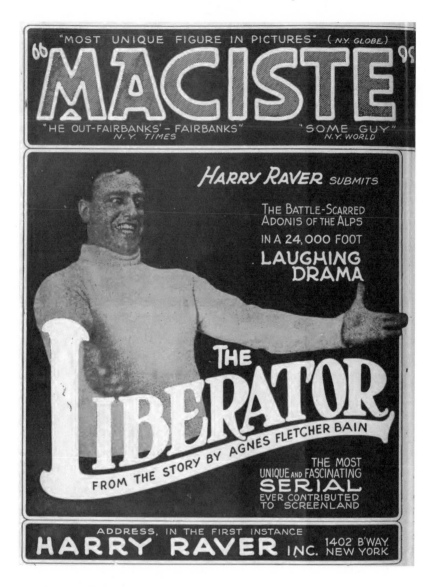

4.5. Advertisement for *The Liberator* in
Motion Picture World, 7 December 1918, 1014.

From the author's personal collection.

battle-scarred adonis of the alps in a 24,000 foot Laughing Drama," and "The Soldier-Hero, D'Annunzio's discovery whose Herculanean exploits in 'Cabiria' and 'The Warrior' amazed the world. Maciste, once believed dead comes back in 'The Liberator' to gladden and thrill the millions who worship at his shrine" (fig. 4.5).[104] Comparisons to Fairbanks continued, with references to earlier *New York World* exclamations, such as "He Out-Fairbanks' Douglas Fairbanks, and the *New York Times'* proclamation of Maciste as "The Douglas Fairbanks of Italy."[105] Yet Maciste's uniqueness as product and star transferred to the marketing of *The Liberator* as well. In a direct appeal to exhibitors titled "The 'Selling Value' of 'Maciste'" in *Moving Picture World,* Raver wrote: "As a distinctive personality, there is not a man, woman or child who has forgotten 'Maciste.' He stands today as the most unique figure in pictures, a sure-fire star of the first water, backed by a 'whale' of a production in 'THE LIBERATOR.'"[106] Even Maciste himself got into the act with his own "direct appeal" to distributors in the same publication: "I am Maciste. Millions know me as the Giant Slave in 'Cabiria' and as The Warrior in 'The Warrior.' Now I am 'The Liberator' and have come back to America for a stay of twelve weeks in your theatre – to amuse and thrill your patrons. Signed, Earnest Pagani."[107] Allowing Maciste to "speak" for himself was a technique that Raver would also use to attract another audience demographic: those of Pagano's compatriots living in the United States.

MACISTE AND ITALIANS IN AMERICA

Raver astutely carried over Maciste's wide appeal by marketing the films to Italian immigrants living in Manhattan, their geographic center as well as his base of operations. This effort was not unique to the United States during the war; other Allied countries followed the same strategy. In Great Britain and France, for instance, distribution and exhibition of the Maciste films was indicative of a patriotic-oriented programming trend aimed at Italian communities living abroad. On Flag Day, celebrated on 7 October 1915, the West End Cinema chose to exhibit the long-delayed *Cabiria,* accompanied by a fervently patriotic speech by Tullio Sambucetti, the secretary of the Italian Chamber of Congress in London.[108] And, as in the United Kingdom, the film had a particular resonance for Italians living in France. A contemporary notice in *La Cinematografia Italiana ed Estera* also reported on the premiere on 14 March 1917 at a fund-raiser for an Italian orphanage in France, confirming that the Italian immigrant population most likely participated in the benefit.[109]

Giorgio Bertellini has argued that for Italian spectators in the United States watching imported Italian films, there was a close correlation between patriotism and moviegoing. According to Aldo Bernardini, almost sixteen hundred Italian films made their way to American shores by 1915.[110] Nonfiction and fiction films alike that referenced, directly or indirectly, Italian colonial enterprises and participation in both the Italo-Turkish War and World War I became sources of Italian American pride and patriotism, ways in which "cinema could compensate for racial prejudice."[111] Italian Americans, particularly in the film industry's initial capital of New York, flocked to theaters to see the historical epics, many imported by George Kleine, like *Quo Vadis?* and *The Last Days of Pompeii*, that populated American screens, preceding *Cabiria*. As one review of *Cabiria* in the Italian periodical *La Follia di New York* stated: "No Italian should miss going to the Knickerbocker to touch, or better, to witness the 'new miracle' of [Italian] national art and industry."[112] Before Italy's entrance into the war, Italian dramas such as *Il tesoro dei Louzats* (*The Treasure of the Louzats*, Itala Film, 1914, released in the United States in December 1914) and *L'onore di morire* (*The Masque of Life*, Edoardo Bencivenga, Ambrosio, 1915, released in the United States in November 1916), continued their success in the United States. During the war, imports of feature films from Italy slowed to a trickle, although some films did make it over, including the animated children's fantasy *La guerra e il sogno di Momi* (Segundo de Chomón, 1917), which was exhibited in New York at the Strand Theatre under the title *The Hand of the Hun*.[113] Documentaries about the Italian front appeared in cinemas as early as 1916, and this trend continued upon the American entrance into the conflict with films such as the official Italian government's *The Italian Battlefront* (*Giornale della guerra d'Italia*, Regio Esercito-Sezione Cinema, 1917), which played to packed houses in New York, Chicago, Pittsburgh, and Buffalo; *Italy's Flaming Front* (Italian Official War Pictures, 1918), and *Behind the Lines in Italy*.[114] America's largest circulating Italian daily based in New York,

Il Progresso Italo-Americano, featured an advertisement (in Italian) for *Sul Fronte d'Italia* (*On the Italian Battlefront*), announcing a forty-piece orchestra accompaniment and admission prices from twenty-five cents to the luxury two-dollar seats. The ad concludes with a direct exhortation to Italians to come see the film: "ITALIANS! Do not miss the chance to flock en masse to applaud the achievements of our brothers – bring Americans with you – and help spread the word about and popularize the heroism and Glory of our Italy in America."[115]

Advertisements for *Maciste* (billed with its original Italian title) appeared in August 1917 in *Il Progresso Italo-Americano* only after the successful release of *The Warrior.* It was exhibited, "fresh from its Broadway run," in two New York City cinemas aimed at the local Italian population – Acierno's Gotham Theatre on 125th Street and 3rd Avenue, and the People's Theatre in the Bowery. This delay suggests that Raver's decision to market *The Warrior* to Italians in the United States stemmed from the wartime alliance between the two countries as a potential box-office draw to that demographic group. Once that strategy proved prosperous, the subsequent exhibition of *Maciste* was a profitable afterthought.[116]

As in the case of *Cabiria,* Italian-language newspapers advertised the English-language premiere of *The Warrior* at the Criterion in July 1917. Similar to the promotional strategy with *The Liberator,* Raver employed direct address to Italian spectators in the advertising campaign that sold *The Warrior* in Italian-language newspapers in New York. One advertisement, accompanied by an image of Maciste in his *Cabiria* toga, read: "I am Maciste, who played the Giant in D'Annunzio's *Cabiria.* I'm fighting for your cause and for mine on the Italian battlefield, but you can see me in action at the Criterion Theatre where they are playing my most recent film, *The Warrior.* Greetings from the frigid Alps, Ernesto Paganini (Maciste)" (fig. 4.6). What is noteworthy is how this ad and subsequent articles in the Italian American press framed Raver's overall promotional strategy – the connection to D'Annunzio (who did not work on *Maciste alpino*) and the myth of Pagano in combat at the Italian front – within decidedly Italian and American nationalistic terms: Maciste and "Paganini [*sic*]" are fighting for both the American and the Italian American cause: the ambiguity of the possessive "your cause" (*la causa vostra*) in an Italian-language newspaper potentially addresses American citizens

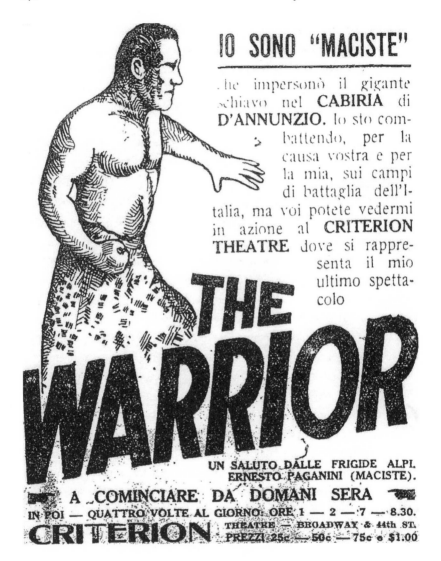

4.6. Advertisement for *The Warrior* in *Il Progresso Italo-Americano*, 15 July 1917, 5.
From the author's personal collection.

and Italian American readers. Thus Maciste functioned as a unifying symbol in the Italian American newspapers for the shared war experience between the two countries as well as American citizens and Italian immigrants.

At the same time, the film's promotional strategies had a much more nationalist bent aimed at praising the film as a decidedly Italian triumph. A description of *Maciste* encouraged the spectator to see the film for patriotic reasons: "No one fails to admire this splendid masterpiece of Italian film art."[117] "We have already referred to the great, Italian war cinema," read a short piece in *Il Telegrafo*, a daily Italian-language paper, about *The Warrior*, "a new masterpiece by Gabriele D'Annunzio – which stars Maciste, the giant of 'Cabiria' in the role of the wild, modern Italian warrior, and whose real name is Ernesto Pagani and is right now fighting on the Italian-Austrian front."[118] Another praised *The Warrior* as a film "in which the achievements of Italy at war are described as only they can be in a film made with the cooperation of the great poet of Italy and the Italian government."[119] Despite his nonparticipation in the film's making, D'Annunzio's increasingly public presence in the war effort further emphasized the product's Italianness for a sympathetic audience.

With *The Liberator* the importation cycle of Maciste films into the United States ended for almost a decade, when in 1928 several of the last films Pagano made in character – the 1926 films *Maciste nella gabbia dei leoni* (released in 1929 as *The Hero of the Circus*), and *Maciste in Hell* (with American distribution in 1931) – came to various venues.[120] For the most part, however, Maciste disappeared from American screens, displaced by Tarzan and other male serial stars, and suffering the fate of other Italian films as the industry began to further decline. But Maciste's successful yet brief sojourn on American soil is an example of how an Italian star and character experienced and interacted with other national systems of production, distribution, and exhibition at a crucial time in the industry's development. The fact that Maciste's films came to the United States in the first place had to do with the entrepreneurial vision of Harry Raver, who, like Giovanni Pastrone, recognized in Maciste an additional exploitable commodity from his highly profitable distribution of *Cabiria* for American markets. The circumstances of the war, and the United States' eventual intervention on Italy's side, provided another, more timely occasion for economic gain. Films are popular at specific times and places for even more specific reasons, and Maciste's heyday ultimately coincided with the war years and their immediate aftermath. As a character, Maciste, like Douglas Fairbanks both on and off screen, addressed a need for a combination of virile strength and moral goodness and certitude at a time of turmoil and uncertainty on national and international levels. Maciste's wartime exploits, while visually coded in realist filmmaking, nevertheless supplanted the visible violence and casualties of war with a sensational yet harmlessly comedic interpretation of that very real threat. While the triumph of the serial form in the 1910s and early 1920s is certainly one avenue of explanation for the transatlantic success of the Maciste series, the character's popularity spoke to a wider constituency: male and female, young and old, middle and lower class, rural and urban, and, lastly, Italian and American. Maciste became a motivational symbol, like other stars, of the wartime alliance between Italy and the United States and of national pride, especially for Italians living in New York. That goodwill would not last long, despite the two nations' mutual victory against the Germans and Austrians, as Italy suffered what it came to call a "mutilated victory," not gaining its promised land and, perhaps more importantly, the international respect it felt it deserved for having sacrificed so greatly during the war years. In the crucial years after the war, Maciste's continued presence on Italian screens would provide the metaphoric salve on wounded national pride as it passed through one of the most tumultuous and politically unstable periods of the twentieth century.

FIVE

Love, Labor, and Leadership

THE MACISTE SERIES AND MODERNITY, 1919–1922

ON 24 OCTOBER 1918, ON THE EVE OF OFFICIAL CESSATION OF combat in World War I, Gabriele D'Annunzio published a poem in the newspaper *Corriere della Sera* titled "La preghiera di Sernaglia" (The Prayer at Sernaglia, referring to the town in the Veneto region where he delivered the address). Phrased as a series of numbered questions and statements, the exhortation spelled out D'Annunzio's utopian vision of Italy's just rights to obtain its deserved fruits after a hard-fought war. He concluded the poem with his prediction of Italy's triumphant future:

> Our victory will not be mutilated.
> No one can break our knees or clip your wings
> Where are you running? Where are you climbing?
> Your race is beyond the night. Your flight is beyond the wind. What was said about God can be summarized: "The Heavens are less wide than your wings."[1]

For the Italian nation it was in fact a mutilated victory, resulting in the loss of territories promised to Italy when it had joined the Allies in the 1915 secret Treaty of London. After the 1919 Paris Peace Conference, the incredibly turbulent period that followed in Italy between 1919 and 1920 known as the *biennio rosso* (Red Biennium) produced resentment against the Americans, the British, the French, and Italy's own government. It prompted D'Annunzio's ultimately unsuccessful takeover of the Adriatic city of Fiume, a fifteen-month military and political standoff with large popular support.[2] It also resulted in deep and dire economic problems and labor strife, particularly in the north and in cities like Turin, home to Maciste and Itala Film.[3] During the Red Biennium there were thousands of strikes and work stoppages. Union participation exploded – membership in the CGL (the General Confederation of Labor, founded in 1906) increased from 250,000 in 1918 to two million by 1920; the CIL (Italian Confederation of Labor) was established in 1919 with more than one million members; and violence flared as the emergent Fascist Party and *fasci di combattimento* (the Fascist fighting leagues) took their vehement anticommunism to the streets.[4] Turin became a hotbed of labor unrest, witnessing the emergence of Antonio Gramsci as one of its leaders. It was the geographical starting point of the ultimately unsuccessful September 1920 factory occupation that spread to the rest of northern Italy, during which Prime Minister Giolitti took the workers' side and resisted intervention, further incurring the growing Fascist movement's wrath.[5] Thus, rather than united by victory, the populace grew even more fragmented regionally, economically, and politically, buoyed by select economic gains during the war. The rich became richer while the middle and working class suffered the most with the rampant inflation that followed the war's conclusion.[6]

Yet not only was the country itself "mutilated," but so was the male body. World War I was the first major conflict in which the presence of the war wounded, ubiquitous on the streets of Europe, was palpably and visibly experienced, revealing that the body was no match for the bellicose machines of modernity and its modern weaponry.[7] As Maurizia Boscagli has argued, the "hyper-masculine corporeality of the athlete-soldier-strongman" simultaneously disavowed and bore "traces of abjection," in this case connected to the bloodied, disfigured, and maimed male bodies that returned from the war.[8] In Italy it would have been difficult not to notice the mutilated bodies, because they populated both the urban streets and the countryside, as well as the many newly formed organizations, governmental and private, that emerged to aid those returning from the fronts, such as the apolitical but vocal Associazione Nazionale fra Mutilati e Invalidi di Guerra (ANMIG, National Association of War Invalids, established in 1917); Associazione Nazionale Combattenti (ANC), a more politically oriented group emerging out of the *combattentismo* movement; and the highly bureaucratized and ineffectual Opera Nazionale Combattenti (National Institute for War Veterans, established in late 1918).[9]

On the big screen, however, the damaged and disfigured male body had an important foil, whose physicality, goodness, and increasingly reactionary and right-wing politics began to reconstruct the national body politic and right the injustices of the mutilated victory: that foil was Maciste. The muscled male body in action and motion, this time not against the backdrop of the war but rather its aftermath, became the antidote to the mutilated victory and mutilated soldiers. In a period of flux and upheaval, on screens Maciste provided a strong, solid figure of continuity, at once modern and antimodern, who consistently engaged and conquered the destructive forces he encountered with humor, strength, and, increasingly, leadership.[10]

In this chapter I trace the trajectory of the restored, integral male body first from biennio rosso up through the March on Rome in October 1922 that cemented Fascism's early rise to power. In the extant films that the Itala Film Company made starring Maciste during the turbulent period between the end of World War I in November 1919 and 1922, his last with the studio that launched him, Maciste engaged with the ongoing social and political unrest and an uncertain political future as issues of class, labor, and ideology superseded race in relation to his character. In Romano Luigi Borgnetto's *Maciste innamorato* (Maciste in Love, 1919), Maciste, in addition to falling in love, sides with the ruling class, who favors the workers while the managerial class is ripe with graft and corruption. The muscled male body becomes a way of managing the masses, a topos that develops further in the films made during the Fascist period. Directed by Carlo Campogalliani, *La trilogia di Maciste* (The Maciste Trilogy, 1920) was an American-style serial of three films – *Maciste contro la morte* (Maciste Conquers Death), *Il viaggio di Maciste* (Maciste's Voyage), and *Il testamento di Maciste* (Maciste's Last Will and Testament) – with a unified narrative arch. Here questions of leadership and governance come to the fore as the issues of rightful government and political corruption merge with the modern serial form. In Borgnetto's *Maciste in vacanza* (Maciste on Vacation, 1921), Maciste engages with the most increasingly ubiquitous of modern machines – the automobile – as he attempts to escape the drudgeries of fame and fortune as well as, ironically, the trappings of modernity. Its northern Italian setting, specifically Turin, entitles a convergence of the fledgling Italian automobile industry, the avant-garde's preoccupation and quasi-obsession with speed and mechanization, and the film industry as the most modern of contemporary representational forms.

What emerges in these films is a problematic relationship among Italian cinema, the Maciste series, and modernity, as the films progressively engaged with industrialization, politics, and the mechanical world.[11] Just as American cinema adapted the comic film to cater to the changing tastes and experiences of popular audiences, so did the Maciste series. In these popular forms, Rob King argues, "The operational aesthetic formed an inevitable part of the self-expression of a society both committed to technological progress and disturbed by its consequences."[12] Each of the films under examination here engages with issues of modernity from divergent perspectives. Mechanized industrialization, effective sovereign rule, and active engagement in foreign affairs were all ideals to which Italian modernity aspired, yet all of these posed serious challenges in their implementation in a country already arriving relatively late to the modern age.

MACISTE INNAMORATO: LOVE IN THE AGE OF INDUSTRIALIZATION

Maciste innamorato recounts the series' primary love story against the backdrop of Turin's labor unrest during the Red Biennium.[13] It is also one of the first Itala films made under the auspices of the UCI, Unione Cinematografica Italiana. Constituted on 30 January 1919 and funded by the Banca Commerciale d'Italia (BCI) and the Banca Italiana di Sconto (BIS), the UCI was one of several unsuccessful attempts to create a trust of production, distribution, and exhibition in the form of various government-sponsored and private initiatives. The organization brought together many different production houses, including Itala Film. The idea was to bring money, regulation, and consolidation to the film business as a whole, producing a series of titles that could then be distributed to domestic and foreign markets.[14] In terms of distribution, the ENAC (Ente Nazionale per la Cinematografia) was created to facilitate agreements with other European national cinemas (those of Germany in particular).

C.I.T.O.-Cinema, a film distribution spinoff of the Compagnia Italiana Traffici con l'Oriente, was aimed toward opening the markets to the east of the Italian peninsula. But as these institutions began to fail during the economic crises of the 1920s, so did many of these initiatives. The 1921 collapse of the Banca Italiana di Sconto was one indicator of the beginning of the UCI's ultimate demise, as was its films' failure to attract a wide audience, since its predominant emphasis was on the waning popularity of the extremely costly historical epics.[15]

This downhill trajectory is part and parcel of the history of the Italian film industry in the 1920s; production fell precipitously from a high of 371 films in 1920, to 66 in 1924, to a mere 8 in 1930.[16] Scholars generally agree on the factors that contributed to the industry's downfall, the first of which, as mentioned above, was the failure of the UCI. Other factors were as follows: (1) industry disorganization and lack of centralization, despite the efforts of the UCI and other organizations and institutions; (2) the precipitous rise in production costs; (3) loss of foreign distribution markets, which had reached an apex during 1914–1915 and in the 1920s virtually disappeared; (5) the greater presence of American and German films that flooded the marketplace; (6) an utter deficiency of, and resistance to, technical and artistic advancements, particularly in narrative complexity and montage; (7) a lack of a national source for raw film stock; (8) a dearth of national financial support; (8) overtaxation on the part of the Italian government and lack of laws stimulating production; and (9) mass emigration, particularly in the second half of the decade, of talent (directors, actors, technicians) to other, more profitable European film industries. As the director Augusto Genina told experimental and early film theorist Anton Giulio Bragaglia, "The re-birth of Italian cinema is happening in Berlin."[17] The Maciste series, however, was an economic anomaly in Italian silent cinema of the 1920s: a continued commercial success among an industry in disarray.[18]

As per custom, *Maciste innamorato* opens with Maciste filming a scene of his subsequent Itala Film production, directed by none other than the film's director, Romano Luigi Borgnetto, in a cameo appearance. *Maciste innamorato* was the first film in the series with Borgnetto, a frequent Pagano collaborator and confidant, receiving sole top billing as director. Born in Turin and originally a painter by profession, Borgnetto had been involved with the film industry and Itala Film from its inception, working with Giovanni Pastrone behind the scenes. He was responsible in part for the success of *Cabiria* (he designed many of the sets and the costumes) as well as the nurturing of such stars as Pina Menichelli and Italia Almirante Manzini.[19]

The characteristic film within the film that opens *Maciste innamorato* features Maciste saving a damsel in distress and capturing her pursuers with his usual brute strength. The locus is the picturesque villa of the wealthy industrialist Thompson (Orlando Ricci). As Maciste lifts one of the perpetrators high in the air, he spies Thompson's daughter Ada (Linda Moglia) "off-camera" and is immediately thunderstruck, allowing his film enemy to fall violently (and comically) to the ground. It was the first time in the series that spectators had seen Maciste so visibly attracted to the opposite sex; in *Maciste* (1915) he and the unnamed heroine exit arm-in-arm at the film's end, but throughout the narrative they function more as collaborators than as star-struck lovebirds.

The love story in *Maciste innamorato* intertwines with a tale of labor sabotage. Three of Thompson's trusted managers – Sbrendoli, Stringhini, and Ercole, humorously and corruptly inept villains who secretly collaborate with Thompson's business rival Bethel – immediately appear as exaggerated types (their names onomatopoetically sound playfully silly in Italian with a connotation of "messy" as well). Bethel's "war" against Thompson's company begins with the managers' attempt to incite a worker's strike (and receive 3,000 lire from Bethel). Maciste and Thompson calm the worker uprising through brute strength (Maciste) and economic incentive (Thompson); the workers will get a bonus if they finish the government contract before the fifteenth of the month. In the meantime Ada is kidnapped, held by the purely villainous Guercio and his wife, Benzina, at the behest of the three conspirators, whom Maciste immediately suspects. After he asks Thompson for permission to rescue Ada, Maciste is captured, breaks free, is captured again, and escapes as he is about to be thrown down a well. He ultimately ensnares Sbrendoli, Stringhini, and Ercole as well as Bethel after he convinces Thompson of their guilt. In the film's climatic sequence, Bethel is ridiculed in front of his wealthy compatriots, and Ada is liberated only to return to her secret lover. Maciste, rejected and scorned, hastily leaves the villa in secret.

The film situates the narrative within the context of northern Italian industrialization and the labor strife that followed World War I. Although the film takes pains to set up the workers as pawns in Bethel's greater exploitative plan to make the insurrection appear spontaneous, the representation of the mob clearly presents them as a menacing force. When the workers are shut out of the factory, a panoramic long shot reinforces their sheer numbers as well as their restlessness once they gather outside the factory gates.[20] As they march on Thompson's villa, the camera stays fixed on the seemingly endless parade of angry workers who shake their fists menacingly, also reinforced in the shot of Thompson at the window watching the crowd approach from below, a window later broken by the workers' ire. Thompson, however, maintains faith in the workers' goodness and their trust in him, saying he has always treated them as "comrades." He addresses the crowd that has gathered outside the villa gates, proclaiming he will work with them toward a solution if they return to the factory. Already beyond control (and further incited by Bethel's men), they attack him anyway with stones, requiring Maciste to save the day. Even after seeing the damage the strike has caused, Thompson remains the workers' ally, proclaiming that "the majority [of workers] are good" and that these uprisings are the work of "a few self-interested scoundrels." Maciste's muscles and Thompsons's good faith restore the proper hierarchical order.

Yet all is not rosy between the workers and the ruling class, as personified in the figure of Ada, who is the mouthpiece of antilabor sentiment. It is she who voices the fear of the strike – "Lord no, a strike" – and who calls the workers "scoundrels" as they begin their attack on her father, employing the same word in a generalized fashion that her father subsequently uses to characterize only a few nefarious individuals. Through strategically edited reaction shots, she smiles and rejoices in Maciste's acts of violence against them. Clearly Ada's social status is at odds with the forced labor she must endure when held prisoner, but her antipathy and resistance to the working and service classes present her as an aloof reactionary. Although women were a growing presence in the public sphere after World War I, and increasingly within the labor movement, Ada constitutes an oppositional view to the socialist agendas of gender equality and emancipation.

Maciste's attitude toward the crowd has more in common with Ada than with Thompson, although it reflects the strong moral compass inherent in his character rather than antipathetic class privilege. He interprets the conflict as a chivalric battle between right and wrong rather than class antagonism. When Ada expresses her fear of the strike, his protective instinct comes into play. His ironic chastising of the crowd for their behavior – "I see that you don't lack courage! Everyone against two! Shame on you!" – speaks to his characteristic principled integrity. At the same time, however, it evokes a desire, increasingly present in the series, to protect or restore the status quo, particularly when it comes to questions of governance and leadership.

It is not, however, Maciste's ability to conquer the mob with his strength, literally tossing and flinging the striking workers left and right, that ultimately wins them over; it is his fame as film star (fig. 5.1). One of the workers recognizes him as the popular actor, and word quickly spreads throughout the crowd, resulting in their proclamation of "*Viva Maciste!*" Thus Maciste's celebratory fame ultimately convinces the workers to do the right thing and calmly return to their work in the factory.[21] With Maciste as star and the workers as his adoring fans, the film continues the series' self-conscious play with character and actor, icon and audience, putting his star persona, as well as his dominating physical presence, to use as a means of pacifying the crowd and subduing the rebellion. It also prefigures the protagonist's central relationship with the crowd in the films made during the first years of the Fascist government.

The fact that Maciste's heroic ideal and star persona are integrated with images of modernization potentially sets up the binary opposition of man versus machine, privileging brute individual strength over industrial might. Maciste's power, however, is clearly in service to the industrialist class and aligns him with its imperatives. Moreover, Maciste's rule and law supersedes the police. When he finally has the proof to convince Thompson of the managers' true nature, Thompson wants to go to the authorities, but Maciste prefers his own revenge, which he promises will

5.1. Maciste and the crowd in *Maciste innamorato* (1919).

be "amusing" (*divertente*) as well as efficacious. He lets Sbrendoli, Stringhini, and Ercole continue about their business, knowing that despite his
threats they will betray Thompson again and lead them to Bethel, which
they do, in front of an elaborately staged gathering, where the police
await to arrest the culprits. The trap functions as an amusing spectacle
onto which Maciste projects his ultimate power just as he preserves the
economic and social status quo.

The two narratives – the love story and the tale of industrial sabotage – have their locus in the same physical site: the Thompson villa,

which is situated on the same property as the factory, geographically anchoring and binding domesticity and business, love and work, and the public and the private to the exact spatial orbit. Rather than virilize him, however, Maciste's infatuation with Ada emasculates him on both an emotional and a social level. Although he dresses the part with his characteristically fashionable suits (more on that below), he never quite integrates socially with Ada and her companions. He is unsure of himself at the lunch table, physically awkward in his manners and mannerisms as the other men in the scene ridicule his voracious appetite and thirst: "Let's hope he won't eat us!" read the intertitles mockingly. Maciste at one point is so taken with Ada that he uncharacteristically forgets to eat, preferring instead to stare longingly at her and failing to notice that the servant has cleared his uneaten food.

Yet while his behavior is not in synch with its environment, Maciste's body remains spectacularly present as the object of constant fascination and admiration. The film frames these scenes in long and medium long shot, featuring the muscular male body front and center, explored in its wholeness and integrity as opposed to the mutilated bodies of returning soldiers that populated both urban and rural Italy at the time. As the group goes off for lunch, Ada's male companions marvel at Maciste's bulging biceps and hold on to him as he carries them up the stairs, one on each arm. At the lunch, Ada's female friend remains in awe of the size of his hands and strokes them appreciatively. Maciste's body, like those of factory workers as theorized by Gramsci, is a desexualized, functional body in service to the labor machine.[22]

Maciste's feelings for Ada indicate a weakness, an Achilles heel that is new and unique to the series. Accordingly, the scenes in which he pines for Ada distract him from his heroic missions and usually result in setbacks rather than accomplishments. About to leave the villa after his initial visit, he gazes forlornly through its gates, clearly struck by love at first sight; when the strike breaks out, he is idly admiring Ada as they lounge in luxury after coffee, seemingly neglecting the ensuing uprising. The film strategically intercuts the mob scenes with these images of love and leisure. Later, in his first rescue attempt of Ada, he is so overcome with emotion that her captor easily knocks him unconscious, recaptures Ada, and liberates the other villains whom Maciste had bound and contained. His humiliation continues as the kidnappers and their collaborators taunt and tease Maciste with ironic toasts to his well-being. Subsequently, after freeing himself and finding Ada again, he is recaptured and thrown, fully bound, down a well deep in the isolated woods. Clearly these impediments create the suspense that is characteristic of the series and of the serial films upon which it was modeled, as intertitles such as this one reinforce: "Removed from the place where he was rushed unconscious, tied up like a salami, Maciste is condemned to a very unhappy end." Yet Maciste maintains his calm demeanor and sense of humor throughout his trials and tribulations.

Clothing continues to make the man, and Maciste remains a dapper figure in his fashionably cut suits that barely wrinkle despite his acts of physical prowess. At the same time, however, they also indicate his social estrangement and exile in this milieu, epitomized in the tails and gloves he must wear to his celebratory dinner at the film's conclusion and with which he struggles to adorn: the gloves are too tight and the collar constricting. His discomfort is exacerbated when Ada enters his dressing room and begins to laugh, although she subsequently reassures him that he cuts a handsome figure. Maciste reluctantly enters the party as the guest of honor, towering over all and moving stiffly among his admirers. His uneasiness is both physical and social; he escapes the party and exclaims, "God! What an effort!" as he collapses in a chair, removes his gloves, and loosens his collar. This physical distress turns emotional when Maciste resolves to confess his true feelings to Ada and, after a brief stop at the buffet to fortify himself, spies her as she reunites with her secret lover.[23] Maciste's pain causes a moment of grief and self-doubt as he looks in the mirror – "On the other hand, she is right. . . . Have you ever seen a gazelle arm in arm with a pachyderm?" – and ultimate disgust at his own behavior (plate 12).[24] The film concludes on an uncharacteristically melancholy note: in its last shot he crushes the now-dried flower Ada had given him as he stares forlornly out the window of the car that shuttles him away from the Thompson saga. Although he remains thoroughly masculine through his physical superiority, Maciste reveals, for the first and only time, an emotional vulnerability that, during a period of highly charged class strife in Italy, is linked to his social and economic position. Ada's rejection additionally reestablishes the social and political equilibrium, with the industrialists solidly in power.

Publicity for the film followed the pattern for previous entries in the series: advertisements began to appear in film periodicals in January 1919,[25] with the characteristic attempt to build word of mouth through an advertisement without the title but only the word "Maciste," several question marks, and the tagline: "A new story in four parts is ready, filled with thrilled adventures and pulsating appeal," as well as below the title a line billing Borgnetto as director.[26] More details appear in subsequent issues, first with the film's title, still surrounded by question marks as if to underscore disbelief in the subject matter, and then with a new tagline: "The peak of hilarity, the maximum of marvels."[27] Reviews were mixed at best; the periodical *Film* proclaimed it to be one of the better Maciste films but with a script that had "little value."[28] The film critic Bertoldo's review in *La Vita Cinematografica,* also citing a weakness in the plot, chastised the filmmakers for descending into farce and for "losing sense of any refinement and finesse, that truly principled, artistic range that he had in *Maciste Alpino*." He also found the love story secondary, not the "emotion that dominates the comedy," and one that is irrelevant to the film's main objective: to showcase Maciste and his exploits.[29] In fact, these exploits remain for the most part devoid of the irony that characterized previous films, a tendency that would evolve further in future films.

The intertwining of the two plots – labor strife and love sickness – occurs in such a way as to solidify the status quo at the expense of historical realism. While the representation of the strike required the suspension of disbelief with respect to its plausibility, given the various machinations needed to provoke it and the facility with which the villains achieved it, the fact that a strike would be set in Turin, the hotbed of socialist anarchism and activism, was at the time a perfectly mimetic narrative device. Bertoldo's criticism, however, reveals the left-leaning sympathy toward the workers that the film decidedly lacks – on screen they are fickle, easily manipulated, and easily provoked toward violence, attributes that those in Turin, at the center of the worker's movement, would unsurprisingly condemn.

Maciste redeems the workers in the eyes and guise of the narrative, presenting, as much of the series does, an ambivalent relationship toward modernity, engaging with the country's own experience of the changes brought about by industrialization and the end of World War I. As the first film in the series released after the war's end (and presumably shot during its final days), the main character's moral, ethical, and corporeal integrity functions, as in the previous Maciste films, as the unifying element around which the film rallies in its support of Italy's changing labor landscape and political instability. In the end the film preserves the economic and amorous status quo as it restores the power to the legitimate (and uncorrupt) ruling class, who form an alliance with the workers in order to quell the insurrection of the managerial/bourgeoisie. These ideological conflicts surface again under the question of leadership and sovereignty in the next series of films.

LA TRILOGIA DI MACISTE (1920): SERIALITY AND SOVEREIGNTY

The three films that make up what it is known *as La trilogia di Maciste* unfold against the backdrop of claims of political succession and the right to govern at a time of great social instability.[30] Involving issues of power, authority, and geographical boundaries, the notion of sovereignty arose during sixteenth- and seventeenth-century Europe as a reaction against papal authority and theocratic rule, eventually entailing various possibilities of state authority – monarchic, constitutional, and democratic – within the conscription of particular territorial boundaries. While sovereign authority depends on the claim to power, the state needs various apparatuses to enforce its laws both nationally and internationally: "Authority commands, power executes."[31] *La trilogia di Maciste* (henceforth, *La trilogia*) is about the abuse of power by those scheming to disturb monarchical sovereignty, followed by restoration of proper order and the status quo, with the rightful leader supported by the people. The films, however, were not an overt attempt to enter into a dialogue with the political turmoil of the Red Biennium. Rather, the questions of leadership within the context of good and bad government well suited the serial form's preoccupation with heroism and might, through Maciste's own muscling of political force to bring out the successful transition of power in a fictitious nation.

La trilogia was an experiment in American-style serialization, one that differed from the previously discussed, American-produced film *The Liberator* (see chapter 4). It was neither a rehashing nor a recycling of previously filmed materials adapted for American screens, but rather a series of three new feature-length films interconnected in setting, plot, and characters. They were released at a time when the highly profitable serial form in the United States was shifting away from the serial queens who dominated in the early to mid-1910s to the male protagonists in the 1920s. Characters such as Tarzan, played by Elmo Lincoln (the "Yankee Maciste," as he was billed); athletes like James J. Corbett (*The Midnight Man,* Universal, 1919) and Jack Dempsey (*Daredevil Jack,* Pathé, 1920); and serials starring the physical culturalists like Eddie Polo (*Lure of the Circus,* Universal, 1918, and *The King of the Circus,* Universal, 1920) began to populate both American and Italian screens. Actors such as Charles Hutchinson, star of the Pathé serials *Wolves of Kultur* (Western Photoplays/Pathé, 1918), *The Whirlwind* (Allgood Pictures, 1920), and *Hurricane Hutch* (Pathé, 1921), achieved fame with the serial form. Harry Houdini, in addition to acting in six feature films, made a fifteen-chapter serial in 1919 titled *The Master Mystery,* produced by Octagon Films and directed by Burton King and E. Douglas Bingham. Carlo Campogalliani, *La trilogia's* director, likely would have seen and been influenced by many of the American serials that were being exhibited around Italy at the time.

As a result of the gender shift in protagonist, there was also a swing in the serials' primary audience toward the male spectator and, as the decade progressed, an increasingly younger male audience. They were moved to second- rather than first-run theaters and shown on Saturday afternoons to better exploit the intended audience. Female characters became a subordinate presence yet still subject to the often sadistic violence that was characteristic of the early female-dominated serials.[32] Most of these later serials departed from the predominantly realistic locales of those of their female counterparts, setting the action in the world of fantasy, jungles, science fiction, and the American West. And as they drifted away from the melodramatic emphasis of the serial queens, despite their reliance on the continuity of the cliffhanger, they became progressively distant from and ambivalent toward modernity, partly a result of various individual state-sponsored censorship initiatives reacting against their representations of crime, violence, and torture.[33]

Yet serials remained one of the most modern forms of cinematic expression, on and off screen, through their intertextual linkages, cross-platform promotional strategies, and preoccupations with the new sensations and experiences of modern life. Their Italian counterparts, like Emilio Ghione's Za la Mort series (see chapter 1), followed a comparable industrial and artistic pattern. Itala Film and UCI intended the films within *La trilogia,* like their American counterparts, for a large, international audience. Internal communications between Itala and the UCI dated 31 October 1919, however, reveal a realization that the films were not of the same caliber. The UCI's initial action was to break down the second episode into two, thus resulting in a trilogy due to the original second film's excessive length. This change presented issues concerning distribution, for the film had already been sold to distributors, who had in turn began to publicize it with just two episodes. The correspondence pertaining to the shift reveals how delicate and intricately connected the postproduction process was to the era's distribution and exhibition practices and how the UCI had the last say in whether these changes could be made (plate 14).[34]

Critical and public reaction to *La trilogia* was mixed. *La Vita Cinematografica's* lengthy review did not mince words, citing its implausible plot, terrible script, and lack of cohesive narrative structure, although the reviewer did have kind words for the acting and cinematography: "The authors, as we can see, have created absurd, illogical, unsustainable, inconceivable situations, and the mise-en-scène has exacerbated and even discovered their absurdity, their lack of logic, their unsustainability, and their inconceivability."[35] A review in *La Rivista Cinematografica,* on the other hand, praised it for what it was: an entertaining series with a wide popular appeal: "We are not big fans of this type of film, but we must agree that we are dealing with popular films, made for a special, numerous audience and that have the quality of marketability. That being said, we must agree that the two authors [Campogalliani and Colloni] could

not have made a more organic, interesting, and we confess, more entertaining film for Maciste." The article also praised Campogalliani as an
up-and-coming *metteur en scène* with an excellent command of division
of scenes and the strategic use of close-ups.[36]

The series had a more positive reception in the United Kingdom,
where it appeared under the following titles: *Facing Death, A Perilous Voyage,* and *The Fatal Hour.*[37] A review in the British film publication *Bioscope*
exclaimed: "Even though one finds oneself confronted with an ingenu-
ous concept, this passionate serial is an excellent spectacle, sometimes
entertaining and sometimes thrilling. The action is fast, the episodes
varied and numerous and the scenic design always realistic and realized
with a cornucopia of tricks."[38] Publicity brochures with copy written simultaneously in three languages – Italian, French, and English – indicate
an intention to market it beyond Italy's borders. Documents pertaining
to its distribution also signal exhibition in Greece, Egypt, Spain, Portu-
gal, Cuba, Sweden, Norway, Denmark, and Switzerland.[39]

The three films that make up *La trilogia* followed the American-style
exhibition format, released in close chronological proximity to one another across the country (plate 13). One poster from Milan announces
their screening on consecutive nights between 13 and 17 February 1922.[40]
Each episode concluded with a visual and textual cliffhanger that would
leave the viewer in suspense, and then each new film began with a summary of the previous film accompanied by scenes illustrating the titles.
The most striking addition *La trilogia* brings to the series is the character
of Tito Fabrizi, played by Campogalliani, who shares the top billing
with Maciste in the film's narrative. In a future film, *Maciste imperatore*
(1924), Maciste would have a sidekick (Saetta), but rarely would he share
the spotlight. Tito provides the brains to Maciste's brawn as the more
intellectual hero; there are multiple shots of Tito reading or staring off
into space contemplating the events unfolding on screen. More than
just a sidekick, however, Tito both directs the action and participates
it. But in contrast to Maciste, whose exhibitions of might are filmed as
much in medium and medium long shot as they are from a distance,
Tito is consistently shot from extreme long shot in order to show that
Campogalliani was actually performing the stunts himself, a fact already

understood by the audience, who were well schooled in Pagano's athletic prowess and strength.

In addition, *La trilogia* departs from the previous Maciste films in that it does not begin with the pretext of Maciste shooting a film (that device would resume in the subsequent *Maciste in vacanza*), but rather with a framing device of a young girl reading a book titled *Maciste* in the opening shot of the first film, *Maciste contro la morte;* it is an image that returns as the last film's concluding shot. This scene follows a still shot of a bare-chested Maciste with his arms folded, reminiscent of his first moments on screen in *Cabiria.* The book as framing device was common in silent cinema, appearing in, among other films, *La guerra e il sogno di Momi* (1917, discussed in chapter 3). The fact that a young girl performs the initial act indicates that, like the American serials, the audience for this type of entertainment was shifting toward younger viewers.

This first film's primary plot centers on the machinations of the prime minister of the fictitious nation of Livonia (Emilio Vardannes) and his rogue (Felice Minotti) to marginalize its sovereign rulers: the king, who eventually dies, and his daughter Maria Laetitia (Letizia Quaranta), who in the first episode leaves college to travel around Italy accompanied by her friend Countess Henriette Litsoky (Ria Bruna) and a chaperone. In her travels she meets Tito, the editor of the newspaper *Corriere Italico* and his "'brother,' precious friend and factotum," Maciste. They save the women from the prime minister's henchmen, but her regal identity remains unknown to the two men. When Maria Laetitia is kidnapped, Tito and Maciste rescue her, but the gentle giant remains behind, is knocked unconscious, and, after being wrapped up and bound, is tossed off a cliff into perilous waters. He manages to escape and board the villain's train, and an American-style train battle ensues, much like the one in episode 13 of *The Hazards of Helen* (1915), that leaves Maciste wounded on the ground. But *Maciste contro la morte*'s final intertitle does not leave the audience in much suspense, reassuring filmgoers that Maciste is not dead and that they will see him again soon, stronger than ever.

The only thing mortally wounded at the opening of the second film of *La trilogia, Il viaggio di Maciste,* is the hero's beloved pipe. Throughout the three films the pipe is his most cherished object ("Maciste's joy") and quasi-fetish, another unifying and humorous element that links the films, similar to the character's familiar ravenous appetite and consistent preoccupation with food. It would become more and more characteristic for Maciste's traits to be altered from one film to another during the series, because Giovanni Pastrone was no longer its controlling artistic force. But the pipe never quite leaves, becoming a fixture in its own right, especially in *Maciste all'inferno* and *Maciste nella gabbia dei leoni,* a metonymic symbol of Maciste's avuncular propensity and heroic masculinity.

This film's second conflict centers on the overarching issue of sovereignty. Maria Laetitia's father, the king, is gravely ill; her cousin Luitpoldo (Vittorio Rossi Pianelli), also the minister of war, scolds the prime minister for disregarding his orders to avert Maria Laetitia and bring her home. At the port as she and Henriette are about to depart, much to the strongman's chagrin, Maciste spies her enemies boarding the same ship and stows away on board, eventually convincing the captain to allow him to work in the ship's engine room stoking the fires. Once the ship docks in Livonia, large, welcoming crowds greet Maria Laetitia as she rushes to the side of her ailing father. At the same time, Maciste informs Tito of his whereabouts and the situation on the ground. The king dies and the princess prepares for her coronation. The prime minister impedes Tito from seeing her and, convinced she is in danger, Tito and Maciste scheme to warn her. When they are captured, the prime minister gives Tito and Maciste twenty-four hours to leave Livonia. Simultaneously, he threatens Maria Laetitia to expose her to scandal for her "lascivious" behavior with Tito, which will compromise the nation's sovereignty if she does not sign the order of exile. Soldiers accompany and guard Maciste and Tito as they board the ship to take them away from Livonia, and Maria Laetitia spirits herself away in a solitary castle to escape the nefarious prime minister. This second film's last intertitle teases: "Evil seems to have the upper hand over good, but will it end like this? Maciste does not think so . . ." This lead-in assures viewers of a third episode, which will be "the richest in surprises and emotions."

On the ship Maciste meets a young black-skinned boy and "baptizes" him Cioccolatino – Little Chocolate. The boy becomes Maciste's adorable and dependable sidekick and reintroduces the issue of race into

5.2. Maciste and Cioccolatino in the engine room in *Il viaggio di Maciste* (1920).

the series. Cioccolatino is played by Pierre Lepetit, one of the many
child stars of Italian silent cinema and one of the many young characters
paired with Maciste, drawing on the original paternal pathos established
in *Cabiria*.[41] When Maciste encounters him for the first time, the boy is
being manhandled and abused by the other workers in the ship's engine
room. As defender of the innocent and weak, Maciste threatens anyone
who hurts him. What is particularly interesting about this scene, in addition to its tinted red hue saturating the flame-stoked room, is that
Maciste is bare-chested and almost blackened from the engine's soot,

recalling the bare-chested and blackened Maciste from *Cabiria,* a film that continued to circulate nationally and internationally in the 1920s (fig. 5.2). Cioccolatino is a projection of othered racial difference that this film then normalizes through behavior and costume. His manners pass from primitive child to more civilized accomplice (although he often eats at Maciste's feet as the latter pats him on the head), and his dress changes from colorful Oriental robes to Anglicized sailor-style whites.[42]

The last film in *La trilogia, Il testamento di Maciste,* features its most spectacular stunts and jam-packed action as the plot's conflicts – Will Maria Laetitia's honor be saved? Will the prime minister be prevented from destroying the kingdom of Livonia? Will Maciste survive his fate? – arrive at their final resolution. Maciste singlehandedly combats soldiers while Tito and Maria Laetitia escape on horseback. Ultimately, however, the Livonian army captures Maciste and condemns him to death by firing squad. Despite the gravity of the situation, irony and humor abound: Maciste is happily reunited with his pipe – "Thank God it's safe" – while awaiting his death (and even smokes as he is bound to a post in front of the firing squad). He consistently laughs and jokes during the moments before his intended execution, set for six in the morning. When the hour arrives and there appears no sign of Luitpoldo and Maria Laetitia, Tito takes it upon himself to stop time, literally, by physically impeding the clock from reaching the predestined hour – as long as the bell-tower clock does not strike six, Maciste cannot be executed. Eventually shot down from the tower by the executioners, Tito survives his breathtaking fall, the rescuers arrive in time to save Maciste, and the strongman captures and binds the prime minister and his henchman to the very pole that was intended for his execution. Ultimately, Maria Laetitia renounces the right of succession in favor of her cousin, and Henriette, Maciste, and Cioccolattino speed away from Livonia on a train, eating sweets to celebrate the restoration of order.

In *La trilogia* Maciste is all integral man, one not fractured or dismembered by recent historical events, ever ready to fight the battle for moral goodness and the just cause. Throughout the series the films normalize Maciste into the muscular, adventurous, bourgeois hero who is more typically seen on American screens. Maciste even has an Americanized profession: he is a professor of physical culture. A scene in Ma-

5.3. Maciste in his office in *Maciste contro la morte* (1920).

ciste's office in the first film, *Maciste contro la morte*, features a mise-en-scène complete with baseball bats, weights and pulleys, boxing gloves, and medicine balls. A framed photograph of a bare-chested Maciste as well as banners from Yale and Texas (and even one that reads "Genova") adorn the walls (fig. 5.3). Throughout the serial he appears as he always has – well dressed and coiffed, smoking his pipe. As the spectator soon learns, he is more of a flirt and openly attractive to the opposite sex, particularly Henriette, who pines for Maciste when he reciprocates her feelings in her presence. This Maciste, as opposed to his incarnation in *Maciste innamorato*, seamlessly floats between classes, adept and adaptable to any situation. More sexually confident, Maciste, unlike his previous incarnation in *Maciste innamorato,* is comfortable among the jet set and nobility, and he attends the carnival party dressed appropriately and willingly in white tie and tails. Not necessarily a tale of class mobility, this Maciste clearly distances himself from his (and Pagano's) humble origins: he is part of, rather than sole enabler of, the emerging upper-middle class.

The films have a much more sophisticated and complicated editing style than previous installments, featuring avid use of the crosscut for suspense and a triangular structure for narrative unity. In their attempt to rescue Maria Laetitia in the first film, Tito is tied to a wood mill, about to be sawed in half unless Maciste can impede the water wheel from functioning. Intercutting between shots heightens the episode's tension, with Maciste gradually destroying the wheel as the bound Tito's head, shot increasingly in perilous close-up, approaches the saw. In another instance, Maciste, perched above on an overpass, ensnares the car carrying the prime minister and his entourage in a large net, creating a pulley with his own strength and muscles and ultimately suspending it in midair. Crosscutting between shots of the car approaching and then being suspended in the net and Maciste heaving the rope enriches the suspense and the display of the strongman's strength.

Many action-packed sequences involve symbols of modernity, including several car chases and hand-to-hand combat atop a moving train. In the series' climactic sequence, the shots oscillate between Maciste in front of the firing squad, Luitpoldo and Maria Laetitia speeding in the car toward the castle, and Tito hanging from the clock to suspend time. Even Maria Laetitia is far from a helpless damsel in distress as she disguises herself and gallops on horseback to inform her cousin Luitpoldo about the evildoings at the castle and Maciste's impending death. Here she clearly channels her on-screen serial queen predecessors: the star Pearl White, for instance, was extremely popular in Italy at the time, with domestic distribution of her film series by the mogul Stefano Pittaluga, who later would go on to produce and distribute the last films in the Maciste series.

La trilogia's constant threat of peril through violence, imprisonment, or imminent death drew on the sensational bombardment typical of

American serial queens and kings. The violence tends more toward the American style, with many incidents involving firearms, which are usually absent from Maciste films. Bullets fly during Maria Laetitia's kidnapping, even piercing a newspaper read by her young companion. When Maciste and Tito are captives on the boat, Cioccolattino emerges from a suitcase, guns blazing, to save the day. There are nonetheless some spectacular scenes showcasing Maciste's brute strength, such as his single-handed takedown of the Livonian army in the second film, even carrying several men on a ladder and throwing them into a lake.

In *La trilogia*'s last installment, the aptly titled *Il testamento di Maciste*, Livonia is in chaos; the prime minister has usurped his authority, imprisoned the princess in order to impede the right of succession, and is determined to rule the country himself. When she escapes and engages her cousin Luitpoldo for help, he does not turn to violence or revolution but rather to the Livonian Consiglio dei Ministri (the Cabinet or Council of Ministers) for support to remove the prime minister from his post. During the rather long procedural scene, Luitpoldo explains: "That man is fatal to our country, and I invoke a measure from the high Council that frees us from the threat of his wild ambition." He gives an impassioned speech in front of the cabinet, seated at a table. The evocative image is one of solemnity and gravity, complete with Luitpoldo's emphatic but not exaggerated hand gestures and rigid body posture, emanating control, power, and determination. Reaction shots of the ministers around the table, also conveying the occasion's seriousness, confirm Luitpoldo's mandate to remove the prime minister. Although performed behind closed doors in a crowded room (and thus eliminating any popular involvement in the governing process), the scene reads as an allegory for good government and rightful leadership, which Maria Laetitia then confers upon him. Because of Luitpoldo's actions and demeanor, this transfer of power appears rightful and just, not nepotistically corrupt.

The question that begs examination at this point is why there existed such a preoccupation with leadership against the backdrop of a fictitious nation and within the context of the American serial form in Italy. American serial queens of the 1910s did engage with pressing historical events, particularly intervention and preparedness in World War I, although the serial kings of the postwar era departed for distant lands and

futuristic times, abandoning mimetic involvement with current historical, social, and political contexts. *La trilogia* draws more on those earlier
female models in its recourse to the sensational and the modern while
simultaneously focusing on questions of sovereignty at a time when Italy
was decidedly lacking in leadership. Maciste preserves the sanctity of
Livonia's autonomy through his muscular might and lighthearted humor
but without the irony that had been an essential part of the first Maciste
films. Yet Maciste as a leader is not the supreme authority, but rather in
service to it; with his muscles and might he enables the rightful leader to
govern through parliamentary authority. As the 1920s progressed, however, the issue of leadership would arise again in the series, when Maciste
would take a much firmer and more independent stance as popular leader
(*Maciste imperatore*) and colonizer (*Maciste nella gabbia dei leoni*) (see
chapter 6). Modern nations possess great leaders, and Maciste would fit
the bill. But for the time being, Maciste needed a vacation from labor
strife and political intrigue. *Maciste in vacanza* engages with many of
the same issues of Italy's experience with modernity, this time through
the personal rather the political – the automobile – and that machine's
relationship to both Italian industry and the modernist avant-garde.

MACISTE IN VACANZA: MACISTE AND
THE MECHANICAL AGE

In the 1909 preamble to his "Futurist Manifesto," published in *Le Fi-
garo* on 20 February, F. T. Marinetti evokes the vehicle as symbols of
the movement's embrace of speed, technology, and modernity in his
recounting of an evening with friends in Milan: "the terrifying clatter of
huge, double-decker trams jolting by, all ablaze with different-colored
lights, as if they were villages in festive celebration"; "the sudden roar of
ravening motorcars"; and "three panting beasts" with "burning breasts."
He exclaims, "I stretched myself out on my car like a corpse on its bier,
but immediately I was revived as the steering wheel, like a guillotine
blade, menaced my belly." Even when Marinetti swerves to avoid two
cyclists and winds up in a muddy ditch (based on an actual incident
that occurred on 15 October 1908), he revels in the car's power and glory:
"When I got myself up – soaked, filthy, foul-smelling rag that I was – from

beneath my overturned car, I had a wonderful sense of my heart being pierced by the red-hot sword of joy." This exaltation in the car, in "the beauty of speed," and the man at the helm of the machine spells itself out in points four and five of the manifesto: "A racing car, its bonnet decked out with exhaust pipes like serpents with galvanic breath . . . a roaring motorcar, which seems to race on like machine-gun fire, is more beautiful than the Winged Victory of Samothrace."[43] It would also play a fundamental role in futurist painting, particularly the works of Umberto Boccioni and Giacomo Balla.[44]

What the passages from the "Futurist Manifesto" make clear is that the car alone was not the focus of its discourse. Just as important was the driver, who dominates the feminized vehicle with, among other things, the virilizing power of the wheel's shaft: "We wish to sing the praises of the man behind the steering wheel, whose sleek shaft traverses the Earth, which itself is hurtling at breakneck speed along the racetrack of its orbit."[45] The car, however, is superior to flesh, more beautiful than the shapely, flowing Ancient Greek sculpture of the goddess Nike (*Winged Victory of Samothrace*). The futurists sought to abolish the Romantic fusion of "Woman and Beauty," advocating instead "the idea of mechanical beauty," in which the male would become one with his car: "We have therefore to prepare for the imminent, inevitable identification of man with his motorcar, so as to facilitate and perfect an unending exchange of intuitions, rhythms, instincts, and metallic discipline."[46] It is a fusion of both the modern and the primitive that, according to Christopher F. Forth, is at the heart of the twentieth-century ideal of Western masculinity: "the new man would be both organic and machine-like, a heady amalgam of flesh and metal in which the male regeneration incorporated both the distant past and the near future."[47]

The futurist avant-garde, the automotive industry, and cinema coincided in Italy at the dawn of the twentieth century. Geographically, this took place principally in northern Italy, not only in Marinetti's Milan but also in Maciste's Turin. Italy lagged behind in the development of the country's automobile industry in comparison with other European nations, despite various initiatives in the nineteenth century with engines and primitive vehicles. Between 1894 and 1918 there were thirty-nine active car manufacturers all over Italy, producing a total of 124,828 vehicles, about one-third of which were exports.[48] But Turin quickly became its center, with the birth of FIAT (Fabbrica Italiana Automobili Torino) in 1899, and several other companies quickly following suit. Turin's viability as an automotive center was obvious, with the Piedmont region's strong history in manufacturing, abundance of electricity, long tradition of vehicle production, proximity to France, and open environment for capital investments.[49] During World War I the government co-opted the automobile industry for defense contracting and arms manufacturing as national wartime needs predicted production output. After the war, cars became a necessity of work and not just a leisure pastime; production turned more functional and utilitarian, yet the Italian automobile industry, at least in the early 1920s, still lacked a mass-produced automobile for the masses akin to Henry Ford's Model T.[50]

The first Italian auto race was held in Turin, with an approximately 57 kilometer round trip to Asti, on 28 May 1895, the same year of the first public screening of the Lumière brothers' Cinématograph. From an international perspective, transportation and the invention of cinema converged in various forms, from the Lumières and their trains, travelogues of urban landscapes featuring the vehicular trappings of modernity (streetcars, trolleys, and trams), to the different perspectives that the moving camera offered as it captured the point of view of vehicles in motion. Films featuring various means of transportation were sources of wonder and amazement, harbingers of peril and danger, and means of creating narrative suspense through exciting chases and rescue scenes. They often simultaneously involved multiple means of traditional and new forms of transportation with efficiency and speed both celebrated and mocked.[51] Within the Italian context they were a staple of early Italian film comedies, which, for the most part, took place in urban environments and yet had, for Gian Piero Brunetta, a much less problematic relationship with vehicular modernity: early Italian comics on screens were less afraid, most likely because, as latecomers to the party, they were less exposed to automobiles.[52]

The Maciste who takes front and center stage in *Maciste in vacanza* epitomized the convergence of modernity and the mechanical as cars were becoming an increasingly popular commodity among everyday Italians (fig. 5.4). As modernity created new modes of behavior and "hab-

5.4. Maciste driving his car in *Maciste in vacanza* (1921).

its of urgency and speed," the role of machines represented the ideals of freedom and leisure.[53] As the early film theorist Ricciotto Canudo wrote in 1909, cinema as a plastic art in movement possessed two distinct aspects, one symbolic and one real. The symbolic, for Canudo, was speed: the movement of images and rapidity of representation, particularly the gestures and movements of the characters/people on screen, are at essence an expression of modernity: "Cinema satisfies even the most tenacious hater of slowness."[54]

This impossible velocity, which found expression in the mathematic precision of movements and their beautiful rapidity on screen, could easily describe Maciste's magnificent gestures as well as his muscularity. The new car culture required muscles rather than the decayed mechanized body associated with the industrial factory and urban life; just getting the car to run necessitated brawn and strength to crank the engine and replace flat tires. Driving as a sport or a means of physical exertion was thought to increase respiration and promote circulation.[55] Maciste incarnated the modern ethos of industriousness, speed, and strength that was emblematic of the shifting modern spirit. His movements on screen are quick, deliberate, and powerful. In addition, Canudo's comparison with car culture, and the driver in particular, is not gratuitous. Velocity is infectious and permeates the driver's physiology as he experiences the rapid sensations of film in the same way as the driver experiences movement and speed. The car becomes, in a sense, a "surrogate body," providing "a visceral sense of empowerment" as well as "the armor for the male while allowing him to revel in the powerful sensation of speed."[56]

Maciste in vacanza was one of three Maciste films released in 1921; the other two, *Maciste salvato dalle acque* (Maciste Saved from Drowning), and *La rivincita di Maciste* (Maciste's Revenge), comprising a two-part serial directed by Romano Luigi Borgnetto, have been lost, although documentation remains on the first film in the archives of the Museo Nazionale del Cinema in Turin.[57] That year also saw the rerelease of *Cabiria*, according to the trade journal *La Rivista Cinematografica*, which featured an article on *Cabiria* as well as a two-page advertising spread. It was, and would be, one of many times the film recirculated after its original 1914 debut.[58] *Maciste in vacanza* was made with a total cost of 192,600 lire, on the high side for the era's production, mostly due to the actors' salaries, which comprised 38 percent of the film's total budget. At this point Maciste was one of the highest-paid actors working in films in Italy; according to Itala Film's accounting books, he was making 16,666.66 lire per month, almost eight times more than anyone else in the company. One person involved in the film's creation, and not on Itala Film's usual payroll, was Alessandro De Stefani, the film's well-known screenwriter. De Stefani was the director of the film section of Turin's Studio Letterario Italiano, an agency dedicated to the promotion of screenwriters and their work as well as to connecting screenwriters to production companies to create new or adapt existing material for the screen.[59] A 1920 advertisement in *La Rivista Cinematografica* features a one-page advertisement by the studio with De Stefani's name at the top promoting a list of the twenty-one screenplays he had written up to that time.[60] At one point during *Maciste in vacanza*'s promotional campaign he became upset when an advertisement for the film mistakenly attributed the screenplay to Borgnetto.[61] The film does feature more intertitles than previous Maciste films in existence today, perhaps pointing to the fact that the screenplay was an important part of the film's production and marketing strategy. It is also one of the better-written films (and De Stefani's sole contribution to the series), harking back to the ironic style of *Maciste alpino*, with its contrast between word and image, and the addition of pithy repartee, especially between Maciste and his leading lady, Miss Edith, played by Henriette Bonard. This rapid-fire banter, along with the film's fast-paced editing à la American serials (as in *La trilogia*), translates the modern notion of speed into the form and language of cinematic expression.

Maciste in vacanza began development in the summer of 1920, with production in the fall under less than ideal weather conditions; many telegrams from the set to the main office elucidate the difficulties in shooting on the outskirts of Turin with intense fog and rain. One letter from the set dated 1 November 1920 recounts these difficulties:

> Shooting on "MACISTE IN VACANZA" is already at a good point. The interior scenes are almost complete: we are only missing two for which we need sun. Rain, which has abundantly plagued us during the entire month of October – and today even snow – has impeded us from proceeding.[62]

The correspondence between the UCI and Itala Film, and between both entities and the production crew, reveals the complicated relationship and the added layer of bureaucracy that was partly responsible for the UCI's eventual downfall. A strike disrupted the film's postproduction (mentioned in correspondence dated 8 January 1921), which did not produce the final negative until 24 March 1921. The UCI was not happy with the final product and asked for modifications, further delaying the film's release.

The filmmakers saw a potentially wide audience for this easily promotable film. An emphasis on internationalism infused *Maciste in vacanza*'s distribution in postproduction correspondence, most significantly beyond Europe's borders. Although there is no evidence of the film's distribution in American newspapers, a series of epistolary exchanges in June 1921 among Giuseppe Barrattolo (Itala's representative in the United States), Itala Film, and the UCI discuss the need for English titles for the film's New York exhibition. So as not to "offend" the Americans in the film's satire of American morals via the portrayal of Miss Edith, the title altered her domicile from Philadelphia to Liverpool and changed all other national references to her character from American to British.

Maciste in vacanza returns to the series' origins as it opens with the actor in character filming a scene from an upcoming movie at the Itala Film studio, like in the original *Maciste* (1915).[63] Itala had certainly grown in size since then, and the shots of the studio's interiors and exteriors reinforce its status as one of Turin's premiere film production centers. At this point, however, rather than the intervention of war or love, the inciting incident is the arrival of Maciste's latest purchase: a car, a Diattolina, referred to throughout the film and even billed in the film's titles as *la sposa* (the wife).[64] The play on words begins with the intertitles, which first refer to "Maciste's secret." After finishing up the shooting of his rescue sequence, he tells his female co-star, "I took a wife," one that "he had custom made"; the intertitle refers to the first "caress" upon the car's delivery. The tongue-in-cheek humor continues as one of his co-stars jumps behind the steering wheel before Maciste can try it out, and the strongman warns, "You already want to play the friendly neighbor but I'm keeping an eye on you!" The intertitles reveal the evident truth: that he had finally realized his dream of the ideal wife, and now it's time, as his co-star says, for the "honeymoon." He approaches the studio head, feigning weakness and exhaustion (despite breaking a table in the office in the process), and receives some vacation time.

The fact that the film's opening scene takes place at the Itala studio speaks to the role the automobile and cinema played in representations of Italian modernity. The featured car was a Diatto, introduced in the intertitles as "Mrs. Maciste," nay "*Diattolina*." The Italian diminutive attached to Diatto, "*ina*," intends both the fact that this was a lighter-model version of the car, which was specifically designed for this film, as well as a term of endearment. The Diatto company, in existence since 1835, was one of Italy's oldest transportation establishments, manufacturing carriage coaches, elegant railway cars, tramlines, and streetcar lines. The car company was founded in 1905 with investment from the French and had various incarnations and names up through 1919, when it became the

5.5. The Diattolina/Signora Maciste in *Maciste in vacanza* (1921).

Automobili Diatto S.A. in 1919. It participated actively in early racing-car circuits, manufacturing stealthily designed vehicles, and had success during the war making lighter-weight trucks. After the war, working with, among others, Ernesto Maserati, it designed both race cars and those intended for the general market.[65] Internal references promoting Diatto abound in the film; for example, when explaining to Borgnetto, who makes a cameo as the car salesman in the film, why he chose this car, the title reads, "Of all the cars he had seen at the factory he wanted the 'DIATTO' . . . with only one seat!" The Diatto insignia adorns the car's front grate as it did on actual models (fig. 5.5)

Even the correspondence exchanged between Diatto and Itala Film to secure the vehicle's placement in the film jokingly played on the car-as-wife paradigm.[66] The letters are in fact quite amusing and seem to revel in continuing the pun from screen to page, playing on both Maciste's strength and the "age difference" between "husband" and "wife." On 13 December 1920, Diatto wrote, presumably in a letter accompanying the car's delivery to the set:

> My chief tester Signor Almerigi has the honor to present you with my latest creation, the Signora Diattolina, all dressed-up and ready to wed your Signor Maciste.
>   Given the groom's Herculean strength, we suggest that he keep in mind not only his wife's delicateness (even though of healthy constitution) but also her small stature that will need to be treated with suitable care.
>   And we hope the union will take place and be happy even though we are dealing with a minor! But neither you nor I will denounce Signor Maciste to the appropriate authorities!
>   Once the nuptials are over I am certain that Diattolina will return proudly and without shame to her paternal home.[67]

The sexual innuendos rampant in the correspondence, while continuing the film's running gag, echo with the futurist fusion of man and machine and the mockery of the bourgeois institute of marriage, which Marinetti and the futurists abhorred.

The car that arrived on the set, however, had a few defects, and the jokes continued to fly back and forth. On the same day, Itala Film responded:

> My Dearest Friend,
>   The gracious DIATTOLINA has arrived happily at her future husband's house and she was received with all the honors worthy of her grace and beauty . . .
>   But the bride has – like all wives – some defects. And the Diattolina even has the advantage that her defects derive from her husband.[68]

The letter goes on to state that Borgnetto and Pagano, referred to once again as Maciste, will visit the Diatto factory to explain what kind of car they need, which turned out to be Model 10 HP, a modified, lightened version of the most popular Diatto being manufactured at that time. The good relations between Itala Film and Diatto did not last long, however. At the completion of production, a dispute ensued as to who actually owned the car, with Itala Film stating they believed the car to be theirs and Diatto in complete disagreement and furious about the condition of the car after production had ended. Eventually Turin's mayor had to be brought in to settle the dispute.

What the film and internal correspondence relating to it reveal, in addition to the fact that Borgnetto and Pagano were shooting several Maciste films at once, is Pagano's complete and utter erasure: he is never referred to by his own name in the exchanges between Itala Film and Borgnetto, only by Maciste, even when the correspondence deals with personal matters. One telegram, dated 16 March 1920, sent from Borgnetto to the Itala Film studios during the production of *Maciste salvato dalle acque,* states, "Today only Maciste leaves – he wants to stay in Genova for a few days." Another recounts that Borgnetto and "Maciste" are going to Sardegna, where *Maciste salvato dalle acque* was filming, and asks the studio for letters of presentation so that they can get preferential treatment. Borgnetto and Pagano did have a very close working relationship from their early days at Itala Film, so the use of the name Maciste could have been a term of endearment. On the other hand, advertising and promotional materials pertaining to the 1921 films, as well as all the correspondence between Itala Film and the Diatto car company, indicate the total merging of the person with the *personaggio* (character).

The showcasing of Maciste's sculpted physical form together with the Diattolina reinforces the connection between manliness and the machine as espoused by the futurists, among others. Maciste plays the entire opening sequence shirtless, his muscles and hairy chest on prominent display, and he literally becomes one with the car, because it has space for only a single occupant: the driver. While there is little talk of the parthenogenesis that Marinetti advocated in his 1910 novel, *Mafarka the Futurist,* the message is one that unites car leisure culture with sexual and social male autonomy.[69]

Maciste's "vacation" takes place in the countryside surrounding Turin, where the film highlights the picturesque landscapes through extreme long shots and panorama shots featuring the protagonist happily driving his car, adorned in his fashionable driving attire. This distinction between city and country would become a focus of cultural debates during the Fascist period, but here the point is that as Italy's most popular star, Maciste can never really get away from it all. His vacation itself is far from restful and relaxing, because he is bombarded wherever he goes by large crowds of adoring fans and those seeking or needing his kindness, goodness, and superhuman strength – from complaints about oxen who rebel and overbearing wives to a request to physically transplant a house from the country to the city. Of course being a star does have its perks, and Maciste receives preferential treatment at a busy restaurant, although he is unable to dine in peace when the crowd forms around him to regale in his voracious appetite, and is later serenaded awake outside the town's hotel by his adoring fans. What is clear is the character's immense popularity and fame even within the remotest of populations: "Wherever he went, the same inevitable fame awaited him," proclaims the intertitle. As he spies an isolated castle on a hill during his drive along the country roads, he comes across a young peasant girl with an ox and hopes she will be able to give him information without recognizing him, saying to himself, "Perhaps this one has never been to the movies before."[70] After she tells him that the castle is uninhabited, she screams, "Maciste!!!," his cover blown once again. This brief interlude self-reflexively and satirically exposes two phenomena: the ubiquitous and ever growing presence and influence of film on the everyday lives of Italians, and the role that stardom increasingly played in its popularity.

The film's second part disrupts Maciste's brief tranquility as the film introduces the damsel in distress: an American, Edith Moak, played by Henriette Bonard, who had been abducted by masked bandits à la Fantômas and Za la Mort. Bonard had an exclusive contract with Itala Film from February through July 1920, for which she received 3,500 lire per month and during which time she had also performed in *Maciste salvato dalle acque*. Itala Film then extended her contract through the end of the year at a salary of 4,500 lire per month for two more films, including *Maciste in vacanza*.[71] Bonard's persona, which seeps into her portrayal of Edith, is that of a modern woman with a blasé attitude, one in keeping with her stated purpose of acting in films purely for the money.[72] The main culprit in Miss Edith's kidnapping, it turns out, is one of her two suitors, Count Baiardi, who arranged the abduction in order to play the hero upon her rescue. The other suitor is the poet Dasti, a small, ridiculous man compared to our superhero. His vacation disrupted, Maciste now becomes embroiled in Miss Edith's affairs. The jokes about the car continue: Edith says she is compromised because they spent the night together under the same roof, which, according to American morals, means they must marry; Maciste replies that he already has a wife. Although Maciste bemoans his "matrimonial" infidelity as well as his loss of solitude and peace, he begins to waver as Edith presents him to her family as her betrothed: he appreciates her beauty, and although she is not "custom-made" like the Diattolina, she does smell better. What this inner and outer dialogue reveals, aside from its sexual innuendo, is the reinforcement of the vehicle's product placement; the intertitles mention the car's brand twice within the span of five minutes, and many more times throughout the film.

His beloved car stolen, Maciste subsequently finds himself trapped in a well with both of Miss Edith's suitors. With his strength he manages to enable the two suitors to climb out of the well, but they ultimately abandon their "rival" and run away to court Miss Edith. Eventually he is able to escape on his own, and after a shoot-out and a car chase, the film reveals the bandit to be a mysterious Spanish thief, one of the many men Miss Edith had met in her travels to sow her oats before settling down in matrimony. The thief had been following her around the world, murdering potential rivals for her hand. Maciste devises a plan to have Miss Edith and her Spanish suitor meet at the villa, where he tricks them into spending the night under the same roof, thus freeing him of his own obligation to marry her. The film concludes with Maciste thankfully reunited with his "wife," the Diattolina, pledging to renew their vows. Vacation over, man and machine drive off into the sunset with Maciste telling his wife, "Can you believe what kind of vacation this has been? Dear wife, let's get married again at home while we work." Happily ensconced in his car, Maciste's body is again at one with the machine, both integral elements in the reconstitution of the fragmented nation and the mutilated male body at the end of World War I.

* * *

Maciste in vacanza, as with *Maciste innamorato* and *La trilogia di Maciste,* had an ambivalent relationship with modernity. Modern forms of industrialization and labor organization, governance, and transportation met with ambiguous acceptance and complicated implementation in their cinematic representations. Modernity for Italy would have to wait, as Ruth Ben-Ghiat has argued, for the centralizing and reclamatory agenda of Fascism.[73] Many of the preconditions for modernity were not yet applicable to the Italian situation. For instance, while mass migration and immigration were extremely prevalent, urbanization was predominantly localized in the north. In addition, industrial production did rise during World War I, buoyed by the transportation industry with FIAT, for instance, becoming the leading producer of cars and trucks.[74] And while nationalism was on the march, the proliferation of new technologies and transportations was sporadic and also geographically skewed toward the north. Even as women entered the public sphere, the family unit still remained the dominant institution. And all of these developments were chronologically behind those of other European countries.

Despite the increasing self-reflexive presence and power of the male star and the Maciste series' reliance on the serial form, Italian cinema itself had yet to fully realize its technical and artistic potential. In August 1920 the magazine *Film* published a three-part series of articles titled "The Crisis of the Industry." Its conclusions at the beginning of the decade proved to be prescient for the next ten years: that the Italian film industry would collapse unless money was invested wisely in it and those investments were overseen properly, and that long-term as opposed to short-term profit should be the goal. In return, the artists involved in the film industry should make better films, looking to smaller studios and individual artists rather than large conglomerations, and not be so preoccupied with consolidation, monopolies, and trusts. The article railed against the UCI, saying that only by dissolving such organizations would there be hope that "a new period would begin that will be newly golden for Italian cinema."[75] Unfortunately, rather than changing the present, the article predicted the future: the more initiatives the industry created, the more it fell into a quagmire. The author was also correct about what would save the industry and, by extension, the country: individual initiative, as personified by Maciste and, subsequently under the auspices of Fascist state intervention in the 1930s, Benito Mussolini.

The Italian cinema's sorry state set the stage for Pagano's decision to move his career to Germany. Pagano signed a contract with Jacob

Karol in late 1921 to make four films with Borgnetto by his side; a notice first appears in the October issue of *La Vita Cinematografica* of that year announcing the deal.[76] Karol had strong ties with the Italian film industry. He was a distributor in Central Europe and the Balkans for the UCI before settling in Berlin to run various film studios.[77] The four films, in chronological order, were *Man soll es Nicht für Möglich Halten*. *Maciste und die Javanerin* (Karol Film Gmbh, 1922), released in 1922 in Italy as *Non si dovrebbe crederlo possibile ovvero Maciste e la giavanese/ Maciste umanitario* (Maciste the Humanitarian); *Maciste und die Tochter des Silberkönigs* (Karol Film Gmbh, 1922), released with such different titles as *Maciste e la figlia del re dell'argento* or *Maciste e la figlia del re della Plata* (Maciste and the Daughter of the Silver King); *Maciste und der Sträfling Nr. 51* (Karol Film Gmbh, 1922), or *Maciste giustiziere* (Maciste the Avenger); and *Maciste und die Chinesische Truhe* (Karol Film GmbH, 1923), known as *Maciste e il cofano cinese* (Maciste and the Chinese Trunk).[78] Maciste was by far not the only strongman to test the German waters: Luciano Albertini (Sansone) and Domenico Gambino (Saetta) came to reap the benefits of a profitable film industry there, as did many other stars, writers, and directors.[79] It was not uncommon at the time; Germany's film industry was thriving at the precise moment that Italy's was collapsing, with innovative film styles and genres like German Expressionism; more popular-oriented dramas such as the *Kammerspielfilm* (chamber play film) and *Strassenfilm* (street film); historical and period pieces; and the *Sensationfilm*, films that integrated high doses of spectacle and action. During the war, increased national production, both propagandistic and entertainment-focused, had witnessed in 1917 the foundation of the UFA (Universum Film–AG), the major postwar studio that through vertical integration became the dominant industrial presence in German cinema of the 1920s. Italian films had a widespread popularity and notoriety in Germany in the previous decade, due to the phenomenal success of *Cabiria*, and serials (*Serienfilm*) were also popular during and after the war. Unlike American films and more like their Italian counterparts, these films did not consist of two-reel serialized cliffhangers, but preferred the feature-length serial format, making the Maciste series, and other Italian strongmen films, the perfect product for the growing German market.[80]

Inadvertently, perhaps, *Maciste in vacanza* set the stage for the Maciste entries made after the 1922 March on Rome and the early years of the Fascist *ventennio* when Pagano returned to Italy to resume his career there. Il Duce himself was also a big car aficionado – he had a distinct penchant for Alfa Romeos, particularly after the attempt on his life on 11 September 1926 while driving a Fiat.[81] Moreover, the movie within a movie that Maciste is filming at the beginning of *Maciste in vacanza* appears to be some sort of historical drama, with Maciste rescuing a damsel in distress in historical costume and Maciste shirtless and in primitive pants. Perhaps a coincidence, but with Pagano's return to the Italian film industry after the rise of Fascism, Maciste's films would take a greater turn toward the historical and the fantastic. As the movement's anti-bourgeois orientation coalesced in the October 1922 March on Rome, it is not surprising that Maciste, as both political and national symbol, would shed his middle-class uniform in favor of even more symbolically oriented costume dramas. Although the sign of the muscled torso remained visible, the signified would shift, evoking instead a different, soon-to-be ubiquitous and much more serialized masculine presence – that of the Duce himself.

SIX

Muscling the Nation

BENITO MUSSOLINI AND THE
MACISTE FILMS OF THE 1920S

FOR THE RELEASE OF THE 1924 *MACISTE IMPERATORE* (MACISTE the Emperor, 1924), *Films Pittaluga,* the distribution arm of Turin's FERT studio, published a humorous cartoon to promote the film (plate 19). In it, a diminutive Mussolini threatens the military-clad, gigantesque Maciste: "You want to be Emperor? Watch out: I've got something for you, too!" With the threat written in both Italian and French (*Films Pittaluga* was a promotional publication directed toward an international audience), Mussolini indicates that Maciste will be on the receiving end of his violent ways, either with his *manganello* (club) or *olio di ricino* (castor oil), both of which were favored weapons of the violent Fascist squads that helped sweep the party into power in October 1922.[1] But Mussolini's pocket-size caricature mitigates the threat, one of many comic and mocking representations that circulated at the time. With his smiling sidekick Saetta at his side, Maciste reduces Mussolini to an embarrassing parody.

In an interview in the same periodical, Bartolomeo Pagano, on the other hand, had this to say about Mussolini: "In the near future I become an emperor. But only in Turin and only on the screen, you know, and Mussolini has nothing to fear from me!"[2] These contradictory statements constitute the only contemporary references I have found of a representational "exchange" between Maciste/Pagano and Benito Mussolini. Unfortunately, little or no definitive documentation exists of a relationship between the two, who became models of 1920s Italian masculinity. Mussolini never mentions Pagano, Maciste, or references any of his films in his published speeches and discourses, nor do the definitive biographies ever refer to either the character or the actor.[3] Since this cause-and-effect relationship is very difficult to establish without archival proof, the connection between the two might reside, as Marcia Landy astutely summarized, "in a fantasmatic cultural and political matrix that was congenial to the cinema of the silent years, with its emphasis on the body, and, beyond that, to the power of the media to materialize mythology."[4]

Landy's quote constitutes an excellent point of departure for unpacking the relationship between Maciste and Mussolini. Whether Maciste directly influenced Mussolini and the presentation of comprehensive proof of that relationship are beyond the scope of this project. What is clear is that their various on-screen representations drew on common discourses, images, and commodities that circulated in Italy in the 1920s: the resurgence of *romanità*, the cult of the muscled male body, nationalism, colonialism, stardom, and fashion. Maciste appears on screen as a likeable, popular, and charismatic representation of Italian masculinity in fiction, and Mussolini, in his early on-screen incarnations, appears as a likeable, popular, and charismatic representation of Italian Fascist masculinity. Moreover, Maciste's previously established muscularity took on additional ideological meaning with the Fascist appropriation and quasi-obsession with sports and the athletic body.

After his permanence in Germany, upon resuming his role as Maciste in Italian film productions with Turin's FERT film production house, within the span of three years Pagano made six extremely popular "superfilms" – expensive, elaborate, highly promoted tent-pole films – four in 1926 alone: *Maciste e il nipote d'America* (Maciste and His American Nephew, 1924), directed by Eleuterio Rodolfi; Guido Brignone's *Maciste imperatore; Maciste contro lo sceicco* (Maciste against the Sheik,1926), directed by Mario Camerini; and three films directed by Guido Brignone: *Maciste nella gabbia dei leoni* (The Hero of the Circus, 1926), *Maciste all'inferno* (Maciste in Hell, FERT-Pittaluga, 1926), and *Il gigante delle Dolomiti* (The Giant of the Dolomites, S.A. Stefano Pittaluga, 1926). In that same year (1926), documentaries and newsreels funded and produced by the Fascist government, under the auspices of the Istituto Luce

(L'Unione Cinematografica Educativa), became obligatory predecessors to the screenings of feature films in Italian theaters.

In these newsreels, another divo began to emerge on screen: Benito Mussolini. The figure of Mussolini as charismatic leader as well as political and cinematic star has received much scholarly attention, making parallels and immediate comparisons between Il Duce and popular film stars and characters of the era, including Maciste. Among the first Italian critics to engage in this discussion was Renzo Renzi. In his 1974 "letter" to Fellini, published as "Il fascismo involontario" (Involuntary Fascism) and written in response to the release of *Amarcord* (1974), the director's personal recollection of the Fascist period, Renzi observed:

> The comic element of Fascism, it is worth repeating, if considered today, certainly rests in the disproportion among imperial intention, the actual condition of the nation and the awareness of the final result: in short, in the unmasked lie of historical-political discourse. Such a disproportion is made particularly evident because it expressed itself theatrically in its leader, Mussolini, since his was, more often than not, an out-of-date style of acting, that needs to be connected to D'Annunzian theater and the cinema of the divas, and that found a contemporary, popular correspondent in Za la Mort.[5]

Renzi continues with comparisons between Mussolini and Emilio Ghione, the actor who played the previously discussed Za la Mort (see chapter 5); the ubiquitous Douglas Fairbanks, especially the later costume dramas such as *Robin Hood* (Allan Dwan, 1922), which appeared on Italian screens in 1924;[6] and Leopoldo Fregoli, the turn-of-the-century *transformiste* who was renowned for his lightning-quick costume changes (chapter 1).

Renzi wrote this essay at the beginning of what would be a time of wholesale critical and scholarly reassessment of both the Fascist period and its documentary and feature film productions, which in the immediate postwar period had been dismissed as mere propaganda, parenthetical political and cultural aberrations, and blips on the radar of the great Italian nation.[7] Although not specifically mentioned by Renzi, subsequent Italian and Anglo-American scholars have invoked Maciste's name as the supreme point of convergence between Italian feature film

production of the 1920s and Mussolini's political stardom.[8] The Duce
was a ubiquitous visual presence on screen and in photographs, and later,
with the advent of sound, an aural one as well, a product neatly packaged
for consumption by a (mostly) adoring public.

In this chapter I examine how stardom, both political and cinematic,
converged in these two figures in a dialogical process. My discussion
wanders back and forth between politics and cinema and between political and cinematic stardom as it seeks to explore both Mussolini's status
as divo on screen, as well as the textual shifts in the Maciste series in
light of changes in the political and cinematic climate of 1920s Italy. One
might argue that Mussolini is more a celebrity than a star if one adopts a
strict historical definition of "*divismo*" to apply only to the screen – that
is, Italian silent film stardom. In relation to power, celebrity and stardom
take on added signification. As P. David Marshall has argued, personalities in turn create public subjects, which is a term that designates "the
relationship of the celebrity to modern collective and social forms that
are expressed through particular individuals in the public sphere."[9] Since
so much of Mussolini as "public subject" was based on his visual representation, I argue that his stardom is more relevant than his celebrity
status.[10]

My focus here is on the films and the primary sources accompanying the Maciste films' release as I address what happened to them as
they passed from Itala Film to FERT between the years of 1924 and 1926,
the years of what Renzo De Felice has termed the "conquest of power"
(1921–1925) and "the organization of the Fascist state" (1926–1929).[11] I
also look at how they enter into a dialogue with developments in Italian
cinema, fiction and nonfiction, and Fascist ideology during that precise
time. While many scholars have made inferences about the Maciste/
Mussolini connection, few have examined the Maciste films themselves
due to their previous inaccessibility and the poor condition of the available prints. Recent restoration efforts by the Museo Nazionale del Cinema (Turin), the Cineteca di Bologna, and the Cineteca Italiana (Milan)
have now made this possibility a reality, allowing the scholar to closely
examine the texts for convergences between their star personae. I have
also chosen to look at select films from the Istituto Luce from 1922 to
1928 in a search for contemporary and simultaneous convergences and

continuities in the representation of Mussolini's and Maciste's masculinity on screens, rather than confirmation of a direct influence.

On the other hand, what is clear from the films, newspaper articles, promotional materials, and archival documents is that the Maciste series did not need Mussolini's support to maintain its popularity: Pagano was a recognizable, bankable star, whose films continued to be successful even as the fortunes of the Italian film industry declined. As one article promoting *Maciste all'inferno* stated, "Maciste is more than an actor: he is an institution," perhaps even exaggerating in saying that "no Italian is more well-known abroad than he is."[12] Nevertheless, I argue that there was a gradual "Mussolinification" of Maciste in the 1926 FERT films as they became increasingly more violent and disengaged from modernity and lost the irony and humor of the original character. The films of the immediate post–World War I period had revealed a growing conservative and reactionary turn as they attempted to restore the fragmented nation and male body and became increasingly preoccupied with the preservation and restoration of order. In the Mussolini era Maciste shed his realistic milieu in favor of big-budget costume dramas with exotic settings that continued and gradually increased this authoritarian line. In *Maciste imperatore* Maciste defeats a cruel dictator and arises as a leader chosen by the masses to lead the fictitious nation of Sirdagna, but not without a cautionary moral on the excesses of power and the proper way to govern. *Maciste all'inferno* returns to the historical epic tradition in Italian cinema as it invokes the nationalized, symbolic role of Dante in contemporary Italian culture to present a highly stylized and special effects–laden representation of the struggle between good and evil and the abuse of power. *Maciste contro lo sceicco* and *Maciste nella gabbia dei leoni* interact with questions of leadership within a colonialist discourse, precisely at the time when the Fascist regime attempted to expand its reach in that realm. The racialized, colonized other is a threat that must be violently eliminated (the sheik) or tamed (the lions, as a metaphor for the crowd) in order to guard against dilution of the race through, respectively, miscegenation or primitivism.[13]

What unites these films, besides their production (by FERT), chronology, and consistency of character is an increasing attention to and eventual preoccupation with the crowd. The role of the crowd, and how to best control and manipulate it for ideological and political purposes, became the subject of much thought and debate at the dawn of the twentieth century, and crowd theorists such as Gustave Le Bon held a major influence over Mussolini and Hitler. Thus essential to a concept of the political stardom, or the public self in the political sphere, is how the leader constructs the ideological self in relation to the masses, who as a result idealize and idolize the charismatic leader.[14] In the 1920s Maciste films, whether at a rally in support of an emperor, in the gates of hell, or the audience of a circus, the masses are a force to be reckoned with and must ultimately, like the lions in the circus, be tamed.

MUSSOLINI AS DIVO

The year 1924 saw the release of *Maciste e il nipote d'America* and marked Pagano's return from German to Italian film production. The film was directed by Eleuterio Rodolfi, an actor, director, and prolific contributor to Italian cinema's nascent years, and scripted by Giovacchino Forzano, a noted and successful playwright and librettist (he was the author of Puccini's *Gianni Schicchi,* among other operas).[15] It was also one of several big new FERT "superfilms" that signaled both the studio's reopening after having been shut down for more than a year and a shift from the studio's previous sentimental dramas and comedies to action and adventure featuring the strongmen Maciste, Saetta, and Galaor. The man primarily responsible for FERT's resurrection, and all of the post-German Maciste films, was Stefano Pittaluga, the most prominent private film industrialist at the time. Before the war, Pittaluga began opening and acquiring movie theaters, with the ultimate goal of creating a vertical monopoly of production, distribution, and exhibition, as well as controlling the importation of foreign films. In 1919 Pittaluga founded the Società Anonima Stefano Pittaluga (SASP), which focused on film distribution. He was also one of the major financial backers of FERT, established in 1919 by Enrico Fiori, who had previously worked with Itala Film, among other companies. The SASP eventually absorbed FERT's Turin and Rome operations and centralized production to the northern city. Their film output was minimal and not of great artistic significance, especially for the international market, which Pittaluga consistently kept his eye on, and the studio remained dormant for much of 1922 and 1923. In 1925 the studio was renamed FERT-Pittaluga, and it was there that the rest of the Maciste films were made and distributed by SASP. In 1926 Pittaluga absorbed what remained of the UCI, with its two hundred theaters. Between the distribution of foreign and domestic films, 80 percent of what was shown on Italian screens was furnished by Pittaluga. He also gained control of the Cines, Celio-Palatino, Itala, and Caesar Film studios.[16]

The SASP and FERT utilized multiple means of promoting their films beyond the traditional advertisements in trade papers and posters. They started their own publicity machinery, with the periodical *Films Pittaluga* in 1923 for the general public; their own *Bollettino di informazioni* (1924), with more specific details on the films, intended for trade use; and wide coverage in the popular Turinese periodical *Al Cinemà* (1922–1927), intended largely for female readers who were eager to learn more about stars.[17] It also received American press coverage in the Italian-language paper *Il Corriere d'America*, with special attention paid to the character of Maciste (without mentioning Pagano's name), evoking his "insuperable" presence in *Cabiria*.[18]

Unfortunately lost, *Maciste e il nipote d'America* constitutes the only Italian transatlantic production embarked upon during the 1920s, with some scenes filmed among New York's skyscrapers.[19] Shot in the fall of 1923, the action takes place and was filmed on Navigazione Generale Italiana's transatlantic ship *Duilio* on its inaugural voyage from Genoa to New York on 1 November 1923. Advertisements for the film prominently showcased and promoted the ship, as they did the Diatto car in *Maciste in vacanza* (plate 6). The troupe, which included Pagano, the actress Diomira Jacobini, and Oreste Bilancia, reportedly spent approximately ten days shooting in New York City and on location at the FERT studio.[20] The film's title appears in publicity under both *Il nipote d'America* and *Maciste e il nipote d'America*, perhaps an indication of the ongoing lawsuit between Itala Film and Pagano over the rights to the character's name (see chapter 1). It also plays on the cultural capital attributed to having an American uncle in Italy: "*lo zio d'America.*" What makes this film particularly unique is that the main character is not Maciste, but rather Bartolomeo Pagano, who is determined to marry off his beloved daughter, Liliana, to his nephew, Vittorio Pagano, who lives in America, despite Liliana's refusal to marry and Pagano's own reluctance to travel by sea. His daughter, however, is in love with her timid piano teacher, Luigi, and Vittorio has secretly married a woman named Clara, unbeknownst to our hero. Also unbeknownst to him Vittorio and Clara board the ship at Naples, and since uncle and nephew have never met they do not recognize each other. Pagano the uncle falls for Clara, and the two newlyweds, Vittorio and Clara, devise a plan to win him over to approving their matrimony. Ultimately, as might be expected, Luigi and Liliana are united.[21]

In its promotional material, FERT announced that this film was the first that FERT-Pittaluga would make with Maciste, soon to be followed by two others: *Maciste imperatore* and *Maciste all'inferno*. But alterations in the FERT-Pittaluga version of the Maciste character were already manifest. FERT's publicity bulletin, *Bollettino di informazioni,* described Maciste as being "still the same unrepentant ladies man, admirer of every beautiful, feminine grace." Maciste had never suffered from seasickness as he does in this film, even though audiences had seen him on boats in *La trilogia di Maciste* (see chapter 5) and soon would continue to do so in *Maciste imperatore,* in which he is aboard multiple ships.[22] What these shifts signal was FERT's desire to exploit the Maciste brand regardless of consistency of character, something that Itala Film had attempted to preserve, with a few exceptions, and to compete with other cinematically present masculine figures on Italian screens: Douglas Fairbanks, whose films Pittaluga himself imported, and the new star of the day, Benito Mussolini.[23]

As I have argued elsewhere, Fascism and its relationship to culture, and feature film production in particular, was not one of supreme government control over the industry; one cannot really speak of a Fascist cinema, but more of an ideologically influenced and oriented production output.[24] Nor did Mussolini's rise signal a radical, immediate break in terms of cultural policy. It cannot be termed a cinema of dictatorship, because the dictatorship did not yet exist. There were, in fact, more continuities than ruptures with pre-Fascist film policies, although that would change with the coming of sound in 1930. Before the October 1922 March on Rome, the Italian government had begun to show signs, albeit small, of interest in the film industry, creating in 1920 an advisory panel for the film industry, with the intention of gathering data on and promoting film production, distribution, and exhibition in Italy. Although the panel consisted of a wide swath of film industry players, it never had much of an impact.[25] The feature film industry's relationship to the emerging Fascist movement and regime was "sporadic," with small, uncoordinated initiatives throughout the 1920s but no major overhauls until 1930, and mostly involved protection of limited interests in distribution and exhibition.[26] Early government interventions included modest modifications to existing censorship practices, still mostly focused on moral rather than political issues,[27] and corporativist enterprises – a Fascist "corporation" of participants in the film industry, officially constituted in 1926; and the founding of the Istituto Internazionale del Cinema Educatore (International Institute for Educational Cinema, 1928).[28] Another indication of political involvement was the birth in the major industrialized cities of *fasci artistici,* whose goal was moral and material help to those producers who might find themselves in difficulty. In Turin's *fascio artistico* the vice president was Domenico Gambino, the actor who played the popular acrobatic strongman Saetta and Maciste's co-star in *Maciste imperatore;* at one point in 1924 there was even talk about making a film titled *Saetta fascista (Saetta the Fascist).*[29]

In terms of production, there was, and in fact would continue to be, a decided lack of early Fascist propaganda feature-length films. As during World War I, many films were made about the Risorgimento, intending to establish a historical continuity between the hero of Italian unification, Giuseppe Garibaldi, and Mussolini,[30] and a few nationally and colonially tinged film productions surfaced, including Mario Camerini's *Kif Tebbi* (1928). Only *Il grido dell'aquila* (The Cry of the Eagle, Mario Volpi, 1923), about the March on Rome and released by the short-lived Istituto Fascista di Propanda Nazionale (Fascist Institute of National Propaganda), stands out, a film that mixed documentary footage with a never-completed film on World War I. It would later inspire the overtly propagandistic *Camicia nera* (Black Shirt, Giovacchino Forzano, 1933) and Alessandro Blasetti's *Vecchia guardia* (Old Guard, 1934).[31]

There were two documented efforts to involve Benito Mussolini into feature film production after the March on Rome. In early 1923 the UCI asked him to aid in the screen adaptation of his own bodice-ripper serialized novel, *Claudia Particella, l'amante del cardinale* (Claudia Particella, the Cardinal's Lover), an anti-Catholic feuilleton published between 1910 and 1911; the UCI also tried to engage Mussolini to write the intertitles for the 1924 remake of *Quo Vadis?*[32] Although both attempts were ultimately unsuccessful, Mussolini did star in numerous documentaries and newsreels promoted by the Istituto Luce. Founded in 1924 as the Sindacato Instruzione Cinematografica (SIC) by Luciano De Feo and Giacomo Paulucci di Calboli as a private enterprise, the regime co-opted the organization in 1925 as part of an ultimate program to establish government control over official forms of mass media. Propaganda films were a priority, but the newsreels for which the Istituto Luce and Mussolini became (in)famous did not fully develop as a film form until 1927, when production rapidly evolved to three to four per week. Although they prominently showcased Mussolini, his policies, and his star persona, the majority of newsreels produced by Luce in the early years, many of which are now available online at the Archivio Luce's web archive (http://www.archivioluce.com/archivio), had much in common with pre-Fascist nonfiction films, such as the documentaries by Roberto Omegna, who also continued to make films during the early 1920s.[33]

Mussolini was, above all, the primary "star" of these films. His visual and aural presence, however, predates the Fascist years. From his early participation in the Socialist movement, as well as his political and journalistic activism, Mussolini had a formidable public authority as a charismatic leader, although it would go through various ups and downs after his expulsion from the party in 1914, the aftermath of World War I, and ultimately the rise of the Fascist political movement.[34] Building on an Italian cultural trajectory of heroic leadership from Giuseppe Garibaldi, the mythologized military commander of Italian unification, much of Mussolini's charisma was not derived from innate qualities, but "manufactured" through his relationship to mass media, and in particular film. As Stephen Gundle has argued in his work on stardom during Fascism as well as the cult of Mussolini, "The construction and projection of the Mussolini personality occurred within a framework in which the collective consciousness had already been shaped and conditioned by certain real enterprises and by certain archetypes of popular literature and film."[35] Many early film performers began their successful careers in the theater and crossed over to film, the most famous example being Eleonora Duse and the film *Cenere* (Ashes, Società Anonima Ambrosio, 1917). Literary figures such as Gabriele D'Annunzio and the futurist Filippo Tommaso Marinetti already presented themselves, through their writings and carefully manipulated performances and stagings, as political and poetic personae. Mussolini actively and consciously played up his charisma with the projection, as Gundle and Lucy Riall have argued, of a new idea of a "strongman" through his physical appearance and sexuality.[36] In a period when, as Simonetta Falasca-Zamponi has argued, "the culture of character" began to morph into the "culture of personality," Mussolini fit the bill. Citing contemporary writings and images, Falasca-Zamponi notes how the myth of Mussolini combined his image as charismatic leader, astute politician, and a "real man," deifying him as omnipresent, omnipotent, and immortal.[37] It was the birth of the cult of Mussolini, one that would last far beyond his violent death.[38]

By 1924 Mussolini had become the most photographed man in history.[39] In addition to numerous biographies devoted to him in print culture from 1923 onward, visual representations of him circulated in postcards even before he was appointed prime minister in 1922.[40] These postcards, mostly produced by private companies, indicated that as a commodity, the visual image of the Duce, like those of Pagano and other movie stars, was in demand, with tens of millions of photographs in circulation.[41] What distinguished Mussolini's iconographic ubiquity from other leaders at the time was that his private life was as much the subject of political iconography as his public presence.[42] It was also this propensity toward the public manifestation of the private self that differentiated him from D'Annunzio, who remained "remote and aristocratic" while Mussolini presented himself as "virile, charismatic, and populist."[43]

This collapse of public and private, however, does not intend an equation between appearance and reality. Mussolini was a master performer who assumed various roles both on and off screen to build and then maintain his popularity. He was the star, as scholars have argued, of his own serial in various adventures, including some already seen in the Maciste series: Mussolini the aviator, Mussolini the race-car driver, Mussolini the soldier/army man, Mussolini the patriarch, and even Mussolini the athlete, to appropriate an exact Maciste title.[44] He also presented himself as being the supreme, capable leader of the people and at the same time one of them, especially in the early years of consolidation.[45] Like the extra-cinematic discourse surrounding Pagano, Mussolini played off his humble origins as a man of the people, and his was the model of Italian masculinity destined to be imitated by his adoring fans, who packed the Piazza Veneto to watch him. The balcony was his privileged stage on and off screen, a defined cinematic space where he could freely gesticulate with his body and, later, with the advent of sound, articulate with his voice. Nicola Mazzanti and Gian Luca Farinelli note how Luce films employed the shot reverse shot, with low-angle shots of Mussolini on the balcony intercut with high-angle shots of the crowd, making him appear larger than life. The films also position him as the idol of adoring fans; they are spliced with a plethora of reaction shots of both the Duce and the people. His frequent speeches from the balcony aligned him with another ubiquitous leader, the pope, thus adding an element of divine anointment and otherworldliness.[46]

These techniques, which would become aesthetic markers of Luce films, are already visible in the 1925 SIC-produced documentary *Il III anniversario della Marcia su Roma solennemente celebrata a Milano* (The Third Anniversary of the March on Rome Solemnly Celebrated in Milan), which opens with a divo-like painted portrait of the Duce complete in iris shot to present the star of a silent film to the audience. Long pans highlight the crowd awaiting his arrival at Milan's Piazza del Duomo, described in the intertitles as a *"marea umana"* (human sea). There are no close-ups of Mussolini on the balcony, but rather a shot reverse shot alternating from high and low angles that reinforces the submissive fervor of the crowd and the Duce's mesmerizing power and control over it. The film also features many in the crowd bearing arms and raising them as a sign of their devotion and the regime's might.

In almost all of the available early newsreels and in still photographs, Mussolini consistently occupies the center of the frame, whether surrounded by Fascist officials or the crowd. The optical points of focus are his body, his face, and, perhaps most significantly, his gestures, including the unique (and much parodied) Mussolinian way of holding his body, contorting his face, and using his arms to convey his message. The theatrical and exaggerated use of the body was common practice not only

6.1. Mussolini with his arms crossed.

From the author's personal collection.

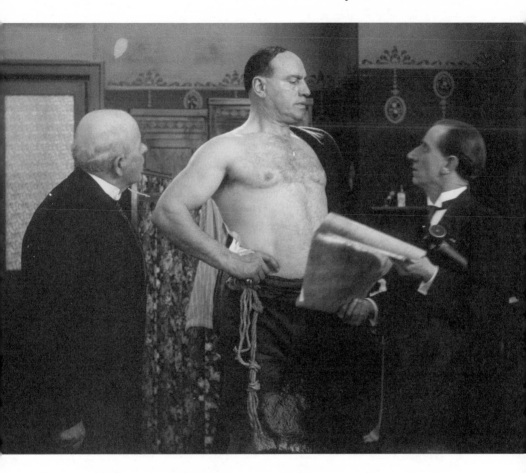

6.2. Maciste in a classic pose in *Maciste imperatore* (1924).

in the previous decade's mainstream theater but also in the acting style
of the era, particularly that of the histrionic divas, who relied on pan-
tomime and dance, among other cultural practices, to convey emotion
on the screen. Because of Italian silent cinema's penchant for the long
shot and long take (editing and close-ups became more widely used in
the late 1920s), the body and the gesture were the primary instruments
used to convey emotion and message.[47] Mussolini's preferred gesture
is his arms crossed, which appeared early on in the SIC and Luce films,
as in the 1923 documentary *A Noi!*, assembled from newsreel footage of
the time and directed by Umberto Paradisi, a well-respected nonfiction

filmmaker, journalist, and later s a s p's head of the press office (fig. 6.1). Another favorite statuesque pose has Mussolini with his hands on his hips, as when he surveys the talented young athletes performing their athletic and gymnastic routines in another 1925 film.[48] These poses potentially evoke, of course, Maciste's first on-screen appearance in *Cabiria* on the rocks (see chapter 2) and the publicity stills FERT released for *Maciste imperatore* of Pagano bare-chested with his hands on his hips (fig. 6.2).[49]

Mussolini's performances on the multiple stages necessitated the ability to both wear and change not only masks but also, like Fregoli and then Maciste, costumes with frequency and agility.[50] His omnipresence through the visual image allowed him to dress the part, and it began early in his political career. Like D'Annunzio, Mussolini was a man of fashion. He had a penchant for spats and stiff collars; hats were one of his essential accessories, and in the early years he preferred the bowler (fig. 6.3). In his first years as Italy's prime minister he avoided being photographed in military or Fascist attire, even though the Fascist black shirt did take on a symbolic, unifying meaning of the movement's emphasis on action and combat.[51] Even in the above-mentioned *A Noi!*, when surrounded by fellow black-shirted Fascists, Mussolini remains in civilian garb, wearing a sport coat and knickers or a fashionable overcoat, top hat, and suit with a white shirt. On the other hand, Augusto Turati, the secretary of the PNF (the Fascist National Party), almost always appeared in the Luce films in black-shirted uniformed splendor.[52]

As a self-proclaimed man of the people, Mussolini's dress varied depending on the occasion, and, like Maciste, he depended on the well-fitted suit to assimilate with the middle class. Ever the mannequin, the Duce changed costumes quickly and easily to play the aviator, the soldier, or the driver, always impeccably dressed.[53] In the 1925 *La battaglia del grano* (The Battle for Wheat), which emphasized the regime's policy on autonomous grain production, Mussolini is shown in the first shot wearing what appears to be a fashionable trench coat and a fedora hat as he runs his fingers through a stack of grain, later turning to a bowler hat and dark overcoat as he surveys the fields. Significantly, he is dressed like those around him, signaling his status as one of the masses, although he remains at center frame.

6.3. Mussolini as a man of fashion.

From the author's personal collection.

Aware of the power of the male body, Mussolini also strategically featured his own physical form as a testament and declaration of his virile image. Here the parallels with Maciste are striking. The Maciste films center on the muscled male body, whether clothed or undressed, as a national symbol of power, strength, and virility. During the years of Italian Fascism these representations took on additional ideological and political symbolism. Even from its earliest days, the regime mobilized the male and female body in service to its ideological imperatives. It aimed to counter the perceived weakness of Italian men who were ill prepared for battle and its consequences during World War I with the goal of "restoring a sense of virility, comradeship, and discipline."[54] The glory of the Italian empire, the order and efficiency of the regime, and the prosperity of the nation were all tied up in the image of happy, robust, fit, reproductive Italian men and women. Physical education became a requirement in the schools and the focus of many extracurricular group activities. Although these activities were aimed primarily at boys and men, women were also encouraged to participate in such sports as tennis, skiing, roller-skating, and, of course, rhythmic gymnastics, which would create lithe and supple bodies as well as instill grace. In the regime's latter years, these talents were showcased in the *sabato fascista* (Fascist Saturdays), in which Italians of all ages, in the splendor of their Fascist uniforms, would participate in a variety of activities intended to instill military, political, and athletic values through homogenization.

The Fascist government invested heavily in sports on both a financial and ideological level; athletic success became a propagandistic tool. Continuing in the French tradition that sports was the "peacetime continuation of war,"[55] the government poured massive amounts of money into creating "fitter bodies and occupied minds."[56] The push toward modernization is closely related to the growth of mass participation in and spectatorship of sports, with cycling and soccer becoming the most popular by 1945.[57] During the *ventennio,* the regime set out, with varying degrees of success, to "fascistize" sports organizations, targeting children from their formative years up through adolescence and adulthood in order to create exemplary future Fascist leaders. It shut down Catholic and socialist sporting clubs that had begun to proliferate during the early twentieth century and established its own institutions, including the

CONI (National Olympic Committee) and the Accademia di Educazione Fisica (Academy of Physical Education) in Rome. In the regime's first ten years the goal was to instill courage, discipline, and strength in men and grace and strength in women. The government also invested heavily in sports infrastructure on Fascist, national, and regional levels, creating in 1929 the first national soccer league and in 1926 a massive project to build sports stadiums as a showcase for architectural and athletic prowess, the first project being the Bologna stadium and sports facility.

The Luce films, even the early ones, featured Mussolini's body in motion, and often athletic motion, conveying the notion of masculine strength as linked to the strength of the leader and thus the nation. Mussolini himself repeatedly appeared fencing, riding a horse, swimming, skiing, and shooting. The irony, however, is that Mussolini suffered from poor health for much of his life but saw the importance of persuading the national, and later international, audience of his athletic prowess.[58] Shots of his presence at gymnastic and athletic displays, as in the 1925 Luce film *Mussolini e Farinacci al saggio ginnico organizzato dalla Milizia Volontaria della Sicurezza Nazionale* (Mussolini and Farinacci at the Gymnastics Display Organized by the Voluntary Militia for National Security) show him walking and conversing with the athletes, surrounded by them but dominating the center of frame. The meaning is clear: as a man of action and movement himself, he feels at home among the young athletes. Even in films that display scenes of others' athletic prowess as he looks on – as in, for instance, the 1928 Luce newsreel *A Roma Mussolini visita la caserma della Guardia di Finanza* (Mussolini Visits the Barracks of the Financial Guard in Rome) – he is sutured into the action. Scenes of the guards running, jumping, and performing feats of strength alternate with reaction shots of a pleased and snappily dressed Mussolini, captured in medium and long shot and always in center frame.[59]

Mussolini was clearly a ubiquitous physical presence, as was his reproduced image on posters, postcards, artwork, and architecture. He became the supreme icon of Fascism and the Italian nation, and his image had close to two thousand official representations and millions upon millions of reproductions in various form.[60] The fact that postcards of his likeness circulated abundantly from the beginning, and that most of them, like those of similar movie stars of the day were, according to

6.4. Maciste as athlete in *Maciste imperatore* (1924).

Enrico Sturani, purchased as keepsakes and not intended to be mailed, were "like holy images, like the saints or the stars."[61] This association with Mussolini and the sacred would play an essential part in the sacralization of politics that would be so endemic to the regime's creation and maintenance of popular consensus in the later years. The early Luce newsreels, however, were more preoccupied with establishing Mussolini as a man of the masses, who acted and dressed like everyone else but who at the same time possessed the necessary charisma, strength, and virility to lead the Italian nation to greatness. This duality is at the essence of Maciste's character and continues in Pagano's Mussolini-era on-screen incarnations as the series dialogued with the contemporary issues of leadership, charisma, and the masses (fig. 6.4).

MACISTE IMPERATORE: LEADING BY EXAMPLE

Pagano's next film for FERT, *Maciste imperatore,* was the first to engage with questions of governance at the time of dictatorship. It was not, as the title might lead one to believe, a wholesale endorsement of totalitarian rule. Much less humorous and ironic than the Itala films, *Maciste imperatore* is a cautionary tale of what can go wrong in an excessively repressive government based on ceremony and despotic rule.[62] With its lack of the parliamentary procedures that figured into the portrayal of rightful leadership in *La trilogia di Maciste,* the film's presentation of proper rule is decidedly monarchical. Originally part of the Kingdom of Sardinia before Italy's unification, Turin had deep historical ties to the Italian monarchy and the Piedmont House of Savoy, led at the time by King Vittorio Emanuele III.[63] Moreover, as the center of FERT's film production, Turin's politically charged atmosphere reflected its pro-worker, leftist leanings. Many of its denizens continued to resist Fascism even after the March on Rome, resulting in the three-day December 1922 Turin Massacre, in which Turin's Fascists killed eleven people and injured many more.[64] That is not to say that the film is anti-Fascist or anti-Mussolini. On the contrary, this film provides multiple episodes of convergence between Maciste and Mussolini, with the cinematic strongman as the proposed model leader taking the right and righteous potential path of benevolent rule.

Maciste imperatore was the first film in the series to be directed by Guido Brignone, a long-established director in Italian silent cinema (and beyond into the 1950s) who would be at the helm of the majority of the Maciste films made by FERT during the Fascist period. Brignone would go on to direct several key ideologically oriented films during the Fascist period, including the patriotic World War I drama *Passaporto rosso* (Red Passport, 1935) and the colonialist *Sotto la croce del Sud* (Under the Southern Cross, 1938). *Maciste imperatore* was written by the playwright and screenwriter Pier Angelo Mazzolotti, billed in the intertitles as an "adventurous romance," and reflected FERT's emphasis on action and adventure films. Although Pagano continues to receive top billing, he is uncharacteristically credited with his given name first: the title card reads "Bartolomeo Pagano (Maciste)" and is repeated with his first appearance on screen in the reverse, "Maciste (Sig. Bartolomeo Pagano)." In most films he is either not given a title card at all, or if listed in the cast of characters, his character name is emphasized. Among possible explanations for this emphatic repositioning are these two: (1) that having recently won the court case to keep the rights to his character's name, Pagano wanted to reinforce the connection; or (2) that Pagano's name was indeed becoming more recognizable as a commodity in and of itself, particularly after the success of *Maciste e il nipote d'America.*

Despite the new face behind the camera, *Maciste imperatore* is the only one of the FERT films to hark back to the series' origins with the usual premise of Maciste on a film set. He is filming a production clearly inspired by Charlie Chaplin's *The Kid* (1921, distributed in Italy in 1923 by SASP as *Il monello*), in which he comes to the aid of a poor boy, dressed remarkably like the original film's Jackie Coogan.[65] Not only does Maciste dispose of the perpetrator by throwing him down a manhole, but he also adorably hugs and kisses the little boy, giving him money as well. After Maciste drives off the set in his car, the FERT logo appears prominently in the background.

The other novelty in *Maciste imperatore* is the addition of Saetta as Maciste's cinematic sidekick. Saetta was a franchise star in his own right. Played by Domenico Gambino, his first foray into cinema began in 1909 in an Itala Film–produced comic series based on his acrobatic feats. He remained with Itala Film for eight years, working on the Cretinetti series (often in drag) and then various films until his first appearance as Saetta in the 1920 *Saetta salva la regina* (Saetta Saves the Queen, Delta Film). He consistently insisted on doing his own stunts throughout his career, opting to increase their difficulty and thus their spectacularity.[66] Saetta's nimble athleticism was the perfect complement to Maciste's brute strength. The film introduces him getting dressed in a mirror and, upon hearing Maciste's car drive by, jumping out the window to land perfectly in its backseat as it continues on the road. Saetta was the other major star around whom FERT built its future success; along with *Maciste e il nipote d'America, Saetta impara a vivere!* (Saetta Learns to Live!, 1924),

also directed by Brignone, was the second of FERT's major productions
of its relaunched studio in 1924. *Maciste imperatore* had an alternate title
that integrated that market plan: *Maciste imperatore e Saetta suo scudiero*
(Maciste the Emperor and Saetta His Squire).[67] Regardless of the title,
their double billing ensured a large audience, even though Saetta is secondary to Maciste in the narrative and disappears for much of the film.[68]

The majority of *Maciste imperatore* takes place in the fictitious kingdom of Sirdagna. The play on Sirdagna/Sardegna (Italian for Sardinia)
lends a pro-monarchical reading to the film's cautionary tale of abuses
in power and ultimate rightful leadership. Sirdagna is a land suffering
under the corrupt rule of the Reggente Stanos (Armando Pouget), whose
excessively extravagant style of governing "contrasts," as the intertitles
state, with the "pitiful condition of the masses," who are shown begging for food at the palace's gate. It is the second foray into the representation of the masses in the Maciste series after *Maciste innamorato*,
in which the factory workers are depicted as easily manipulated and
tamed. In Sirdagna, on the other hand, they suffer unjustly at the hands
of a despotic ruler. The viewer soon learns that Maciste is old friends
with Sirdagna's exiled prince Otis (Renato Mayllard), the illegitimate
son of the deposed deceased king, Lothar VIII. Otis lives incognito in
another "foreign land," where two of his father's faithful servants watch
over him: Count Oultz (played, incidentally, by Giuseppe Brignone, the
director's father) and Baron Riembergk. The use of fictitious countries
was not unusual to silent cinema or the Maciste series. However, the
narrative solution does create a roman à clef situation with the extra-
cinematic reality as it doubly removes the action from any connection
to contemporary Italy.

Rather than concentrate on his studies, Otis is fascinated with the
celebrated mime Cinzia (played by the popular femme fatale Elena
Sangro),[69] who is conspiring with Stanos's henchman Osram (Oreste
Grandi) to ensnare Otis in a trap to be rid of him once and for all. Otis in
fact does fall for Cinzia and flees with her one week later, when Maciste
and Saetta have already returned to work. Oultz and Riembergk pursue
Maciste to help rescue Otis, revealing his true status as the future king
of Sirdagna, and Maciste enlists Saetta as his partner in restoring rightful rule. They create a plot to have Maciste pose as Otis, stabilize the

country, and then complete the transfer of power. Through their skill, athletic prowess, and might, Maciste and his gang are able to rescue Otis from Cinzia and Osram's clutches, with some comical and suspenseful mishaps along the way, and reveal to him his true identity as the future king of Sirdagna.

When approached by Otis's guardians, Maciste is in costume, wearing an outfit similar to the toga he wore in *Cabiria*. It was a popular image of Maciste that continued to circulate in postcards throughout the 1920s and was used to publicize the film (fig. 6.5). It also recalled the resurgent interest in all things Ancient Rome that continued to appear on Italian screens (the remake of *Quo Vadis?* in 1924 being the most infamous). The visual and metaphorical presence of the cult of romanità, the heritage of Ancient Rome and its significance for national restoration, became especially relevant during the Fascist regime.[70] Rather than a nostalgia for the very distant (Ancient Rome and Renaissance Italy) as well as the recent past (the Risorgimento), romanità was, as Joshua Arthurs has argued, a "revolutionary project of modernity, a coherent language with which to articulate aspirations for the contemporary world," one that intended a new man, "the epitome of the virile citizen-soldier."[71] Part and parcel of that modernization of the Roman myth was the muscled, male body in relation to the new modernist, nationalist body politic.[72] One review of *Maciste imperatore* indeed noted the classical proportions of Maciste's body: "his body remains, even taut in exertion, full of balance and of an astonishing plasticity."[73] An interview with "Maciste" published in Pittaluga's promotional *Films Pittaluga* similarly commented on his body's "plasticity of form and elasticity of movement."[74]

Maciste imperatore also harks back in some ways to *La trilogia di Maciste,* in which Maciste partners with a dear friend to help ensure the sovereignty and political stability of a foreign nation. Yet several factors distinguish the two films. In *La trilogia,* Maciste takes a backseat, in many ways, to Tito, who is the brains behind the operation. In *Maciste imperatore,* however, Maciste is clearly positioned as the go- to and can-do man in charge, with Saetta at his side. Second, in *Maciste imperatore* the masses play a much larger role. Stanos is clearly an evil despotic ruler; his brutal reign over the people of Sirdagna, shown in his disdain for their suffering, is accompanied by an ornate devotion to excessive pomp

6.5. Maciste in his toga in *Maciste imperatore* (1924).

and circumstance of both everyday governance and the "prince's" return to the kingdom. A series of dissolves, for instance, reveals elegant guardsmen on horseback at the ornate palace's entrance, beautifully coiffed and dressed ladies in waiting, and the full seat of government awaiting his arrival. The film takes pains to show the suffering of the Sirdagnan masses at his cruel hand. Rather than lumped together as an anonymous mass as in *Maciste innamorato* or *La trilogia,* they are individualized and even given a voice by those most innocently effected by their fate: it is a child who tells the indifferent guard at the gate, "We are hungry." The use of the plural indicates the universality of their plight and their eventual solidarity once they choose the rightful leader.

But the people also have a political defender on Sirdagnan ground: the characters of Lothar's democratic advisor the marshal (Gero Zambuto) and his daughter, Ginevra (Lola Romanos). The film takes pains to show that despite their wealth these royals are in sympathy with the people: the marshal has written a memo about the "liberal aspirations of the people" and warns Stanos, who has just torn it up, that the masses have been tyrannized for too long and will soon revolt. Both are dressed in their military uniforms, but the marshal's clothing is white compared to that of the darker, and more evil, Stanos. Ginevra goes directly to the people, handing out money to the poor and wretched. They set the example of good governing that Maciste/Otis must follow. When Maciste disguised as Otis takes the stage as the presumed leader, with the real (and diminutive) Otis at his side, he is also in a light-colored uniform, shot from low angle so as to heighten his power and authority. A series of reaction shots size up Maciste. The admiring gazes from the women are highly eroticized (even the parliamentarians agree that he is "magnificent"). When one meek-looking officer expresses his disapproval – "he is too big" – Maciste uses the occasion as a way to flex his physical and political muscle, picking up the insubordinate by the collar and escorting him from the room.

The group that accepts Maciste/Otis unequivocally are the masses, shown eagerly awaiting his address from the balcony; here the parallels with the Luce films in which Mussolini was beginning to and would appear are conspicuous (fig. 6.6). Although Maciste/Otis comes to the

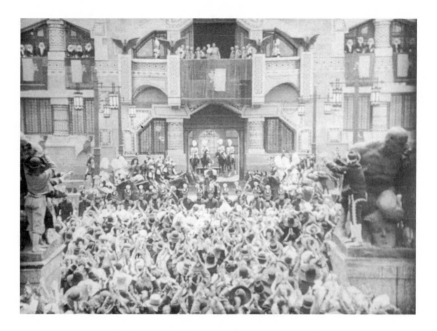

6.6. Maciste and the masses in *Maciste imperatore* (1924).

throne through "birth," the film presents him as a leader chosen by and at one with the people. He meets their cries of "We want to see the prince!" not with the disdain expressed on Stanos's face, but with "I want to meet the people whom I sincerely love," an attitude that is clearly intelligible in his expression and demeanor. He, like Mussolini in *A Noi!*, appears on the balcony in extreme long shot in center frame, with the adoring and cheering crowd in front of him. Reaction shots of young and old alike, alternating with a smiling Maciste, strengthen his acceptance as rightful leader: "But he is not a prince . . . he is . . . a true emperor!" and "Long live our emperor!" The people's jubilant willingness to accept him and even elevate him to benevolent absolute ruler place him firmly with both a democratic and imperialistic rule. He reiterates to Stanos that he will present the document that solidifies his ascension to the throne only when the masses have come to know and love him. With justice as his guiding principle, he wishes only to be known as their friend, not their leader, thus establishing himself, as did Mussolini, as one of them. When the real Otis assumes the throne, he too has the people's blessing as the masses wildly cheer outside the palace.

Another revealing similarity between Maciste as emperor and Mussolini is their physical regimen: Maciste/Otis's "daily morning gallop." One of the very first Luce newsreels from May 1928 features Mussolini on horseback at the Villa Borghese as well as at an equestrian facility, where he guides his horse through jumps and other maneuvers with ease.[75] Printed reports at the time substantiated these activities. One 1923 article in the newspaper *Domenica del Corriere* recounts Mussolini's morning routine, which included a daily horseback ride. Describing him as a "passionate" and "indefatigable" horseman, the article notes how his endurance can easily exhaust more than one horse, just as subsequent propaganda would make insinuations about his insatiable sexual appetite. The article also equates his muscularity with his ability to govern: "The honorable Mussolini has trained as an equestrian, from the moment when he forked the government between his robust legs. And now he is an expert, as he is in fencing, which he has sacrificed recently for his newest passion."[76] This routine is displayed in motion in the 1928 Luce newsreel *Mussolini a cavallo lungo la via Appia* (Mussolini on Horseback along the Appian Way). Of course he wears his impeccable riding garb, complete with perfectly folded handkerchief in pocket and classic fedora hat. Yet the fashionable athletic Duce also exudes a paternal image, thus reinforcing what would become another carefully constructed and ideologically loaded role that he played as father and father figure of the nation; he gives his young son Romano Mussolini a brief ride on the horse with him and salutes the children as they "receive the Duce's good word."[77] It also creates a iconographic bridge between Mussolini and the "father" of the Italian nation, Giuseppe Garibaldi, whose reproduced image in painting and sculpture often featured him on horseback with his red shirt and white horse.[78]

Maciste's exercise routine reveals, like Mussolini's, that the people are his primary concern but in an even more direct and active way: he rescues a man whose leg is trapped under a boulder as the indifferent and cruel official guards look on and even beat a woman begging for their assistance. This is but one example in which Maciste proves himself both exemplary and model leader. At another point he orders food to be distributed to the poor and hungry at the palace gates as the film contrasts the "before" and "after" scenarios. "It is good that the poor receive help and protection from us" precedes images of mothers and children eating and smiling, a scene that would play out later, coincidentally or not, in the Fascist period with the creation of the ONMI, the Opera Nazionale Maternità e Infanzia, inaugurated in 1925 for the protection and social assistance of women and children.

Although Saetta's stunts are lighthearted in *Maciste imperatore,* most of Maciste's spectacular displays are increasingly vicious, without much of the humor and irony that characterized the majority of the Itala films. The threat of violence persists throughout the film in the guise of Stanos's evil dictatorship, but the film's conclusion includes ferocious acts shown in more detail than ever before in the Maciste series' extant prints. In one scene our hero is trapped in a room with six mysterious men adorned in head-to-toe armor and burnishing swords against an unarmed Maciste. Eventually he is able to arm himself with sword and shield, but one soldier manages a deep cut on Maciste's neck; it is the first time in the series that an enemy has drawn blood (Maciste also returns the favor). Stanos's men also stuff Otis in a bag, tie him up, and throw him in the canal surrounding the castle; Saetta jumps in and saves him while simultaneously ensnaring his captors. Others violently arouse Oultz and Riembergk from their slumber and, after much struggle and torture, throw them in a secret jail. These confrontations occupy more than six minutes of screen time and are shown in great detail, including strategic close-ups of a wounded Maciste and spilled blood. As discussed above, violence was an essential component of Fascism's appeal, along with its rise and ultimate preservation of power, and played an important role in its mythology. In addition, the ability to endure pain was considered a sign of national fortitude. As Christopher F. Forth has shown, during this period the notion of pain was central not only to the creation of manly men but also in the creation of nations. The ability to endure pain differentiated the weak individual from the strong, and strong, cohesive nations from weaker ones. If the nation was a living (and gendered) being "bound up in the physical and moral identity of its citizenry," duels were "affronts to the body politic" as experienced through the private body.[79]

6.7. *Maciste imperatore* (1924) and the Fascist salute.

Maciste thrives not only because of his strength but also because he has the strength to bear pain.

As further potential proof of the connection to the extra-cinematic political context, there are several scenes in which Maciste appears to give the Fascist Roman salute (fig. 6.7). This gesture's meaning, while typical of Mussolini and the Fascists and ubiquitous in the Luce documentaries, is ambiguous. As the real Otis takes his rightful place on the throne in front of a humiliated Stanos and a shocked crowd, Maciste, at his side, raises his arm in what could be read as the Roman salute. He does not directly salute the new leader, but rather directs it at the raucous and surprised crowd that has assembled, and he repeats it when directly asked what his role in the farce was. It appears more as an attempt to calm and placate the crowd than a political gesture. Maciste's real salute to Otis's power is more regal than Fascist; he kneels down at Otis's feet and proclaims his humble servitude. Yet the iconographic reference to the salute's contemporary ubiquity leaves open the possibility for a more reactionary reading.

Notwithstanding the cartoon analyzed at the beginning of this chapter, publicity materials that FERT and SASP released for the film steer clear of the politically charged situation. The sole comment was left to Pagano in the cartoon quotation above about Mussolini having nothing to fear in Maciste. The photo spreads and interviews with Maciste/ Pagano and other members of the cast and crew focus on the large-scale production, the revived FERT studio, and information about exciting location shoots. Even the film reviews, which were decidedly negative, avoided any comparison of Maciste to Mussolini or vice versa. "It is not a work of art, thus it does not lend itself to a close dissection and a detailed criticism," wrote "Il Rondone" in *La Vita Cinematografica*. "A film rich with ingredients, good ideas, mixed with expertise, sustained by a considerable force but lacking that fire that no one knows what it is or what it's worth, but that elevates a work to the virtue of art," opined "Gulliver" in *La Rivista Cinematografica*.[80] What the critics did agree on and notice was the delighted audience that consistently packed the theaters. Thus, just as the Sirdagnan masses rejoiced in their leader, Italian audiences heaped their approval on their ever popular strongman, and they would continue to do as he made his next journey into the bowels of hell.

MACISTE ALL'INFERNO: TEMPTATION, CHAOS, AND ORDER

Maciste all'inferno, from its special effects–laden opening scenes of the underworld, constitutes a novelty in the series, an allegorical tale of good and evil that was like nothing Italian audiences had ever experienced before.[81] At the same time, it harks back to the series' origins in the historical epic and, with its fable-like tale about right and wrong, the preservation of order against the threat of chaos. It was, of course, not the first on-screen incarnation of Dante's *Divine Comedy*. Dante was an early source of inspiration: Milano Films produced *L'inferno* (*Dante's Inferno,* Milano Films, 1911), a film that, along with *La caduta di Troia* (*The Fall of Troy,* Itala Film, 1910), ushered in the golden age of Italian silent cinema.[82] *L'inferno* is also perhaps the best-known of the Maciste films, thanks in great part to Federico Fellini's multiple citations of it as one of his first cinematic memories and one of the primary fonts of inspiration throughout his career.[83] The film was the next in FERT-Pittaluga's series of super-productions after *Maciste imperatore,* initiated in 1924, when it was shown at the annual Milan Fair in March of that year to great acclaim: a rave review published in *La Vita Cinematografica* that month validates the production and distribution chronology.[84] Advertisements and other promotional materials begin to appear in film magazines such as *Al Cinemà* and *La Vita Cinematografica* in January 1925, but censors intervened, and the film ultimately received their approval in March 1926 and appeared in theaters soon thereafter.[85]

In *Maciste imperatore,* representations of leadership and rule took on an additional ideological resonance during the Fascist ventennio. Similarly, Dante's iconic text became an integral Fascist symbol. On a personal level, Mussolini saw Dante as a guiding spirit throughout his political career. During his youth, according to his biographers, Mussolini would walk through the streets of Forlimpoli, where he attended high school, shouting stanzas of *Inferno* and *Purgatorio,* with a particular penchant for Dante's political invectives. Later, after his rise to power, he frequently invoked Dante in numerous speeches as a symbol of both the glories of Italian culture and its political ambitions.[86] Linguistically, the regime sought to unify the country through the elimination of dialects and the adoption of Dante's Florentine Italian as the national language. On a symbolic and sacred level, Dante was glorified as a literary national icon, eclipsing the Petrarchan model that had dominated the intellectual imaginary through the eighteenth century. In nationalistic terms the regime sought to exploit his imperial vision for Italy.[87] In 1924 the author Salvatore Gotta rewrote the lyrics to Fascist youth anthem "Giovinezza," adding an invocation to Dante: "The valour of thy warriors / The virtue of thy pathfinders / The vision of Alighieri / Shines now in every heart" ("Il valor dei tuoi guerreri / La virtù dei pioneri / La vision dell'Alighieri

/ Oggi brilla in tutti i cuor"). In 1925 its recital became obligatory at public performances on the 21 April national holiday honoring the birth of Rome.[88] Between 1938 and 1940 the regime began construction on the Danteum, intended to be built in the center of Rome as not only a monument to the poet but also an intellectual center for Dante studies.[89]

Dante himself does not make an appearance in *Maciste all'inferno*, and the film is far from a faithful adaptation of the *Inferno*. Rather, it divides its time between this world and the underworld while harking back to the historical epics that populated the golden age of Italian cinema, with many allusions to *Cabiria*. Like the previous decade's films, it featured a cast of hundreds, elaborately constructed sets, and magnificent costumes. On a technical level the film marked the return of Segundo de Chomón, the special-effects wizard, to the series, and his representations of hell feature, among many other techniques, appearing and disappearing smoke and flames; desperately doomed flying souls on the Acheron River; a floating octopus representing the temptations of vice; flying dragons, including a spectacular aerial point-of-view shot; a screen within a screen so that hell's inhabitants can witness earth's happenings; and a decapitation and subsequent re-capitation of the many of hell's denizens who battle Maciste. The elaborately designed intertitles fluctuate between standard prose and hendecasyllabic verse, reconstructed from archival documents (plates 24–26).[90]

Billed as a *"Diavoleria in cinque atti di 'Fantasio'"* (A piece of mischief in five acts of Fantasio), the narrative quickly sets up Maciste as the natural enemy of the forces of the netherworld that consistently try to infiltrate it. Far from contemporary Italy – or even Sirdagna, for that matter – the film's first scene shows Maciste violently returning the evil spirits sent to corrupt the earthly paradise, described in the film's intertitles as "an oasis of Peace" (*un'oasi di Pace*), where animals, families, and vegetation happily coexist, and dense, bucolic foliage fills the mise-en-scène. With further echoes to the Garden of Eden and the original sin, Maciste is a gardener in love with his beatifically beautiful neighbor Graziella (Pauline Paulaire). The film's sets and costume evoke a nineteenth-century German Romanticism, linking it to the other guiding literary spirit over the text: Goethe's *Faust*.[91]

The film is rife with references not only to the above-mentioned *Cabiria,* with Maciste as the savior and protector of feminine innocence, here the wronged woman rather than the pure young girl.[92] It also travels beyond Italy's borders for its sources of inspiration. Barbariccia bears a strong resemblance to Robert Weine's Dr. Caligari, as does the technique of duplicity of identity. Another clear muse is Georges Méliès, even though de Chomón and the early French filmmaker were great rivals: the devils as they depart for earth appear jumping and infantile in a line, as did the wizards in *A Trip to the Moon* (1903), also a film about extraterrestrial exploration. Barbariccia's transformation into his Caligari-like earthly appearance employs the same tricks as Méliès's stop-motion editing.[93]

The film presents hell itself in political turmoil, with tension among its king, Pluto (Umberto Guarracino), and Gerion (Mario Saio), the prime minister of its "absolute" government. Barbariccia, portrayed by the noted Italian actor Franz Sala, who specialized in playing the villain, represents the political opposition. Elena Sangro returns to the Maciste series to play the femme fatale Proserpina, Pluto's wife, who along with his daughter, Luciferina (Lucia Zanussi), become rivals for Maciste's attention once he journeys to hell. How he finds himself there is through Barbariccia, whom Pluto sends to earth in search of souls to corrupt. Maciste quickly recognizes him for his real identity and refuses to make a Faustian pact with the devil (he even nominates Goethe's character in his rejection of temptation). Barbariccia instead sets his eyes on Graziella's chaste soul as he creates a violent storm in which Graziella is forced to give refuge to Giorgio, a stranger who mysteriously appears, thus compromising her moral purity. First pregnant and abandoned and then desperate after Barbariccia has made her young son disappear, Graziella remains pure and good throughout the film. Although not unique to representations of the fallen woman in Italian cinema, here the exaltation and beatification of mother and child, regardless of marital status, coincided with the regime's political agenda of procreation. Giorgio does ultimately return, but only after Maciste threatens him if he does not "do the right thing." After Proserpina thwarts Maciste's departure from the bowels of hell by kissing him, thus dooming him to eternal damnation, he is saved by the Christmas prayers of Graziella and Giorgio's son. The holy family – beatifically represented in bucolic, snow-covered splendor as church bells chime and humble denizens celebrate the birth of Christ (a setting that would be evoked later in *Il gigante delle Dolomiti*) – is ultimately blessed by an angel who signals the end of the allegorical tale.

Maciste's eventual confrontation with Barbariccia becomes a battle between, as the intertitles state, the former's "force" and the latter's "unlimited power" and leads the spectator to the most successful parts of the film: Maciste's struggles in hell. Maciste's feats of strength are reserved predominantly for his sojourn to the underworld, where his force is truly tested. Still dressed in his worldly garb, his otherworldly fate is to constantly do battle with the multitudes of lost souls and to defend the weak who are unjustly punished. His Achilles heel is sexual temptation: if he kisses a she-devil within three days of his permanence in hell, he is doomed to remain there, and Proserpina ultimately ensnares him in this trap. Thus this Maciste is a sexualized and desirous Maciste, not only in a pure and chaste way (he loves Graziella even after her dalliance with Giorgio) but also as one tempted by the flesh of females, who are clearly attracted to him as well. The sexualized gaze in hell is a reciprocal one; both Proserpina and Luciferina delight in their lustful voyeurism of Maciste's body and he in the scantily clad feminine souls who ogle him. The fact that Maciste's virility extends into the sexual realm reveals a Jekyll-and-Hyde side of his character: it is weakness that ultimately dooms him to eternal damnation.[94] Yet Maciste in hell is infinitely more powerful (and more interesting) than he is on earth. His strength is magnified a hundredfold, and in his costume he bears a marked resemblance to contemporary incarnations of Tarzan. His skin is darkened, iconographically assimilating him into hell's milieu and simultaneously recalling the character's origins in *Cabiria*. His torso is not completely naked, however, because Pagano was beginning to lose his youthful physique and needed more coverage of his growing stomach (fig. 6.8).

Nevertheless, his physical might is put to good use as a weapon to calm the insurrection, and once again Maciste finds himself in the position of defending a king and preserving the status quo.[95] Violence, increasingly present in the series (and no exception in this film), is necessary to quell the masses and gain popular support, but not without the

6.8. Maciste as condemned soul in *Maciste all'inferno* (1926).

crowd itself constituting a peril of its own. Civil war breaks out in hell as Barbariccia's forces battle for control against Pluto, and Maciste is able to quash the rebellion singlehandedly. As in *Maciste imperatore,* the masses are desperate and ripe for strong leadership, and the intertitles inform the reader, "And, as usual, the masses side with the strongest one." To cries of "Down with Barbariccia" and "Long live Maciste," Pluto's reign is secure and he grants Maciste his wish to return to earth.[96] But there is a fundamental difference between Maciste as leader in the two films: *Maciste all'inferno'*s damned souls are not as consistently supportive of

6.9. An illustration of Maciste in *Al Cinemà* 4, no. 13 (1925): 5.

Maciste the leader as is the crowd in *Maciste imperatore* – they fight back
and easily switch allegiances.

Although clearly not a propaganda film, *Maciste all'inferno,* like Fascism itself, turned to past glories to mythologize the present.[97] The film's
nationalism lies in its reliance on the historical epic, which, as I argued in
chapter 1, served to create an allegorical base on which to construct the
new Italian nation in early twentieth-century Italy. Maciste becomes a
sacred figure at the film's conclusion, bathed in light and welcomed back
to his earthly paradise as defender of the weak, the purveyor of justice,
and, like Dante and Mussolini, a sacralized symbol of the nation. In

the 1925 magazine *Al Cinemà,* an article promoting the film featured an illustration of Maciste that bears an incredible likeness to the Duce, a sketch based on the above-mentioned promotional postcard for *Maciste imperatore* (figs. 6.5 and 6.9).[98] This connection was destined to become more apparent with the 1926 Maciste films, the first to be produced under the totalitarian regime, in which Maciste engages with the enemy – this time not the devil, but the menacing, and often rebellious, colonial other.

ADVENTURES IN COLONIALISM: *MACISTE CONTRO LO SCEICCO* AND *MACISTE NELLA GABBIA DEI LEONI*

The post-1925 Maciste films were among the first Italian films to acknowledge the newly constituted totalitarian regime's imperialist ambitions in a colonial setting. It was a particularly brutal period for Italian colonialist enterprises. Mussolini and the Fascists expanded and consolidated their power in Somalia and Libya through the violent suppression of native uprisings. While arguably not "colonial films" in and of themselves, since they do not portray life in the Italian colonies, *Maciste contro lo sceicco* and *Maciste nella gabbia dei leoni,* both partially set in Africa, articulated a need for dominance over the exotic, colonial other against the backdrop of two very different genres: the pirate film and the circus film.[99] Richard Dyer has argued that the champion or "built body" within a colonial setting in the Tarzan, Hercules, and Rambo films "set the terms for looking at the naked white male body": "the built body in colonial adventures is a formula that speaks to the need for an affirmation of the white male body without the loss of legitimacy that is always risked by its exposure, while also replaying the notion that white men are distinguished above all by their spirit and enterprise."[100] Just as Mussolini must tame the colonies, Maciste must rid the literal and metaphoric colonies of corruption through violence, protect the purity of the white race, and save the innocent, even those racially othered, from the menacing forces of evil.[101]

These two films are not, however, the first films in the post-*Cabiria* series to deal with the racialized other. In *La trilogia di Maciste* the adorable Cioccolatino provides several scenes of comic tenderness, showcasing Maciste's frequent goodness and kindness toward children and offering a normalizing path of de-Orientalization. Things do not turn out so well in *Maciste imperatore:* the two young African men, also dressed in sailor suits, attempt to impede Maciste's rescue of the future prince Otis and subsequently receive a brutal beating. It is not Maciste but Saetta, rather, who doles out their sentence, at one point putting his foot on one of their faces and pulling the other out of the water by his hair. After their capture, Maciste takes pity on them, letting them loose with a warning never to get under his feet again. Moral goodness triumphs over racial superiority, but in the post-1925 films the two become fused into an equation of moral and racial superiority.

In *Italian Fascism's Empire Cinema*, Ruth Ben-Ghiat traces the history of colonial cinema back to the silent period, in which cinema relied on the representation of the primitive to affirm the modernity of the film apparatus. Early documentaries on the colonies in Italy by Luca Comerio demonstrate that they became a space where "older fantasies of movement and conquest came together with the new culture of violence made possible by changes in military technologies." Themes in Comerio's films of the 1910s and 1920s embrace many of the characteristics of what Ben-Ghiat terms "Italy's empire cinema": the camera as a weapon of war and imperialism, violence as a masculine rite, the ability of modern technologies to tame and vanquish nature, performance as a lens into the primitive, and the privileged position of the camera and cameraman in its representation. Films such as Mario Camerini's *Kif Tebbi* (1928) gained the most notoriety, but one can make the case, as Ben-Ghiat does, that these films belong to what Ella Shohat has called the "orientalist genre," which "revolve around fantasies of rescue and domination" in which the male protagonist saves the damsel in distress from the vicious othered male.[102]

Maciste contro lo sceicco was in fact billed as an "Orientalist adventure." It also in many ways echoes the pirate film, an increasingly popular genre at the time, to which the international success of Douglas Fairbanks's *The Black Pirate* (Albert Parker, 1926) would soon attest. There had already been two adaptations of Emilio Salgari's canonical novel *Il corsaro nero* (The Black Pirate, 1899), part of a cycle of pirate films that

Plate 3. Italian poster for *Maciste alpino* (1916) by Leopoldo Metlicovitz.

Plate 4. Films preserved at the Film Archive of the
Museo Nazionale del Cinema in Turin.

Plate 5. Nitrate negative reel of *Maciste alpino* (1916), with the evidence
of decayed emulsion visible in the bubbles formed on its coils.

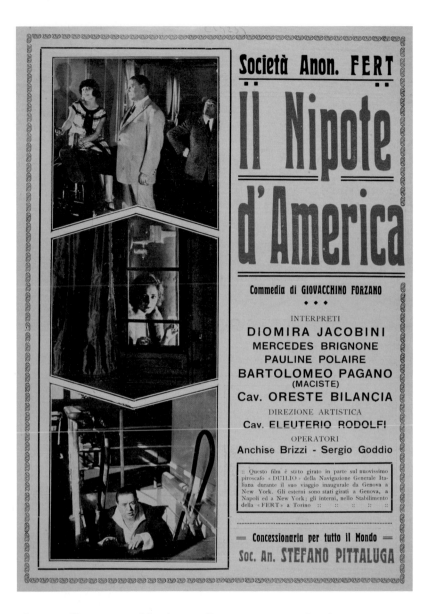

Plate 6. Publicity material for *Il nipote d'America,* now considered
lost. In such cases, extra-cinematic materials are the only
evidence left to reconstruct the film's plot and structure.

Plate 7. Frame from the Dutch nitrate copy of *Maciste* (1915), the basis for the film's restoration. The scene shows the double-coloration technique employed at the time, with stencils. The imperfect correspondence between the image's borders and the blocks of color was a common problem with this type of coloration. (Nitrate print from the EYE Film Institute, Netherlands.)

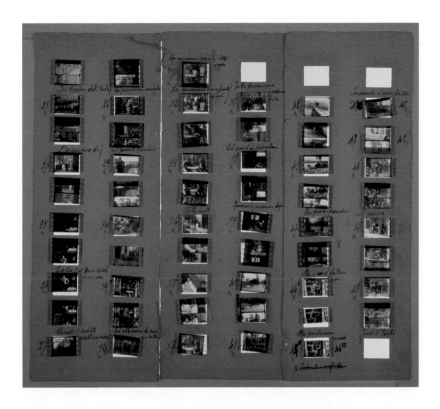

Plate 8. Color sampler from *Maciste* (1915): colored frames sewn onto perforated cardboard. The sampler served as evidence of the film's editing order at the time of the film's release. Visible on the frame are notes indicating the intertitles' positioning.

Plate 9. Maciste at attention in front of a high-ranking official who resembles King Vittorio Emanuele III; under his shoe lies the Austrian prisoner Fritz Pluffer. This publicity photo reproduces a sequence absent from the 2000 restoration of *Maciste alpino* (1916). The sequence was recently discovered and subsequently integrated into the 2014 restoration.

Plate 10. Maciste and a fellow soldier force the Austrian Fritz Pluffer to eat spaghetti. This publicity photo reproduces a sequence absent from the 2000 restoration of *Maciste alpino* (1916). The sequence was recently discovered and subsequently integrated into the 2014 restoration.

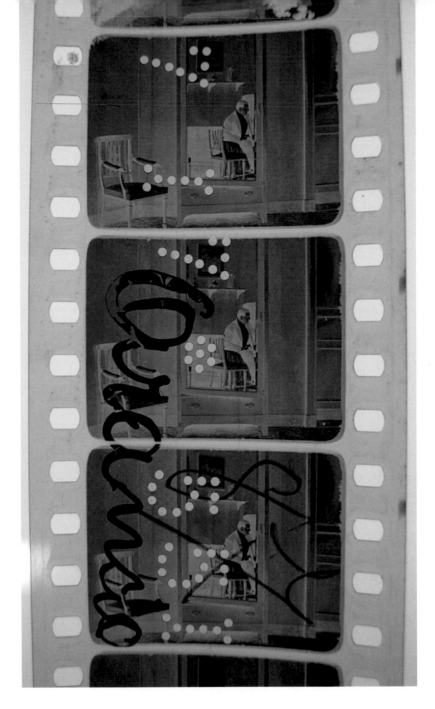

Plate 11. Section of the French negative of *Maciste innamorato,* one of the prints upon which the restoration was based. (Nitrate print from the Cinémathèque Française, Paris.) Punctured codes appear on the filmstrip. *"Arancio"* (orange) indicates coloration; the "X" indicates the positioning of the appropriate intertitle.

Plate 12. Maciste at the mirror in the restored copy of *Maciste innamorato* (1919). These frames were reintegrated into the restored print thanks to the nitrate negative housed in Paris.

Unione Cinematografica Italiana
✦ ROMA ✦

LA TRILOGIA
DI MACISTE

PRIMO EPISODIO

MACISTE CONTRO LA MORTE

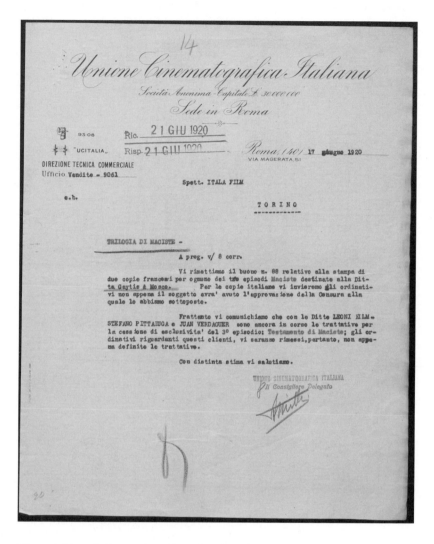

Plate 13. (*facing*) Cover of a publicity brochure for *Maciste contro la morte* (1920), the first episode of *La trilogia di Maciste* (1920).

Plate 14. A letter sent from the Unione Cinematografica Italiana to Itala Film dated 17 June 1920, which, among other things, references the French copy divided into episodes destined for the Gatys & Mosco Company. The film thus circulated in France with the prescribed divisions into three separate full-length films. The nitrate print at the root of the restoration, the version in which the three films were integrated into one full-length film, is thus a subsequent release.

Plate 17 and Plate 18. Comparison of the original intertitles from a film produced by FERT-Pittaluga (*Caporal Saetta*, nitrate print housed at the Fondazione Cineteca Italiana, Milan) and the electronic reproduction of the same graphic, used in the restoration of *Maciste imperatore* (1924).

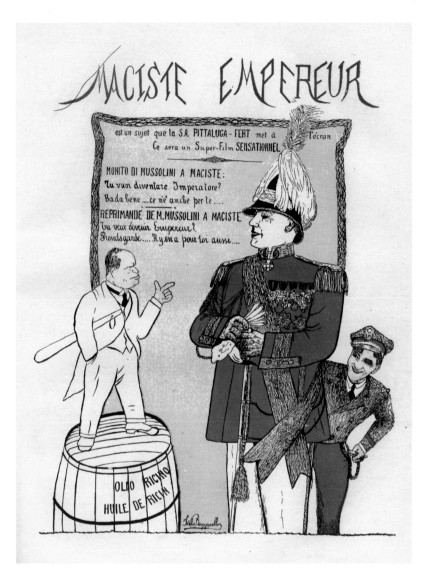

Plate 19. Satirical cartoon in which Benito Mussolini directs a vague threat to Maciste, who wears his imperial uniform from *Maciste imperatore* (1924). The cartoon appeared in *Films Pittaluga* 2, no. 15 (1924).

Plate 20. A still from *Maciste nella gabbia dei leoni* (1926).

"Datemi le forbici!"

PRODUZIONE

"PITTALUGA - FILM"

Plates 21a–f.
A series of frames from *Maciste nella gabbia dei leoni* (1926), with intertitles.

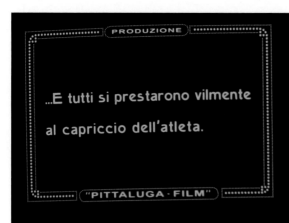

PRODUZIONE

...E tutti si prestarono vilmente

al capriccio dell'atleta.

"PITTALUGA · FILM"

Plate 22 and Plate 23. Frames reproduced from the restored copy of *Maciste contro lo sceicco* (1926). The difference in quality is evident in the grain and contrast. The first image (plate 22), which was printed on a duplicate negative from the previous restoration, is of good quality and has nice hues of gray, while the second (plate 23) was printed from the 16mm print owned by Bruno Boschetto, and has a stronger contrast that renders details in the darker areas indistiguishable.

Plates 24, 25, and 26. Intertitles from the 2009 restored copy of *Maciste all'inferno* (1926), reconstructed on the basis of the positive nitrate print, with Portuguese intertitles, housed in Brazil.

Caron dimonio con occhi di bragia,

il vecchio bianco per antico pelo,

nocchiero della livida palude.

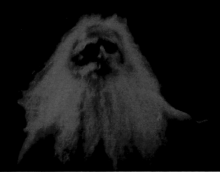

(PAULINE POLAIRE)

PITTALVGA FILM

Graziella, la dolce vicina

di Maciste.

(PAULINE POLAIRE)

PITTALVGA FILM

Rosa Films produced between 1921 and 1922, all directed by Vitale De Stefano – *Il corsaro nero* (1921); *Iolanda, la figlia del corsaro nero* (Iolanda, Son of the Black Pirate, 1920); and the two-part *Gli ultimi filibustieri* (The Last Prodigies, 1921 and 1922) – as well as Augusto Genina's very successful 1923 *Il corsaro* (The Pirate, Artisti Italiani Associati, 1923).[103]

Maciste contro lo sceicco is, like *Maciste all'inferno,* set in the nineteenth century, this time with Italy as a solid geographical point of reference. The film is clearly a period piece, featuring elegant costumes, horse-drawn carriages, and antimodern settings. The wealthy, young heiress Anna Del Fusaro is the subject of an arranged kidnapping by her greedy guardian uncle, the Count Lanni, to be sold to an Arab sheik so that Lanni and his lover, Marina, can live off her fortune. She is sent off on a ship to Africa with a circumspect captain/pirate, Ricon, under whom Maciste is employed. Although loyal to his commander, Maciste is clearly disapproving of this plan. When the captain takes ill, the ship's sailors, led by the second in command, Lopez, begin to mutiny and to harass Anna, who is at first defended, albeit weakly, by Pietro, an aristocratic political refugee in disguise, and then forcefully by Maciste, who takes both of them under his protection. While on the ship, Anna and Pietro begin a courtship. The sailors, however, capture Maciste and Pietro and deliver Anna to the sheik, Abd-El-Kar. Maciste and Pietro rescue her after a prolonged journey across the desert, a violent confrontation with the Arab and his men, and a suspenseful desert chase and battle sequence.

Mario Camerini was at the director's helm of *Maciste contro lo sceicco,* and he wrote the script as well. He had begun his film career assisting his cousin, the director Augusto Genina, as a scriptwriter and assistant director and began to direct on his own in the early 1920s, his first feature being *Jolly, clown da circo* (Jolly, Circus Clown, 1923). He worked frequently for Pittaluga's FERT Studios and SASP, directing such films as *La casa dei pulcini* (The House of Chicks, 1924), the last film starring the prematurely deceased and popular actor Amleto Novelli; *Voglio tradire mio marito!* (I Want to Cheat on My Husband, 1925), an Italian "version" of Cecil B. DeMille's *Why Change Your Wife* (1920); and the above-mentioned *Kif Tebbi. Rotaie* (Wheels, 1929) remains his fundamental and lasting contribution to this era, a film marked by its connection to the German *Kammerspiel* films as well as its innovative use of strategically placed sound effects and musical track.[104]

Maciste contro lo sceicco does in fact have a different feel from the other Pittaluga super-productions directed by Brignone. Its shooting locations feel distant and remote; the first intertitle, for instance, employs "in an isolated location . . ." as its "Once upon a time." There are many more shots of the landscape than in previous Maciste films, suggesting remoteness and distance from the historical present. The film begins with a montage of landscape pans and tilts of the Fusaros' castle, showcasing not only its isolation but also nature's physical brutality (the high, rocky cliffs and the tumultuous sea below it). Much of the action takes place in coastal settings and exotic locales, evoking borders and boundaries that are often the focus of imperialist discourse. When the ship finally arrives in Africa, a montage of views of the exotic and primitive coastline, much like early cinema's touristic *actualités,* sets the stage for what will be the sheik's Orientalist form of brutality.

The film's tone is much more serious than that of previous Maciste films, with few or no moments of comic relief. It is also a much more metaphorical film than previous entries. Shots of adorably innocent animals contrast with the nefarious ways of pirate life: a dog with newborn puppies becomes the bait that lures Anna into the room where the pirates trap her. Images of the innocent puppies, some sucking at the mother's teat, alternate with those of a screaming, desperate Anna as the ship departs. A black cat that had previously crossed Ricon and Maciste's path as a premonition against embarking on their crime later reappears as a menacing (and moralizing) reminder, superimposed on Ricon as he has a heart attack. A profound religious subtext of sin and redemption permeates the narrative when Ricon becomes ill and sees the error of his ways, ultimately sacrificing himself to save Anna. Plays on light and shadow, religious citations (St. John, for instance), and Catholic imagery pervade the film as well.[105]

Maciste in *Maciste contro lo sceicco* is pure strength and goodness, described as both a lion and a lamb, but he is lacking in the intelligence and irony that characterizes, albeit to a lesser extent, the character's other 1920s films. He seems more of a dolt, dependent and subservient

6.10. Anna being threatened by the sheik in *Maciste contro lo sceicco* (1926).

to Ricon, but, as in his other films, he enforces that others respect the institutional hierarchy on the ship and the captain's authority. For Steven Ricci, the film's first shots of Maciste – a close-up of his muscular forearms in action as they untangle an anchor – reference Pagano's off-screen working-class background and origins as a stevedore.[106] In contrast, the savage menace takes two forms in this film: the African pirate, who is among the ship's more nefarious passengers, and the eponymous sheik. The African is always shirtless, wears a turban, and smokes a long pipe, thus further signaling his alterity. The sheik, on the other hand, is clothed head-to-toe in feminized robes (fig. 6.10). Their major threat is not violence, as Maciste's strength and goodness will conquer all, but rather miscegenation, which is prefigured through the other's menacing gaze. When Anna is alone on the deck and cornered by the sailors, the film

6.11. Anna being threatened by the African in *Maciste contro lo sceicco* (1926).

presents the African as the greatest threat, despite the fact that Lopez has instigated the assault and is the first to touch her. Anna's naked calf is visible from under her skirt, shown in a fetishized close-up from the African sailor's point of view (fig. 6.11). As his hand reaches out to touch her, she violently kicks him away, but the danger is clear. Even clearer is the fact that the film constructs the second act as the more nefarious, not only because of the violent reaction that it provokes but also because it finally arouses the emasculated Pietro, who has remained immobile at a distance, to act in her defense.[107]

Pietro is an interesting character who does not immediately assimilate either into Maciste's masculine ethos or the pirate's lascivious ways. He spends most of his time reading, not working, on the ship, distancing himself from their sexual and criminal exploits. Nor does the narrative immediately establish why Pietro is on the ship; the film eventually reveals him to be a political refugee of nobility who had to escape

Marseilles on the first ship available. Before his intervention on behalf of Anna, the only clue as to his moral composition, aside from his race, is the scene in which he leads a Sunday sermon and prayer with the soldiers "once again"; and "with the reading of divine words, he reawakened devotion and goodness in those souls" as the sailors bow their heads in prayer. Notably absent among the participants is, of course, the African sailor, who laughingly and mockingly observes them, smoking his long (read foreign) pipe.

The sheik does not figure into the narrative until the film's second half, but in a flash-forward it sets up his threat to Anna's preestablished purity: when the count signs the agreement with Ricon to deliver Anna to the sheik, the film previews what will be several key scenes in Anna's capture and internment. The configuration of his compound, with its desert setting, tents, as well as his costume, acknowledges the most famous of Arab screen incarnations at the time: Rudolph Valentino, whose own *The Sheik* (George Melford, 1921) was released in Italy in 1924 to great acclaim. Like Maciste and Mussolini, as Giorgio Bertellini has argued, Valentino was a model of transatlantic Italianness and also, as I have written elsewhere, of Italian muscularity.[108] Although this sheik is decidedly lacking in good looks and sexual charisma – he is all villain – the editing in the attempted rape scene in the Italian films bears a striking, structural resemblance to that of the American film.[109] Valentino, however, had a problematic relationship with the Fascist government, especially after he renounced his Italian citizenship in 1925, and a nationalist reading of Maciste's triumph over the sheik betrays a superiority of the pure Latin Italian over the Americanized Latin (lover).

This superiority, in terms of the film's violence, finds expression not only in Maciste's usual weapon of choice – his fists and his strength – but also in guns and ammunition. As soon as they land in Africa, Maciste and Pietro wrestle arms and horses from two of the sheik's men and use them frequently in their efforts. The film also returns to the battlefield, but this time it is a colonialist setting. When Maciste, Pietro, and Anna flee, disguised as Arabs, they come across a European tent encampment. An epically staged battle begins between the Europeans and the natives, with, naturally, the Arabs in ultimate retreat and many men, including the sheik, mortally wounded. In this first film set in Africa, Maciste has begun to make the official passage from colonized, in *Cabiria*, to colonizer and recurring symbol of national and nationalist pride, one that he would complete in his next film.

In *Maciste nella gabbia dei leoni*, the hero returns to the site of origin for many of the strongman films: the circus (the film is subtitled *"Vita da Circo"* [Life in the Circus]). Written by Brignone as well under the pseudonym Ginn Bill, the film portrays Maciste as the lion tamer of the Karl Pommer circus. Pommer is a kind and benevolent man who is having heart problems and must leave the circus in the hands of his son Giorgio while he seeks a cure at the lakes. Meanwhile, the star attraction of the circus, the equestrian Sarah (Elena Sangro once again) conspires with Strasser (Franz Sala as well), the circus manager, to take over its reins by seducing Giorgio (Alberto Collo), who only has eyes for Sarah and not a mind for running the business. Maciste, in the meantime, is off hunting lionesses in Africa for his act while this sabotage plays out. During the excursion he saves the life of a young African woman named Seida, played by a blackfaced Mimy Dovia, who was only seventeen when she took on this role. She secretly follows him back to Italy, where, being the kind and gentle giant that he is, he takes her under his wing. Sullivan (Umberto Guarracino), a competing strongman in the circus, lustfully watches Seida, who, in defending herself from his subsequent sexual assault, scratches him. He then humiliates her by cutting her nails while the rest of the circus members cheer him on. Maciste arrives in time to save Seida from further harm and to deliver Sullivan a brutal punishment. Seida becomes Maciste's assistant as a lion tamer, and as she learns the ropes she falls in love with Giorgio. Eventually Pommer returns and gives Giorgio an ultimatum: he must choose either Sarah or the circus. He chooses Sarah, but then, thanks to Seida, discovers Sarah and Strasser's evil plan. Ultimately, Seida becomes a circus star, Giorgio abandons the femme fatale in favor of Seida, Sarah meets a violent death, and the police arrest Sullivan for various crimes, including attempting to sabotage the circus.

In this film the specific reference to the colonies occurs in the film's first act when Maciste is on his hunting expedition in search of lions. The natural scenery of Africa would become standard to the colonial film, and it is both tranquil and terrifying. The film's landscape shots, especially while Maciste is on the river with his cargo, set up the romanticization of the primitive, accompanied by intertitles evoking the "solemn poetry of that African sunset." When Seida follows him to Italy, he warns her that "you will enter into a world that could make you regret what you are abandoning," both elegizing the unsophisticated colony and bemoaning the fallen world of civilization. The colony is both a mesmerizing and menacing place, and the film clearly positions Maciste as commander of the savage animal and colonial wilderness, dressed in his safari best among the scantily clothed natives (fig. 6.12). Just as he captures the lioness with firepower and force, he rescues Seida from her would-be captors, firing and brandishing the machete, a movement he later replicates in the lion's cage at the circus.

This film also features compelling visual evidence of the synergistic relationship between Maciste and Mussolini. As Simonetta Falasca-Zamponi has shown, Mussolini became associated with lions and lion taming from early in his administration. In 1923 a circus owner offered him a cub as a gift, and for a time he kept it at his Roman domicile in Palazzo Tittoni, later donating it to a zoo. He named the cub Italia and continued to be photographed with her, at one point shown driving with her in a car. He was even featured on *Time* magazine's cover in July 1926, stroking her fur. For Falasca-Zamponi, the association of Mussolini with the wild beast "initiated the vogue of Mussolini as tamer."[110]

Like the lion tamer, Maciste restores order throughout the film after various insurrections. Pommer's circus, with its connotations of difference and otherness, becomes a stand-in, as do the lions themselves, for Italy's colonial territories. The circus itself is a spectacular setting, with connotations of difference and alterity, power struggles between management and the workers, potential insurrections, and unruly crowds that must consistently be tamed by the proper forces. It is also highly sexualized, with the female body on constant display as showcased in multiple shots of women in various states of dress and undress and Sullivan's attempts to rape Seida. As the moral compass of the circus and as physical enforcer in opposition to Strasser and Sullivan, Maciste is the good, gentle "animal tamer," who is more than willing and able to crack the whip, literally and figuratively, to keep the natives in line. The film enables this geographic displacement, as does *Maciste contro lo sceicco,*

6.12. Maciste and his gun in *Maciste nella gabbia dei leoni* (1926).

6.13. Maciste and Seida in *Maciste nella gabbia dei leoni* (1926).

through the strategic use of African signs in the form of geography and racial types. The circus itself is a multiracial configuration, with Africans performing various subservient functions, such as accompanying the camels and donkeys, marching in the city streets to promote Sarah's feats, and acting as servants to Pommer and Maciste.

The racialized character of Seida, however, reveals how fears of miscegenation in the colonial world are a one-way street (fig. 6.13). A supremely sympathetic character, much like Maciste himself was as a slave in *Cabiria* (and with a clear acknowledgment of that fact), she engages audience empathy through her childlike innocence as well as her spunk and resilience. Much as Sullivan is the anti-Maciste, she is the anti-Sarah. Clearly enamored of Giorgio from the first moment she lays eyes on him, the film ultimately allows for him to choose the right woman despite her racial otherness. This pattern of a darkened Italian actress playing the racialized female love interest would continue in such colonial films as Brignone's subsequent *Sotto la croce del Sud* and *Jungla nera/l'esclave blanc* (The Black Jungle, 1936), directed by Jean-Paul Paulin.[111] In *Maciste nella gabbia dei leoni,* Seida provides a model for the civilizing of the savage, gradually becoming domesticated into a proper Western woman, as evidenced in her change of costume from dirty, barely clothed savage to sophisticated, Westernized dress when she is coupled with Giorgio at the film's end. [112]

Continuing the pattern of the FERT films, the violence in *Maciste nella gabbia dei leoni* is highly pronounced, takes place in multiple settings, and once again involves a potentially menacing mob. In the series' passage from *Maciste imperatore's* benevolent crowd, whom the leader must win over and serve, the masses in *Maciste nella gabbia dei leoni* are to be feared and distrusted. At the film's end, Sullivan lets loose an untamed lioness as the grand circus performance is under way. A panicked escape from the theater ensues, resulting in dismemberment and death, and victims are later shown as lifeless corpses being loaded into awaiting cars. Sarah meets a particularly brutal and violent death when she is jostled and trampled to death by the crowd. Just as in *Maciste imperatore* the protagonist had a double and evil foil as a negative model of leadership (Stanos), in this film he has an equally nefarious doppelganger, Sullivan. Guarracino, who played King Pluto in *Maciste all'inferno,* gained success as the monster in *Il mostro di Frankenstein* (Frankenstein's Monster, Albertini Film, 1920), starring the strongman Luciano Albertini as Frankenstein. Like other strongmen, Guarracino transferred to the German film industry, where, commencing in 1921, he was billed as "Cimaste," a play on and an acknowledgment of the German reputation of Maciste. Bald, toothless, and hairy, he represents, in Stella Dagna's view, the anti-Maciste, a possible Mr. Hyde to Maciste's Dr. Jekyll.[113] There are two standoffs between the characters, each with

6.14. Sullivan and Maciste in *Maciste nella gabbia dei leoni* (1926).

their chests puffed out and arms on hips, much like the iconic pose Mussolini would assume in many photographs and films (fig. 6.14). The film neatly delineates not only between good and evil but also between good and evil muscularity, violence, and force. Maciste's pummeling of Sullivan after he has sadistically cut off Seida's nails is particularly graphic (plates 21a–f), with repeated blows to his bloody face. It also shows that the fickle and brutal crowd, like in *Maciste all'inferno*, will follow the strongest; at first they cheer on Sullivan as he maims Seida, and then Maciste as he gives Sullivan his just due.[114]

Promotional materials and contemporary film reviews for all three of the 1926 films under examination in this chapter were quick to draw on their potential as national products promoting what they saw as a newly revitalized Italian film industry. In terms of promotional strategies, Pittaluga marketed them to a wide audience. For *Maciste nella gabbia dei leoni*, Pittaluga-Films' *Rassegna di programmazioni* included every possible genre in its exhortation to distributors: "This subject has all the characteristics of refinement, of fascination, of sentimental, dramatic and adventurous attraction."[115] For *Maciste contro lo sceicco*, however, the brochures advertising the film were more specific in the film's significance and appeal as a colonial film. The copy for one brochure reads, "A dramatic, adventurous plot whose beginning in Italy moves further and further away, orienting itself first to the sea and toward the land of Africa.... The characteristics of Arab life, picturesque horseback, phantasmagoric warlike uproars and very lively flights across the boundless desert."[116] A "delight and a lesson at the same time," said one reviewer in Bologna.[117] The films were, in fact, enormous national and international successes and were embraced as national productions that provided hope for the sagging Italian film industry. In America, Universal's Thrill Picture Company acquired *Maciste nella gabbia dei leoni*, redubbed it *The Hero of the Circus*, and released the film in 1928 to great acclaim.[118]

Many Italian reviews echoed the comments made about *Cabiria*, other historical epics, and Maciste/Pagano a decade earlier. In a review of *Maciste all'inferno*, one journalist opined: "As an exceptional artist with natural gifts and a love of art, Maciste honors, in Italy and elsewhere, our Cinema and our Country."[119] Reviews of that film after its premiere at the 1924 Milan Fair in the Milanese press were equally effusive on nationalist grounds. "*Maciste all'Inferno* constitutes one of the greatest achievements that Italian Cinema has produced in recent years," wrote the newspaper critic of *L'Ambrosiano*. Similarly, the periodical *Il Secolo* exclaimed, "It is consoling to see that, in a period of severe crisis in our film industry, one Italian studio can create, with exclusively Italian capital and Italian components, such a complete masterpiece."[120] The same was said of *Maciste contro lo sceicco:* "Unquestionably an air of renewal blows through our national production!"[121]

For one critic, however, Maciste had morphed into something beyond the national: "Maciste, the strong and gentle Italian giant, courageous and generous, is a 'type' of international cinema, such as he is able to conquer the public's greatest favor." Thus Maciste had come full circle from *Cabiria*. He had transformed from a *tipo*, a specimen, a symbol of racial and national masculinity, to an international type and star in his own right. Part of this shift owed itself to Pittaluga-Films' intense marketing and distribution of the films simultaneously in different European territories. At the same time, it indicates how Maciste singlehandedly attempted to rescue and redeem the Italian film industry in the 1920s from ruin, although that stay was, unfortunately, only temporary.

*   *   *

In the unpacking of the often-cited Maciste/Mussolini relationship, what comes to the fore is a convergence of visual and political culture, mass media and ideology, and masculinity and national identity. The multiple roles that Mussolini assumed both on and off the screen (father, aviator, soldier, leader, for example), complete with costume changes, constituted its own form of serial, with Mussolini as the star whose heroic gestures ultimately expressed a desire for and the institution of order and authority. Their physical differences notwithstanding – Pagano was much taller (parodied in the cartoon), and in much better health, than the somewhat diminutive Mussolini – they both occupied a similar space in contemporary Italian culture, as icons of 1920s Italian masculinity.

The bodies of the strongman and the Duce collide as the representation of the white, muscled, and virile body assumes an ideological positioning that aligns it with gendered ideological imperatives. What the representations of Maciste and Mussolini on film and in still photography share is a common referent to Ancient Rome; a connection to the masses and the crowd; and the showcasing of the active, athletic male body as a symbol of virility and national pride. The bodies of both the Duce and the film star functioned as national symbols of regeneration, constituting an avenue of continuity as opposed to rupture, one that, in the Italian context, spanned two centuries of representation, from visual culture to the plastic arts and, ultimately, in the persona of Maciste, the cinema.

Conclusion

IN ITS LAST FILM, *IL GIGANTE DELLE DOLOMITI,* THE MACISTE series returns to its roots, heading back to the snowcapped peaks of *Maciste alpino* with a bucolic yet modernized tale of espionage and intrigue. Echoes of that earlier film begin from its opening shots of the majestic mountainous landscape and a low-angle shot of Maciste, complete with pipe and smile, as he blends into the rugged background. What immediately comes to the fore is a fusion between Germanic and Italian culture that was typical of the Tyrol region. Italy had regained the southern Tyrol territory after World War I, and the film is in many ways a celebration of that irredentist victory. As one promotional article states, "From the Dolomites' high peaks, haloed in glory from the Italian army's most recent victories." The "giant" in the title is a play on words: it can refer to Maciste himself or to the "passo del Gigante," which was the treacherous mountain pass that separates the southern and northern Tyrol regions.

In this film Maciste lives at the Three Crosses Pass in the Dolomites, found today in the Ampezzo Dolomites Natural Park, near Cortina d'Ampezzo. An alpine guide by profession, he is guardian to his nephew Hans (Aldo Morus), the "joy of his life" (fig. C.1). In the same area resides Riccardo Ewert, an engineer whose recent discoveries and experiments in aviation have the potential to result in major gains for the nation's air force. He is the object of affection of the English artist Maud Faie (Dolly Grey), who also takes care of Maciste and Hans. Standing in her way is the seductive Vanna Dardes (Elena Lunda), who, with Giorgio Muller (Luigi Serventi), is conspiring to steal Riccardo's technical plans. Vanna sets her lustful eyes on Riccardo while Giorgio aggressively pursues a

C.1. Maciste and Hans in *Il gigante delle Dolomiti* (1926).

C.2. Maciste and Hans in *Il gigante delle Dolomiti* (1926).

very reluctant Maud. Although the authorities are following the suspicious couple, it takes Maciste in the end to foil their nefarious plot to steal the aeronautical documents. His collaborator on righting the wrongs is Freddy Humbert (Augusto Poggioli), who like, Maciste, has personal reasons to seek revenge: he was married to and abandoned by Vanna Dardes, also known as Hannah Humbert. Although the film allows Maciste to confront the film's and the character's antagonist, Giorgio, and justice enables the correct coupling (Riccardo/Maud), it is God, rather than Maciste, who doles out punishment as he creates a storm that ultimately dooms the villains' escape.

The film highlights the native alpine sport movement as well as Italy's increasing status as a tourist destination. Abundant shots feature happy, healthy men and women skiing by day and socializing by night in the elegant splendor of the mountain resort. Guests partake in local culture not only through skiing but also through typical local dance. One scene features Maciste and his compatriots, at the annual party for the alpine guides, dancing "La Tirolese" (the local dance) in traditional costume. *Il gigante delle Dolomiti* bears a resemblance to the German genre of the mountain film (*Bergfilm*), whose influence was already apparent during Maciste's voyage to hell. In terms of its editing and structure the film is more advanced than others of the series; it has much smoother transitions between the shots and a more complex parallel editing structure, although the plot remains traditionally torn between right and wrong, good and evil, and morality and corruption. Like *Maciste all'inferno*, the film is replete with Catholic imagery, from its initial shots of snow-covered crosses to the initials "K.M.B." that adorn Maciste's front door, meaning *Christus/Kristus mansionem benedicat*, or Christ Bless this house. *Il gigante* bears an additional similarity to that earlier film with Maciste's sidekick, his adorable nephew. Once again Maciste is in a paternal role without paternity, although he is related by blood to the adorable young tyke.

The film also sets the stage for future feature film production during the Fascist period in that it clearly delineates between the good, virtuous woman (Maud) and the evil temptress (Vanna/Hannah). Maciste uses his might to protect feminine virtue, although Maud is far from helpless, reminiscent of the series' first film heroine in *Maciste*. Haunting the backstory as well is another maternal angel, Maciste's sister and young Hans's mother, who had died of "pain and shame" when abandoned by the man who had deceived and betrayed her (none other than Giorgio Muller). Similarly, the film employs the Fascist "*voi*" for formal, second-person address instead of the traditional "*lei*" in the intertitles.

The omission of Maciste's name from the title, the only one in the series in which it does not appear, resonates in the film's structure; what is strikingly different about the film is just how superfluous Maciste is to the narrative. Consistency of character remains – the intertitles refer to him as "A courageous guide, strong like a lion, gentle and good like a

little boy" – but he has very little actual screen time. Most of his acts of
bravery do not occur until the film's second half, when he rescues Maud
from Giorgio's sexually predatory advances by digging her out of her
snow-trapped home with his bare hands and fends off a pack of wolves
who threaten to devour her. Despite his consistent good humor, Maciste's feats of strength in this film do not bear his traditional humoristic
imprint, although he does hang one character by the seat of his pants
in an echo of his wartime alpine adventure. In the end, only God, not
Maciste, can render justice, and God does punish those who are guilty
of wrongdoing (Giorgio and his sidekick, Schultz), on the giant's pass.
Despite the deus ex machina rendering of justice, more earthly and more
modern means of combat emerge in the film. Guns are the weapon of
choice for all but Maciste, and much of the plot revolves around sur-
veillance: Maud learns of Vanna's plans when she spies her through a
window. The hotel bellman provides comic relief throughout the film as
he observes the guests' comings and goings.

As a summa of his previous films, however, *Il gigante delle Dolomiti*
retains the consistent connection between male stardom and Italian
nationalism as the embodiment of heroic masculinity passed from the
historical epic in *Cabiria* to the iconographically ubiquitous political
persona of Benito Mussolini. Maciste became the model Italian to lead
the relatively young nation by heroic and entertaining example, and in
this film this metonymic relationship between character and landscape
reifies that bond. The various discourses of nationalism and stardom
coalesced in the figure of the masculine, in particular the chiseled hero
who came to embody the new Italian nation through muscular might.
No cinematic figure would better epitomize this convergence of Italian
vigor, virility and vitality than Maciste. As symbol of the nation, Maciste
restored and maintained the status quo, even as that status quo shifted
from pre – World War I nationalism, to postwar reconstruction, to Fascist consolidation. The Maciste films used the mechanisms of stardom
and film genre to create a popular icon who, through his goodwill and
humor, charmed his way to the top of the box-office charts and into the
Italian popular imaginary.

Maciste's influence, however, does not end in 1926. Pagano himself made three additional films after the demise of the Maciste series:

Il vetturale di Montecisio (The Coachman from Montecisio, 1927), *Gli ultimi zar* (The Last Czars, 1928), and *Giuditta e Oloferne* (Judith and Holofernes, 1928), all produced by the Società Anonima Stefano Pittaluga and directed by Baldassarre Negroni. Although the character is not present, the connection between Maciste and Pagano remained so strong that publicity materials consistently referenced Maciste, either in parenthesis next to Pagano's name or within the film intertitle itself. But even with the demise of the character, the series' films were redistributed throughout the 1920s and later, in the 1930s and 1940s, with added sound. Maciste was later reborn in the sword-and-sandal peplum films of the 1960s, and the legend continues in Italian fiction – Lorenzo Beccati's *Il barbiere di Maciste* (Maciste's Barber, 2002), Roberto Bolaño's *Una novelita lumpen* (*A Little Lumpen Novelita*, 2002, translated into English in 2014), and in children's literature – *Il galletto Maciste* by Anna Sarfatti (Maciste the Rooster, 2004).

Maciste's impact has the potential to live on in what is hoped will be the eventual rediscovery of new prints, archival sources, and, most importantly, film restoration. As the following interventions in the appendix detail, film restoration is in itself an ongoing, serialized process that in turn opens up future avenues of exploration for film scholars and thus for film audiences all over the world at museums, festivals, and online. The possibilities, while not endless, exist, and I anticipate that this study is only the beginning of a long journey, one that combines film studies, film restoration, and film exhibition in a symbiotic synergy for future generations.

Appendix

CLAUDIA GIANETTO *&* STELLA DAGNA
Museo Nazionale del Cinema, Turin, Italy

Translated by Maria Elena D'Amelio

The Restoration of the Maciste Series

Cabiria was an enormous success, and it is clear that the character most beloved by the audience was Maciste, due to the particular characteristics that the author imbued in him, for the special dramatic situations in which the author placed him, and also for Pagano's effective performance.

In order to exploit that success Itala Film decided to produce a series of action films called "Maciste," in which it developed the daring and humorous adventures of the good-hearted strongman with solid muscles and valiant heart – either as policeman, athlete, alpine soldier, or other personifications – who represented, in the most varied times and places, the same, typical figure of the super-strongman in service to just and generous causes.[1]

RESTORATION: WHAT WE DON'T KNOW

The history of cinema is also and especially the history of films. It is a story made from stories, since films themselves are not abstract ideas but material works from a tangible, variable, reproducible base, which are born, altered, and nonetheless eventually destined to disappear. Briefly, the history of cinema is also the material history of the actual print (in film for the first one hundred years of production, but also in video and digital formats today). Often it is the responsibility of the restorers and archivists, who work in the shadows, so to speak, to create the necessary conditions so that scholars and film lovers alike can see the films that make up the history of the so-called seventh art.

Restoring a film means giving it back to the public but also, to varying degrees depending on the circumstances, making choices that will dramatically affect the way spectators view it. For this reason we believe it is essential that the practices of film restoration do not remain the sole prerogative of film specialists. Knowing what you are looking at is useful for all types of audiences, but for those whom cinema is an object of study that awareness is especially crucial. As a commercial practice, to present a "restored" film often means to exploit a kind of brand, an indicator that would want to guarantee the best possible visual quality. More often than not, however, details of the restoration process are not proffered to the public, on the assumption that it is unnecessary for the uninitiated to engage with a specialized area that is often considered too complex and too boring. The result in these cases is that the viewer takes a leap of faith and assumes that the restorers always know the best procedures necessary to achieve maximum results in returning movies to their "original splendor." It would certainly be nice if that were really the case. Looking at things a little closer, however, it is easy to see that a mastery of technique does not guarantee absolute certainty in the restoration process and that you can get very close to the film's "original splendor" without ever being able to completely fill in those gaps created over time.[2]

Familiarizing the reader with the general restoration process permits access to a wealth of valuable information: Was that color or that light native to the print, or are they effects of modern reprinting technologies? Was a specific intertitle's interesting hint about contemporary womanhood present in the original, or is it the result of a translation from a foreign print? Was the script really lacking a coherent plot, or is the print incomplete and therefore missing long sections that could clarify some obscure points? Acquainting oneself with the concepts of "print," "preservation," and "reconstruction" can offer additional opportunities to understand the history, style, and message of a film. The political subtext of *Maciste all'inferno,* for instance, was not as pronounced in circulating prints that had different intertitles than those that appeared in the original (see the section on *Maciste all'inferno* in part 2 of the appendix). Similarly, the plot of the recently restored *La trilogia di Maciste* appears illogical, but judging by contemporary reviews, the screenplay was not coherent even in 1920 upon the film's original release. Yet the only print known today, used as the master of the recent restoration process, had been reduced to about half of its original total length for a subsequent French re-edition. This reduction certainly contributed in making an already complex plot even more confusing. And so on.[3]

Film restoration, often based on philological assumptions as well as the mediation between the original material's physical condition and the use of new technologies, does have its rules and its fixed theoretical points. One of the main objectives of this essay and of the "In Focus" section of this appendix is to invite scholars and film lovers to venture into the practice and theory of this process by asking themselves this question as they watch their beloved films: "What am I really watching?" Thus it is important that these contributions appear at the end of a volume that, while extremely well documented from a historical perspective, also analyzes films from a social and anthropological standpoint. For these reasons the dialogue between the field of cultural studies and the philology of restoration that takes place in this volume is a necessary one, and one that should occur in the shadow of Maciste, the most well-known giant of silent cinema.

The character of Maciste, played by Bartolomeo Pagano, had such an important impact on popular cinema and its audience that there is no doubt he deserves the special commitment we dedicated between 2006 and 2011 to the recovery of his films. At the Museo Nazionale del Cinema we worked in collaboration with the Cineteca di Bologna and the Immagine Ritrovata laboratory on the retrieval and restoration of all the extant Italian titles in the Maciste series. It was a long and complex project with its own history and philosophy that this essay now presents in detail. If sometimes nonspecialists underestimate the impact of film preservation and restoration practices, it is equally true that collecting data and specific information on these topics often can be an odyssey or at least a difficult and frustrating search. Publishing accounts of film restoration is not systematic; there is not a standard descriptive form for this process; and the belief that it is preferable to separate film restoration from film analysis instead of working from an interdisciplinary perspective does not contribute to the opening of spaces for public debate.[4] Perhaps an experiment such as this one – that is, the inclusion of an appendix dedicated to film restoration in a volume of film history and textual analysis – will set a small precedent that contributes to the demolition of the barriers that still divide historians and restorers, as well as laboratory technicians and semioticians. We are convinced that this process of breaking down disciplinary walls will bring mutual satisfaction and unexpected results to all parties involved.[5]

CABIRIA: A CERTAIN IDEA OF THE "EXCEPTIONAL"

It all started with Cabiria (plate 1). It was in that movie that Maciste appeared on screen for the first time, stealing the show from better-known actors and quickly conquering the audience. As is well known, after that success, Cabiria's director/producer, Giovanni Pastrone, decided to dedicate a spin-off to the African freedman Maciste, who, in reality was neither a freedman nor an African and would become the hero of one of the longest and most successful film series of Italian silent cinema.

Nearly a century later the story in a certain sense repeated itself. In 2006 the Museo Nazionale del Cinema (MNC) restored both the silent (1914) and the sound versions (1931) of Cabiria. This was one of the most challenging restorations in the history of the museum for its exceptional, daunting commitment and high profile.[6] Cabiria's restoration accelerated the recuperative program of the restoration of Turin's silent film patrimony that was already under way at the museum, and it contributed to individuating Pagano's Maciste films as a priority. It is no coincidence that the restoration of Maciste (1915), the first film of the series, was screened only a few months after the public presentation of the restored version of Cabiria.

From Cabiria to Maciste, then, the passage appears brief. In fact, it is not. It involved going from a film production of high cultural aspirations to a popular one and from a restoration event to a multiyear continuative preservation project.

We have referred to Cabiria and its restoration as an "exceptional" event. There are very few films for which this adjective is so pertinent. At the time of its release, absolutely everything in Cabiria was out of the norm: the mise-en-scène, the directing, the budget, the publicity campaign, its spectacularity, and its technical innovations (plate 2). The scientific and financial work required in the film's restoration was similarly exceptional. Even the time and place of the restored version's screening was unusual: it was held during the winter Olympics hosted by the city of Turin, which wanted to reinforce its role as a cultural destination in a postindustrial age.

Compared to this "film-monstrum" and its extraordinary restoration, the *Maciste* series is exceptional for distinct yet complementary reasons: the longevity of the series, its flexibility and adaptation, its capacity to win over a wider audience, and its influence on sound films decades later. At the same time, the exceptionality of the restoration rests in the continuity, conventions, and recognition of the cultural validity of popular cinema, as well as the privileged status that allows restorers the time to specialize in an entire corpus of films.

This exceptionality has the power to amaze, allure, and even fascinate, and yet if we are talking about the restoration and safeguarding of cultural heritage, it can also contain some risks, especially if the exceptionality is evoked too frequently and lightly. We often hear that it is essential to invest resources in projects that ensure great media visibility in order to attract a potential wide audience of nonspecialists and private funds. One must always remember, however, that artistic and cultural patrimony requires substantial investment and commitment aimed at the entire collection as opposed to individual films. In addition, the scientific approach to restoration needs to be independent from political and financial pressure. Without this continuous commitment, in a few years we might end up without any material to valorize.

In the case of *Cabiria*, the "event" of the restored film's first public presentation was the natural outcome of many years of research, study, and cataloguing of materials dedicated to Turin's silent film production. During the silent era Turin was the capital of filmmaking, a cinematic city par excellence, with – and perhaps even more so than – Rome. It is not by chance that the MNC's most precious archival collections are those that are dedicated to this golden age. In 2006, therefore, the museum decided to restore Pastrone's film not only because of its fame but also because this choice was consistent with the museum's history and its collections.[7] The fact that the restored *Cabiria*'s first screening took on the form of an important film premiere was clearly very positive, as was the fact that the popular magazines and newspapers that dedicated their pages to it brought attention to silent film culture.[8] This visibility was a means of spreading film culture, not an end in and of itself.

In our opinion the exceptional event in the film restoration and conservation world makes sense only if it is the culminating moment of a continuous project. In the case of *Cabiria*, the valorization of Turin's silent film tradition and the cataloguing and analysis of the collections should extend toward the future, taking advantage of the opportunity to reach a wide audience to create the best conditions for the restoration and preservation of films of even less spectacular appeal.

A SERIAL RESTORATION

When we began the restoration of *Maciste*, we did not immediately think about restoring the entire series.[9] Simply the film was important, closely linked to Pastrone's colossal *Cabiria*, and the Dutch Film Museum, now called the EYE Film Institute Netherlands, had a good color nitrate print. *Maciste*'s restoration seemed a logical and natural choice. When completed, the film's pace, quality, and freshness were a surprise even to those who had already seen the terrible black-and-white print that circulated prior to the restoration. At the time of the film's initial release, the character of Maciste, even in modern clothing, was at the height of his fame, so we decided to verify how many and which other prints of Maciste films remained in the world. In the museum's collection we had only the mediocre reprint of the first *Maciste* and the nitrate print of the film *Maciste alpino*, which already had been restored in 2000.

The search was successful. Various archives across the world had Maciste films never before seen in recent years because they were printed on the era's flammable film stock and thus unable to be screened.[10] Thus was born the idea for a long-term project about the restoration of all the Italian productions in which Bartolomeo Pagano played the part of the heroic strongman par excellence. It may be called a "serial restoration," with the goal of preserving all the existing films in the Maciste series with the best technical tools available.

This commitment required a good dose of bravery, considering the amount of time and resources that would have been, and in fact were, necessary. It became one of the main restoration projects of the MNC for the next five years.[11] This modus operandi produced enviable working conditions, allowing the restoration staff to devote attention to the historical and archival materials as well as the analysis of the film materials so that we were able to gradually yet steadily improve our knowledge of the entire series, as if year after year each film added a piece to the fresco to slowly render it clearer and more visible.

At first, however, came the choice of what exactly to restore. If we accept the idea that film archives and restorers contribute to writing film history by creating the material conditions for the films of the past to be visible again, it is clear how such decisions must be considered strategic. The belief that everything can be preserved and that the archives should not in any way be selective is – in the majority of cases – purely utopian. Restoration and preservation require substantial resources and often just enough to ensure the conservation of existing collections. Unfortunately, choice is necessary. But based on what criteria?

The avenues of research opened up by *Cabiria* were numerous: we could select the historical films, Itala Film's productions, and the films inspired by Gabriele D'Annunzio, just to name a few. Why focus just on Maciste? The reasons were basically two. The first, which we have already mentioned, was the historical, social, and cinematographic relevance of the series and its relation to the collections that were already housed at the museum. The second reason, perhaps less acknowledged, was that the Maciste films needed to be restored.

Many historians and scholars have investigated the phenomenon of the strongman in Italian silent cinema.[12] Nevertheless, they had to rely on a limited availability of accessible prints. However brilliant, their research was based more on extra-cinematic material than the actual films, which were often visible only on damaged or incomplete prints. Before our project, only three Maciste films had been restored: our print of *Maciste alpino*, and *Maciste contro lo sceicco* and *Maciste all'inferno*, both at the Cineteca di Bologna.[13] There existed only incomplete black-and-white prints of *Maciste* and *Maciste in vacanza*, with missing sequences and translated intertitles, and for present-day audiences it might be difficult to understand why these films were so successful when they were released. Of the other titles, we were faced with only ghosts and fragments of the original images.

To this date, in addition to *Cabiria* there are twelve restored Maciste films available (counting separately the three episodes of *La trilogia di Maciste*), ten of which have been restored by the MNC and in the Cineteca di Bologna between 2006 and 2010.[14] These are all Italian productions, more than half of the total filmography. The results of this multiyear restoration project are also important because, as we shall see, it was a technically demanding effort, which included looking for available material, the reintegration of the Italian intertitles, the collation of different prints, and complex laboratory work.

To be able to restore half of the films of the series might not seem like much, but if one considers that the estimated percentage of extant silent films is only approximately 20 percent of the total output, with the Maciste series the ratio of restored films to unrestored films is clearly above average.[15] The preservation of motion pictures is not something that should be taken for granted. This is another of those discussions that should merit greater debate outside of this small circle of specialists: that films survive over time is in the interest of anyone who loves cinema. To think that today the problem is solved by new technologies is highly naive. Conversely, because of the ephemeral nature of digital technologies, it is likely that the percentage of images produced today and still viewable a hundred years from now will be far less than 20 percent.[16] Perhaps, as Paolo Cherchi Usai writes, we are not yet sufficiently aware that film history is primarily the story of film destruction.[17]

BEYOND THE MASTERPIECES

Reflecting on the criteria for selecting films for restoration, it would be natural to think that films considered to be masterpieces – that is, the era's best and most successful films – should be saved first. Which begs the question, are (all) the Maciste films masterpieces?

This seemingly reasonable question is in reality based on a weak premise. Before answering it we must interrogate the notion of the "masterpiece" itself. It is not so easy to decide which films fall into this category. Experience teaches us that tastes change over time, so movies ignored for years are all of a sudden rediscovered as classics, and titles that at one point were considered essential have been forgotten. Value judgments may change, and, lest we forget, the canon is built on what is in a condition to be discovered. Just think how easy it is to discover great unknown films if you venture into marginal national filmographies. The second yet equally important objection to the criterion of the "masterpiece" is which films are considered part of a country's cultural heritage. The question to ask is if only those of high art and high quality deserve to be preserved, or whether popular cinema, which is often a better indicator of the taste of a historical period and reaches a wider audience, also merits this fate.

Of course, no one denies that films recognized as cinematic milestones should be prioritized. However, our idea is that the history of cinema is built not only by jumping from one artistic peak to another but also by trying to explore the valleys of popular and middle-brow productions. From this perspective, the serial nature of the Maciste restoration project allowed us to see how the best movies of their time are always in a dialogue with contemporary popular production. The project's objective was recuperative: to best restore all the films available, independent of critical judgment of their cinematic value. In our opinion, two out of the ten Maciste films are worthy to be considered classics, for their stylistic rigor and effectiveness of expression: *Maciste alpino* (plate 3) and *Maciste all'inferno,* both restored, perhaps not coincidentally, before 2006. The remaining titles are mostly good films, with some parts better than others. In a few cases Pagano's charisma and acting cannot even save them.

Maciste imperatore, for example, even though it contains a few spectacular images and a discreet mise-en-scène, is slowly paced, has a confusing screenplay, and, above all, features uninspiring characters. Considering the film only through aesthetic criteria, one might ask whether the time and resources invested in its restoration were actually well spent. The answer is in the analysis that Jacqueline Reich has dedicated to the film in relation to its political and social implications in this book. *Maciste imperatore* is a key film to understanding the true nature of the relationship between Benito Mussolini and Maciste and the ideological transformation that the series underwent in the 1920s. Without its restoration it would have been more difficult to contextualize Maciste within Italian cinema and society during the years of the Fascist regime's consolidation of power.

Finally, the assumption that only masterpieces of cinema are worthy of restoration would deny us the joy of discovery. Most of the films involved in the project were not in viewable condition before the restoration, so it was impossible to know in detail the real value of the films. Both *Maciste in vacanza* and *Maciste nella gabbia dei leoni* were a pleasant surprise.

RESTORATION AND PRESERVATION

Film restoration does not have an established tradition like that of other visual arts and, in many respects, is still trying to define its own language. The word "restoration" can be used to refer to very different processes, and unlike what happens in painting, sculpture, and architecture, the restored object will always be a completely new artifact compared to its starting materials.[18]

Restoration may be limited solely to "preservation": a new copy of the film is printed from the original master without changing editing, intertitles, or other characteristics of the film's internal structure. It is not an easy mechanical process. The original print, often in flammable cellulose nitrate, must first be cleaned and repaired patiently frame by frame. During the printing phase, in the analog process, laboratory techniques may be used and designed to obtain the best possible image quality, such as wet-gate printing, which temporarily coats the negative in order to minimize scratches and other physical defects. Today it is becoming increasingly frequent that this work is carried out through digital technology. In such cases, however, it is not preservation, but digital restoration.

Our work on the Maciste series is part of a more complex type of restoration, often called "reconstruction," in which the restoration team works on the internal structure of the film in order to obtain a version that is as close as possible to the print that was chosen as a reference, usually the version shown at the first public screening in the country of production. One example of restoration through reconstruction is "collation," which is when the editing order of shots is obtained from several different prints: a key scene can be more complete in source A, the next one may be of much better quality in source B. The restorer may shift the priorities that will guide his or her choice from case to case (see the sections on *Maciste innamorato* and *Maciste contro lo sceicco* in part 2 of this appendix). Another typical example of reconstruction is the restoration of the original intertitles. Almost none of the nitrate prints of Maciste films had Italian intertitles; global success produces such consequences as Bartolomeo Pagano, the Genovese dockworker, "speaking" Dutch in the surviving prints. The texts of the original intertitles, found among various archival documents, are often far more accurate, witty, and full of puns and idioms than those prepared for foreign distribution. Examples worth noting are the Italian-Spanish medley spoken by the suitor of Edith Moak in *Maciste in vacanza,* or the "Dantesque" tercets spoken by Maciste in *Maciste all'inferno.*

Reconstruction may take very different paths, depending on the state of the initial materials. In *Maciste* the restoration work limited itself to the reintegration of the Italian intertitles, while in *Maciste innamorato* integration between different sources was very complicated and extremely difficult. In part 2 of this appendix we offer some examples to recreate at least in part the variety and complexity of individual cases.

When one intrudes this way into a film's narrative fabric, there is always a degree of arbitrariness to the intervention, no matter how rigorous. The original source is manipulated, albeit on the basis of precise criteria. The risk of creating a hybrid, or worse, a fake, exists. Debates on this topic among the experts are quite lively. Some argue that if the passage of time has left its traces on the film, it is important to respect the organic integrity of the evidence as we found it. If *La trilogia di Maciste* presently exists only in the 1920 heavily reworked French version, the argument would be that the only philologically correct approach is to preserve that very same version. If the only extant prints of *Maciste all'inferno* are in Portuguese, so they should remain in the restored print, in order to avoid "false" digitally reconstructed intertitles.[19]

These objections pose serious problems, and we struggled repeatedly with them during the course of the restoration project. The fact that we chose to proceed without limiting ourselves to preservation is

not because we were unaware of the risks involved in too creative a restoration, but rather because it seemed that the working conditions and
the materials at our disposal offered the opportunity to substantially
increase our understanding of the films and the way they entertained,
moved the audiences, and told their stories. In doing so, the availability
of outstanding extra-filmic material related to the Maciste series was
crucial. In general, the information pertaining to the film under restoration really makes a difference; for instance, the story of *Maciste innamorato* was not complete and intelligible in any of the two prints used for
the restoration. Only their collation allowed for the integration, albeit
partially, of narrative meaning and rhythm. And so it was in many other
cases, including *La trilogia di Maciste,* perhaps the films about which we
debated the most as to whether to proceed with the restoration, without
attempting to reintegrate the intertitles and the original structure. Our
choice in the end, still open to a critical debate, was to run the risk of
manipulating the original, paying the utmost attention to the sources,
both filmic and extra-filmic. As with most things in life, every choice has
advantages and disadvantages. In the case of restorations, the ideal solution in theory does exist: to preserve the original print (or prints) as discovered and at the same time to work on a hypothetical reconstruction.
Unfortunately, the costs of such a practice would be difficult to sustain.

We chose to disclose all the details of the restoration process and the
related documentation in order to contribute to the discussion and open
up future possibilities of improving and amending our work.[20] The prints
and their history must always be respected, but when possible a film as
a story in and of itself deserves to see its capacity to communicate to an
audience reestablished. The important thing in our view is that there is
room for debate and discussion. The viewer must know how what she
has before her eyes has come to be what it is, here and now, after a long
and perilous journey.

TREASURE HUNT

The first thing to do, once it has been decided which film to restore, is to
look for it – that is, to identify all the prints still existing in the world – reconstruct its story, and select the most useful elements for the restora-

tion process according to their age, condition, and completeness. At the time of the worldwide success of the Maciste series, prints of the films bounced from one theater to another in numerous countries, only to later be lost to disintegration, fire, slow decay, or even in a handful of cases to remain reeled up for decades on shelves, in boxes, and in cellars until finally landing in archives all over the world. It is not surprising, therefore, that our research revealed that only a few original prints were conserved in Italian archives. Moreover, it is particularly strange that just one or two prints are left of films that were so popular in their time. But as we have seen, the actual film material was bulky, flammable, and dangerous, and the very idea of a film archive, a place to preserve films of cultural significance, was not yet a common practice in the 1920s (plate 4).

This treasure hunt in search of old film prints, however, would have been almost impossible until two decades ago. If nowadays we can follow Maciste's footsteps to different continents, it is mainly because of the spirit of cooperation and coordination among film archives from around the world, and because of the logistical support provided by organizations such as the Association of Moving Image Archivists (AMIA),[21] and especially the Fédération Internationale des Archives du Film (FIAF).[22] In practice, the first step is to consult FIAF's database, Treasures from Film Archive, to which member archives signal their possessions of prints of films produced during the period ranging roughly from the beginning of cinema to the advent of sound films.[23] It is an essential starting point, even if the data obtained should always be double-checked directly with the archive that has the original print and supplemented by a more targeted search. Many archives have contributed to our project by generously providing their prints and their skills. The archive of Bois d'Arcy, for example, kept a print of a Maciste movie whose exact title had not been entered into the database because it had not been identified. However, having recognized the unmistakable main character, it was possible to identify the print as the reduced version of the three episodes of *La trilogia di Maciste*. The nature of our "serial restoration" has triggered a true virtuous cycle; the restoration and presentation of each Maciste restored film year after year have allowed researchers and colleagues from other archives to know about our project and report any titles, data, and information available on their prints.

Once found, the prints must be analyzed in order to identify what might actually be useful to the restoration. In Turin, for example, we kept a black-and-white print of *Maciste* that, according to our research, has proven to be a reprint from the 1960s of the beautiful colored nitrate positive preserved in Amsterdam. At this point our print has been shelved, and the selected print to be restored was of course the original Dutch, which was older, more complete, and of much higher quality.

IN THE LABORATORY

The Maciste films migrated from the archives to Bologna and the laboratory of L'Immagine Ritrovata. The project was also a good example of a fruitful collaboration between laboratory technicians and archivists. This synergy not only makes the job more enjoyable but also, and above all, is crucial for the success of the restoration, an activity that requires a meticulous analysis of the sources and, simultaneously, a familiarity with the most advanced technologies available for the treatment of the film material.

Cooperation between laboratories and film archives is even more important today, because the availability of new digital intervention techniques in film risks being poorly implemented due to a dangerous split in competency. The background of someone who has been working with film stock is certainly very different from that of a qualified digital restorer or color-correction technician (way more than that of an archivist/restorer with respect to an analog technician who is adept, for instance, in reparation and printing), but not to the point of taking for granted the impossibility of a real dialogue. A respectful and fruitful collaboration is possible.

The best base for the restoration of a film is usually the oldest print, one that has undergone the fewest reprints. In the case of the Maciste films, at best it comes down to using prints that are close to one hundred years old. Time does not pass without leaving a trace of its path, not even on film. Today, film is the material that has the longest life expectancy, so that with some adjustments, an original print from the early twentieth century can be shown on a modern projector. However, the material film might be dirty, broken, or damaged, and these are only a few of the mechanical injuries accumulated over the years that can befall the "body" of a film (plate 5). In the laboratory, technicians spend dozens of hours in the film's company, armed with scalpels, scissors, special tape, and cleaning liquid, showing how the direct relationship between the artisan and the film is an essential element of the restoration, even with such an easily reproducible art form like cinema.

Once the films selected for collation are repaired, a duplicate negative is printed and assembled according to the instructions of the technical *découpage*.[24] This negative will serve as the base for the restored positive prints. In the restoration of the Maciste films between 2006 and 2010, we did not employ digital techniques, which, at the time, were not as widely used and were more costly than they are today. The lone exception was for the reconstruction of the intertitles, which had initially been reproduced analogically with the *truka* and then recreated later at the computer.[25] The 2014 restoration of *Maciste alpino* called for digital intervention.

Perhaps a scan of the images and their digital "correction" would have allowed us to obtain "cleaner" results, especially when the original prints did not permit an optimal photographic rendition. Such was the case of some passages of *Maciste innamorato* and the images from the 16mm print of *Maciste contro lo sceicco* (see the section on *Maciste contro lo sceicco* in part 2 of the appendix). The analog process, however, produced an excellent result, maintaining an essence that was a closer version to the original's material reality.

NOT JUST FILMS

Every film, especially the successful ones, leaves behind a trail of various related materials: photos, articles, advertising, gadgets, but also documents such as screenplays, correspondence, production notebooks, editing notes, contracts, censorship visas, laboratory notes, and so forth. These sources are extremely important for the film context but also extremely rare to find. Usually one does not give enough importance to what these sources are able to tell us. Certainty their extreme variety does not help, so much so that to reference them one can't help but use a negative term, in defining them in what they are not: extra-cinematic or extra-filmic materials. At the same time, their problematic availability does not help valorize their importance as a historical source; at the time of release, no one ever thought of preserving films, let alone film stills or lab receipts. From this point of view, we in Turin have an extremely privileged point of departure. Thanks to its founder, Maria Adriana Prolo, the MNC has a rich collection of extra-cinematic materials, particularly related to the preservation of these types of non-filmic materials, that over the years has produced major works of cataloguing, film digitization, and online publication.[26]

The archives of Itala Film and Pittaluga-Films, producers of all the Italian Maciste films, are among the museum's more prominent collections. For restorers, this was an information gold mine, and the availability of the films and their related documentation helped support the Maciste restoration project. We are not referring here to general historical information, but to real technical information that has been useful to guide the restoration of the film's original structure. This systematic use of extra-cinematic materials in film restoration uniquely characterizes the restoration of the Maciste series and of the restoration activities of the MNC in general.[27] Over the years, the opportunity to work with the films themselves as well as a coherent and vast body of documents has permitted us to elaborate a highly effective style and practice in our craft. The detailed study of the documents related to the silent films helps to understand the dynamics of the era's production and distribution, familiarizing us with practices, fonts, and names and simplifying the decoding and understanding of abbreviations, technical terms, and codes.

Silent film restoration, however, is not a standardized process – each case is different. At the end of the 1910s, for example, it was not possible to print a duplicate negative from a positive, so the only base for printing new copies was the "camera negative" (or negative cameras if the film was made with more than one camera). Sometimes the prints for the international distribution were prepared by the home production company, as evidenced by numerous letters in which Itala Film managers complain about the gross mistakes in the intertitles' translation; other times the negatives were sent to foreign laboratories for the printing of new prints. The only negative of *Maciste innamorato* was sent for this purpose to an English laboratory after it had been lightly damaged by the French. It came back, however, severely damaged, which, of course, led to a series of epistolary complaints from the production company to the British laboratory in 1920. One very meticulous Itala Film technician compiled a document describing all the damage to the negative and the length of each segment,[28] which in turn became a valuable resource for us to verify film length as well as gaps. It was also a confirmation of how the artistic and commercial success of Itala Film's productions was based on the extreme attention to detail at all levels of production. The document describing the damages to the *Maciste innamorato* negative print is a unique source, linked to the history of that particular film.

In general the compilation of materials to document a film's production was standard practice. From the production notes we could retrieve the Italian intertitles, their order, and sometimes the different colors envisioned for tinting and toning; from the censorship certificate we could discern the original length of the film; from the *descrizione dei quadri* (a kind of screenplay) we could find the presence of gaps or editing mistakes; the intertitles' photographic slides (glass plates with the letters used to compose them) offered a faithful source to rebuild the font and the borders of the original intertitles; and the "color samples" indicated the coloration of the different shots, the editing order, and in some cases the position of the intertitles.

If studied with the proper attention, such documents tell us so much about the film and its production practices, even beyond their specific use in the reconstruction. For example, they are fundamental to those who want to get a feel for the missing Maciste films. Certainly nothing can replace viewing a film that no longer exists, and no secondary source is worth more than direct contact with images on screen. Failing all else, however, reading a lost film's intertitles and plot summary may recreate with good approximation the narrative structure and the characters' traits, as well as provide fundamental data, which helps to correct different filmographic inaccuracies in traditional sources.

In this light, we realized that *Maciste e il nipote d'America* is the film whose loss we feel the most. For the first time, Maciste is depicted in not an entirely positive vein, but rather as a stubborn and selfish uncle, ready to force two young people into an arranged marriage if the beauty of his nephew's true love had not forced him to change his mind at the end.[29] Nothing remains but the hope of a lucky discovery to give vision to what is today only words (plate 6).

WHERE THE FILMS GO

At the end of the restoration process we have a new film. On the shelves of our archives are kept, well-aligned, the reels of all the Maciste films we worked on in recent years. Polyester film should ensure a life expectation much longer than a century (and especially for their duplicated negative). The goal of preserving their memory for the future is achieved for now. If we think of a film, however, it is not usually a print of the film that comes to mind, but a story through images. The film lives through projection, and this aspect should not be underestimated. To screen the restored films we have usually chosen two of the most important festivals of silent cinema: Il Cinema Ritrovato Festival in Bologna and Le Giornate del Cinema Muto in Pordenone.[30] These venues guaranteed us not only an encounter with an audience already in love with films of the past but also the ability to present the results of the restoration process in the best possible conditions – for instance, in a theater with the right projection apparatus and with live musical accompaniment. Film's performative dimension was even more accentuated in the silent era: no eventual passage to television or home video. Silent films were made to be seen only in theaters, and that influenced the mise-en-scène and the style. How many small details, for example, are lost on the small screen in the long shots of *Cabiria*!

The need to preserve and promote occasions of silent film viewing "as they should be seen" does not negate compromise with new technologies to reach a wider audience. In the MNC Bibliomediateca you can see all the films restored in recent years on DVD and video.[31] In 2009 the first edition of *Maciste* was released in DVD for the Cineteca di Bologna collection.[32] The important thing to consider when you watch a silent movie on DVD, on YouTube, or on VHS is that what you are watching is just a shadow of what viewers saw in their time. It is certainly better than nothing, but it should not prevent us from watching them on the big screen if the opportunity presents itself. The music, theater, and film will inevitably be far from those of the early twentieth century (hoping that old means of projection are maintained), but it would still provide that collective experience that we believe is related to the great success of the gentle giant Maciste, even when, years later, in the 1960s, he would no longer have the open smile of Pagano, but the sculpted muscles of some body builders.

> The film ended with Maciste leaving on horseback uttering the famous phrase: "Wherever a strong man tramples on a weak one, my place is there." That caused a ten minute applause and the famous comment of Bigattone, "Then you have to walk miles, Maciste."[33]

The use of force in service to the weak is a story whose charm is destined never to get old, even today, on our screens and in our archives, in our histories and in our lives.

Maciste: In Focus

MACISTE (MARVELOUS MACISTE, 1915)

Restoration Notes

The restoration of *Maciste* was carried out by the Museo Nazionale del Cinema in Turin (MNC) and by the Cineteca del Comune di Bologna (CB, now Fondazione Cineteca di Bologna), from a nitrate positive, tinted and toned print with Dutch intertitles, preserved at the Nederlands Filmmuseum in Amsterdam (now EYE Film Institute Netherlands). The texts of the Italian intertitles were reconstructed according to the censorship certificate, the production notes, and the photographic slides of the intertitles preserved at the MNC. A duplicate negative and a positive copy colored by the Desmet method were printed. The work was carried out at the laboratory L'Immagine Ritrovata (IR) in 2006. In the restoration of the Maciste series it was decided to insert ten black frames to signal the missing parts. They constitute barely perceptible brief flashes that seek to signal important discoveries in the film's reconstruction without compromising the pleasure of storytelling.

Reproducing Painted Colors

Silent films were often colored with techniques that required the application of dyes on the positive print; tinting and toning were the most common techniques. Tinting involved soaking the film in tubs filled with dye so that the whites would become colored and the dark parts would remain as such. In toning, the film was immersed in a chemical solution that reacted with and colored only the black colors. In this way, except for cases in which the two techniques were combined, each shot appeared monochrome, but at that time the public was accustomed to color codes: blue for night scenes, red for fire, yellow for the artificially lit indoor scenes. For one of the key scenes of *Maciste,* however, a special solution was chosen. When the unnamed young protagonist takes refuge in a movie theater to escape her pursuers, the shot shows the crowded movie theater while *Cabiria* is projected on the screen (see chapter 2). The theater's interior is blue, while the "screen within a screen" is first red and then, in successive shots, yellow (plate 7). This two-tone effect is obtained with a stencil applied frame by frame on the original film stock and utilizes the same principle of stencil color process used in the early years of cinema and no longer in use in 1915.

The film's "color sampler," one of the rarest production documents from the silent era, confirmed that the colors on the Dutch copy of *Maciste,* including the two-tone frame, were precisely the original ones. The color sampler consists of perforated sheets on which colored frames, indicating the beginning and end of the different sequences in order of editing, are sewn or glued; their intertitles are marked in pen at their expected position in the film. The color sample sheets were used by technicians of the era to check colors, editing, and intertitle insertion (plate 8). In addition to being a document of great beauty, the color sampler is a blessing for the restorer, who can cull an enormous amount of useful information for the film's reconstruction: the order of the sequences, identification of gaps, and, of course, information on color.

Even with a valid reference point for the color reproduction, technical problems still arise, because the coloration process involved in the direct dyeing of the film is difficult to reconstruct in today's laboratories. The traditional methods used at the time can be recreated now on an experimental basis but not on a large scale, because it would be too costly and complex a process. At the same time, the color print of a tinted and toned film often does not produce acceptable results: the bright and lively aniline colors would become dull, and the dark colors would lose their depth and definition. The two-tone scene in the theater, with its double coloration, was even more complex to restore.

To obtain a chromatic effect similar to that of the original, in the restoration of *Maciste* the colors of the era have been reproduced through Desmetcolor, a technique that prints the duplicate negative on black-and-white film and then subjects the positive copy to a process of flash printing in order to allow for the reproduction of homogeneous and brilliant colors. For the two-tone theater scene, the lab technicians experimented with a process that called for the successive exposure of the positive copy to two flashes of different colors. The resulting image is very close to the original colorization, including the irregular and "trembling" border.

MACISTE ALPINO (THE WARRIOR, 1916)

Restoration Notes

The restoration was carried out by the Biennale di Venezia in collaboration with the MNC, departing from a negative camera fragment and a positive nitrate copy preserved at the museum, integrated with two positive nitrate prints held at the Fondazione Cineteca Italiana (CI) in Milan and the British Film Institute (BFI) in London, all of which were scanned in 4K. The original intertitles were reconstructed from production documents, intertitle plates held at the MNC, and by title blocks used by Itala Film on coetaneous films.

The original coloration was reproduced from the CI print, the notes inscribed directly on the negative, and on the documents pertaining to editing and tinting held at the MNC. The restored copy was completed with missing images from versions of the film previously available, such as the 2000 restoration carried out by the MNC and the municipality of Valtournenche. It measures 1,444 meters, compared to 2,084 meters of the first, original print, verified by the official document certifying the film's original length, no. 12240 from 21 November 1916, before certain scenes were removed by different censorship interventions.

The IR laboratory carried out the restoration in 2014.

Fragments Found: Reinstatement of the "Cuts"

The recovery of films and materials pertaining to the silent period (and beyond) can bring about fascinating discoveries, even for already well-known films. *Maciste alpino* is one of the best-known films in the Maciste series and, not surprisingly, was the first to have been restored by the MNC in 2000.

Recently, however, in the MNC archives a negative fragment of the film was found with previously unseen images. To be precise, the images had never been seen in the context of the film's restored copy realized in 2000; however, two publicity photos already preserved in the museum's photo library anticipated the recently discovered episode. In the first one our hero, Maciste, dragging Pluffer with him, greets a military officer whose features and, above all, his stature are very reminiscent of the king of Italy, Vittorio Emanuele III (plate 19); in the second there is Maciste forcing Fritz Pluffer to eat a plate of spaghetti (plate 10).

The fragment, inserted into the new restoration, shows Maciste, who, after having captured the Austrian soldier, takes him to the camp of the alpine troops. Maciste receives the greetings of the visiting king (no intertitle mentions King Vittorio, but the parody is clear) and then places the prisoner in his cell and forces him to end his hunger strike. The evil and treacherous Pluffer first reveals to Maciste how the count of Pratolungo was punished by the Austrians for facilitating the escape of Italian prisoners; then Pluffer pretends to be sick in order to be admitted to the military hospital, only to attack a nurse and run away. This sequence makes the narrative of the film much clearer; the intertitles corresponding to the fragment are confirmed in all the archival documents. The shots belong in the end of the film's third part, from the capture and escape of Pluffer.

The reason why this sequence was cut from the film, however, probably was because of the censors (see chapter 3), who might not have liked both the violence of the scene in which the Austrian attacks the nurse and the good-natured parody of the king. Research into this hypothesis is ongoing. The main objective, in any case, is to clearly declare the restoration's goal, and in particular which version of the film the restorer attempts to reconstruct.

MACISTE INNAMORATO (MACISTE IN LOVE, 1919)

Restoration Notes

The restoration of *Maciste innamorato* was realized by the MNC and CB from a tinted and toned positive nitrate print with English intertitles, preserved at the British Film Institute (BFI) in London, and from a duplicate negative without intertitles held by the Cinémathèque Française (CF) in Paris. The texts of the Italian intertitles were reconstructed according to the information in the censorship certificate and in the production documents preserved at the MNC; an analysis of Itala's other contemporary film productions provided the model for the intertitles' design. The missing parts are signaled with ten black frames. A duplicate negative and a positive copy colored with the Desmet method were printed. The IR laboratory carried out the work in 2006.

Same Movie, Different Prints: Collating

At the beginning of each restoration, the first item on the agenda is to search for all the prints of the film that are preserved in the world's many archives. Many films of the silent era have been lost; others survived only in one copy. When multiple prints of the same film are available, we proceed to a comparison and, if the materials call for it, eventually to a "collation," which is the selection of the best shot from the originals, depending on the quality. The differences between two prints of the same film can vary wildly.

The French negative print of *Maciste innamorato* is incomplete, without intertitles, and is primarily made up of small unbound reels. At the time, indeed, the negative was not edited before the positive processing, while today the positive copies are assembled after the color process. During the production phase, this procedure required that information could be clearly passed among the director, the technicians working on the editing, and those involved in coloration. In order to facilitate communication and to guarantee that no precious directions were lost in the process, all the information was written on the material film itself (plate 11). Therefore, the negative print of *Maciste innamorato* requires some deciphering: a cross on the frame indicates where an intertitle would be placed, a number between perforations signals the order of editing, and writing on the images shows the color of the frame or sequence.

The analysis of the English positive print, however, at first seemed to undermine the importance of the information reported on the French negative, since apparently it looked like a complete copy that did not seem to require special integration. In these cases, however, one should never rely on first impressions. At the end of the movie, for instance, Maciste discovers Ada with another admirer, so he flees to his room, packs his bags, and runs away in distress at his first amorous delusion. In the English version the sequence is linear, and we would not think there to be any possible gaps. The negative print, however, contains a shot of that sequence that was lost in the positive print; in it Maciste is ready to pack and leave, but then suddenly he stops to look thoughtfully at his reflection in the closet mirror (plate 12). In this case it is clear that the frame belonged to the sequence of his departure because of its location (the hotel room), Maciste's outfit, and his behavior. If there had been any doubts, the position would have been confirmed by the numeric code marked on the image, originally made for the editing staff. A cross indicates the position of the melancholy intertitle: *"D'altronde, essa ha ragione . . . s'è mai visto la gazzella a braccetto col pachiderma?"* (On the other hand she is right. . . . Have you ever seen a gazelle hand in hand with a pachyderm?) The last question was how to restore the original color to the black-and-white negative copy. The response lay once again in deciphering the clues on the film itself. Where "orange" is written on the negative in Italian (*arancio*), the frame of restored copy was tinted that color, and so on. The fact that the writing is in Italian seems to further confirm that these instructions came from the film company itself (plate 11).

LA TRILOGIA DI MACISTE (THE MACISTE TRILOGY, 1920)

Restoration Notes

La trilogia di Maciste was restored by the MNC and the CB from a tinted and toned nitrate print with French intertitles preserved at Les Archives

Françaises du Film Centre National de la Cinématographie (now Centre National du Cinéma et de l'Image Animée, or the CNC) of Bois d'Arcy. That copy was a rerelease made for the French market, in which the film's three episodes were combined into a single feature film. The restoration has reinstated the original division into three episodes, signaled the gaps with ten black frames, and reconstructed and repositioned the Italian intertitles on the basis of archival documents preserved at the MNC. The IR laboratory carried out the restoration in June 2010.

Divisions: The Restoration of the Episodes

La trilogia di Maciste consists of three separate films, distributed as chapters of the same story (plate 13). This is a unique characteristic, not found in any of the other existing films of the series. This serial structure, however, was completely lost in the only surviving copy of the film. The episodes had been thoroughly cut and reassembled, apparently to distribute the film as a single movie.

This edition had used the original French intertitles with their unique border and the Itala–U.C.I. production company icon, yet repositioned in a creative way. In the original episodes, at the beginning of the second and third movies there was a summary of previous episodes. Many of the intertitles contained in this summary were obviously more concise than those included in the actual movie; these recapitulatory intertitles have been used to describe the more glaring cuts in the French version.

When the only available copy of a film presents such different presumed characteristics from when it was released, the restorer has to decide whether to preserve it in its present, existing form or try to recreate a supposed "original" version. In the case of *La trilogia di Maciste* the choice was facilitated by the availability of copious production documents, which could help us reconstruct a good approximation of the story and its various episodes in the film's initial distribution (plate 14). It was therefore decided to restore the original division into chapters, reinserting the Italian intertitles reconstructed on the basis of the "list of intertitles." These historical documents are typewritten sheets that served as a guide during the film's production for the preparation of the intertitles and the translations for the foreign versions.

The main problem posed by this choice has been what to do with the story's gaps: of more than four hours of the original projection – the total length of the three episodes at their first distribution – less than half remain. Some narrative passages were unclear and, more important, many of the original intertitles in the French version relating to subplots or deleted gags were unintelligible. It was decided, however, to signal the missing parts with ten black frames, to reinstate the original intertitles whenever possible, and to include new, written summaries only when it would be otherwise impossible to understand the narrative's development. All of these choices are philologically documented but still make the vision of the three restored episodes less fluid and more complex than that of other films in the series. In a certain sense we sacrificed an ease of understanding for the possibility to approximate the structure of the era's films, restoring the episodic nature that distinguished *La trilogia di Maciste* from the other films in the series.

MACISTE IN VACANZA (MACISTE ON HOLIDAY, 1921)

Restoration Notes

The restoration of *Maciste in vacanza* was carried out by the CB and the MNC in collaboration with the Cineteca Nazionale (CN) in Rome and the Film Library of Madrid, based on a tinted and toned nitrate positive print with Italian intertitles preserved in Rome; on a sound duplicate negative without intertitles and on nitrate negative fragments preserved at the Filmoteca Española in Madrid; and eventually on a positive safety copy derived from the Madrid negative and housed in Turin. The texts of the Italian intertitles were reconstructed according to the information contained in the censorship certificate and productions notes housed at the MNC. The gaps have been signaled with ten black frames. A duplicate negative and a positive copy colored with the Desmet method were printed. The restoration was carried out at IR laboratory in 2008.

What Is Missing: The Treatment of Gaps

The nitrate copy of *Maciste in vacanza* from Rome presents characteristics that make it a valuable source for the restorer: it has the original Italian intertitles with graphics from the period, and it has maintained brilliant and well-preserved colors (plate 15). Nevertheless, the footage measures 1,325 meters, thirty minutes less than the copy projected in 1921. We know this thanks to the censorship certificate, in which was reported, along with a list of intertitles, the exact length of the approved copy for projections so that it was not possible, after the granting of authorization, to add forbidden images without the possibility of verification.

When a copy is incomplete, it is almost certain that the missing parts are the beginning and the end of the film, as they are the most vulnerable to cuts and damages both during editing and projection. *Maciste in vacanza* is no exception. One of the most incomplete parts of the positive copy in Rome is the film's beginning, when Maciste anxiously awaits the delivery of a new car on the set of his film (see chapter 5). The Madrid duplicate has allowed us to reconstruct much of the missing sequence, in which we see, among other things, the director showcasing the set where Maciste will be performing soon (plate 16). Despite this discovery, the opening shots of *Maciste in vacanza* should be considered lost. The gap is evidenced by the first two frames glued onto the color sampler with images that do not exist in the prints: Maciste in a plastic pose inside a circular matte and Maciste deep in thought against the background of the film stage. These frames suggest that the film would open with an iris on Maciste fantasizing about his new car.

Sometimes the gaps are clearly identifiable because they interrupt the narrative flow; in other cases, like the one just analyzed, it is not so easy to perceive that "something is missing," and only the extra-cinematic documentation can help us to notice it.

MACISTE IMPERATORE (MACISTE THE EMPEROR, 1924)

Restoration Notes

The restoration of *Maciste imperatore* was carried out by the CB and the MNC from a tinted and toned nitrate positive print with Dutch intertitles preserved at the Nederlands Filmmuseum in Amsterdam. The texts of Italian intertitles have been reconstructed from the censorship certificate and from the list of intertitles housed in the MNC archives; the intertitles' graphics were reconstructed by analyzing the copies of the FERT-Pittaluga films produced during the same period. The gaps identified have been signaled with ten black frames. A duplicate negative and a positive copy colored with the Desmet method were printed. The work was carried out at the IR laboratory in 2007.

Style Matters: The Graphic Design of the Intertitles

There was only one existing copy of *Maciste imperatore*, a positive print in the Netherlands. In these cases, from the point of view of the image, one should try to get the best quality out of the only existing reference, whatever it may be. There is, however, one element that can be modified, if one is lucky enough to have production documents or censorship information available: the intertitles, the film's most easily manipulated element. The foreign versions, in particular, had to modify them for their audience, perhaps with different nuances that would be more understandable in the context of another country. Sometimes it was the same film production company that prepared the foreign versions of their films; other times this task was delegated to the distribution companies. In the latter case, the graphics of the frame and the font of the writing could be completely different from that of the first distribution. This is the case of the Dutch copy of *Maciste imperatore*.

Contrary to what one might think, graphic designs are not an accessory. A simple font without a border may have a completely different visual impact from a floral font in an Art Nouveau–style border. Often the graphic designs of the intertitles were the "brand" of the film company, which in turn wanted to keep them elegant and recognizable. One of the goals of the restoration of *Maciste imperatore* was the restoration of Italian intertitles' original graphics. But how could it be done without any Italian prints as a reference?

Assuming that the production companies tended to maintain a recognizable style in their intertitles, the restoration team tried to track down original prints of films produced in 1924 by FERT-Pittaluga – it was a real "hunt" that, thanks to the cooperation of the other FIAF archives, was very successful. *Treno di piacere* (Pleasure Train) and *Caporal Saetta* (Chief Saetta), both released in 1924 by FERT, have intertitles with dotted borders in which the FERT-Pittaluga logo is clearly seen (plate 17). So this is the graphic that has been reproduced electronically for the printing of the intertitles of the restored copy of *Maciste imperatore* (plate 18). The digital reproduction, however, maintains a fixity that a trained eye can easily spot. Even an accurate philological approach cannot avoid leaving traces of its own aesthetic in the film, revealing both the possibilities and limits of ever newer technologies at our disposition.

Unfortunately we were not able to find an effective reference for the "inserts," those written messages that appear in the film in the form of a letter, telegram, or ticket. In the original they were penned on backgrounds that accurately reproduced the form in which they had been entered. Certainly the precious parchment that attests to the legitimacy of the emperor of Livonia was no exception. The original insert definitely had a realistic background that certified the importance of the document; the restored one had to settle for a neutral font on a sober light background.

MACISTE NELLA GABBIA DEI LEONI
(MACISTE IN THE LIONS' DEN, 1926)

Restoration Notes

The restoration of *Maciste nella gabbia dei leoni* was realized by CB and the MNC, based on two tinted nitrate positive prints found at the Cinemateca Brasileira in São Paulo and now preserved at the CB. The text of Italian intertitles was reconstructed based on the Italian censorship certificate and the list of intertitles preserved at the MNC; the graphic design of the intertitles and the inserts were reconstructed by analyzing the FERT films produced in the same period. The comparison between the prints and the production documents highlighted some gaps and small editing mistakes. A duplicate negative and a positive copy colored with the Desmet method were printed. The work was carried out at the IR laboratory in 2007.

Assumptions and Certainties: The Editing of Intertitles

The success of the Maciste film series was international, but it may appear strange that the only two surviving prints of an Italian film from the 1920s are both from across the ocean in South America. The reasons why this can happen are several: chance, a collector's passion, and the distraction of a distributor who forgets the reels in storage. The two Brazilian nitrate prints of *Maciste nella gabbia dei leoni* have Portuguese intertitles, very different from one another, as a further proof of how silent films were particularly easy to manipulate, cut, and reassemble. The restoration of a film must take into account the often complex past history of the prints in order for the restorers to make the right choices. The right choices, however, cannot always be made without prevailing doubts.

In a scene from *Maciste nella gabbia dei leoni*, Sullivan attacks the young Seida by forcibly and violently cutting her nails (plate 20 and plates 21a–f). Compared to the two Brazilian nitrate prints, the Italian version accentuates the collective dimension of the violence on the girl. In the production documents, indeed, there is an intertitle (number 79) that is absent in both Brazilian prints of the film: "And everyone cowardly followed the athlete's whim" ("*E tutti si prestano vilmente al capriccio dell'atleta,*" plate 21d).

Reconstructing an intertitle during the course of the restoration poses the difficulty of not only restoring both text and graphics, but also, and especially, of the identification of the right place to insert them. It is a sensitive choice because intertitles' insertion can affect the film's pace. Sometimes "physical" elements in the original prints may help, such as crosses drawn on the frame, or punching or splices that reveal an original insertion. None of these traces, however, were in either of the prints of *Maciste nella gabbia dei leoni*. In order to position the intertitle that refers to the lack of solidarity of the circus people toward Seida, we had to rely on the diegesis. There are several moments in which the phrase might be relevant: in the sequence where the frightened girl looks around and sees the crowd around her laughing, or when a woman in the group blocks her escape and throws her back into the aggressor's arms (plate 20).

Luckily, our location choices are limited by the need to comply with the order in which the intertitles are given in the production documents. In this case, the number 79 is preceded and followed by two sentences spoken by Sullivan. The position in which the Brazilian equivalents were placed seemed incongruous. We decided, therefore, to insert the two intertitles after a medium shot of Sullivan that shows him talking. Then the new intertitle has been inserted in the sequence section between numbers 78 and 80: before a long shot of the group laughing at the girls' aggression. The result is consistent and seems to respect the style of the period (for example, the presence of an intertitle after a close-up). However, this is only a hypothesis. In film restoration we aim for neutrality and objectivity, but sometimes we are forced to operate without absolute certainty. That is why it is so important that the restorations are documented in detail. Like the restoration of paintings and sculptures, subsequent discoveries and new technologies will allow future generations to amend the possible mistakes of our interventions.

MACISTE CONTRO LO SCEICCO (MACISTE AGAINST THE SHEIK, 1926)

Restoration Notes

The new restoration of *Maciste contro lo sceicco,* carried out by the MNC and the CB, restored the original Italian intertitles thanks to the production documents preserved at the MNC. Some shots were also reinstated thanks to a copy kept in the Archivio Bruno Boschetto in Turin. The restoration was carried at the IR laboratory in June 2009.

Behind the Lines: The Incongruity of Original Materials

Small-gauge prints such as 16mm were often not considered fit for restoration. Their resolution is lower than that of a 35mm print, not to mention that, in the case of silent films, those are often prints projected over and over again in churches, clubs, associations, and art house cinemas. Each analog printing transfer causes loss of quality and definition. In addition, multiple projections result in scratches, dirt, and breakage to the film.

Yet it is often in the 16mm prints that frames lost in any other source may be found. In the case of *Maciste contro lo sceicco*, the 16mm print from the Boschetto collection completely lacked a large portion of the first part of the film yet contained the most complete version of the scene where the sailors on the deck of the ship harass Anna (see chapter 6). In the restored version it is not difficult to recognize the frames that came from the reduced-size print footage: the contrast is high, the lines create a kind of spiderweb on the images, and, in general, the quality is much lower. Thus Anna turns suddenly, captured in some good quality, clear black-and-white frames, while soon after we can see scratched and damaged images showing a partial point-of-view shot from the perspective of the threatening sailors (plate 22 and plate 23).

There are analog techniques that can reduce the lines on the image – for example, wet-gate printing, which can guarantee only marginal, limited improvement.

Today, just a few years after the restoration of *Maciste contro lo sceicco*, the availability of digital techniques would allow the restorers to further improve the quality of the footage from 16mm. This possibility, rich with positive consequences, also holds a hidden danger: to modify old movies according to our taste, eliminating any sign of the material history that distinguished them.

MACISTE ALL'INFERNO (MACISTE IN HELL, 1926)

Restoration Notes

In the new restoration of *Maciste all'inferno,* carried out by the MNC and the CB, we reinstated the original intertitles that describe the underworld in poetic tercets, clearly inspired by the style of Dante Alighieri and based on the information found in historical documents preserved in Turin. The restoration was performed at the IR laboratory in 2009.

Dante's Tercets: How an Intertitle Can Change a Movie

The most recent restoration of *Maciste all'inferno* was in 2009. The film, however, had already been restored in 1993. Fifteen years is not much, considering that the goal of the restoration is to preserve the film in the long term. Why return to a film if copies of an accurate restoration already exist?

The reason was the discovery of the original list of intertitles prepared during the film's production stage. For the 1993 restoration the texts of the intertitles were translated from a Brazilian print, retaining part of the graphics. A comparison between this translation and the original Italian texts shows how the story itself does not change much; what does change, however, is the atmosphere created by those alterations.

When Maciste descends into hell, the laconic intertitle reads: "In the beginning Maciste does not understand his surroundings" ("*Al principio Maciste non comprende ciò che lo circonda*"). The Dantesque intertitle in the Italian version is more suggestive because it is in poetic tercets: "With great confusion in the head / Maciste at first does not understand / like a person forced out of bed" ("*Con grande confusione nella testa / Maciste a tutta prima non capisce / come persona che per forza è desta*"). This poetic style in rhyme characterizes almost all the scenes in hell, while the sequences on earth are in prose. This disparity is designed to highlight the difference between the earthly kingdom and the kingdom of darkness and was almost completely lost in the restored copy of 1993. The frequent references to Dante in the film were lost as well, such as when Maciste, indecisive about Proserpina's proposal, is "Like the ones who are suspended" ("*Tra color che stan sospesi*") as Dante defines the souls in limbo. A little later the scene ends with an embrace between Maciste and Proserpina because "Fasting was stronger than fear" ("*Poscia più che il timor poté il digiuno*"), referring to the tragic episode of Count Ugolino, which in this scene assumes a malicious tone, perhaps alluding to the fact that until then Maciste had never really kissed any of his on-screen female co-stars.

Some intertitles, as mentioned, retained the original graphics of the Brazilian copy. There are painted backgrounds with recurring country landscapes, a devil who dominates the writing with outspread wings, and a frame with demons winking (plates 24–26). The designs are beautiful, but how could we be sure that they were the original backgrounds, and not, as sometimes happened, prepared especially for the foreign market? Several factors have helped us: in all the designs the Pittaluga-Films logo appears, a typical feature of the original intertitles; the font used for the lettering is the same that was usually employed in Pittaluga films; the symbol of the Brazilian distributor, when present, is off-center and therefore seems to be added at a later time; the sequence number marked on the film footage corresponds to the one of the production documents; and in one of the drawings the author signed "Giannini," a name that seems to belong to an Italian artist. The devils soon nodded from the intertitles of the restored copy. Their creative contribution to the film was considered so important as to justify the investment of resources in a new restoration.

Filmography

THE FOLLOWING FILMOGRAPHY LISTS THE CREDIT INFORMA-
tion for all the films in which Bartolomeo Pagano plays the character of
Maciste, from *Cabiria* (1914) to *Il gigante delle Dolomiti* (1926).

The primary source for information on a particular film is listed directly following the data in abbreviated form in parenthesis. Whenever
possible, we verified the information directly with the original materials, especially those housed at the MNC. Some additional information
appeared in different sources, and in these cases we chose to identify
only what we considered to be the most significant. As a source, priority
was given to the lists of intertitles compiled for a production – which
often reported the names of the principal actors and technicians – over
the films themselves and advertising materials of the period as sources
for identification. When two different sources appear next to a name, it
means that one source identified the name and the other source identified the pseudonym or the film character.

When it was not possible to verify the data from the era's original
sources, widely accepted bibliographic references have been used. The
main reference works for any filmography on the Italian silent cinema
are *Bianco & Nero*'s volumes dedicated to the Italian film production
between 1905 and the end of the 1920s, edited by Aldo Bernardini and
Vittorio Martinelli and published in the 1980s and 1990s. In these fundamental volumes the authors compiled a filmographic sheet for each film
and, whenever possible, excerpts from contemporary film reviews. When
the data reported in *Bianco & Nero* contradicted the information in the
documents of the period, the latter has been given priority. The spelling

of the names, if the sources were not in agreement, has been standardized according to the version considered more reliable, which we established after crosschecking the various sources in question.

Information that was not possible to verify through archival documents has been reported in brackets. Such is the case, for instance, regarding the collaboration of Segundo de Chomón on several films of the Maciste series. For this specific case the main source of information was the filmography edited by Simona Nosenzo and published in *Manuale tecnico per visionari. Segundo de Chomón in Italia, 1912–1925* (Turin: F.E.R.T., 2007).

Paolo Caneppele, from Österreichisches Filmmuseum of Vienna (the Austrian Film Museum), provided film data sheets published in the magazine *Paimann's Filmlisten. Wochenschrift für Lichtbild-Kritik* (Paimann's Film List. Weekly for Photo-Criticism), which were extremely useful to verify the information about the German productions. To complete this information we have consulted Vittorio Martinelli, *Il cinema tedesco degli anni Venti e la critica italiana* (Gemona: Cineteca del Friuli, 2001) and the website www.filmportal.de.

The information regarding censorship has been verified through the censorship certificates, and then through the online database www .italiataglia.it, based on the documents concerning the film revisions held in the archives of the Direzione Generale per il Cinema del Ministero per i Beni e le Attività Culturali (General Cinema Office of the Ministry of Heritage and Culture). Whenever other sources were not available, we reported the information published in the *Bianco & Nero* volumes.

Cabiria's filmographic data had been revised on the occasion of the 2006 publication of Silvio Alovisio and Alberto Barbera's anthology *Cabiria & Cabiria* (Turin: Museo Nazionale del Cinema, 2006); a condensed version of its credits has been reprinted here.

In two cases the titles of the films are capitalized. *THE LIBERATOR,* a film advertised in the American magazines of the time, is not an individual film shot by Bartolomeo Pagano for Itala Film, but a reedited compilation of different films then prepared for the American market. *MACISTE AFRICANO,* on the other hand, is the Italian title of a hypothetical German film production, on which censorship data are reported in the database of www.italiataglia.it. However, the film information has not been found in any of the period sources consulted.

Extant prints allowed us to identify and verify the most recognizable actors; Gianna Chiapello, a specialist in Turin's silent film production, provided additional information to the existing filmography.

We have identified the archival location for each film; for the films restored by and housed at the MNC there is also a brief description of the restored copy.

ABBREVIATIONS

Institutions

MNC: Museo Nazionale del Cinema di Torino

CB: Fondazione Cineteca di Bologna

CN-CSC: Cineteca Nazionale–Centro Sperimentale di Cinematografia, Roma

Contemporary Documents

doc.ed: list of intertitles

doc.no: censorship certificate

doc.sog: subject

doc.cor: correspondence

doc.c: folder

rec: contemporary reviews

PFL: *Paimann's Filmlisten*

pub: publicity materials

Bibliography

M2001: V. Martinelli, *Dal Dott. Calligari a Lola – Lola. Il cinema tedesco degli anni Venti e la critica italiana* (Gemona: Cineteca del Friuli, 2001).

BN: V. Martinelli, *Bianco & Nero* issues on Italian silent cinema filmography.

—— *Il cinema muto italiano. I film del dopoguerra/1919* 41, no. 1–3, ed. Vittorio Martinelli (January–June 1980).

—— *Il cinema muto italiano. I film del dopoguerra/1920* 41, no. 4–6, ed. Vittorio Martinelli (July–December 1980).

—— *Il cinema muto italiano. I film degli anni venti/1921–2* 42, no. 1–3, ed. Vittorio Martinelli (January–June 1981).

—— *Il cinema muto italiano. I film degli anni venti/1923–1931* 42, no. 4–6, ed. Vittorio Martinelli (July–December 1981).

—— *Il cinema muto italiano. I film della grande guerra/1918* 50, no. 1–2, ed. Vittorio Martinelli (1989).

—— *Il cinema muto italiano. I film della grande guerra/1917* 50, no. 3–4, ed. Vittorio Martinelli (1989).

—— *Il cinema muto italiano. I film della grande guerra/1916, prima parte* 51, no. 1–2, ed. Vittorio Martinelli (1990).

—— *Il cinema muto italiano. I film della grande guerra/1916, seconda parte* 51, no. 3–4, ed. Vittorio Martinelli (1990).

—— *Il cinema muto italiano. I film della grande guerra/1915, prima parte* 52, no. 1–2, ed. Vittorio Martinelli (1991).

—— *Il cinema muto italiano. I film della grande guerra/1915, parte seconda* 52, no. 3–4, ed. Vittorio Martinelli (1991).

—— *Il cinema muto italiano. I film degli anni d'oro/1914, prima parte* 53, no. 1–2, ed. Vittorio Martinelli (1992).

—— *Il cinema muto italiano. I film degli anni d'oro/1914, seconda parte* 53, no. 3–4, ed. Vittorio Martinelli (1992).

N2007: *Manuale tecnico per visionari. Segundo de Chomón in Italia 1912–1925*, Simona Nosenzo (Turin: Associazione F.E.R.T., 2007).

F2008: Alberto Friedemann, *Fert. Storia di un nome, di due società e di tre stabilimenti* (Turin: Associazione F.E.R.T., 2008).

Websites
Itt: www.italiataglia.it
Fp: www.filmportal.de

Identification
id: individual identification by specialists.

Cabiria
(Italy, 1914)

Dir: Giovanni Pastrone – Intertitles and characters' names: Gabriele D'Annunzio – Cinematography: Augusto Battagliotti, Natale Chiusano, Segundo de Chomón, Vincent C. Dénizot, Carlo Franzeri, Giovanni Tomatis – Scenography: Luigi Romano Borgnetto [Camillo Innocenti] – Special effects: Segundo de Chomón – Cast: Lydia Quaranta (Cabiria, Elissa), Marcellina [Bianco] (young Cabiria), [Carolina Catena] (young Cabiria), Teresa [Gina], Marangoni (Croessa), Dante Testa (Karthalo, Moloch priest), Umberto Mozzato (Fulvio Axilla), Bartolomeo Pagano (Maciste), Raffaele Di Napoli (Bodastoret), Edouard Davesnes (Annibale, Asdrubale), Italia Almirante Manzini (Sofonisba), Vitale De Stefano (Massinissa), Alexandre Bernard (Siface), Enrico Gemelli (Archimede), Didaco Chellini (Scipione), Emile Vardannes (Batto), Signora Davesnes (Cabiria's mother), Gino-Lelio Comelli (Lelio), Bonaventura W. Ibañez (Marcello) – Music: Ildebrando Pizzetti (*Fire Symphony*), Manlio Mazza – Censorship certificate: n. 3035 (request 31 March 1914; certificate: 10 April 1914) – First screening: 18 April 1914, Theatre Vittorio Emanuele of Turin e Lyric Teatre of Milan – Original length: 3,364 m – Production: Itala Film.

Restored copy:
Italian version: 35mm, positive, polyester, 3,102 m, 169' a 16 f/s, color (Desmetcolor), Italian intertitles, mute (MNC, restoration 2006).

English version: 35mm, positive, polyester, 3,037 m, 166' a 16 f/s, color (Desmetcolor), English intertitles, mute (MNC, restoration 2006). In 2006 the MNC also restored the 1931 sound version of *Cabiria*.

Maciste
(Italy, 1915, released as *Maciste and Marvelous Maciste* in the U.S.)

Dir: Vincent C. Dénizot, Luigi Romano Borgnetto (BN) – Supervision: Giovanni Pastrone (BN) – Cinematography: Augusto Battagliotti (BN), Giovanni Tomatis (BN), [Segundo de Chomón] (N2007) – Special effects: [Segundo de Chomón] (N2007) – Cast: Bartolomeo Pagano (Maciste) (id), Clementina

Gay (the girl) (BN), Felice Minotti (a bandit, the helper of uncle Alexis) (id), Amelia Chellini (the girl's mother) (id), Didaco Chellini (the uncle, Duke Alexis) (id), Leone Papa (BN) – Censorship visa: 9875 del 01.6.1915 (first approval) (doc.no) – Original length: 1,968 m (doc.no) – Production: Itala Film (doc.no).

Restored copy: 35mm, positive, polyester, 1,377 m, 67' a 18 f/s, color (Desmetcolor), Italian intertitles (MNC, CB, restoration 2006).

Maciste alpino
(Maciste the Alpine Soldier, Italy, 1916, released as *The Warrior* in the U.S.)

Dir: Luigi Maggi (BN), Luigi Romano Borgnetto (BN) – Supervision: Giovanni Pastrone (a.k.a. Piero Fosco) (rec, doc.ed*) – Subject and screenplay: Giovanni Pastrone (BN) – Cinematography: Giovanni Tomatis (BN), Carlo Franzoni (BN), Augusto Battagliotti (BN) – Special effects: [Segundo de Chomón] (N2007) – Cast: Bartolomeo Pagano (Maciste) (id), Fido Schirru (Fritz Pluffer) (rec), Enrico Gemelli (Count of Pratolungo) (rec), Marussia Allesti (Giulietta, Young Countess of Pratolungo) (rec), Sig. Riccioni (Alpine officer) (rec), Riccardo Vitaliani (Austrian officer) (rec), Evangelina Vitaliani (BN), Felice Minotti (restaurant maître, Alpine officer) (id) – Censorship certificate:12240 of 11.21.1916 (Itt) / 12240 of 06.27.1917 (doc.no)** – Original length: 2,084 m (Itt) – Production: Itala Film (doc.no).

Restored copy: 35mm, positive, polyester, 1,944 m., 95' at 18 f/s, color, Italian intertitles, silent / DCP 4K, 95' a 18 ft/s, color, Italian intertitles / DCP 4 K, 95' a 18 ft/s, color, English intertitles.

(La Biennale di Venezia with the collaboration of MNC; 2014 restoration.)

*Before the scenes that take place in the high mountains, an intertitle says: "*Piero Fosco queste gesta italiche ricostrusse per opera dell'arte nuova in laude dell'alpino forte e generoso*" (Piero Fosco reconstructed these heroic actions through this new artistic medium to honor the strong and generous alpine trooper).

**A censorship certificate discussing a 22-meter sequence that was supposed to be added at the end of *Maciste alpino* is at MNC. The description of the scene says: "*In terra un gran soldato tedesco con intorno i piccoli soldati che lo hanno atterrato. Apparizione di Maciste con un soldato americano che sventola la sua bandiera*" (A big German soldier is lying on the ground, surrounded by the small Italian soldiers who knocked him down. Maciste appears, along with an American soldier waving his flag).

Maciste poliziotto
(Maciste the Policeman, Italy, 1918)

Dir: Roberto Leone Roberti (BN) – Cinematography: Giovanni Tomatis (BN), [Segundo de Chomón] (N2007) – Special effects: [Segundo de Chomón] (N2007) – Cast: Bartolomeo Pagano (Maciste) (doc.ed), Italia Almirante Manzini (Bianca Suardi) (doc.ed), Ruggero Capodaglio (Eusebio Cavicchioni) (doc.ed), Claudia Zambuto (doc.ed), Vittorio Rossi-Pianelli (doc.ed), Arnaldo Arnaldi (doc.ed) – Censorship certificate:13369 of 3.6.1918 (doc.no) – Original length: 2,520 m (doc.no) – Production: Itala Film (doc.ed).

Maciste atleta
(Maciste the Athlete, Italy, 1918)

Dir: Vincent C. Dénizot (BN) – Supervision: Giovanni Pastrone (BN) – Cinematography: Giovanni Tomatis (BN) – Cast: Bartolomeo Pagano (Maciste) (doc.sog), Italia Almirante Manzini (PFL), Ruggero Capodaglio (Eusebio Cavicchioni) (BN), Giulio Andreotti (BN) – Censorship visa: 12419 of 3.31.1918 (doc.no) – Original length: 2,135 m (doc.no) – Production: Itala Film (doc.no).

Maciste medium
(Maciste the Medium, Italy, 1918)

Dir: Vincent C. Dénizot (BN) – Supervision: Giovanni Pastrone (BN) – Cinematography: Giovanni Tomatis (BN) – Cast: Bartolomeo Pagano (Maciste) (rec), Italia Almirante Manzini (Bianca) (PFL), Ruggero Capodaglio (Eusebio Cavicchioni) (BN), Elettra Raggio (rec) – Censorship visa:13453 of 4.26.1918 (doc.no) – Original length: 1,455 m (doc.no) – Production: Itala Film (doc.no).

THE LIBERATOR
(series) (Italy/U.S., 1918)*

Dir: [Giovanni Pastrone] (rec) – Subject: Agnes Fletcher Bain (rec) – Cast: Bartolomeo Pagano (as Ernest Pagano), Italia Almirante Manzini (as Italia Manzini) (rec), Mark Albro (rec), Anatole Froyez (rec), Dorian Gerain (rec), Julian Bernard (rec), Eduarde Davesnes (rec) – Distribution: Harry Raver (rec).

The Liberator was advertised in American film magazines between December 1918 and January 1919 as a twelve-episode serial. Most likely it is a collage editing of *Maciste atleta, Maciste poliziotto,* and *Maciste medium* for the American market; the female protagonist and the plot summary are the same.

Maciste innamorato
(Maciste in Love, Italy, 1919)

Dir: Luigi Romano Borgnetto (doc. ed) – Cinematography: Alvaro De Simone (BN) – Special effects: [Segundo de Chomón] (N2007) – Cast: Bartolomeo Pagano (Maciste) (id), Linda Moglia (Ada Thompson) (doc.ed), Orlando Ricci (Sig. Thompson) (doc.ed), Leone Papa (Stringhini) (id), Sig.a Frediani (Benzina) (id) – Censorship visa: 14105 of 4. 3.1919 (doc.no) – Original length: 2,005 m (doc.no) – Production: Itala Film (doc.no).

Restored copy: 35mm, polyester, positive, 1,903 m, 93' a 18 f/s, color (Desmetcolor), Italian intertitles (MNC, CB, restoration 2006).

La trilogia di Maciste
(The Maciste Trilogy, Italy,
1920, three episodes)

Episode 1: *Maciste contro la morte* (Maciste Conquers Death)
Episode 2: *Il viaggio di Maciste* (Maciste's Voyage)
Episode 3: *Il testamento di Maciste* (Maciste's Last Will and Testament)

Dir: Carlo Campogalliani (doc. ed) – Subject and screenplay: Carlo Campogalliani (doc.ed), Carlo Pollone (doc.ed) – Cinematography: Fortunato Spinolo (doc.ed) – Cast: Bartolomeo Pagano (Maciste) (id), Letizia Quaranta (Princess Maria Laetitia) (doc.ed), Carlo Campogalliani (Tito Fabrizi) (doc.ed), Emilio Vardannes (prime minister) (doc.ed), Vittorio Rossi Pianelli (Prince Luitpoldo) (doc. ed), Felice Minotti (prime minister's accomplice) (doc.ed), Pierre Lepetit (Cioccolattino) (doc.ed), Ria Bruna (Countess Henriette Litsoky) (doc. ed), P. Berton (Prof. Dupuis) (doc. ed), Gabriel Moreau (pub), Oreste Bilancia (gentleman in the garden) (id), Sig.a Frediani (woman in the ship) (id) – Censorship certificate *Maciste contro la morte* (Episode 1): 15144 of 6.8.1920 (BN) – Original length *Maciste contro la morte*:1,549 m (Itt); Censorship certificate *Il viaggio di Maciste* (Episode 2):15145 of 6.9.1920 (Itt) – Original length *Il viaggio di Maciste*: 1,798 m (Itt); Censorship certificate *Il testament di Maciste* (Episode 3): 15146 of 6.9.1920 (Itt) – Original length *Il testamento di Maciste*: 1,724 m (Itt) – Production: Itala Film, U.C.I. (doc.ed).

Restored copy: 35mm, positive, polyester, 2,664 m (1st ep: 546 m + 2nd ep: 1127 m + 3rd ep: 991 m), 118' a 20 f/s (1st ep: 24' + 2nd ep: 50' + 3rd ep: 44'), color (Desmetcolor), Italian intertitles (MNC, CB in collaboration with CNC–Les Archives du Film de Bois d'Arcy, restoration 2010).

Maciste salvato dalle acque
(Maciste Saved from
Drowning, Italy, 1921)

Dir: Luigi Romano Borgnetto (doc. ed) – Subject and screenplay: Luigi Romano Borgnetto (doc.ed), Camillo Bruto Bonzi (doc.ed) – Cinematography: Augusto Pedrini (doc.ed) – Special effects: Segundo de Chomón (doc.cor) (N2007) – Cast: Bartolomeo Pagano (Maciste) (doc.ed), Henriette Bonard (Miss Elisa Groppara) (doc.ed), Erminia Zago (Miss Dorothy Bulldog) (doc.ed), Guido Clifford (Doctor John Hosbler) (doc.ed), Mario Voller Buzzi (Arnaldo Cambiasi) (doc.ed), Emilio Vardannes (Pedro Garçia, the Spanish) (doc.ed), Leone Heller (Fred, the German) (doc.ed), Gino Comelli (Julot, the Frenchman) (doc.ed), Mario Marcati (Nicolajewich, the Russian) (doc. ed), Colucci (doc.cor) – Censorship visa:15898 of 3.25.1921 (Itt) – Original length: 1,689 m (Itt) – Production: Itala Film, U.C.I. (doc.ed).

La rivincita di Maciste
(Maciste's Revenge, Italy, 1921)

Dir: Luigi Romano Borgnetto (doc. cor) – Subject and screenplay: Luigi Romano Borgnetto (doc.cor), Camillo

Bruto Bonzi (doc.cor) – Cinematography: Augusto Pedrini (doc.cor) – Special effects: Segundo de Chomón (doc.cor) – Cast: Bartolomeo Pagano (Maciste) (doc.ed), Henriette Bonard (Elisa Groppara) (doc.cor, doc.sog), Erminia Zago (Miss Dorothy Bulldog) (doc.cor), Guido Clifford (Doctor John Hosbler) (doc.cor), Emilio Vardannes (doc.cor), Mario Voller Buzzi (Arnaldo Cambiasi) (doc.cor), Leone Heller (doc.cor), Gino-Lelio Comelli (doc.c), Marcati (doc.c), Colucci (doc.c) – Censorship visa: 15907 of 3.29.1921 (doc. no) – Original length: 1,370 m (doc. no) – Production: Itala Film, U.C.I. (doc.no).

Maciste in vacanza
(Maciste on Vacation, Italy, 1921)

Dir: Luigi Romano Borgnetto (doc. ed) – Subject and screenplay: Alessandro De Stefani (doc.ed) – Cinematography: Augusto Pedrini (doc.ed) – Special effects: [Segundo de Chomón] (N2007) – Cast: Bartolomeo Pagano (Maciste) (id), Henriette Bonard (Miss Edith Moak) (doc.ed), Gemma De Sanctis (Miss Dolly) (doc.ed), Mario Voller-Buzzi (Conte Baiardi) (doc. ed), Felice Minotti (Fernando Perez) (doc.ed), Guido Derege di Donato (the poet Dasti) (doc.ed) – Censorship visa: 16028 of 5.6.1921 (Itt) – Original length: 1,907 m (Itt) – Production: Itala Film, U.C.I. (doc.ed).

Restored copy: 35mm, positive, polyester, 1,644 m, 72' a 20 f/s, color (Desmetcolor), Italian intertitles (MNC, CB, CN-CSC), in collaboration with

Filmoteca Española di Madrid, restoration 2008).

Man soll es Nicht für Möglich Halten. Maciste und die Javanerin
(Germany, 1922) (tit. It.: *Non si dovrebbe crederlo possibile ovvero Maciste e la giavanese / Maciste umanitario* [Itt] [trans: Maciste the Humanitarian])

Dir: Uwe Jens Krafft (PFL) – Screenplay: Georg Jacoby (Fp), Robert Liebmann (Fp) – Cinematography: Alfred Hansen (Fp), Giovanni Vitrotti (Fp) – Cast: Bartolomeo Pagano (Maciste) (PFL), Carola Toelle (PFL), Paul Otto (PFL), Arnold Korff (PFL), Manja Tzatschewa (PFL), Georg Baselt (PFL), Arnold Marlé (Fp), Josef Rehberger (Fp), Karl Platen (Fp), Willy Allen (Fp) – German censorship visa: 04.26.1922 (Fp) – Italian censorship visa: 17134 of 06.15.1922 (Itt) – Italian version original length: 1,864 m (Itt) – Production: Jakob Karol–Film Gmbh, Berlin (PFL).

Maciste und die Tochter des Silberkönigs
(Germany, 1922) (tit. It.: *Maciste e la figlia del re dell'argento* (M2001) / *Maciste e la figlia del re della Plata*) (trans: Maciste and the Daughter of the Silver King)

Dir: Luigi Romano Borgnetto (Fp) – Screenplay: Rolf Vanloo (Fp) – Cinematography: Giovanni Vitrotti (rec), Lamberti (rec) – Cast: Bartolomeo Pagano (Maciste); Elena Makowska (Fp), Ludwig Hartau (Fp),

Hans Junkermann (Fp), Otto Treptow (Fp), Heinrich Peer (Fp), Kurt Lilien (Fp), Gerhard Ritterband (Fp) – German censorship certificate: 07.28.1922 (Fp) – Italian censorship visa: 17612 of 11.30.1922 (Itt) – Italian version original length: 1,898 m (Itt) – Production: Jakob Karol–Film Gmbh, Berlin (Fp).

Archival copy preserved at Gosfilm-fond of Russia

Maciste und der Sträfling Nr. 51
(Germany, 1922-M2001]) (tit. It.: *Maciste giustiziere* (Itt).
(trans: Maciste the Avenger)

Dir: Luigi Romano Borgnetto (PFL) – Screenplay: Paul Rosenhayn (Fp) – Cinematography: Robert Baberske (Fp) – Cast: Bartolomeo Pagano (PFL), Karl Beckersachs (PFL), Karl Falkenberg (PFL), Leopold von Ledebur (PFL), Elsie Fuller (PFL), Edith Meller (PFL), Ludwig Rex (M2001) – German censorship visa: 28.11.1922, B.06786 / 28.09.1923, A70 (Fp) – German version original length: 2,072 m (Fp) – Italian censorship visa: 18086 of 04.4.1923 (Itt) – Italian version original length: 1,826 m (Itt) – Production: Jakob Karol–Film Gmbh, Berlin (PFL).

Archival copy preserved at the Cinémathèque Royale de Belgique

Maciste und die Chinesische Truhe
(Germany, 1923) (tit. It.: *Maciste e il cofano cinese* (Itt). (trans: Maciste and the Chinese Trunk)

Dir: Carl Boese (PFL) – Screenplay: Richard Hutter (Fp) – Cinematography: Ludwig Lippert (Fp), Max Grix (Fp) – Cast: Bartolomeo Pagano (Maciste), Elsie Fuller (PFL), Rudolf Lettinger (PFL), Grete Hollman (PFL), Karl Falkenberg (PFL), Ferdinand Martini (M2001), Edwin H. Knopf (Fp), Li Chun Di (Fp), Nien Tso Ling (Fp), Toni Wittels (Fp), Karl Falkenberg (Fp), Jakob Tiedtke (Fp), Gerhard Ritterband (Fp), Sybill Morel (Fp) – German censorship visa: 11.05.1923, B.V.32.23 / 07.05.1923, B.07193 (Fp) – German version original length: 2,072 m (Fp) – Italian censorship visa: 18604 of 08.16.1923 (Itt) – Italian version original length: 1,561 m (Itt) – Production: Jakob Karol–Film Gmbh, Berlin (PFL).

Archival copies preserved at Cinémathèque Royale de Belgique, and the CN-CSC.

MACISTE AFRICANO
(African Maciste, Germany, 1923)]*

Italian censorship visa: 18709 of 09.21.1923 (it) – Italian version original length: 1,561 m (Itt)

*The censorship visa data are available on the www.italiataglia.it website (Itt), which reports the information of the archives of the General Cinema Office of the Ministry of Heritage and

Culture. This hypothetical film title, however, has not been found anywhere else.

Maciste e il nipote d'America / Il nipote d'America
(Maciste and His American Nephew, Italy, 1924)

Dir: Eleuterio Rodolfi (doc.ed) – Subject and screenplay: Giovacchino Forzano (doc.ed) – Cinematography: Anchise Brizzi (doc.ed), Sergio Goddio (doc.ed) – Cast: Bartolomeo Pagano (Maciste) (doc.ed), Diomira Jacobini (Clara Pagano) (doc.ed), Mercedes Brignone (Aunt Bianca) (doc.ed), Pauline Polaire (Liliana Pagano) (doc.ed), Oreste Bilancia (teacher Cherubini) (doc.ed), Eleuterio Rodolfi (doc.ed) (Vittorio Pagano), Giuseppe Brignone (secretary Blount) (doc.ed), Augusto Bandini (BN) – Censorship visa: 19303 of 2.29.1924 (Itt) – Original length: 1,940 m (Itt) – Production: FERT-Pittaluga (rec).

Maciste imperatore
(Maciste the Emperor, Italy, 1924)

Dir: Guido Brignone (doc.ed) – Subject: Pier Angelo Mazzolotti (BN) – Screenplay: Guido Brignone (rec) – Cinematography: Massimo Terzano (doc.ed) – Special effects: [Segundo de Chomón] (N2007) – Cast: Bartolomeo Pagano (Maciste) (id), Domenico Gambino (Saetta) (doc.ed), Elena Sangro (Cinzia, the mime) (doc.ed), Oreste Grandi (Osram) (doc.ed), Augusto Bandini (cadet Paintheroxskoski) (doc.ed), Lola Romanos (Ginevra) (doc.ed), Gero Zambuto, (marshal of Lothar) (doc.ed), Raoul [Renato] Mayllard (Prince Otis) (doc.ed), Armand Pouget (the regent Stanos) (doc.ed), Giuseppe Brignone, (Count Oultz) (doc.ed), Lorenzo Soderini (Baron Riembergk) (doc.ed), Agostino Borgato (gran consultant) (id), Felice Minotti (officer at the court of Stanos) (id), Franz Sala (guard officer) (id), [Andrea Miano] (BN) – Censorship visa: 20004 of 10.18.1924 (Itt) – Original length: 2,134 m (Itt) – Production: FERT-Pittaluga (rec).

Restored copy: 35mm, polyester, positive, 1,710 m, 83' a 18 f/s, color (Desmetcolor), Italian intertitles (MNC, CB, restoration 2007)

Maciste nella gabbia dei leoni
(Maciste in the Lion's Den, Italy, 1926, released in the U.S. as *The Hero of the Circus*)

Dir: Guido Brignone (doc.ed) – Screenplay: Guido Brignone (Ginn Bill) (BN + doc.ed) – Cinematography: Massimo Terzano (doc.ed), Anchise Brizzi (doc.ed) – Scenography: Giulio Lombardozzi (BN) – Cast: Bartolomeo Pagano (Maciste) (id), Elena Sangro (Sarah, the equestrian) (doc.ed), Mimy Dovia (Seida) (doc.ed), Umberto Guarracino (Sullivan) (doc.ed), Alberto Collo (Giorgio Pommer) (doc.ed), Vittorio Bianchi (Karl Pommer) (doc.ed), Giuseppe Brignone (Juliette, the old clown) (doc.ed), Franz Sala (Strasser) (doc.ed), the Pommer circus staff (BN), Augusto Bandini (circus artist) (id), Felice Minotti (circus artist) (id), Andrè Habay (BN), Luigi Serventi (BN), Oreste Grandi (BN) – Censorship visa: 22390 of 1.21.1926 (Itt) – Original length: 2,393 m (Itt) – Production: Società Anonima Stefano Pittaluga (pub).

Restored copy: 35mm, polyester, positive, 2,100 m, 90' a 20 f/s, color (Desmetcolor), Italian intertitles (MNC, CB, 2007)

Maciste contro lo sceicco
(Maciste against the Sheik, Italy, 1926) sott. Oriental Adventures

Dir: Mario Camerini (doc.ed) – Subject and screenplay: Mario Camerini (pub) – Cinematography: Anchise Brizzi (doc.ed), Antonio Martini (BN) – Scenography and costumes: Camillo Pagliucchi (doc.ed) – Cast: Bartolomeo Pagano (Maciste) (id), Cecyl Tryan (Anna Del Fusaro) (doc. ed), Rita d'Harcourt (Marina Dulac) (doc.ed), Lido Manetti (Pietro De Bric) (doc.ed) in intertitles (Count Pietro de Latene), Franz Sala (Count Carlo Lanni) (doc.ed), Alex Bernard (Captain Ricon) (doc.ed), Oreste Grandi (Lopez) (doc.ed), Michele Mikailoff (Sheik Abd-El-Kar) (doc.ed), Armand Pouget (the butler) (doc.ed), Felice Minotti (a sailor) (id), Mario Saio (a sailor) (id), F. M. Costa (BN) – Censorship visa: 22468 of 2.12.1926 (Itt) – Original length: 2,256 m (Itt) – Production: Società Anonima Stefano Pittaluga (pub).

Restored copy: 35mm, polyester, positive, 2,000 m, 88' a 20 f/s, black-and-white, Italian intertitles (MNC, CB, 2009).

Maciste all'inferno
(*Maciste in Hell*, Italy, 1926*)

Dir: Guido Brignone (doc.ed) – Subject: Fantasio (Riccardo Artuffo) (doc.ed) – Cinematography: Massimo Terzano (doc.ed), Ubaldo Arata (doc. ed) – Assistant to the cinematographer: Giulio Lombardozzi (BN) – Special effects: Segundo de Chomón (doc.ed) (N2007) – Cast: Bartolomeo Pagano (Maciste) (id), Pauline Polaire (Graziella) (doc.ed), Elena Sangro (Proserpina) (doc.ed), Lucia Zanussi (Luciferina) (doc.ed), Franz Sala (Barbariccia/ Doctor Nox) (doc.ed), Umberto Guarracino (Plutone) (doc.ed), Mario Saio (Gerione) (doc.ed), Domenico Serra (Giorgio) (pub), Felice Minotti (BN), Andrea Miano (BN) – Censorship visa: 20529 of 03.16.1926 (approval on appeal) (Itt) – Original length: 2,475 m (Itt) – Production: Fert-Pittaluga (doc. ed).

Restored copy: 35mm, polyester, positive, 2,306 m, 101' a 20 f/s, color (Desmetcolor), Italian intertitles (MNC, CB, restoration 2009).

*The film was presented to the film competition of the Milan Fair in 1924; it was censored and distributed only two years later (F2008).

Il gigante delle Dolomiti
(The Giant of the Dolomites, Italy, 1926)

Dir: Guido Brignone (doc.ed) – Subject: Guido Brignone (Gin Bill) (BN + doc.ed) – Cinematography: Massimo

Terzano (doc.ed) – Scenography: Domenico Gaido (doc.ed), Giulio Lombardozzi (doc.ed) – Cast: Bartolomeo Pagano (Maciste, the alpine guide) (id), Aldo Marus (nephew Hans) (doc.ed), Elena Lunda (Vanna Dardos/Hanna Humbert) (doc.ed), Dolly Grey (Maud, the painter) (doc.ed), Andrea Habay (Eng. Richard Ewert) (doc.ed), Luigi Serventi (Giorgio Müller, the adventurer) (doc.ed), Mario Saio (tourist) (doc.ed), Augusto Poggioli (Freddy Humbert) (doc.ed), Augusto Bandini (boy in the elevator) (doc.ed), Oreste Grandi (guide Shulz) (doc.ed), Felice Minotti (a valley dweller) (id), Ernesto Vaser (a tavern guest) (id) – Censorship visa: 23113 of 11.12.1926 (Itt) – Original length: 2,352 m (Itt) – Production and distribution: Società Anonima Stefano Pittaluga (doc.ed).

Copy preserved in the Fondazione Cineteca Italiana, Milan.

Notes

Introduction

1. Throughout this study I have adopted the following procedure to present English-language translations of Italian film titles: I use the American title under which known U.S.-distributed Italian films appeared in the United States in italics; e.g., *La caduta di Troia* (*The Fall of Troy*, Itala Film, 1910), unless the two titles coincide, as in the case of *Cabiria* (Itala Film, 1914). When no American title is available, I have included a literal translation of the title in roman; e.g., *L'ultima battaglia* (*The Last Battle*, 1914). My source for the American titles of Italian films is Aldo Bernardini, ed., *Archivio del cinema italiano*, vol. 1, *Il cinema muto, 1905–1931* (Rome: ANICA: 1991), as well as newspapers, trade journals, and archival sources.

2. See part 3 of the appendix for a detailed filmography of all of Maciste's films.

3. My research is indebted to previous work on the Maciste films, and I draw upon these works throughout the book. Gian Piero Brunetta, *Storia del cinema italiano*, vol. 1, *Il cinema muto, 1895–1929* (Rome: Riuniti, 1993), 87–89,

317–319. Brunetta has written frequently on the silent period in many different venues and languages. The recently released *Il cinema muto italiano* (Bari: Laterza, 2008) is a synthesized, revised edition of his previous work on this subject. See also the entry "Cinema muto italiano" in *Storia del cinema mondiale*, vol. 3, *L'europa. Le cinematografie nazionali*, ed. Gian Piero Brunetta (Torino: Einaudi, 2000), 31–60; *Cent'anni di cinema italiano* (Roma-Bari: Laterza, 1991); *Buio in sala: 100 anni di passione dello spettatore cinematografico* (Venezia: Marsilio, 1989); and *Cinema italiano fra le due guerre* (Milano: Mursia, 1975). For English speakers, the long-awaited translation of Brunetta's work is now available, *The History of Italian Cinema: A Guide to Italian Film from its Origins to the Twenty-first Century* (Princeton, NJ: Princeton University Press, 2009). See also Monica Dall'Asta, *Un cinéma musclé. Le surhomme dans le cinéma muet italien (1913–1926)* (Crisnée: Yellow Now, 1992); "La diffusione del film a episodi in Europa," in *Storia del cinema mondiale*, vol. 1, *L'europa. Miti, luoghi, divi*, ed. Gian Piero Brunetta (Turin: Einaudi,

1999), 277–323; and "Italian Film Serials and (Inter)National-Popular Culture," in *Italian Silent Cinema: A Reader*, ed. Giorgio Bertellini (New Baret, UK: John Libbey, 2013), 195–202. Also see Richard Dyer, *White* (London: Routledge, 1997), 145–183; Alberto Farassino, "Maciste e il paradigma divistico," in *Cabiria e il suo tempo*, ed. Paolo Bertetto and Gianni Rondolino (Milan: Il Castoro, 1998), 223–232; Alberto Farassino and Tatti Sanguineti, eds., *Gli uomini forti* (Milano: Mazzotta, 1983); Michele Giordano, *Giganti buoni. Da Ercole a Piedone (e oltre) il mito dell'uomo forte nel cinema italiano* (Rome: Gremese, 1998); Cristina Jandelli, *Breve storia del divismo cinematografico* (Venezia: Marsilio, 2007), 47–53; Marcia Landy, *Stardom, Italian Style: Screen Performance and Personality in Italian Cinema* (Bloomington: Indiana University Press, 2008), 7–15; Vittorio Martinelli and Mario Quargnolo, *Maciste & Co. I giganti buoni del muto italiano* (Gemona del Friuli: Cinepopolare Edizioni, 1981); Vittorio Martinelli, "Lasciate fare a noi, siamo forti," in Farassino and Sanguineti, *Gli uomini forti*, 9–28; Steven Ricci, *Cinema & Fascism: Italian Film and Society, 1922–1943* (Berkeley: University of California Press, 2008), 81–87; Irmbert Schenk, "The Cinematic Support to National(istic) Mythology: The Italian Peplum, 1910–1930," in *Globalization, Cultural Identities, and Media Representations*, ed. Natascha Gentz and Stefan Kramer (Albany: State University of New York Press, 2006), 153–168; and Mario Verdone, "Il film atletico e acrobatico," *Centrofilm* 17 (1961): 3–36. Denis Lotti has shed new light

on Pagano and the Maciste films in "Il divismo maschile nel cinema muto italiano: protagonisti, film, stereotipi, 1910–1929" (PhD diss., Università degli Studi di Padova, 2011). I graciously thank Denis for sharing his research with me.

4. See the introduction and essays by Adrian Lyttelton, as well as Paul Corner, "State and Society, 1901–1922," in *Liberal and Fascist Italy, 1900–1945*, ed. Adrian Lyttelton (Oxford: Oxford University Press, 2002), 1–16 and 17–43 respectively. See also Martin Clark, *Modern Italy, 1871 to the Present*, 3rd ed. (London: Longman, 2008), and Jonathan Dunnage, *Twentieth-Century Italy: A Social History* (London: Routledge, 2002). For more on the notion of nation and character, see Silvana Patriarca, *Italian Vices: Nation and Character from the Risorgimento to the Republic* (Cambridge: Cambridge University Press, 2010).

5. Suzanne Stewart-Steinberg, *The Pinocchio Effect: On Making Italians (1860–1920)* (Chicago: University of Chicago Press, 2007), 1–20, here 1.

6. The first scholar to examine Maciste's racial transformation was Giorgio Bertellini, and my work owes a tremendous debt to his initial observations and to much of his subsequent work on race and Italian and American cinema. Giorgio Bertellini, "Colonial Autism: Whitened Heroes, Auditory Rhetoric, and National Identity in Interwar Italian Cinema," in *A Place in the Sun: Africa in Italian Colonial Culture from Post-Unification to the Present*, ed. Patrizia Palumbo (Berkeley: University

of California Press, 2003), 255–278, esp. 256–257.

7. I pay homage to the work of Modris Eksteins, who stated: "Coincidence is our term for concurrence that is not consciously willed and that we cannot explain in any definitive sense. However, if we retreat from the restrictive world of linear causality and think in terms of context and confluence rather than cause, then it is undeniable that there were many influences . . . at work in the imaginations." Modris Eksteins, *Rites of Spring: The Great War and the Birth of the Modern Age* (Boston: Houghton Mifflin, 1989), 3.

8. Geoff Eley, "Culture, Nation, Gender," in *Gendered Nations: Nationalisms and Gender Order in the Long Nineteenth Century*, ed. Ida Blom et al. (Oxford: Berg, 2000): 27–40, here 29. For the Italian case, see Ronald S. Cunsolo, *Italian Nationalism: From Its Origins to World War II* (Malabar, FL: Robert E. Krieger, 1990); and Nicholas Doumanis, *Italy* (London: Arnold, 2001).

9. Emilio Gentile, *The Struggle for Modernity: Nationalism, Futurism, and Fascism* (Westport, CT: Praeger, 2003), 2.

10. George L. Mosse, *Nationalism and Sexuality: Middle-Class Morality and Sexual Norms in Modern Europe* (Madison: University of Wisconsin Press, 1985), 1–22.

11. George L. Mosse, *The Image of Man: The Creation of Modern Masculinity* (New York: Oxford University Press, 1996), 5. Similarly, Max Nordau's concept of regenerate "Muscle Jewry," as Todd Samuel Presner has argued, "was not only consistent with the national

goals of the Zionist movement. . . . It was also the crystallization of these goals on the individual body of the Jew" with the goal of achieving "Jewish national goals through corporeal means." Todd Samuel Presner, "'Clear Heads, Solid Stomachs, and Hard Muscles': Max Nordau and the Aesthetics of Jewish Regeneration," *Modernism/Modernity* 10, no. 2 (2003): 269–296, here 269–70.

12. George L. Mosse, *Nationalism and Sexuality: Respectability and Abnormal Sexuality in Modern Europe* (New York: Howard Fertig, 1985), 9–19.

13. Federico Boni, "Sport, mascolinità e media," in *Mascolinità all'italiana. Construzioni, narrazioni, mutamenti*, ed. Elena dell'Agnese and Elisabetta Ruspini (Turin: UTET, 2007), 79–102.

14. Dyer, *White*, 145–183.

15. Maria Wyke, *Projecting the Past: Ancient Rome, Cinema, and History* (London: Routledge, 1997), 25–26.

16. Ibid.

17. Christopher E. Forth, *Masculinity in the Modern West: Gender, Civilization, and the Body* (New York: Palgrave Macmillan, 2008), 117–138, 164.

18. Alberto Abruzzese, "Gli uomini forti e le maestre pedani," in Farassino and Sanguineti, *Gli uomini forti*, 56–66. This emphasis on strength and might found its way into popular literature as well, particularly in Eduardo De Amicis's novel *Amore e ginnastica* and the popular tales of Emilio Salgari. See Giuseppe Valperga, "Mitologie popolari dell'uomo forte," in Farassino and Sanguineti, *Gli uomini forti*, 67–70; and Stewart-Steinberg, *Pinocchio Effect*, 171–176. For more on Salgari, see chap-

ter 2's discussion of his works in relation to *Cabiria*.

19. Charles Hirschman, "The Origins and Demise of the Concept of Race," *Population and Development Review* 30, no. 3 (2004): 385–415. See also George Stocking, "The Turn-of-the-Century Concept of Race," *Modernism/Modernity* 1, no. 1 (1994): 4–16.

20. John Dickie, *Darkest Italy: The Nation and Stereotypes of the Mezzogiorno, 1860–1900* (New York: Palgrave Macmillan, 1999), 2–5; Giuseppe Sergi, *The Mediterranean Race: A Study of the Origin of European Peoples* (New York: Charles Scribner's Sons, 1909), 28–38; and Alfredo Niceforo, *L'Italia barbara contemporanea* (Milan: Remo Sandron, 1898). For Lombroso, see Cesare Lombroso, *Criminal Man,* trans. Mary Gibson and Nicole Hahn Rafter (Durham, NC: Duke University Press, 2006); and Mary Gibson, *Born to Crime: Cesare Lombroso and the Origins of Biological Criminality* (Westport, CT: Praeger, 2002). Similarly, as Gentile observes, "The preponderance attributed to the awareness of a common past in forming the modern concept of nation, understood to be its historic formation and not a natural factor, excluded race from the characteristics determining nationality." Emilio Gentile, *La Grande Italia: The Rise and Fall of the Myth of the Nation in the Twentieth Century,* trans. Suzanne Dingee and Jennifer Pudney (Madison: University of Wisconsin Press, 2008), 31.

21. Nietzsche's concept of the superman is not related necessarily to the muscular body; for Nietzsche, man is at the center of the universe and controls his own destiny, but his materiality is not a physicality. At one point in *Thus Spoke Zarathustra,* drawing on the Greek culture that influenced much of his work, Nietzsche condemns the vanity of the sublime ones who are obsessed with vanity, appearance, and power in their muscularity (the god Theseus) in favor of Dionysus, who for Nietzsche embodies the qualities of the superhero. Friedrich Nietzsche, *Thus Spoke Zarathustra: A Book for All and None,* ed. Adrian Del Caro and Robert Pippin, trans. Adrian del Caro (Cambridge, UK: Cambridge University Press, 2006), 91–92. See also Barbara Spackman, *Fascist Virilities: Rhetoric, Ideology, and Social Fantasy in Italy* (Minneapolis: University of Minnesota Press, 1996), 83–84.

22. Nietzsche's ideas began to circulate in Italy after D'Annunzio was writing his primary works that articulated his concept of the superman. Francesco Piga argues that D'Annunzio's early works laid the foundation for his idea of superuomismo before he came into direct contact with Nietzsche's writings in 1895. Francesco Piga, *Il mito del superuomo in Nietzsche e D'Annunzio* (Florence: Nuovedizioni Vallecchi, 1979), 118–119.

23. Stephen Gundle, "The Death (and Re-birth) of the Hero: Charisma and Manufactured Charisma in Modern Italy," *Modern Italy* 3, no. 2 (1998): 173–189. See also George L. Mosse, "The Poet and the Exercise of Political Power: Gabriele D'Annunzio," in *Masses and Man: Nationalist and Fascist Perceptions of Reality* (Detroit: Wayne State University Press, 1987), 87–103.

24. Andrea Baravelli, "L'immagine virile dell'Italia," paper delivered at the Convegno Sissco, Lecce, 25–27 September 2003.

25. For nineteenth-century philosopher Vincenzo Gioberti, Italians suffered from a disease of the will, "a moral sickness that emasculated and feminized a previously virile people." Patriarca, *Italian Vices*, 25. Patriarca notes how this feminine/weak versus masculine/strong binary was a common metaphor used in national rhetoric.

26. Gigliola Gori, "Supermanism and the Culture of the Body in Italy: The Case of Futurism," *International Journal of the History of Sport* 16, no. 1 (1999): 159–165, esp. 162; Barbara Spackman, *Fascist Virilities*, in particular 9–10. Futurism is another recurring discursive presence in the Maciste series and is discussed in detail in chapters 3 and 5.

27. Although profoundly anticlerical, writers for the modernist Florentine journals *La Voce, Leonardo,* and *Lacerba* believed in the spiritual mission of creating a national Italian culture. The vociani, including Giovanni Papini and Giuseppe Prezzolini, emphasized the religious component to politics, advocating a spiritual nationalism linked to a modernist, cultural rebirth. Walter L. Adamson's work in this field is fundamental. See his "Modernism and Fascism: The Politics of Culture in Italy, 1903–1922," *American Historical Review* 95, no. 2 (1990): 359–390; "Fascism and Culture: Avant-Gardes and Secular Religion in the Italian Case," *Journal of Contemporary History* 24, no. 3 (1989): 411–435; and especially *Avant-Garde Florence: From Modernism to Fascism*

(Cambridge, MA: Harvard University Press, 1993), 182–187.

28. Giovanni Papini, *Maschilità* (Florence: Libreria della Voce, 1919). All page numbers for citations to this work appear directly in the text.

29. Adamson, *Avant-Garde Florence,* 81–90.

30. Dan Streible, *Fight Pictures: A History of Boxing and Early Cinema* (Berkeley: University of California Press, 2008); Luke McKernan, "Lo sport nel cinema muto," *Griffithiana* 64 (October 1998): 80–141; Lee Grieveson, "Fighting Films: Race, Morality, and the Governing of Cinema, 1912–1915," *Cinema Journal* 38, no. 1 (1998): 40–72.

31. Thomas Waugh, "Strength and Stealth: Watching (and Wanting) Turn-of-the-Century Strongmen," *Canadian Journal of Film Studies /Revue Canadienne d'ètudes Cinématographiques* 2, no. 1 (1992): 1–20. See also Thomas Waugh, *Hard to Imagine: Gay Male Eroticism in Photography and Film from their Beginnings to Stonewall* (New York: Columbia University Press, 1996).

32. Cited in Gianni Rondolino, *I giorni di Cabiria* (Turin: Lindau, 1993), 18, originally published as *Torino come Hollywood* (Bologna: Cappelli, 1980).

33. Marcia Landy, *Italian Film* (Cambridge: Cambridge University Press, 2000), 25.

34. For more on the world's fair, see Cristina Della Coletta, *World's Fairs Italian Style: The Great Exhibitions in Turin and Their Narratives, 1860–1915* (Toronto: University of Toronto Press, 2006).

35. Gianni Rondolino, "'Affatica meno e rende di più.' Il cinema muto

a Torino," in Bertetto and Rondolino, *Cabiria e il suo tempo*, 19–30; and Gianni Rondolino, "Il cinema torinese nei primi anni Dieci," in *Cabiria & Cabiria*, ed. Silvio Alovisio and Alberto Barbera (Turin: Museo Nazionale del Cinema, 2006), 274–284. See also Davide Bracco et al., eds., *Torino città del cinema* (Milan: Il Castoro, 2001), in particular Rondolino's essay, "La nascita del cinema a Torino," 25–32.

36. My work here clearly owes great debt to Gaylyn Studlar and *This Mad Masquerade: Stardom and Masculinity in the Jazz Age* (New York: Columbia University Press, 1996).

37. Here I am indebted to the work of Miriam Hansen, Daisuke Miyao, and Giorgio Bertellini. See in particular Miriam Hansen, *Babel & Babylon: Spectatorship in American Silent Cinema* (Cambridge, MA: Harvard University Press, 1991); Daisuke Miyao, *Sessue Hayakawa: Silent Cinema and Transnational Stardom* (Durham, NC: Duke University Press, 2007); and Bertellini, *Italy in Early American Cinema*, as well as his "Duce/Divo: Masculinity, Racial Identity, and Politics among Italian Americans in 1920s New York City," *Journal of Urban History* 31, no. 5 (2005): 685–726, and "The Atlantic Valentino: The "Inimitable Lover" as Racialized and Gendered Italian," in *Intimacy and Italian Migration: Gender and Domestic Lives in a Mobile World*, ed. Loretta Baldassar and Donna Gabaccia (New York: Fordham University Press, 2011), 37–48.

38. Dall'Asta, *Un cinéma musclé*, 81.

39. Throughout this study I use the term "Fascism" with a capital "F" to signify Italian Fascism and its policies, dis-

courses, and ideology; "fascism" with a lowercase "f" refers to the movement in general. And as I have previously argued, I intend not to speak about Fascist film production, particularly during its fledgling period between 1922 to 1926, but rather film production during the early years of the Fascist period due to the lack of solid, ideological control by the government. Nor do I intend to offer a comprehensive historical summary of this highly eventful time. I refer the reader to multiple volumes on the cultural, social, and political history of Fascism that examine numerous facets of this complicated and complex period of Italy's tumultuous past: Philip V. Cannistraro, *La fabbrica del consenso. Fascismo e mass media* (Roma: Laterza, 1975); Victoria De Grazia, *The Culture of Consent: Mass Organization of Leisure in Fascist Italy* (Cambridge: Cambridge University Press, 1981); Victoria de Grazia, *How Fascism Ruled Women, 1922–1943* (Berkeley: University of California Press, 1991); Renzo De Felice, *Fascism: An Informal Introduction to Its Theory and Practice*, ed. Michael Ledeen (New Brunswick, NJ: Transaction Books, 1976); Renzo De Felice, *Mussolini il fascista*. 4 vols. (Torino: Einaudi, 1965–1997); Renzo De Felice, *Antologia sul fascismo* (Bari: Laterza, 1976); Alexander de Grand, *Italian Fascism: Its Origins and Development*, 3rd ed. (Lincoln: University of Nebraska Press, 2000); David Forgacs, ed., *Rethinking Italian Fascism: Capitalism, Populism, and Culture* (London: Lawrence and Wishart, 1986); Adrian Lyttelton, *The Seizure of Power: Fascism in Italy, 1919–1929*, rev. ed. (London: Routledge, 2004);

Giovanni Mira and Luigi Salvatorelli, *Storia d'Italia nel periodo fascista,* 2 vols. (Torino: Einaudi, 1970); Roland Sarti, ed., *The Ax Within: Italian Fascism in Action* (New York: New Viewpoints, 1974); and Zeev Sternhell, with Mario Snajder and Maia Asheri, *The Birth of Fascist Ideology: From Cultural Rebellion to Political Revolution,* trans. David Maisel (Princeton, NJ: Princeton University Press, 1994).

40. Paolo Cherchi Usai, *Silent Cinema: An Introduction,* 2nd ed. (London: BFI, 2008).

41. "Maciste," Traccini.it, http://www.treccani.it/vocabolario/maciste.

42. For more on the Peplum film, see Maria Elena D'Amelio, *Ercole, il divo* (San Marino, Italy: AIEP, 2012); Michèle Lagny, "Popular Taste: The Peplum," in *Popular European Cinema,* ed. Richard Dyer and Ginette Vincendeau (London: Routledge, 1992), 163–180; Maggie Günsberg, *Italian Cinema: Gender and Genre* (New York: Palgrave Macmillan, 2005); Vittorio Spinazzola, *Cinema e pubblico: lo spettacolo filmico in Italia, 1945–1965* (Rome: Bulzoni, 1985); Stefano Della Casa, "Una postilla sul genere mitologico," in *Sull'industria cinematografica italiana,* ed. Enrico Magrelli (Venice: Marsilio, 1986), 171–179; Maria Wyke, "Herculean Muscle!: The Classicizing Rhetoric of Bodybuilding," *Arion* 4, no. 3(1997): 51–79; Robert Rushing, "Gentlemen Prefer Hercules: Desire/Identification/Beefcake," *Camera Obscura* 23, no. 3 (2008): 158–191; Roy Menarini and Paolo Noto, "Dall'economia di scala all'intertestualità di genere," in *L'arte del risparmio: stile e tecnologia,* ed. Gia-

como Manzoli and Guglielmo Pescatore (Rome: Carrocci, 2005), 19–30; Jon Solomon, *The Ancient World in Cinema,* rev. and exp. ed. (New Haven, CT: Yale University Press, 2001); Michael G. Cornelius, ed., *Of Muscles and Men: Essays on the Sword and Sandal Film* (Jefferson, NC: McFarland, 2011).

43. Federico Fellini, "Amarcord Maciste," in Farassino and Sanguinetti, *Gli uomini forti,* 182.

1. The Birth of the Strongman

1. Legal documents pertaining to a 1923 court case seemingly contradict Pagano's place of birth. In the legal decision filed in the case, dated 19 March 1923, the declaration referred to the actor as "Bartolomeo Pagano fu Giuseppe, nato a Napoli e residente a Torino" (Bartolomeo Pagano originally Giuseppe, born in Naples and resident of Torino). My information comes from a copy of Pagano's death certificate, which is the definitive Italian document for this information. See also Marco Grifo, "Alla ricerca del cast perduto: la troupe di *Cabiria,*" in Silvio Alovisio and Alberto Barbera, eds., *Cabiria & Cabiria* (Turin: Museo Nazionale del Cinema, 2006), 110–126.

2. Roberto Chiti, "Bartolomeo Pagano, un uomo chiamato Maciste," catalog from the 41st Festival di Cinema Sportivo (Turin 2–8 December 1985), *Maciste. Omaggio a Bartolomeo Pagano* (Turin: Tepotecnica Ernani, 1985), 1–6; "Un'intervista con il figlio di Maciste," in *Gli uomini forti,* ed. Alberto Farassino and Tatti Sanguineti (Milan: Mazzotta, 1983), 180–181; and Denis Lotti, "Il divismo maschile nel cinema muto

italiano. Protagonisti, film, stereotipi, 1910–1929," PhD diss., Università degli Studi di Padova, 2011. The entry on Bartolomeo Pagano by Roberto Chiti in *Filmlexicon degli autori e delle opere*, vol. 5 (Rome: Edizioni Bianco e Nero, 1962), 231–232, tells a different story: that Pagano was already an actor and actively sought out the role.

3. "Un'intervista con Maciste," *Films Pittaluga* (15 February 1924), 45–46; and "'Maciste, il gigante buono.' Intervista con Bartolomeo Pagano," *Al Cinemà* 3, no. 11 (1924): 8–10.

4. "Un'intervista con Maciste," *Films Pittaluga* (15 February 1924), 45–46; and "'Maciste, il gigante buono.' Intervista con Bartolomeo Pagano," *Al Cinemà* 3, no. 11 (1924): 8–10.

5. A brief report on the court case appears in "Notizie varie," *La Vita Cinematografica* 14, no. 11 (1923): 58.

6. The original quote reads: "Caro Bartolomeo, non sei mica Otello o Cirano e tantomeno Charles Chaplin . . . Maciste è sempre Maciste, ma scaduto il contratto a un Pagano se ne fa un altro, vincono il poeta e le maestranze della Casa." Excerpt from the manuscript (pp. 26–27) of the judgment No. 911 of 27 July 1923 by the Court of Appeals of Turin in the case of the Società Anonima Itala against Bartolomeo Pagano decreed on 27 November 1923. The document is preserved in the State Archives of Turin, United Chambers, Civil and Criminal Court of Turin, Civil Sections, Civil Judgments Volume 1923, Court of Appeal of Turin.

7. Sentenze Civili 1923, 901–950, 27 July 1923. The document is preserved in the State Archives of Turin, United Chambers, Civil and Criminal Court of Turin, Civil Sections, Civil Judgments Volume 1923, Court of Appeal of Turin.

8. The booklet was part of a series known as *I grandi artisti del cinema*. See *I grandi artisti del cinema: Maciste (Bartolomeo Pagano)* (Milan: Gloriosa Casa Editrice, 1926), 2. All subsequent references are cited directly in the text. Among other portrayed stars in the series were Mary Pickford, Jackie Coogan, Rudolph Valentino, Douglas Fairbanks, Sessue Hayakawa, and Charlot (Charlie Chaplin). Maria Jacobini and Rina De Liguoro were the only other Italians (aside from Valentino) who merited their own booklet at the time of this edition's publication. On the series, see Raffaele De Berti, *Dallo schermo alla carta. Romanzi, fotoromanzi, rotocalchi cinematografici: il film e i suoi paratesti* (Milan: Vita e Pensiero, 2000); and Raffaele De Berti and Marina Rossi, "Cinema e cultura popolare: i rotocalchi illustrati," in "Il cinema a Milano fra le due guerre," ed. Francesco Casetti and Raffaele De Berti, special issue of *Comunicazioni Sociali* 10, no. 3–4 (1988): 222–254.

9. Key works on Italian stardom and silent cinema that have influenced my thinking on this subject include Stephen Gundle, "Fame, Fashion, and Style: The Italian Star System," in *Italian Cultural Studies: An Introduction*, ed. David Forgacs and Robert Lumley (Oxford: Oxford University Press, 1986), 309–326; Cristina Jandelli, *Breve storia del divismo cinematografico* (Venice: Marsilio, 2007); Marcia Landy, *Stardom, Italian Style: Screen Performance and Personality in Ital-*

ian Cinema (Bloomington: Indiana University Press, 2008); and Vittorio Martinelli, "Nascita del divismo," in *Storia del cinema mondiale,* vol. 1, *L'Europa. Miti, luoghi, divi,* ed. Gian Piero Brunetta (Turin: Einaudi, 2000), 221–250. My theoretical definition of stars is predominantly influenced by the following works: Richard Dyer, *Stars,* rev. ed. (1979; London: BFI, 1998), and *Heavenly Bodies: Film Stars and Society* (New York: St. Martin's, 1986); Christine Gledhill, ed., *Stardom: Industry of Desire* (London: Routledge, 1991); Paul McDonald, *The Star System: Hollywood's Production of Popular Identities* (London: Wallflower, 2000); Toby Miller, "Stars and Performance," in *Film Theory: An Introduction,* ed. Robert Stam and Toby Miller (Malden, MA: Blackwell: 2000), 595–602; Janet Staiger, *Interpreting Films: Studies in the Historical Reception of American Cinema* (Princeton, NJ: Princeton University Press, 1992), and *Perverse Spectators: The Practices of Film Reception* (New York: New York University Press, 2000); and Gaylyn Studlar, *This Mad Masquerade: Stardom and Masculinity in the Jazz Age* (New York: Columbia University Press, 1996), and *Precocious Charms: Stars Performing Girlhood in Classical Hollywood Cinema* (Berkeley: University of California Press, 2013).

10. Maurizia Boscagli, *Eye on the Flesh: Fashions of Masculinity in the Early Twentieth Century* (Boulder, CO: Westview Press, 1996), 4. Boscagli also acknowledges the flip side of this duality, that "the perverse masculinity inscribed onto the body of the Nietzschean superman can be understood as producing sexual and gender indeterminacy," whereby the muscled body is also "a hysterical body simultaneously disavowing and bearing traces of abjection" (9–10).

11. Gian Piero Brunetta, "Introduzione," in *Metamorfosi del mito classico nel cinema,* ed. Gian Piero Brunetta (Bologna: Il Mulino, 2011), 9–30.

12. Roland Barthes, *Mythologies* (1957; New York: Hill and Wang, 1972).

13. Emilio Gentile, *La Grande Italia: The Rise and Fall of the Myth of the Nation in the Twentieth Century,* trans. Suzanne Dingee and Jennifer Pudney (Madison: University of Wisconsin Press, 2008), 3–15.

14. David Atkinson and Denis Cosgrove, "Urban Rhetoric and Embodied Identities: City, Nation, and Empire at the Vittorio Emanuele II Monument in Rome, 1870–1945," *Annals of the Association of American Geographers* 88, no. 1 (1998): 28–49, here 33. See also John Agnew, "The Impossible Capital: Monumental Rome under Liberal and Fascist Regimes, 1870–1943," *Geografiska Annaler* 80B (1998): 229–240; Peter Bondanella, *The Eternal City: Roman Images in the Modern World* (Chapel Hill: University of North Carolina Press, 1987); and John Dickie, "*La macchina da scrivere:* The Victor Emmanuel Monument in Rome and Italian Nationalism," *Italianist* 13 (1994): 261–285.

15. Emilio Gentile, *Politics as Religion,* trans. George Staunton (Princeton, NJ: Princeton University Press, 2006), xiii. Scholars tend to translate Gentile's concept of *religione civile* as both "civil religion" and "civic religion." I have chosen to use the term "civic reli-

gion" in order to stress the importance of the connections between the religious and the civic, thereby eliminating the English definition of "civil" as courteous or polite.

16. Ibid., xvi. See also Emilio Gentile, *The Sacralization of Politics in Fascist Italy,* trans. Keith Botsford (Cambridge, MA: Harvard University Press, 1996).

17. Scholars have approached film and religion from multiple points of view and a variety of disciplines: religious studies, film studies, anthropology, and sociology. Film scholars concentrate predominantly on representations of religion in film, while religious studies scholars and theologians tend to look at the convergences between film and religion in a search for a potential dialogue between the two disciplines. William L. Blizek, ed., *The Continuum Companion to Religion and Film* (London: Continuum, 2009); Rachel Dwyer, *Filming the Gods: Religion and Indian Cinema* (London: Routledge, 2006); Pamela Grace, *The Religious Film: Christianity and the Hagiopic* (Boston: Wiley-Blackwell, 2009); Robert K. Johnston, *Reel Spirituality: Theology and Film in Dialogue,* 2nd ed. (Grand Rapids, MI: Baker Academic, 2006); John C. Lyden, *Film as Religion: Myths, Morals, and Rituals* (New York: New York University Press, 2003); Clive Marsh and Gaye Ortiz, eds., *Explorations in Theology and Film: Movies and Meaning* (Oxford: Blackwell, 1997); Jolyon Mitchell, "Theology and Film," in *The Modern Theologians: An Introduction to Christian Theology since 1918,* 3rd ed., ed. David F. Ford with Ra-

chel Muers (London: Blackwell, 2005), 736–759; Steve Nolan, *Film, Lacan, and the Subject of Religion: A Psychoanalytic Approach to Religious Film Analysis* (New York: Continuum, 2009); Conrad Ostwalt, *Secular Steeples: Popular Culture and the Religious Imagination* (Harrisburg, PA: Trinity Press International, 2003); Adele Reinhartz, *Jesus of Hollywood* (Oxford: Oxford University Press, 2007); Paul Schrader, *Transcendental Style in Film* (Berkeley: University of California Press, 1972); Pete Ward, *Gods Behaving Badly: Media, Religion, and Celebrity Culture* (Waco, TX: Baylor University Press, 2011); and Melanie J. Wright, *Religion and Film: An Introduction* (London: I. B. Taurus, 2007). The lone collection to ground early cinema and religion historically is *Une invention du diable? Cinéma des premiers temps et religion,* ed. Roland Cosandey, André Gaudreault, and Tom Gunning (Lausanne: Editions Payot, 1992). For religion and Italian cinema, see Aldo Bernardini, "Les catholiques et l'avènement du cinema en Italie: promotion et contrôle," in Roland Cosandey et al., *Une invention du diable?,* 3–11; Ruggero Eugeni and Dario E. Viganò, eds., *Attravarso lo schermo. Cinema e cultura cattolica in Italia,* vol. 1, *Dalle origini agli anni Venti* (Rome: Ente dello Spettacolo, 2006); Elena Mosconi, "Un potente maestro per le folle. Chiesa e mondo cattolico di fronte al cinema," in Eugeni and Viganò, *Attravarso lo schermo,* 145–171; and Stefano Socci, *L'ombra scura della religione* (Fiesole: Cadmo, 2002).

18. Gentile, *Politics as Religion,* 1, 7–8.

19. Edgar Morin, *The Stars*, trans. Richard Howard (1972; Minneapolis: University of Minnesota Press, 2005), 73; emphasis in original. Similarly, "the history of the stars repeats, in its own proportions, the history of the gods. Before the gods (before the stars) the mythical universe (the screen) was peopled with specters or phantoms endowed with the glamour and magic of the double. Several of the presences have progressively assumed body and substance, have taken form, amplified, and flowered into gods and goddesses. And even as certain major gods of the ancient pantheons metamorphose themselves into *hero-gods of salvation*, the star-goddesses humanize them-selves and become new mediators be-tween the fantastic world of dreams and man's daily life on earth" (25; emphasis in original).

20. Scholarship continues to employ religious metaphors in relation to star-dom. The recent Star Decades Series: American Cultures/American Cinema, edited by Adrienne L. McLean and Murray Pomerance and published by Rutgers University Press, features titles that draw on stars' celestial and oth-erworldly status; for instance, Patrice Petro, ed., *Idols of Modernity: Movie Stars of the 1920s* (New Brunswick, NJ: Rutgers University Press, 2010); R. Bar-ton Palmer, ed., *Larger Than Life: Movie Stars of the 1950s* (New Brunswick, NJ: Rutgers University Press, 2010); and Pamela Robertson Wojcik, ed., *New Constellations: Movie Stars of the 1960s* (New Brunswick, NJ: Rutgers Univer-sity Press, 2012).

21. Morin, *Stars*, 84. Today, the noun "diva" (female) and more recently "divo" (male) have become part of Anglo-Saxon vocabulary, deriving from opera but intending a privileged, nar-cissistic performer of music, stage, or screen.

22. See Gian Piero Brunetta, *Storia del cinema italiano*, vol. 1, *Il cinema muto, 1895–1929* (Rome: Riuniti, 1993), 72–91. The term "divismo," or even "stardom," lacks the historical specific-ity necessary, in my opinion, to intend the characteristics of Italian stardom in reference to silent cinema. In this work, borrowing from historiography of the Fascist period in Italy, I employ the word "divismo" to refer to Italian stardom as a whole, much as I have previously used "fascism" (as opposed to "Fascism") to indicate the general political ideology. See Jacqueline Reich, "Mussolini at the Movies: Fascism, Film, and Culture," in *Re-Viewing Fas-cism: Italian Cinema, 1922–1943*, ed. Jacqueline Reich and Piero Garofalo (Bloomington: Indiana University Press, 2002), 3–29. When I refer to "Di-vismo," as does Marcia Landy, I intend the culturally defined, historically spe-cific phenomenon of Italian silent film stardom, focusing on the diva film and female actresses of the period. I choose this terminology in order to historically ground "Divismo" in relation to the specific genres characteristic of this pe-riod. See Landy, *Stardom Italian Style*, 42–43.

23. Borrowing from English, the word "star" (*la star* – feminized) also appears in Italian film periodicals and newspapers of the day, but it is

employed more with reference to Hollywood than popular, native-produced performers. In the United States the first terms used for actors were "posers" and "picture personalities"; in England they were called "bioscope models." See Richard deCordova, *Picture Personalities: The Emergence of the Star System in America* (Urbana: University of Illinois Press, 1990); and Chris O'Rourke, "How to Become a Bioscope Model: Transition, Mediation, and the Language of Film Performance," *Early Popular Visual Culture* 9, no. 3 (2011): 191–201. For more on American stars in the 1910s and the various discourses circulating around them, see Jennifer M. Bean, ed., *Flickers of Desire: Movie Stars of the 1910s* (New Brunswick, NJ: Rutgers University Press, 2011).

24. Martin Loiperdinger and Uli Jung, eds., *Importing Asta Nielsen: The International Film Star in the Making, 1910–1914* (New Barnet, UK: John Libbey, 2013); and Patrice Petro, *Joyless Streets: Women and Melodramatic Representation in Weimar Germany* (Princeton, NJ: Princeton University Press, 1989), 153. On Nielsen in Italy, see Giovanni Lasi, "Italy's First Film Star: Asta Nielsen, 'Polaris,'" in Loiperdinger and Jung, *Importing Asta Nielsen,* 234–246; and Martinelli, "Nascita del divismo," 221–250, here 222.

25. Aldo Bernardini, *Cinema muto italiano,* vol. 3, *Arte, divismo e mercato, 1910–1914* (Rome-Bari: Laterza, 1982), 83; Riccardo Redi, *Cinema muto italiano (1896–1930)* (Rome: Biblioteca di Bianco & Nero, 1999), 69–73; and Mary Wood, *Italian Cinema* (London: Berg, 2005), 4.

26. Bernardini, *Cinema muto italiano,* 3: 50–52. See also Catherine E. Kerr, "Incorporating the Star: The Intersection of Business and Aesthetic Strategies in Early American Film," *Business History Review* 64, no. 3 (1990): 383–410.

27. Martinelli, "Nascita del divismo," 229.

28. Eleonora Duse, an internationally recognized Italian stage actress at the turn of the centuries, made one important contribution to the genre, *Cenere* (Ashes, Ambrosio Film, 1917).

29. On the dive and diva films, see Angela Dalle Vacche, *Diva: Defiance and Passion in Early Italian Cinema* (Austin: University of Texas Press, 2008); and Cristina Jandelli, *Le dive italiane del cinema muto* (Palermo: L'Epos, 2006).

30. Francesco Pitassio, *Attore/divo* (Milan: Il Castoro, 2003), 88–93.

31. "Adriana Costamagna" (signed by Veritas), *La Vita Cinematografica* 2, no. 10 (1911): 1–2. Tragically and ironically, Costamagna was disfigured on set in an encounter with a leopard. See Massimo Scaglione, "Il cinema a Torino. Pochi divi ma tanti comprimari," in *Torino città del cinema,* ed. Davide Bracco et al. (Milan: Il Castoro, 2001), 45–56, here 46. A similar portrait of Lydia de Roberti, one of the early femmes fatales of Italian cinema, describes her along much the same lines, in particular the Greek beauty of her face. "Lydia de Roberti," Veritas, *La Vita Cinematografica* 2, no. 16 (1911): 1.

32. Jandelli, *Breve storia del divismo cinematografico,* 43.

33. Very little, in general, has been written on male stars of the silent era.

Studies such as Landy (*Stardom, Italian Style*) concentrate on non-cinematic figures like D'Annunzio and Mussolini; Jandelli (*Breve storia del divismo cinematografico*) cites Pagano and Emilio Ghione; Martinelli ("Nascita del divismo," 38–39) and Brunetta (*Storia del cinema italiano*, 1: 86–87) devote only a few pages to the phenomenon. It should be noted that the 2008 volume, and the updated version of volume 1, of Brunetta's fundamental four-volume *Storia del cinema italiano* adds a section devoted to Ghione as the only other male star examined in detail besides Pagano (108–110).

34. Morin, *Stars,* 89. Morin notes that in the 1910s in Europe and the United States, male stars were not yet matinee idols, but more the offspring of the male acrobats, comics, and athletes of early short films (6).

35. For magic and its relation to early cinema, see Matthew Solomon, *Disappearing Tricks: Silent Film, Houdini, and the New Magic of the Twentieth Century* (Urbana: University of Illinois Press, 2010).

36. For Monica Dall'Asta, the strongman emerged from the historical epic through his personification of the dialectic relationship between the individual and the collective, between identity and alterity that is at the heart of the historical film. His individual strength is at the service of the good of the people but must be kept within those tightly bound divisions between good and evil. Monica Dall'Asta, *Un cinéma musclé. Le surhomme dans le cinéma muet italien (1913–1926)* (Crisnée: Yellow Now, 1992), 27–44.

37. Elena dell'Agnese, "*Tu vuo' fa l'Americano:* la costruzione della mascolinità nella geopolitica popolare italiana," in *Mascolinità all'italiana. Construzioni, narrazioni, mutamenti,* ed. Elena dell'Agnese and Elisabetta Ruspini (Turin: UTET, 2007), 3–34, here 7.

38. "In difesa dell'industria italiana. I soggetti e le loro esecuzioni = I Divi e le Dive," *La Vita Cinematografica* 9, no. 33–4 (1918): 52–53.

39. "Gli idoli," *La Vita Cinematografica* 9, no. 13–14 (1918): 41.

40. For more on stardom and types, see my "Stardom in Italian Silent Cinema," in *The Companion to Italian Cinema,* ed. Frank Burke (Boston: Wiley-Blackwell, forthcoming 2015).

41. Early cinema and the national was the subject of the 2006 Domitor Early Cinema conference and the excellent anthology that emerged as a result. From the many works therein, in particular the introduction by the conference's organizers and the essay by Tom Gunning, I employ the terminology "national," "international," and "global" to describe the flow, circulation, and articulation of cinema as a historicized phenomenon in relation to the late nineteenth and early twentieth-century manifestations of capitalism, imperialism, and colonialism. See Tom Gunning, "Early Cinema as Global Cinema: The Encyclopedic Ambition," and Richard Abel, Giorgio Bertellini, and Rob King, introduction to Richard Abel, Giorgio Bertellini, and Rob King, eds., *Early Cinema and the "National"* (Eastleigh, UK: John Libbey, 2008), 1–8, 11–16. Also relevant is Elizabeth Ezra and Terry Rowden, "General Introduction:

What Is Transnational Cinema?" in
Transnational Cinema: The Film Reader,
ed. Elizabeth Ezra and Terry Rowden
(London: Routledge, 2006), 1–12.

42. John Welle sees the first years
of Italian cinema as "arriving" from
other nations and being local rather
than national in terms of character and
exhibition. John Welle, "The Cinema
Arrives in Italy: City, Region, and Nation in Early Film Discourse," in Abel
et al., *Early Cinema and the "National,"*
164–171.

43. Sergio Raffaelli, "Quando il cinema era mobile," *La Ricerca Folklorica*
19 (April 1989): 103–112; and Aldo Bernardini, *Cinema italiano delle origini.*
Gli ambulanti (Gemona: Cineteca del
Friuli, 2001).

44. Michele Canosa, ed., *1905: La*
presa di Roma. Alle origini del cinema
italiano – Beginnings of Italian Cinema
(Bologna: Le Mani/Cineteca di Bologna, 2006); and Mario Musumeci
and Sergio Toffetti, eds., *Da* La presa
di Roma *a* Il piccolo garibaldino. *Ri-*
sorgimento, Massoneria e instituzioni:
l'immagine della nazione nel cinema
muto (1905–1909) (Rome: Gangemi,
2007). Both editions are bilingual Ital-
ian/English, and the latter is accompanied by a DVD with the restored versions of *La presa di Roma* and *Il piccolo*
garibaldino (The Garibaldi Boy, Cines,
1909). On the film as a battleground
between state and church power, see
Giovanni Lasi, "La ripresa di Roma/
Recapturing Rome," in *1905. La presa di*
Roma, 41–114, 157–232.

45. Silvio Alovisio, "Il cinema italiano: dalle origini all'avvento del sonoro,"
in Eugeni and Viganò, *Attraverso lo*

schermo, 61–95; Chiara Caranti, "Disordered Traffic: Film Distribution in Italy
(1905–1930)," in *Italian Silent Cinema:*
A Reader, ed. Giorgio Bertellini (New
Baret, UK: John Libbey, 2013), 285–294.

46. Gian Piero Brunetta, *Buio in sala.*
Cent'anni di passione dello spettatore cin-
ematografico (Venice: Marsilio, 1989),
37; Bernardini, *Cinema muto italiano,* 3:
95–96.

47. Bernardini, *Cinema muto italiano,*
3: 62–77.

48. This self-consciousness is not
necessarily unique to Italian comedies. Bernardini, "Appunti sul cinema
comico ialiano," *Griffithiana* 7, no.
24–25 (1985): 21–35, here 33; and Elena
Mosconi, *L'impressione del film. Con-*
tributi per una storia culturale del cinema
italiano, 1895–1945 (Milan: Vita and
Pensiero, 2006), 88–95. Many featured
titles that acknowledged and parodied
popular films, such as *Tontolini Nerone*
(Tontolini as Nero, Cines, 1910), *Kri Kri*
e il "Quo Vadis?" (Kri Kri and "Quo Vadis?," Cines, 1912), and *Cinessino imita*
Fantomas (Cinessino imitates Fantomas, Cines, 1914). Others would take
the spectator directly inside the theater
or film studio, such as *Cretinetti al cin-*
ematografo (Foolshead at the Cinemato-
graph, Itala Film, 1911), *Tontolini scrit-*
tore di soggetti cinematografici (Tontolini
Writes for the Cinema, Cines, 1911), and
Polidor arriva alla Casa Pasquali (Polidor Arrives at the Pasquali Studios,
Pasquali, 1912), allowing spectators a
glimpse of the film studio at work, as
would the first Maciste film.

49. Bernardini, "Appunti sul cinema
comico italiano," 29.

50. Gian Piero Brunetta, "Il clown cinematografico tra salotto liberty e frontiera del West," *Griffithiana* 7, no. 24–25 (1985): 11–20.

51. Deed worked with Georges Méliès before moving to Pathé.

52. It proved to be an astute move by Itala. In 1909 the first Cretinetti films appeared to national and international acclaim, and much of the studio's early success in domestic and foreign markets was due to their popularity. The series had uninterrupted success until the end of 1911 when Deed went back home to France, but he ultimately returned to Italy in 1915 as French film production entered into an economic crisis. Both Emilio Ghione (the future serial star Za la Mort) and Domenico Gambino (the future athletic/acrobatic Saetta, who would appear alongside Maciste in 1924) got their start in films while working with Deed's troupe. Gian Piero Brunetta, *Storia del cinema italiano*, 1: 194; Bernardini, "Appunti sul cinema comico italiano," 29–30; and Jean A. Gili, *André Deed. Boireau, Cretinetti, Gribouille, Toribio, Foolshead, Lehman* ... (Genoa: Le Mani, 2005), 113–133.

53. Deed would go on to star in and direct one of the few surrealist Italian films, *L'uomo meccanico* (*The Mechanical Man*, Milano Film, 1921), and Bartolomeo Pagano played a non-Maciste bit part in *Cretinetti e gli stivali del brasiliano* (Cretinetti and the Brazilian's Boots, Itala Film, 1916). See Gili, *André Deed*, and Paolo Cherchi Usai, "Italy: Spectacle and Melodrama," in *The Oxford History of World Cinema*, ed. Geoffrey Nowell-Smith (Oxford: Oxford University Press, 1996), 123–129, here 125.

54. Instead, the comic one-reelers lived on the tradition of the *comica finale* (roughly translated as "the last laugh"), because from the 1910s onward they continued to be exhibited *after* melodramatic or tragic films, such as the diva films, in order for the audience to experience the necessary catharsis to leave the theater in an appropriately good mood. This way, older films continued to recycle during the silent period and beyond. Bernardini, "Appunti sul cinema comico italiano," 35.

55. Much of the information on serials emanates from the work of Monica Dall'Asta, "La diffusione del film a episodi in Europa," in *Storia del cinema mondiale*, vol. 1, *L'Europa I*, 277–315; "Italian Film Serials and (Inter) National-Popular Culture," in Bertellini, *Italian Silent Cinema*, 195–202; and Dall'Asta, ed., *Fantômas. La vita plurale di un antieroe* (Pozzuolo del Friuli: Il Principe Costante Edizioni, 2004).

56. Denis Lotti, *Emilio Ghione, l'ultimo apache. Vita e film di un divo italiano* (Bologna: Cineteca di Bologna, 2008); Brunetta, *Storia del cinema italiano*, 1: 209; and Dall'Asta, "Italian Film Serials," 196.

57. The length of full-length feature films in Italy did not stabilize until 1913–1914, when the accepted length was between 1,000 and 1,500 meters, approximately one hour. Only in special cases – big spectacles and works of cultural prestige, for instance – did film duration surpass 2,000 meters.

58. Ben Singer, "Serials," in *Encyclopedia of Early Cinema*, ed. Richard Abel (New York: Routledge, 2005), 582–583. Chapter 4, which discusses the

distribution, exhibition, and reception of *Maciste* and *Maciste alpino* in the United States, explores the relationship between American and Italian serials in greater detail, and chapter 5 interrogates *La trilogia di Maciste* in the same light.

59. Richard Abel, *The Ciné Goes to Town: French Cinema, 1896–1914,* updated and expanded ed. (Berkeley: University of California Press, 1998), 43, 264–267. Film D'Arte Italiana also released *Françoise de Rimini* (Ugo Falena, 1910), with Francesca Bertini.

60. Peter Bondanella, *A History of Italian Cinema* (New York: Continuum, 2009), 5–6.

61. James Hay, *Popular Film Culture in Fascist Italy: The Passing of the Rex* (Bloomington: Indiana University Press, 1987), 152. See also Giovanni Calendoli, *Materiali per una storia del cinema italiano* (Parma: Maccari Editore, 1967), 30; and Irmbert Schenk, "The Cinematic Support to National(istic) Mythology: The Italian Peplum, 1910–1930," in *Globalization, Cultural Identities, and Media Representations,* ed. Natascha Gentz and Stefan Kramer (Albany: State University of New York Press, 2006), 153–168. For more on Italy's colonialist ambitions and their repercussions, see Ruth Ben-Ghiat and Mia Fuller, eds., *Italian Colonialism* (New York: Palgrave Macmillan, 2005).

62. "Dai trionfi del palcoscenico agli splendori della cinematografia: glorie italiane," *L'Illustrazione Cinematografica* 1, no. 6 (1912): 350–351.

63. *Il Maggese Cinematografico* 1, no. 1 (1913): 1. For more on the magazine, see

Il Maggese Cinematografico, ed. Marco Grifo (Turin: Biblioteca FERT, 2005).

64. "Film d'arte italiana," *La Vita Cinematografica* 2, no. 23 (1911): 1.

65. Calendoli, *Materiali per una storia del cinema italiano,* 71.

66. Monica Dall'Asta, *Un cinéma musclé,* 27; Maria Wyke, *Projecting the Past: Ancient Rome, Cinema, and History* (London: Routledge, 1997), 25.

67. Played by Bruto Castellani, the character of Ursus was celebrated in the press and by the moviegoing public, including being singled out for praise by the British royal family. Although Castellani remained attached to the historical epic – he continued to appear prodigiously in the genre, culminating in his reincarnation of Ursus in the 1924 remake of *Quo Vadis?* (Gabriellino D'Annunzio/Georg Jacoby, UCI) – Mario Guaita Ausonia, the actor who played Spartacus in the eponymous film, did not and would later go on to star in his own series of strongman films. See Brunetta, *Storia del cinema italiano,* 1: 143–173.

68. The 1908 version was directed by Ambrosio and Luigi Maggi, the 1913 version by Mario Caserini and Eleuterio Rodolfi, also produced by Ambrosio.

69. *La caduta di Troia* involved the collaboration of two individuals who would play important roles in the Maciste series: his creator, Giovanni Pastrone, and Romano Luigi Borgnetto, Pagano's trusted advisor and director of several of the late Itala Maciste films.

70. Bernardini, *Cinema muto italiano,* 3: 151.

71. *La Vita Cinematografica* 4, no. 18 (1913): 42–43.

72. Much of what follows summarizes the wonderful work of previous film historians on the strongman films: Alberto Farassino and Tatti Sanguineti, eds., *Gli uomini forti*; Gian Piero Brunetta, *Storia del cinema italiano*, 1: 87–89, 317–319; Monica Dall'Asta, *Un cinéma muscle*, "La diffusione del film a episodi in Europa," and "Italian Serial Films"; Landy, *Stardom, Italian Style*, 7–15; Alberto Farassino, "Maciste e il paradigma divistico," in *Cabiria e il suo tempo*, 223–232; Michele Giordano, *Giganti buoni. Da Ercole a Piedone (e oltre) il mito dell'uomo forte nel cinema italiano* (Rome: Gremese, 1998); Cristina Jandelli, *Breve storia del divismo cinematografico*, 47–53; Vittorio Martinelli and Mario Quargnolo, *Maciste & Co. I giganti buoni del muto italiano* (Gemona del Friuli: Cinepopolare Edizioni, 1981); Vittorio Martinelli, "Lasciate fare a noi, siamo forti," in Farassino and Sanguineti, *Gli uomini forti*, 9–28; Steven Ricci, *Cinema & Fascism: Italian Film and Society, 1922–1943* (Berkeley: University of California Press, 2008), 81–87; Imbert Schenk, "The Cinematic Support to National(istic) Mythology: The Italian Peplum, 1910–1930," and Mario Verdone, "Il film atletico e acrobatico," *Centrofilm* 17 (1961): 3–36.

73. American serials starring important male actors of the day are treated in detail in relation *to La trilogia di Maciste* in chapter 5.

74. Dall'Asta, *Un cinéma musclé*, 185; and Alberto Farassino, "Anatomia del cinema muscolare," in Farassino and Sanguineti, *Gli uomini forti*, 46–48.

75. Martinelli and Quargnolo, *Maciste & Co.*, 32–36.

76. Bertoldo, review of *Maciste innamorato, La Vita Cinematografica* 10, no. 17–18 (1919): 148–149; emphasis in original.

77. Farassino, "Anatomia del cinema muscolare," 29–40.

78. Ibid., 41.

79. Martinelli and Quargnolo, *Maciste & Co.*, 9–10.

80. Farassino, "Anatomia del cinema muscolare," 38–47.

2. From Slave to Master

1. Benito Mussolini, "Dalla neutralità assoluta alla neutralità attiva ed operante," *Avanti!* (18 October 1914): 3.

2. Peter Bondanella, *The Eternal City: Roman Images in the Modern World* (Chapel Hill: University of North Carolina Press, 1987), 207–208, and Luciano Curreri, "Il mito culturale di Cartagine nel primo Novecento tra letterature e cinema," in *Cabiria & Cabiria,* ed. Silvio Alovisio and Alberto Barbera (Turin: Museo Nazionale del Cinema, 2006), 299–307.

3. Vittorio Martinelli, "D'Annunziana," *Griffithiana* 21, no. 64 (1998): 26–49.

4. This print's 2006 restoration by the Museo Nazionale del Cinema was based on five different existing prints from various film libraries (Pastrone's personal copy from 1932, Gosfilmofond [Moscow], the Museum of Modern Art [New York City], Cinemateca Espagnola [Madrid], and the Hungarian Film Archive [Budapest]) and archival documents pertaining to the filming at the MNC. Of the film's original 3,370 meters, this copy preserves 3,102 meters. The intertitles derive from the libretto

that accompanied the film at its 1914 premiere in various Italian cities. It differs markedly from the American DVD (Kino Video, 2000) but at this point has yet to be released on DVD in either Italy or abroad due to long-standing legal disagreements with the director's heirs. For specific details on the film, see part 3 of the appendix.

5. The literature on *Cabiria* is copious, and I will make reference to these and many other sources throughout this chapter: Alovisio and Barbera, *Cabiria & Cabiria;* Paolo Bertetto and Gianni Rondolino, eds., *Cabiria e il suo tempo* (Turin: Museo Nazionale del Cinema, 1998); Gian Piero Brunetta, *Storia del cinema italiano,* vol. 1, *Il cinema muto, 1895–1929* (Rome: Riuniti, 1993), 173–177; Gian Piero Brunetta, *The History of Italian Cinema: A Guide to Italian Film from Its Origins to the Twenty-First Century* (Princeton, NJ: Princeton University Press, 2009), 33–38; Giovanni Calendoli, *Materiali per una storia del cinema italiano* (Parma: Maccari Editore, 1967), 63–111; Carlo Celli and Margo Cottino-Jones, *A New Guide to Italian Cinema* (New York: Palgrave Macmillan, 2007), 12–16; Angela Dalle Vacche, *The Body in the Mirror: Shapes of History in Italian Cinema* (Princeton, NJ: Princeton University Press, 1993), 27–52; Marcia Landy, *Italian Film* (Cambridge: Cambridge University Press, 2000), 33–40; Pierre Sorlin, *Italian National Cinema, 1896–1996* (London: Routledge, 1996), 35–38; Jon Solomon, *The Ancient World in Cinema,* rev. and exp. ed. (New Haven, CT: Yale University Press, 2001), 47–49; and Maria Wyke, *Projecting the Past: Ancient Rome, Cinema, and History* (London: Routledge, 1997), 25–26.

6. Martin Miller Marks, *Music and the Silent Film: Contexts and Case Studies, 1895–1924* (New York: Oxford University Press, 1997), 103–108.

7. Chiara Caranti, "*Cabiria,* 1914 & 1931: la distribuzione in Italia e nel mondo," in Alovisio and Barbera, *Cabiria & Cabiria,* 148–173, specifically 148–158.

8. Maria Adriana Prolo, "Francesi nel cinema italiano muto," *Bianco & Nero* 14, no. 8–9 (1953): 69–74.

9. Paolo Cherchi Usai, *Giovanni Pastrone* (Florence: La Nuova Italia, 1986). See also Silvio Alovisio, "The 'Pastrone System': Itala Film from the Origins to World War I," in *Italian Silent Cinema: A Reader,* ed. Giorgio Bertellini (New Baret, UK: John Libbey, 2013), 87–96.

10. Cherchi Usai notes that although tracking shots had already been employed in earlier films, including the French *Le pickpocket mystifié* (The Pickpocket Bewildered, Pathé, 1911), *Cabiria*'s camera movements "perform a crucial narrative and descriptive function, and were filmed on a sophisticated system of tracks which allowed for remarkably complex camera movements." Paolo Cherchi Usai, "Italy: Spectacle and Melodrama," in *The Oxford History of World Cinema,* ed. Geoffrey Nowell-Smith (Oxford: Oxford University Press, 1996), 123–130, here 127.

11. De Chomón came to work for Itala Film and Pastrone in 1912. His contributions to *Cabiria* are numerous: special effects, including miniatures, pyrotechnics, and trick photography, as well as the implementation of artificial

lighting. He continued to work at Itala Film for ten years and later returned to contribute to *Maciste all'inferno*. Joan M. Minguet Batllori, *Segundo de Chomón. El cine de la fascinación* (Barcelona: Generalitat de Catalunya, Istitut Català de les Indústres Culturals, 2010), and Simona Nosenzo, *Manuale tecnico per visionari. Segundo de Chomón in Italia, 1912–1925* (Turin: Associazione F.E.R.T, 2007).

12. Chiara Caranti traces the national and international distribution and exhibition of the film's 1914 and 1931 versions. Caranti, "*Cabiria* 1914 & 1931,"160–170.

13. *Corriere della Sera*, 19 April 1914, anthologized in Alovisio and Barbera, *Cabiria & Cabiria*, 384.

14. Ugo Menichelli, "*Cabiria* di G. D'Annunzio e dell'Itala-Film al Lirico di Milano," *La Vita Cinematografica* 5, no. 16 (1914): 74–75, anthologized in Alovisio and Barbera, *Cabiria & Cabiria*, 387.

15. The question of *Cabiria*'s authorship was debated in both scholarly and legal circles. In the 1950s and 1960s there was a protracted battle between Il Vittoriale degli Italiani, the institute in charge of D'Annunzio's literary patrimony, and the Italian film studio Lux Film about who was its true author: Pastrone had conceded the rights to the film to Lux, which at the time, perhaps attempting to take advantage of a renewed and growing interest in historical epics, wanted to reissue a sound version of the film. Ultimately the court sided with Lux, citing Pastrone as the film's true author. Copies of the courts' decisions, including the final appeals

court decision in 1964, are held in the MNC Archives, Fondo Cabiria, A193/1 (sch.inf. 4142). See also articles pertaining to the case, such as "D'Annunzio ha perso la causa per la riedizione di *Cabiria*," *La Nazione*, 27 January 1965, housed in the MNC, Fondo Cabiria, A193/5 (sch.inf. 6570).

16. Martinelli, "D'Annunziana," 26; and Gianni Rondolino, "Gli impacchi taumaturgici dei miti di celluloide," in *Gabriele D'Annunzio: grandezza e delirio nell'industria dello spettacolo. Atti del Convegno Internazionale Torino, 21–23 marzo 1988* (Genoa: Costa and Nolan, 1989), 213–228, here 214–215. For more on D'Annunzio's role in the film, see Silvio Alovisio, "Il film che visse due volte. *Cabiria* tra antichi segreti e nuove ricerche," in Alovisio and Barbera, *Cabiria & Cabiria*, 26, and Paolo Cherchi Usai, ed., *Giovanni Pastrone. Gli anni d'oro del cinema a Torino* (Turin: UTET, 1986). For more on screenplays during the silent period in Italy, see Silvio Alovisio, *Voci del silenzio. La sceneggiatura nel cinema muto italiano* (Milan: Il Castoro, 2005); Francesco Pitassio and Leonardo Quaresima, eds., *Scrittura e immagine. La didascalia nel cinema muto/Writing and Image: Titles in Silent Cinema* (Udine: Forum, 1998); and Sergio Raffaelli, *Cinema film regia. Saggi per una storia linguistica del cinema italiano* (Rome: Bulzoni, 1978). One of several drafts of the original screenplay is also reproduced in Alovisio and Barbera, *Cabiria & Cabiria*, 45–52. For more versions of the various drafts and the final screenplay, see Giovanni Pastrone, *Cabiria. Visione storica del III secolo a. C.. Didascalie di*

Gabriele D'Annunzio, ed. Roberto Radicati and Ruggero Rossi, introduction by Maria Adriana Prolo (Turin: Museo Nazionale del Cinema, 1977). For more on D'Annunzio's role in the making of *Cabiria,* see Gian Piero Brunetta, *Storia del cinema italiano,* 1: 97–103.

17. Nicoletta Pacini, "La promozione di *Cabiria:* i manifesti e le brochure," in Alovisio and Barbera, *Cabiria & Cabiria,* 210–223, here 214.

18. Fondo Cabiria, A193/5 (sch. inf. 6570), Museo Nazionale del Cinema, Turin. This document was later reproduced for the July 1988 catalogue printed on the occasion of a public projection of the film.

19. Michele Giordano, citing an interview with Umberto Aldini, a scholar of Ancient Greek culture, supposes the origin from the Greek *mékistos,* superlative of *makròs,* meaning "large." Aldini also cites verse 289 of Aeschylus's *Agamemnon,* which refers to the mountain "Macistus" (Mákiotos). Michele Giordano, *Giganti buoni. Da Ercole a Piedone (e oltre) il mito dell'uomo forte nel cinema italiano* (Rome: Gremese, 1998), 31.

20. Marco Grifo, "Alla ricerca del cast perduto: la troupe di *Cabiria,*" in Alovisio and Barbera, *Cabiria & Cabiria,* 110–126. This story of discovery differs from the one traditionally accepted by the first generation of Maciste scholars, including Vittorio Martinelli, who claims that Domenico Gambino (Saetta) and Romano Luigi Borgnetto (who would also become a mentor to Pagano throughout his career) were the first to notice him at the Genoa port. Vittorio Martinelli, "Lasci-

ate fare a noi, siamo forti," in *Gli uomini forti,* ed. Alberto Farassino and Tatti Sanguinetti (Milan: Mazzotta, 1983), 9–28, 10. Grifo bases his interpretation on documents relating to the court case between the heirs of D'Annunzio and Pastrone over the rightful ownership of *Cabiria.* The court documents (filed 1953, ultimate court decision 1964) cite the testimony of Cassiano, who said that he discovered and then trained Pagano for the role of Maciste. Documents housed in the MNC Archives, Fondo Cabiria, A193/1 (sch.inf. 4142).

21. Cherchi Usai, ed., *Giovanni Pastrone,* 74.

22. According to Frank Snowden, Ancient Greeks and Romans were familiar with a wide variety of racial types of varying physical characteristics. Frank M. Snowden Jr., *Before Color Prejudice: The Ancient View of Blacks* (Cambridge, MA: Harvard University Press, 1983), 15–17.

23. Popular lore originally held that *Cabiria* was an uncredited adaptation of *Carthage in Flames,* first serialized in 1906 and then published as a novel in 1908. Lorenzo Braccesi, "Salgari e l'antico," *Studi Storici* 46, no. 4 (2005): 955–965. There are differing interpretations. Giovanni Calendoli, *Materiali per una storia del cinema italiano* (87–89) recognizes Salgari's influence on the film, particularly the scenes at the Temple of Moloch, but notes a fundamental ideological difference: in the novel the oppressed Carthaginians are the good guys and the Romans are the villains. Luciano Curreri sees more of an influence of Gustave Flaubert's *Salambô* (1862). According to Lorenzo Brac-

cesi, there is a character in *Carthage in Flames* akin to Maciste – a strong sailor named Sidone, who saves the young girl from being sacrificed by Moloch. For more on this debate, see Luciano Curreri, "Il Fuoco, i Libri, la Storia: Saggio su *Cartagine in fiamme* (1906) di Emilio Salgari," in Emilio Salgari, *Cartagine in fiamme. Romanzo,* ed. Luciano Curreri (Rome: Quiritta, 2001), 315–403; and Raffaele De Berti, "Il film d'avventura italiano tra Salgari e *Captain Blood,*" in *Schermi di regime. Cinema italiano degli anni trenta: la produzione e i generi,* ed. Alessandro Faccioli (Venice: Marsilio, 2010), 128–139.

24. Rosetta Giuliani Caponetto, "'Going Out of Stock': Mulattoes and Levantines in Italian Literature and Cinema of the Fascist Period," PhD diss., University of Connecticut, 2008, 86–88. For a more detailed examination of the sexual politics of colonial Italy, see Barbara Sòrgoni, *Parole e corpi. Antropologia, discorso giuridico e politiche sessuali interrazziali nella colonia Eritrea (1890–1941)* (Naples: Liguori Editore, 1998), 101–125.

25. Monica Dall'Asta, *Un cinéma musclé. Le surhomme dans le cinéma muet italien (1913–1926)* (Crisnée: Yellow Now, 1992), 38–39, 60.

26. An additional question here is whether audiences would have been aware of the character's mixed-race status, and so far I have found no evidence to support that statement.

27. Cristina Jandelli, *Breve storia del divismo cinematografico* (Milan: Marsilio, 2007), 47.

28. In Wyke, *Projecting the Past,* 26. See also Dall'Asta, *Un cinéma musclé,* 37.

29. Cristina Jandelli, "'Per quanto immagini, sono riusciti a farsi amare come persone vere.' Attori, recitazione e personaggi in *Cabiria,*" in Alovisio and Barbera, *Cabiria & Cabiria,* 127–137; Fabio Pezzetti Tonion, "Corpo della visione, corpo della narrazione: Maciste in *Cabiria,*" in Alovisio and Barbera, *Cabiria & Cabiria,* 138–145; Dall'Asta, *Un cinéma musclé,* 36–37; Dalle Vacche, *Body in the Mirror,* 37; and Landy, *Italian Film,* 35–36.

30. In these actions he prefigures the role the athlete/acrobat Saetta would play in *Maciste imperatore* (1924), a film that is discussed in detail in chapter 6.

31. *L'Avanti,* 19 April 1914, anthologized in Alovisio and Barbera, *Cabiria & Cabiria,* 384–385; *Il Maggese Cinematografico* 2, no. 8 (1914), anthologized in Alovisio and Barbera, *Cabiria & Cabiria,* 393.

32. *Il Giornale d'Italia,* 24 April 1914, anthologized in Alovisio and Barbera, *Cabiria & Cabiria,* 391.

33. Brunetta, *Storia del cinema italiano,* 1: 173; Wyke, *Projecting the Past,* 45; Calendoli, *Materiali per una storia del cinema italiano,* 86.

34. Vittorio Mariani, "L'anima italiana in *Cabiria,*" *Il Tirso,* 23 April 1914, anthologized in Alovisio and Barbera, *Cabiria & Cabiria,* 390–391.

35. Wyke, *Projecting the Past,* 20, 165. The colonialist discourse reaches its fruition later in the Maciste series, when Maciste becomes an African colonizer in *Maciste nella gabbia dei leoni* (*The Hero of the Circus,* Pittaluga Film, 1926), to be discussed at greater length in chapter 6.

36. Calendoli, *Materiali per una storia del cinema italiano*, 86; Celli, *New Guide to Italian Cinema*, 12–16; Dalle Vacche, *Body in the Mirror*, 27–52. The Libyan war also found its way into both fiction and nonfiction films during the early 1910s. The Italian film history journal *Immagine – Note di Storia del Cinema* dedicated its third issue (2011) to the subject. See, in particular, Denis Lotti, "La guerra allusa. L'imperialismo nel cinema di finzione italiano tra propaganda e speranza (1909–12)," 11–52; Sila Berruti and Luca Mazzei, "'Il giornale mi lascia freddo'. I film 'dal vero' dalla Libia (1911–12) e il pubblico italiano," 53–103; and Giovanni Lasi, "Viva Tripoli italiana! Viva l'Italia! La propaganda bellica nei film a soggetto realizzati in Italia durante il conflitto italo-turco (1911–12)," 104–119.

37. Lucia Re, "Italians and the Invention of Race: The Poetics and Politics of Difference in the Struggle over Libya, 1890–1913," *California Italian Studies Journal* 1, no. 1 (2010): 1–58, here 6 and 9. Available at http://escholarship.org /uc/item/96k3w5kn.

38. Giorgio Bertellini, *Italy in Early American Cinema: Race, Landscape, and the Picturesque* (Bloomington: Indiana University Press, 2009), 167–181.

39. Gabriele D'Annunzio, "Del cinematografo considerato come uno strumento di liberazione e come arte di trasfigurazione," *Il Corriere della Sera* (18 February 1914). Reprinted in Cherchi Usai, ed., *Giovanni Pastrone*, 115–122. Translated in English as "On the Cinematograph as an Instrument of Liberation and an Art of Transfiguration [1914]," trans. Rhiannon Noel

Welch, with Giorgio Bertellini, in *Early Cinema*, vol. 4, ed. Richard Abel (New York: Routledge, 2013), 262–267, here 264–265.

40. For an excellent analysis of D'Annunzio's rhetorical articulation of imperialism and race, see Jared M. Becker, *Nationalism and Culture: Gabriele D'Annunzio and Italy after the Risorgimento* (New York: Peter Lang, 1994), 75–130. See also Filippo Caburlotto, "D'Annunzio, la latinità del Mediterraneo e il mito della riconquista," *California Journal of Italian Studies* 1, no. 1 (2010). Available at http://escholarship .org/uc/item/7gx5g2n9; Calendoli, *Materiali per una storia del cinema italiano*, 64–77; and Giovanna Finocchiaro Chimirri, *D'Annunzio e il cinema Cabiria* (Catania: CUECM, 1986), 35.

41. *Il Tirso* 23 (April 1914), anthologized in Alovisio and Barbera, *Cabiria & Cabiria*, 387–389.

42. As Jandelli similarly observes, "If Maciste is African, Pagano is Italian." *Breve storia del divismo cinematografico*, 49.

43. "Maciste in persona al *Lirico* nella rappresentazione di 'Cabiria,'" *Corriere della Sera*, 9 May 1914, 4; emphasis added. I would like to thank Cristina Jandelli and Giorgio Bertellini for providing me with this particular reference.

44. Dall'Asta, "La diffusione del film a episodi," in Brunetta, *Storia del cinema mondiale*, vol. 1: *L'Europa. Miti, luoghi, divi* (Turin: Einaudi, 2000), 277–323, here 315. Cherchi Usai observes, "From a political point of view, the strongman who saves the girl underlines a concept of racial and moral superiority." Inter-

view with Paolo Cherchi Usai, quoted
in Giordano, *Giganti buoni,* 19.

45. In addition, he was told to remain
silent, smile broadly at the audience,
and shake hands when requested (as
cited in Cherchi Usai, ed., *Giovanni
Pastrone,* 66). As we shall see below, this
use of African American minstrel culture reemerges in *Maciste.*

46. *Maciste, L'uomo forte* (DVD,
Cineteca di Bologna and Museo Nazionale del Cinema, 2009). The print
found on the DVD, accompanied by a
terrific book of primary and secondary
sources, is the 2006 restored version of
the film, carried out by the Cineteca
di Bologna, the Museo Nazionale del
Cinema, and the L'Immagine Ritrovata
laboratory in Bologna. It derives from
the only surviving nitrate copy held
by the Nederlands Filmmuseum in
Amsterdam, Holland, and the archival
materials housed at the MNC. The
restoration contains only 1,372 meters
of the original print's 1,968 meters. For
more information, see parts 2 and 3 of
the appendix.

47. *La Vita Cinematografica* 5 (Special Issue) (31 December 1914): 78–79;
and *La Vita Cinematografica* 6, no.
26–27 (1915): 42–43. Caranti attributes
this rise to a calculated recycling of one
film's extra-cinematic discourse to promote another. Caranti, "Cabiria 1914 &
1931," 151.

48. Martinelli, "Lasciate fare a noi,"
10. Mario Verdone cites a conversation
he had with Pastrone in 1952 about the
making of *Maciste,* in which Pastrone
claims that the series was his idea but
after making *Cabiria* and then *Il fuoco*
he wanted to take a break. During his

absence, however, one of his colleagues
at Itala Film had begun to make a Maciste film but based the character on
Pagano's origins as a dockworker, not,
as Pastrone had planned, as a civilized
member of society with "hat, tie and
new clothes." Pastrone claims some
of that original footage was used in
Maciste. Archival documents do not
support the veracity of Pastrone's statements, and his memory appears to fail
him, because he claims that *Maciste*
was released before *Cabiria,* which was
clearly not the case. Mario Verdone, "Il
cinema atletico e acrobatico," *Centrofilm* 17 (1971): 8–9.

49. Eric Lott has written brilliantly
on the racial ambiguities of the figure
of American minstrel culture, specifically that of the black dandy, in *Love
and Theft: Blackface Minstrelsy and the
American Working Class* (New York:
Oxford University Press, 1993), 131–135.

50. Calendoli, *Materiali per una storia del cinema italiano,* 104–108. Marcia
Landy notes the ethical dimensions of
Maciste's physical feats. Landy, *Stardom, Italian Style,* 9–11.

51. George Sadoul, "A colloquio con
Giovanni Pastrone," *Centrofilm* 2, no. 14
(1960): 5–13.

52. The scene is viewable at http://
www.museocinema.it/collezioni
/maciste/main.html, *Maciste* Sequenza
#1. Part 2 of the appendix discusses the
difficulty of its restoration.

53. *La Cine-Fono* 10, no. 320 (1916).

54. David Atkinson and Denis Cosgrove, "Urban Rhetoric and Embodied
Identities: City, Nation, and Empire at
the Vittorio Emanuele II Monument in
Rome, 1870–1945," *Annals of the Asso-*

ciation of American Geographers 88, no. 1 (1998): 28–49.

55. Angela Dalle Vacche notes how this scene is one of many featuring a redefinition of female identity in relation to film spectatorship. Angela Dalle Vacche, *Diva: Defiance and Passion in Early Italian Cinema* (Austin: University of Texas Press, 2008), 190.

56. The scene is viewable at http://www.museocinema.it/collezioni/maciste/main.html, *Maciste* Sequenza #2.

57. Sorlin notes how this spotlighting or directed use of natural light was unique to Italian silent cinema. Sorlin, *Italian National Cinema*, 28.

58. For more on the role that costume and clothing play in the Maciste films, see my "Slave to Fashion: Masculinity, Suits, and the Maciste Films of Italian Silent Cinema," in *Fashion in Film*, ed. Adrienne Munich (Bloomington: Indiana University Press, 2011), 236–259.

59. Wanda Strauven, "From 'Primitive Cinema' to 'Marvelous'," in *The Cinema of Attractions Reloaded*, ed. Wanda Strauven (Amsterdam: Amsterdam University Press, 2006), 105–120. On Maciste and the role of disguise and acting, see Alberto Farassino, "Maciste e il paradigma divistico," in Bertetto and Rondolino, *Cabiria e il suo tempo*, 223–232, especially 226–227.

60. Farid Chenoune, *A History of Men's Fashion*, trans. Deke Dusinberre (Paris: Flammarion, 1983), 135–142.

61. Emily Braun, "Futurist Fashion: Three Manifestoes," *Art Journal* 54, no. 1 (1995): 34–41, here 39. Futurism would return to the Maciste series in *Maciste*

alpino (see chapter 3) and *Maciste in vacanza* (see chapter 5).

62. For a discussion on the notion of traffic in relation to American modernity, see Kristen Whissel, *Picturing American Modernity: Traffic, Technology, and the Silent Cinema* (Durham, NC: Duke University Press, 2008), 1–19. The subject of technology, transportation, and the automobile enters into chapter 5's discussion of Maciste and modernity.

63. Luciano Mecacci, "Psicologia e psicoanalisi," in *La cultura italiana del Novecento*, ed. Corrado Stajano and Franca Angelini (Bari: Laterza, 1996), 515–558. See also Glen Gabbard and Krin Gabbard, *Psychiatry and the Cinema*, 2nd ed. (Washington, DC: American Psychiatric Press, 1999), 35–39.

64. I had originally believed that Buffalo Bill Cody's traveling Wild West Show, which toured throughout Italy in the 1890s and then in 1906, might have exposed Italians to blackface performers, since many American performances featured black and blackfaced entertainers. See Joy S. Kasson, *Buffalo Bill's Wild West: Celebrity, Memory, and Popular History* (New York: Hill and Wang, 2000), 213–217; Robert W. Rydell and Rob Kroes, *Buffalo Bill in Bologna: The Americanization of the World, 1869–1922* (Chicago: University of Chicago Press, 2005), 105–117. A recent and brilliant investigative thesis by Stefania Iarlori, however, has painstakingly shown that although the Buffalo Bill shows that passed through northern Italy in 1906 (Genoa, La Spezia, Turin, and Milan) featured a panoply of multiracial characters (Native Americans, Mexicans,

Japanese, and Arabs, just to name a few), they did not feature African Americans or performers in blackface. Stefania Iarlori, "Immagini d'America. Rappresentazioni di Buffalo Bill e Cervo Bianco nella cultura italiana del primo '900," BA diss., University of Genova, 9 July 2008.

65. Barbara L. Webb has examined the transatlantic cross-pollination of the black dandy in American culture, noting that "the Blackface dandy claims a genealogy traceable to the everyday performances of dandies in Europe and their imitators in the United States." Barbara L. Webb, "The Black Dandyism of George Walker: A Case Study in Genealogical Method," *TDR/The Drama Review* 45, no. 4 (2001): 7–24, here 9. See also Hazel Waters, *Racism on the Victorian Stage: Representation of Slavery and the Black Character,* and Monica L. Miller, *Slaves to Fashion: Black Dandyism and the Styling of Black Diasporic Identity* (Durham, NC: Duke University Press, 2009).

66. According to Gerald Butters, 95 percent of all African American roles were played by white actors in American cinema of the 1910s and 1920s. See Butters, *Black Manhood on the Silent Screen* (Lawrence: University of Kansas Press, 2002), 7; and Cedric J. Robinson, *Forgeries of Memory and Meaning: Blacks and Regimes of Race in American Theater & Film before World War II* (Chapel Hill: University of North Carolina Press, 2007), 82–92. For Italian cinema, see Aldo Bernardini's *Cinema delle origini in Italia. I film "dal vero" di produzione estera* (Gemona: La Cineteca del Friuli, 2008); and Riccardo Redi,

Film stranieri sugli schermi italiani, vol. 1, *1896–1911* (Naples: Giannini, 2003).

67. Shelleen Greene makes the connection between Harlequin and Maciste in reference to *Cabiria.* Shelleen Greene, *Equivocal Subjects: Between Italy and Africa – Constructions of Racial and National Identity in the Italian Cinema* (New York: Continuum, 2012), 28. For more on Harlequin and the commedia dell'arte, see Lynne Lawner, *Harlequin on the Moon: Commedia dell'Arte and the Visual Arts* (New York: Harry N. Abrams 1998), 11–102; Robert Henke, *Performance and Literature in the Commedia dell'Arte* (Cambridge: Cambridge University Press, 2002), 153–174; and Allardyce Nicoll, *The World of Harlequin: A Critical Study of the Commedia dell'Arte* (Cambridge: Cambridge University Press, 1963), 67–73.

68. Jane M. Gaines, *Fire and Desire: Mixed-Race Movies in the Silent Era* (Chicago: University of Chicago Press, 2001), 149.

69. This white appropriation of blackface in Hollywood cinema is the central thesis of Michael Rogin, *Blackface, White Noise: Jewish Immigrants in the Hollywood Melting Pot* (Berkeley: University of California Press, 1996).

70. Criticism cited in Alberto Farassino, "Anatomia del cinema muscolare," 44.

71. *La Cine-Fono* 10, no. 320 (1916): 41.

72. Il Rondone, "*Maciste,*" *La Vita Cinematografica* 6, no. 5–6 (1916): 108–109.

3. Maciste Goes to War

1. Michael Paris, introduction to *The First World War and Popular Cin-*

ema: 1914 to the Present, ed. Michael Paris (New Brunswick, NJ: Rutgers University Press, 2000), 1. For more on early cinema and the filming of war, see the recent issue of *Film History* 22 (2010), edited by Stephen Bottomore; and Bottomore, "Il cinema appare nelle guerre balcaniche e boere, dal 1895 al 1914," in *Il cinematografo al campo. L'arma nuova nel primo conflitto mondiale,* ed. Renzo Renzi, with Gian Luca Farinelli and Nicola Mazzanti (Ancona: Transeuropa, 1993), 32–39.

2. Renzo Renzi, "Il detto e il non detto," in *Sperduto nel buio. Il cinema muto italiano e il suo tempo,* ed. Renzo Renzi (Bologna: Cappelli, 1990), 9.

3. Gian Piero Brunetta, "Cinema e prima guerra mondiale," *Storia del cinema mondiale,* vol. 1, *L'Europa. Miti, luoghi, divi,* ed. Gian Piero Brunetta (Torino: Einaudi, 2000), 252–275, 254.

4. Modris Eksteins, *Rites of Spring: The Great War and the Birth of the Modern Age* (Boston: Houghton Mifflin, 1989), 223.

5. Pierre Sorlin, "Cinema and the Memory of the Great War," in Paris, *The First World War and Popular Cinema,* 5–26.

6. Respectively, *La Vita Cinematografica,* numero speciale (December 1916): 271. See also *La Cinematografia Italiana ed Estera* 9, no. 3 (1917): 56; *La Vita Cinematografica* 8, no. 7–8 (1917): 141; *La Cine-Fono* 11, no. 342 (1917): 88; and *La Cine-Fono* 11, no. 341 (1917): 118.

7. Marco Salotti, "Un'intervista con il figlio di Maciste," in *Gli uomini forti,* ed. Alberto Farassino and Tatti Sanguineti (Milan: Mazzotta, 1983), 182.

8. This modernism/traditionalism dichotomy in relation to the war is at the heart of the scholarship of both Giaime Alonge and Gian Piero Brunetta. Giaime Alonge, *Cinema e guerra* (Turin: UTET, 2001); and Gian Piero Brunetta, *Storia del cinema italiano,* vol. 1, *Il cinema muto, 1895–1929* (Rome: Riuniti, 1993), 219–228.

9. Jay Winter challenges the idea that modernism "neatly" left behind eighteenth- and nineteenth-century cultural images derived from religious, romantic, and classical traditions. He argues for an integrative approach to the interpretation of World War I's cultural history, drawing equally on the historiographical tendencies of what he calls the "modernist thesis" – that World War I precipitated "the creation of a new language of truth-telling about war in poetry, prose and the visual arts" – and the "traditional approach," which focuses instead on what modernism rejected: the "classical, romantic, or religious images and ideas widely disseminated in both elite and popular culture before and during the war." Jay Winter, *Sites of Memory, Sites of Mourning: The Great War in European Cultural History* (Cambridge: Cambridge University Press, 1995), 2–3.

10. Giovanna Procacci, "A 'Latecomer' in War: The Case of Italy," in *Authority, Identity, and the Social History of the Great War,* ed. Frans Coetzee and Marilyn Shevin-Coetzee (Providence, RI: Berghahn, 1995), 3–28. See also William A. Renzi, "Italy's Neutrality and Entrance into the Great War: A Re-examination," *American Historical Review* 73, no. 5 (1968): 1414–1432.

11. Opposition crossed political social and economic sectors: the working class, with its deep distrust of government, was more concerned with domestic rather than international issues; the peasants still had little concept of nation or country; the middle class was skeptical after reading about the dangers of the initial conflict in other parts of Europe through widespread newspaper coverage; and political blocks such as the socialists and the Catholics as well as the parliamentary majority opposed it. On the other hand, the radicals, republicans, masons, and nationalists saw the war as a way to advance Italy's territorial and diplomatic credibility on the Continent and create national consensus. Also instrumental were relatives of the beloved Giuseppe Garibaldi, who helped recruit soldiers as early as 1914. Mario Isnenghi, *La grande guerra* (1993; Florence: Giunti Editore, 2000), 34–35.

12. Italy's major military weakness was its own meager navy, which never could have competed against Britain's powerful fleet, and its poorly equipped army, which could never have contended against France. In addition, Italy was dependent on British coal supply. Martin Clark, *Modern Italy: 1871 to the Present*, 3rd ed. (Harlow, UK: Pearson/ Longman, 2008), 218.

13. Mario Isnenghi, *Il mito della grande guerra* (Bologna: Il Mulino, 1989), 106.

14. Amy Boylan, "Maternal Images in Song, Bronze, and Rhetoric: Mercantini's 'Inno a Garibaldi,' Baroni's *Monumento ai Mille,* and D'Annunzio's *Orazione per la sagra dei Mille,*" *Ital-*

ian Studies 66, no. 1 (2011): 40–58. See also Boylan's "Masculinity and Commemoration of the Great War: Gabriele D'Annunzio's *La beffa di Buccari* and Eugenio Baroni's *Monumento al Fante,*" *Italian Culture* 29, no. 1 (2011): 3–17.

15. Gabriele D'Annunzio, "Orazione per la sagra dei Mille. V maggio MDCCCLX–V maggio MCMXV," in Gabriele D'Annunzio, *Per la più grande Italia. Orazioni e messaggi di Gabriele D'Annunzio* (Milan: Fratelli Treves, 1915), 29–30;

16. Originally, King Vittorio Emanuele III was supposed to attend the inauguration. When Salandra, who was charged with previewing D'Annunzio's speech, realized that it amounted to a declaration of war, something only the king could enact, and recognized the persuasive power of D'Annunzio's rhetoric, he was able to persuade the king not to attend the ceremony and to allow D'Annunzio to read his entire speech. Antonino Répaci, *Da Sarajevo al "maggio radioso": l'Italia verso la prima guerra mondiale* (Milan: Mursia, 1985), 377–379.

17. Ugo Ojetti, *D'Annunzio amico, maestro, soldato* (Florence: Sansoni, 1951), as quoted in Répaci, *Da Sarajevo al "maggio radioso,"* 381.

18. This convergence of war mobilization, aggressive masculinity, and war commemoration was emblematic of the cult of the fallen soldier that emerged in the nineteenth century and reached its apotheosis after World War I, constituting both a nationalization and a sacralization of death in warfare: "The cooptation of Christian symbolism and ritual to sanctify the life and death

of the soldier was to play a crucial part in the Myth of the War Experience." George L. Mosse, *Fallen Soldiers: Reshaping the Memory of the World Wars* (New York: Oxford University Press, 1990), 25. Many historians in fact see this speech and the maggio radioso as a whole as precursors to the massive Fascist displays and spectacles that aided in creating cultural consensus during the *ventennio,* many of which, like some of the maggio radioso rallies, also culminated in violence. Répaci, *Da Sarajevo al "maggio radioso,"* 410. For Fascism, see Simonetta Falasca-Zamponi, *Fascist Spectacle: The Aesthetics of Power in Mussolini's Italy* (Berkeley: University of California Press, 1997).

19. Alonge, *Cinema e guerra,* 4, 46. Alonge is indebted to Benjamin, who sees sensorial shock and fragmented vision as constitutive of the modern condition. See *Cinema e guerra,* 12–14.

20. According to the *Archivio del cinema italiano,* vol. 1, *Il cinema muto italiano,* ed. Aldo Bernardini (Rome: Anica, 1991), the film was released on 22 June 1915.

21. Vittorio Martinelli, "Il cinema italiano in armi," in *Sperduto nel buio,* ed. Renzo Renzi, 35–42, here 40.

22. Vittorio Martinelli, *Il cinema muto italiano 1915. I film della grande guerra, seconda parte, Bianco & Nero* 52, no. 3–4: 214.

23. Giovanni Nobili Vitelleschi, "The Representation of the Great War in Italian Cinema," in Paris, *First World War and Popular Cinema,* 162–171.

24. Brunetta, "Cinema e prima guerra mondiale," 256.

25. Riccardo Redi, *Il Christus di Giulio Antamoro e di Enrico Guazzoni* (Rome: Associazione Italiana per le Ricerche di Storia del Cinema, 2002). According to sources in Redi's collection, the poem was commissioned for the film by Giulio Antamoro's brother but not published until 1932, after Fausto Salvatori's death. For more on the story of Christ in the cinema, see the Museo Nazionale del Cinema's online source, *Ecce homo,* http://www.museocinema .it/collezioni/eccehomo/main.html. Similarly, although made after the war, Abel Gance's pacifist film *J'accuse (I Accuse,* 1919), was only one of many works that "appropriated religious images both before and during the war to create a revived form of popular romanticism." Drawing on the revival of popular religious imagery as commodities in nineteenth-century, modern incarnations, Gance's and other religious visual representations sanitized the worst features of the war and presented it as "mythical or romantic adventure." Winter, *Sites of Memory,* 119–144, here 119 and 133, respectively.

26. A brief notice in *La Vita Cinematografica* writes that Itala Film had to slow down its productions because most of its male personnel had been called up to serve in the army. *La Vita Cinematografica* 7, no. 39–40 (1916): 167.

27. An article from the *Bioscope,* the British periodical, republished in *La Cinematografia Italiana ed Estera,* reassured British and Italian spectators of the industry's vitality and viability. Leonard Donaldson, "Our Allies and the Cinema," *La Cinematografia Italiana ed Estera* 9, no. 23 (1915): 40.

According to Paolo Cherchi Usai, the Itala Film studio at one point was used as a hospital at Pastrone's urging. Paolo Cherchi Usai, *Giovanni Pastrone* (Florence: La Nuova Italia, 1985), 84.

28. Riccardo Redi, *Cinema muto italiano* (Rome: Biblioteca di Bianco & Nero, 1999), 111–116.

29. Silvio Alovisio, "Il cinema italiano: dalle origini all'avvento del sonoro," in *Attraverso lo schermo. Cinema e cultura cattolica in Italia*, vol. 1, *Dalle origini agli anni Venti*, ed. Ruggero Eugeni and Dario E. Viganò (Rome: Ente dello Spettacolo, 2006), 61–95. The Turinese film periodical *La Vita Cinematografica* lamented this shift to Rome. Pier Da Castello, "Perchè la sede della cinematografia deve essere a Torino anzichè a Roma," *La Vita Cinematografica* 9, no. 35–36 (1918): 61–62.

30. Vittorio Martinelli and Mario Quargnolo, *Maciste & Co. I giganti buoni del muto italiano* (Gemona del Friuli: Cinepopolare, 1981), 23–24.

31. Monica Dall'Asta, *Un cinéma musclé. Le surhomme dans le cinéma muet italien (1913–1926)*. (Crisnée: Yellow Now, 1992), 69–70.

32. Marco Bertozzi, *Storia del documentario italiano. Immagini e culture dell'altro cinema* (Venice: Marsilio, 2008), 54–58; Nicola Bultrini and Antonio Tentori, *Il cinema della grande guerra* (Chiari: Nordpress, 2008), 28–32; Alovisio, "Il cinema italiano: dalle origini all'avvento del sonoro," 82–83. For Brunetta, these films provided new perspectives in their celebration of modernity and industrialization, as well as new visual sensations with their aerial shots that dislocated traditional space

and modified the "logistics of the audience's imagination." Brunetta, "Cinema e prima guerra mondiale," 260–261. For Giaime Alonge, they reveal the dialectic between the visible and the invisible: what is permissible to see and be seen and what is not. Giaime Alonge, "La guerra come orizzonte e come rappresentazione," Torino D@ams Review (2006), available online at http://www.turindamsreview.unito.it/sezione.php?idart=83. This is also an argument put forth by Pierre Sorlin in reference to Italian fiction films during World War I. Pierre Sorlin, "1914–1918: la guerra invisibile," in *I limiti della rappresentazione*, ed. Leonardo Quaresima, Alessandra Raengo, and Laura Vichi (Udine: Forum, 2000), 153–162. For more on Italian photography and World War I, see Angelo Schwarz, "Le fotografie e la grande guerra rappresentata," in *La grande guerra. Esperienza, memoria, immagini*, ed. Diego Leoni and Camillo Zadra (Bologna: Il Mulino, 1986), 745–764.

33. These and other documentaries are now available on DVD under the title *Doppio sguardo sulla grande guerra. I "dal vero" del 1915–1918 tra cinema, guerra e propaganda* (Gemona del Friuli: Cineteca del Friuli, 2006). The two-DVD set also features a documentary, *Gorizia in trincea*, which features voice-over narration of actors reading from these vivid diaries.

34. There have been two restorations of *Maciste alpino*. The first, in 2000, was carried out by the Museo Nazionale del Cinema in collaboration with the Fondazione Cineteca Italiana in Milan and the Municipality of Valtournenche.

A duplicate negative and color copies were printed from a tinted and toned nitrate positive preserved at the MNC. The work was performed in 2000 at the Blue Film Laboratory in Milan. The second, just recently restored in 2014 in order to integrate newly discovered fragments, was carried out by the Venice Biennale in collaboration with the MNC, departing from a negative camera fragment and a positive nitrate copy preserved at the museum, integrated with two positive nitrate prints held at the Fondazione Cineteca Italiana in Milan and the British Film Institute in London, all of which were scanned in 4K. The original intertitles were reconstructed from production documents, intertitle plates held at the MNC, and by title blocks used by Itala Film on coetaneous films.

35. The original title reads: "Ai popoli generosi, ai figli della civiltà che combattono contro la barbaria tedesca, quale omaggio, questa rievocazione." Titoli, quaderno di produzione, con indicazione di didascalie e numero delle parti, relativo a film dell'Itala del 1915–1918, MNC online archives, *Maciste alpino*, "Documenti archivistici," http://www.museocinema.it/collezioni /Muto.aspx, A160/9. This opening intertitle, reconstructed from the script but not appearing in extant prints, is confirmed in the review of the film in *La Vita Cinematografica* 8, no. 3–4 (1917): 79–83.

36. Leslie Midkiff DeBauche, *Reel Patriotism: The Movies and World War I* (Madison: University of Wisconsin Press, 1997), 59; Daniel J. Leab, "Total War On-Screen: The Hun in U.S. Films,

1914–1920," in *"Huns" vs. "Corned Beef": Representations of the Other in American and German Literature and Film on World War I*, ed. Thomas F. Schneider and Hans Wagener (Göttingen: V & R Unipress, 2007), 153–184; Andrew Kelly, *Cinema and the Great War* (London: Routledge, 1997), 13.

37. Alonge, *Cinema e guerra*, 72–73.

38. For more on the uniform in *Maciste alpino*, see my "Slave to Fashion: Masculinity, Suits, and the Maciste Films of Italian Silent Cinema," in Adrienne Munich, ed., *Fashion in Film* (Bloomington: Indiana University Press, 2011), 236–259.

39. The scene is viewable at http:// www.museocinema.it/collezioni /maciste/main.html, *Maciste* Sequenza #6.

40. The one significant exception to this paradigm is *Maciste innamorato*, discussed in detail in chapter 5.

41. Manelli, "*Maciste alpino* e l'Itala Film,'" *Film* 3, no. 36 (1916): 4.

42. Brunetta, "Cinema e prima guerra mondiale," 268. For Nobili Vitelleschi, the hybrid stylistic codes and attention to visual effects make it modern. Nobili Vitelleschi, "The Representation of the Great War in Italian Cinema," 165–167.

43. The scene is viewable at http:// www.museocinema.it/collezioni /maciste/main.html, *Maciste* Sequenza #4.

44. Mosse, *Fallen Soldiers*, 139–142. See also, for the Italian case, Antonio Gibelli, *Il popolo bambino. Infanzia e nazione nella Grande Guerra a Salò* (Turin: Einaudi, 2005), 134–148.

45. Cited in Giaime Alonge, *Il disegno armato. Cinema d'animazione e propaganda bellica in Nord America e Gran Bretagna* (1914–1945) (Bologna: CLUEB, 2000), 57. Alonge has written widely on this film. See his "Giocando con i soldatini. *La guerra e il sogno di Momi* tra propaganda e mercato," in *Nuovo spettatore* 1, no. 1 (1997): 167–178, as well as *Cinema e guerra*, 7–8; and "La guerra come orizzonte," 8–10. In *Il disegno armato* Alonge also makes the argument that although *Momi* is a patriotic film, there is no reference to Italy at all, that the film instead is a synthesis between the nationalism of war propaganda and the internationalism of the market. Alonge theorizes that the film's indistinguishability of both enemy and hero was a deliberate attempt to create an ambiguity that could aid in the film's exportation. *Momi* was in fact exported to Great Britain under the title *Jackie in Wonderland* and in the United States in 1918 as *The Hand of the Hun*.

46. "For many, gas took the war into the realm of the unreal, the make-believe. When men donned their masks they lost all sign of humanity, and with their long snouts, large glass eyes, and slow movements, they became figures of fantasy, closer in their angular features to the creations of Picasso and Braque than to soldiers of tradition." Eksteins, *Rites of Spring*, 163.

47. Mosse, *Fallen Soldiers*, 7.

48. Mosse analyzes this tendency in religious terms; many monuments featured the dying soldier in the image of Christ as symbol of the power of resurrection and redemption. Mosse, *Fallen Soldiers*, 104. On Italian war monuments in particular, see Renato Monteleone and Pino Sarasini, "I monumenti italiani ai caduti della grande guerra," in Leoni and Zadra, *La grande guerra,* 631–662.

49. The documentary *Azione del R. Marina nel golfo di Trieste* (1917) goes as far as to conclude with a colored (tinted) shot of the three-colored flag on top of a triumphant submarine.

50. Sergio Raffaelli notes how the film's linguistic realism embraces the language of patriotism in many of the references cited above. Sergio Raffaelli, *L'italiano nel cinema muto* (Florence: Franco Cesati Editore, 2003), 72–81.

51. On Maciste's connection to the arditi and futurism, see Dall'Asta, *Un cinéma musclé, 63,* 70–74. Dall'Asta extends the connection between the strongman film and futurism to some of the postwar stars such as Saetta (Domenico Gambino) and Sansone (Luciano Albertini), among others, 129–133.

52. In contrast to popular opinion both leading up to and during the war, many Italian intellectuals, including those in the film industry, embraced intervention believing that the war would not have lasted long. Eksteins has argued that the war was more than just a conflict of nations; rather, "The war, it seemed, was run on the basis of assumptions, on reflex responses that were engendered by a code of values and ideas, not solely about war itself but about civilization in general." Eksteins, *Rites of Spring,* 174. He notes that in addition to spurring a flurry of artistic activity, the war prompted many artists to join the war effort as fighters, writers, and propagandists.

53. Mosse, *Fallen Soldiers,* 53–54.

54. "Futurism and the Great War," originally published in Italian in *L'Italia Futurista* (8 July 1917). Here reprinted in *F. T. Marinetti: Critical Writings,* new ed., ed. Günter Berghaus, trans. Doug Thompson (New York: Farrar, Straus & Giroux, 2006), 245–246. See also Mosse, *Fallen Soldiers,* 20–22, 60–61, 72–73.

55. Emilio Gentile, *The Struggle for Modernity: Nationalism, Futurism, and Fascism* (Westport, CT: Praeger, 2003), 35–36. Mosse notes the similarities between futurism and German Expressionism as two youth movements that saw in war an opportunity to end bourgeois complacency, tyranny, and hypocrisy. Mosse, *Fallen Soldiers,* 55–57; see also Isnenghi, *Mito,* 180.

56. F. T. Marinetti, "The Foundation and Manifesto of Futurism," originally published in *Poesia* 5, no. 1–2 (1909), here reprinted and translated in Berghaus, *F. T. Marinetti,* 11–17, here 13. For more on a discussion of futurism, the machine, and speed and the mechanized man, see Maurizia Boscagli, *Eye on the Flesh: Fashions of Masculinity in the Early Twentieth Century* (Boulder, CO: Westview Press, 1996), 129–164. In her work Boscagli interprets the futurist male body as both a laboring and desexualized, automatic body.

57. "Extended Man and the Kingdom of the Machine," in Berghaus, *F. T. Marinetti,* 85–88, here 86. In the "Technical Manifesto of Futurist Literature" (1912), which advocates the total abolition of syntax, structure, and the eradication of the "I," Marinetti calls for the creation of "a mechanical man, one who

will have parts that can be changed." Berghaus, *F. T. Marinetti,* 113. For more on the relationship between the male body, Maciste, and cars, see the discussion of *Maciste in vacanza* in chapter 5.

58. "Extended Man," 87. In Christine Poggi's synthesis of Marinetti's mechanical body, the futurist man, as "superhuman hybrid" and "sportsman, aviator, or warrior," would be "capable of astounding feats of physical prowess." Christine Poggi, "Dreams of Metalized Flesh: Futurism and the Masculine Body," *Modernism/Modernity* 4, no. 3 (1997): 19–43, here 20. As in the futurist taxonomy, women have no place in Maciste's world, particularly when he is engaged in warfare.

59. The scene is viewable at http://www.museocinema.it/collezioni/maciste/main.html, *Maciste Sequenza #6.*

60. Marco Armiero, *A Rugged Nation: Mountains and the Making of Modern Italy* (Cambridge, UK: White Horse Press, 2011), 5. See also Alessandro Pastore, "La patria, la guerra e la montagna. Identità nazionali e conflitti politici nella rete associativa dell'alpinismo italiano (1913–1927)," in *Alla conquista dell'immaginario. L'alpinismo come proiezione di modelli culturali e sociali borghesi tra Otto e Novecento,* ed. Michael Wedekind and Claudio Ambrosi (Treviso: Edizioni Antilia, 2007), 143–167.

61. On Soffici and the Alps, see Walter L. Adamson, *Avant-Garde Florence: From Modernism to Fascism* (Cambridge, MA: Harvard University Press, 1993), 209; for Jahier, see Isnenghi, *Mito,* 187–190, as well as Piero Jahier, *Con me e*

con gli alpini (Rome: Edizione La Voce, 1920). Another important treatment of war in the Alps is Emilio Lussu's *Un anno sull'altipiano* (Milan: Mondadori, 1971), published first in France in 1938 and then in Italy in 1945.

62. Mosse, *Fallen Soldiers,* 114–119. He also discusses the German mountain films by Luis Trenker and later Leni Riefenstahl that became so popular in Germany after the war: "The myth of mountains as Arcadia did not point to flowering fields or country churchyards, but to an innocence that implied hardness, domination, and conquest among individuals and nations." Mosse, *Fallen Soldiers,* 116. The mountain movie culminates in the last film of the Maciste series, *Il gigante delle Dolomiti* (1926), examined in this book's conclusion.

63. Recent scholarship in environmental history and film studies has focused on the role of landscape in the shaping and construction of Italian national identity. Giorgio Bertellini, *Italy in Early American Cinema: Race, Landscape, and the Picturesque* (Bloomington: Indiana University Press, 2009), and "The Earth Still Trembles: On Landscape Views in Contemporary Italian Cinema," *Italian Culture* 30, no. 1 (2012): 38–50; Rosalind Galt, "Italy's Landscapes of Loss: Historical Mourning and the Dialectical Image of *Cinema Paradiso, Mediterraneo,* and *Il Postino,*" *Screen* 43, no. 2 (2002): 158–173; and Noa Steimatsky, *Italian Locations: Re-inhabiting the Past in Postwar Cinema* (Minneapolis: University of Minnesota Press, 2008).

64. Brunetta, "Cinema e prima guerra mondiale," 267–268; Dall'Asta, *Un cinéma musclé,* 61–63.

65. Luca Cottino notes the religious elements in the film in his "La novità di *Maciste alpino,*" *Italian Culture* 27, no. 1 (2009): 43–59.

66. Martinelli, "Il cinema italiano in armi," 35.

67. Denis Lotti surmises that the censorship board imposed these cuts to stress the chivalric principles to which the Italian army inspired, even in battle. Denis Lotti, *Il divismo maschile nel cinema muto italiano. Protagonisti, film, stereotipi, 1910–1929,* Tesi di Dottorato di Ricerca, Università degli Studi di Padova (2011). A notice about the film's final clearance from the censors appears in *La Vita Cinematografica* 7, no. 43–44 (1916): 129.

68. The defendants also stated that since they did not attend the screening when the censorship board saw the film in Rome, they could not be sure of the version screened. The entire judgment is reproduced in *La Vita Cinematografica* 8, no. 17–18 (1917): 103–104.

69. See, for instance, the invective by the French actor Turlupin, "Censura," in *La Cine-Fono* 11, no. 344 (1917): 92.

70. *La Vita Cinematografica* 8, no. 17–18 (1917): 110.

71. *La Vita Cinematografica* 7, no. 17–18 (1916): 50–51. The ads are repeated in the next three issues, when publicity strategy switches to the full title and the tagline, "La più alta vetta . . . cinematografica è raggiunta da *Maciste alpino,* Imminente Pubblicazione." The Ditta Stefano Pittaluga in Genoa, the film's distributor, publicized the film in

much the same way, although without the irony: "D'imminente programmazione, *Maciste alpino* dell'Itala Film. Il più grandioso lavoro ed il più clamoroso successo della stagione." *La Vita Cinematografica* 8, no. 33–4 (1916) and 7, no. 39–40 (1916), respectively. Ads appear in *La Cinematografia Italiana ed Estera* around the same time. See *Cinematografia Italiana ed Estera* 10, no. 17 (1916): 19.

72. *La Vita Cinematografica* 7, no. 39–40 (1916): 108–109, and 7, no. 41–42 (1916): 18–19.

73. Brochure del cinema Bios di Bologna, 29 January 1917. MNC online archives, *Maciste alpino*, "Materiali pubblicitari," P41392, http://www.museo nazionaledelcinema.it/collezioni /Muto.aspx?id=795.

74. Thomas Row, "Mobilizing the Nation: Italian Propaganda and the Great War," *Journal of Decorative Propaganda Arts* 24 (2002): 140–169.

75. Postcards, already widely circulating in the late nineteenth century, became another way to both represent and manage the war, opting for the humorous and the motivational over the realistic. Rarely did images of the brutal, bloody deaths common to all areas of combat appear in photos or artistic renderings; when the injured were depicted, their wounds were slight or heavily bandaged. Many had religious imagery imbued in their iconography, especially in Italy, with Christ looking down on the sufferers and protecting them. Mosse, *Fallen Soldiers*, 128–135. For examples of postcards depicting the war in Italy, see Enrico Sturani, *Cartoline. L'arte alla prova della cartolina* (Manduria [Taranto]: Barbieri Editore, 2010), 157–161.

76. For more on Metlicovich, see *Metlicovich, Dudovich. Grandi cartellonisti triestini. Manifesti dalla Raccolta "Achille Bertarelli" del Castello Sforzesco di Milano*, ed. Giovanna Ginex (Milan: Skira, 2001). I would like to thank Nicholas Lowry of Swann Galleries in New York for helping me to identify positively Metlicovich's authorship of the Italian poster for *Maciste alpino*.

77. Fabrizio Romano, "Les Premières. *Maciste Alpino* (Itala-Film) al Gran Salone Ghersi di Torino," *La Vita Cinematografica* 8, no. 3–4 (1917): 80.

78. Angelo Menini, "I grandi avvenimenti d'arte. *Maciste Alpino* dell'Itala Film a Torino (al Salone Ghersi)," *Film* 4, no. 3 (1917): 12.

79. Roland de Beaumont, "Les nouveautés ciné–théâtrales Italiennes," *La Vita Cinematografica* 7, special number (December 1916): 201–205, trans. Hélène Volat.

80. Menini, "I grandi avvenimenti d'arte," 12.

81. *La Vita Cinematografica* 8, no. 1–2 (1917): 126.

82. Walter L. Adamson, "The Impact of World War I on Italian Political Culture," in *European Culture in the Great War: The Arts, Entertainment, and Propaganda, 1914–1918*, ed. Aviel Roshwald and Richard Stites (Cambridge: Cambridge University Press, 1999), 308–329, here 323; Clark, *Modern Italy*, 226; and Emilio Franzina, "Il tempo libero dalla guerra. Case del soldato e postriboli militari," in Leoni and Zadra, *La grande guerra*, 161–230.

83. Isnenghi, *Mito,* 13. The writers for the Florentine literary and cultural periodicals *La voce* and *Lacerba* in particular saw the war as an opportunity to revolutionize and remake Italy. The journalism, novels, poetry, and essays of the avant-garde writers, including Giuseppe Prezzolini, Giovanni Papini, and Ardengo Soffici, expressed disgust with the previous Giolitti government and its policies of appeasement. Soffici took a decidedly anti-German and anti-Austrian position in making his case for war; Prezzolini and Papini were more nuanced, seeing the war as a confrontation between French and Germanic cultures, arguing instead in favor of the supremacy of French culture and its affinities with Italy and as a cure for Italian society's many ills. Adamson, *Avant-Garde Florence,* 192–193; and Clark, *Modern Italy,* 208–210. See also Emilio Gentile, *The Struggle for Modernity: Nationalism, Futurism, and Fascism* (Westport, CT: Praeger, 2003), 27–40.

84. De Beaumont, "Le success de 'Maciste Alpin,'" *La Vita Cinematografica* 8, no. 1–2 (1917): 88.

85. Romano, "Les Premières," 80.

86. Ibid., 83.

87. Angelo Ventrone, *La seduzione totalitaria. Guerra, modernità, violenza politica* (1914–1918) (Rome: Donzelli, 2003), 151–164.

88. Brunetta, "Cinema e prima guerra mondiale," 254. On Henny Porten, see Ramona Curry, "How Early German Film Stars Helped Sell the War(es)," in Karel Dibbets and Bert Hogenkamp, eds., *Film and the First World War* (Amsterdam: Amsterdam University Press, 1995), 139–148. See

chapter 4 for more on stars and American cinema during World War I.

89. *La Cinematografia Italiana ed Estera* 11, no. 7–8 (1917): 43.

90. Dall'Asta, *Un cinéma musclé,* 63.

91. Procacci, "A 'Latecomer' in War," 6.

92. John Keegan, *The First World War* (New York: Alfred A. Knopf, 1999), 224–229. The majority of Italian combatants were in fact not from the northern region but rather southern peasants unaccustomed to the harsh conditions.

93. "It was a sullen, often illiterate, ill-equipped army, torn away from its homes and fields to fight on a foreign soil for incomprehensible reasons." Clark, *Modern Italy,* 225.

94. Mark Thompson, *The White War: Life and Death on the Italian Front, 1915–1919* (New York: Basic Books, 2008), 381. There were 29,000 Italian soldiers tried by military courts between 1915 and 1919. While about 40 percent of them were acquitted and many pardoned after the war, 750 were executed. Jonathan Dunnage, *Twentieth-Century Italy: A Social History* (London: Pearson, 2002), 45.

95. Procacci, "A 'Latecomer' in War," 19–21. After the calamitous losses at the Battle of Caporetto, there was increasing suppression of dissent and revolt (22).

96. *La Vita Cinematografica* 8, no. 17–18 (1917) and 8, no. 23–24 (1917): 95, respectively. In Brazil, a publication directed at Italians living abroad was "Il Maciste Coloniale." Danúsia Torres dos Santos, "L'immigrazione italiana a Rio de Janeiro: tracce storiche," available

online at Emigrazione-notizie.org /download.asp?dl=77.

97. Pierluigi Ercole, "'Little Italy on the Brink': The Italian Diaspora and the Distribution of War Films in London, 1914–1918," in *Cinema, Audiences, and Modernity: New Perspectives on European Cinema History,* ed. Daniel Biltereyst, Richard Maltby, and Philippe Meers (London: Routledge, 2011), 154–165. The citation is from "Maciste, Hercules, Samson: One of the Great Films of 1917: A Sensational Screening at the Alhambra," *Kinematograph and Lantern Weekly,* 2 August 1917, 82. I thank Pierluigi Ercole for graciously sharing the article with me.

98. Brochure del Théâtre du Vaudeville, [1915–1916], MNC online archives, *Cabiria,* "Materiali pubblicitari," http://www.museocinema.it/collezioni/Muto .aspx, P01367.

99. Emmanuelle Toulet, "Il cinema muto italiano e la critica francese," Vittorio Martinelli, ed., *Cinema italiano in Europa, 1907–1929* (Rome: Associazione Italiana per le Ricerche di Storia del Cinema, 1992), 11–36, especially 19–22; the review is cited on 21.

100. Colette, "Maciste alpin," *Le Film* (18 June 1917): 26, anthologized in Colette, *Colette at the Movies: Criticism and Screenplays,* ed. Alain and Odette Virmaux, trans. Sarah W. R. Smith (New York: Frederick Ungar, 1980), 28–29. I would like to thank John Welle for bringing this source to my attention.

101. Both the request and its approval are housed in the Museo Nazionale del Cinema's archives. MNC online archives, *Maciste alpino,* "Documenti

archivistici," http://www.museocinema .it/collezioni/Muto.aspx, A173/94.

4. Over There

1. Giaime Alonge, "La guerra come orizzonte e come rappresentazione," Torino D@ams Review (2006), 22, available at http://www.turindams-review.unito.it/sezione.php?idart=83. The file appears at the archives of the Ufficio Storico dello Stato Maggiore (AUSSME, F-1 fondo *Comando Supremo – vari uffici,* b. 299) and is presumably from 1918.

2. Jennifer Bean, "Technologies of Early Stardom and the Extraordinary Body," *A Feminist Reader in Early Cinema,* ed. Jennifer Bean and Diane Negra (Durham, NC: Duke University Press, 2002), 404–443; Mark Garrett Cooper, "Pearl White and Grace Cunard: The Serial Queen's Volatile Present," in *Flickers of Desire: Movie Stars of the 1910s,* ed. Jennifer Bean (New Brunswick, NJ: Rutgers University Press, 2011), 174–195; Monica Dall'Asta, "Il serial," in *Storia del cinema mondiale,* vol. 2, *Gli Stati Uniti,* ed. Gian Piero Brunetta (Turin: Einaudi, 1999), 289–336; Ben Singer, *Melodrama and Modernity: Early Sensational Cinema and Its Contexts* (New York: Columbia University Press, 2001), in particular 221–260; Shelley Stamp, *Movie-Struck Girls: Women and Motion Picture Culture after the Nickelodeon* (Princeton, NJ: Princeton University Press, 2000), 102–153; and Raymond W. Steadman, *The Serials: Suspense and Drama by Installment* (Norman: University of Oklahoma Press, 1977), 3–49. For more on serial production during the war, see

Craig W. Campbell, *Reel America and World War I: A Comprehensive Filmography and History of Motion Pictures in the United States, 1914–1920* (Jefferson, NC: McFarland, 1985), 47; and Kalton C. Lahue, *Continued Next Week: A History of the Moving Picture Serial* (Norman: University of Oklahoma Press, 1964), 38–65. In an interesting parallel, the novelization of *Cabiria*'s plot was serialized in a variety of American newspapers, including Wisconsin's *Janesville Daily Gazette* (January 1915) and *Eau Claire Leader* (October 1914).

3. I am indebted, in my intermedial understanding of the nature of early stardom, to the work of Richard Abel, in particular *Americanizing the Movies and "Movie-Mad" Audiences, 1910–1914* (Berkeley: University of California Press, 2006), 3–11, 231–252; and "G. M. Anderson: 'Broncho Billy' among the Early 'Picture Personalities,'" in Bean, *Flickers of Desire*, 22–42.

4. I am not completely comfortable, as others have insinuated (Brunetta and Dall'Asta), in drawing a causal conclusion that the success of the Maciste films in the United States gave rise to the popularity of the male serial stars in the 1920s, because I have not yet found any definitive proof of such a thesis. However, I do see the Maciste series, *The Warrior* in particular, as having an impact on the American public as well as the male action-hero genre.

5. "Gossipy Bits – Elmo Lincoln Has Been Called the Yankee Maciste," *Sandusky (OH) Star Journal*, 8 July 1919, 12; "Elmo Is Said to be Stronger than Maciste," *Billings (MT) Gazette*, 13 July 1919, 2. Lincoln had already gained some notoriety in D. W. Griffith's *Intolerance* (1916) as the Mighty Man of Valor. Vernell Coriell, "Elmo the Mighty" (1968), reprinted in Marci'a Lincoln Rudolph, *My Father, Elmo Lincoln: The Original Tarzan* (N.p.: Empire Publication Services, 1999), 27–43.

6. Gaylyn Studlar, *This Mad Masquerade: Stardom and Masculinity in the Jazz Age* (New York: Columbia University Press, 1996), 10–89; and Scott Curtis, "Douglas Fairbanks: Icon of Americanism," in Bean, *Flickers of Desire*, 218–241.

7. "Death of Maciste Denied," *Philadelphia Inquirer*, 10 March 1918, 18.

8. Unlike Sessue Hayakawa and Rudolph Valentino, Pagano did not come to the United States to find employment in the American film industry. Others, such as the boxer Luigi Montagna, who later became the actor Bull Montana, preceded; not only was Montagna Fairbanks's personal trainer, but he also became a successful comic player in his own right. Luciano Albertini, the strongman who played Sansone in Italy, came to the United States in the 1920s to make what appeared to be an unsuccessful serial titled *The Iron Man* (Universal, 1924). Giuliana Muscio, *Piccole Italie, grandi schermi. Scambi cinematografici tra Italia e Stati Uniti, 1895–1945* (Rome: Bulzoni, 2004), 58–59.

9. Daisuke Miyao, *Sessue Hayakawa: Silent Cinema and Transnational Stardom* (Durham, NC: Duke University Press, 2007), 8–9.

10. Giorgio Bertellini, "Duce/Divo: Masculinity, Racial Identity, and Politics among Italian Americans in 1920s

New York City," *Journal of Urban History* 31, no. 5 (2005): 685–726, here 688.

11. The notion of emasculation and the spectacle of foreignness comes from Dale Hudson, "'Just play yourself, "Maggie Cheung"': Irma Vep, Rethinking Transnational Stardom and Unthinking National Cinemas," *Screen* 47, no. 2 (2006): 213–232.

12. Giorgio Bertellini, "George Beban: Character of the Picturesque," in Bean, *Flickers of Desire,* 155–173, as well as his "Black Hands and White Hearts: Italian Immigrants as 'Urban Racial Types' in Early American Film Culture," *Urban History* 31, no. 3 (2004): 375–399.

13. Robert Eberwein, *Armed Forces: Masculinity and Sexuality in the American War Film* (New Brunswick, NJ: Rutgers University Press, 2007), 9–13. See also Eberwein's introduction to *The War Film,* ed. Robert Eberwein (New Brunswick, NJ: Rutgers University Press, 2005), 2–3.

14. For more on the debate over what constitutes the discursive formation of a war film, see J. David Slocum, "General Introduction: Seeing Through American War Cinema," and Steven Neale, "War Films," both in *Hollywood and War: The Film Reader,* ed. J. David Slocum (London: Routledge, 2006), 1–21 and 23–30, respectively. For more on the Spanish-American War in cinema, see also, in the same volume, James Castonguay, "The Spanish-American War in United States Media Culture," 97–108.

15. Gian Piero Brunetta, "'Over There': La guerra lontana," in *Storia del cinema mondiale,* vol. 2, *Gli Stati Uniti,*

ed. Gian Piero Brunetta (Turin: Einaudi, 1999), 267–288.

16. Campbell, *Reel America and World War I,* 37–39, 44–50. See also Andrew Kelly, *Cinema and the Great War* (London: Routledge, 1997), 15–28.

17. Leslie Midkiff DeBauche, *Reel Patriotism: The Movies and World War I* (Madison: University of Wisconsin Press, 1997), in particular xvi and 34–48; "The United States' Film Industry and World War I," in *The First World War and Popular Cinema: 1914 to the Present,* ed. Michael Paris (New Brunswick, NJ: Rutgers University Press, 2000), 138–161. For more on the war and American cinema, see Kevin Brownlow, *The War, the West and the Wilderness* (New York: Alfred A. Knopf, 1979), 1–171; and Michael T. Isenberg, *War on Film: The American Cinema and World War I* (London: Associated University Presses, 1981).

18. For *Hearts of the World* within the context of World War I, see James M. Welsh, "The Great War and the War Film as Genre: *Hearts of the World* and *What Price Glory?*" in *Hollywood's World War I: Motion Picture Images,* ed. Peter C. Rollins and John E. O'Connor (Bowling Green, OH: Bowling Green State University Press, 1997), 27–38.

19. Richard deCordova, *Picture Personalities: The Emergence of the Star System in America* (Urbana: University of Illinois Press, 1988); Catherine E. Kerr, "Incorporating the Star: The Intersection of Business and Aesthetic Strategies in Early American Film," *Business History Review* 64, no. 3 (1990): 383–410. See also Jennifer Bean, "Introduction:

Stardom in the 1910s," in *Flickers of Desire*, 3.

20. Charlie Keil and Ben Singer, "Introduction: Movies and the 1910s," in *American Cinema of the 1910s: Themes and Variations*, ed. Charlie Keil and Ben Singer (New Brunswick, NJ: Rutgers University Press, 2009): 1–25.

21. Gaylyn Studlar, "Theda Bara: Orientalism, Sexual Anarchy, and the Jewish Star," in Bean, *Flickers of Desire*, 125.

22. "Movies Mobilized to Aid in War Work," *New York Times*, 28 July 1917, 8.

23. Suzanne W. Collins, "Calling All Stars: Emerging Political Authority and Cultural Policy in the Propaganda Campaign of World War I," PhD diss., New York University, 2008, 3–4, 9. See also Larry Wayne Ward, *The Motion Picture Goes to War: The U.S. Government Film Effort during World War I* (Ann Arbor, MI: UMI Research Press, 1985).

24. Collins, "Calling All Stars," 223–237. See also Sue Collins, "Bonding with the Crowd: Silent Film Stars, Liveness, and the Public Sphere," in *Convergence Media History*, ed. Janet Staiger and Sabine Hake (New York: Routledge, 2009), 117–126.

25. Midkiff DeBauche, *Reel Patriotism*, 79.

26. Miyao, *Sessue Hayakawa*, 9–15, 127–135. See also his updated article, based on the recent restoration of select Hayakawa films, "Sessue Hayakawa: The Mirror, the Racialized Body, and *Photogénie*," in Bean, *Flickers of Desire*, 91–112. For Hayakawa's participation in the Liberty Loan campaign, see Campbell, *Reel America and World War I*, 89 and Collins, "Calling All Stars,"

312. Hayakawa's popularity extended beyond the United States to include France, Germany, and Russia as well, laying bare the contradictions between the West's simultaneous embrace of Orientalist and Japanese culture and fear of the yellow-periled other.

27. The notice of the *Maciste* premiere in New York appears in "More Thrills by Maciste: New Movie Play Women around the Slave in 'Cabiria,'" *New York Times* (20 March 1916), 9; for *Maciste alpino*, see *Evening Telegram – New York* (8 July 1917), 10.

28. "Harry R. Raver," *Moving Picture World* 21 (15 August 1914): 943; and "The Exclusive Supply Corporation," *Moving Picture World* 21, no. 2 (1914): 261.

29. Giorgio Bertellini, "Risuscitare la storia: *Cabiria* e gli Stati Uniti," in *Cabiria & Cabiria*, ed. Silvio Alovisio and Alberto Barbera (Turin: MNC, 2006), 174–180. The film later transferred to the Globe Theater, still commanding a high ticket price (25 cents).

30. Advertisement in *Moving Picture World* 21, no. 8 (1914): 1059.

31. Bertellini, "Risuscitare la storia"; Eileen Bowser, *The Transformation of Cinema, 1907–1915* (Berkeley: University of California Press, 1990), 251; Bernard Hansen, "D. W. Griffith, Some Sources," *Art Bulletin* 54, no. 4 (1972): 493–515; Miriam Hansen, *Babel & Babylon: Spectatorship in American Silent Cinema* (Cambridge, MA: Harvard University Press, 1991), 175–178; and Davide Turconi, "G. P. & D.W.G.: Il dare e l'avere," in *Pastrone e Griffith. L'ipotesi di una storia*, ed. Guido Cincotti (Rome: Bianco e Nero, 1975), 33–39.

32. "What They Stand For: Harry Raver," *New York Dramatic Mirror,* 11 August 1917, 15.

33. Cited, respectively, in "Produce Italas Here: 'Maciste, the Giant of 'Cabiria,' and Other Stars in Films Made in America," *New York Dramatic Mirror,* 26 May 1915, 24; and "Itala Company's Plans," *Moving Picture World* (31 July 1915): 800.

34. "Itala Company's Plans," 800; "To Produce in America: Famous Studio Will Have Studios Here – Definite Arrangements Not Announced," *Moving Picture World* (5 June 1915): 1582, and "Harry Raver Gives Luncheon," *New York Dramatic Mirror,* 25 August 1915, 24. The credits for the American review of *Maciste* appear in *Variety,* 20 August 1915, 19. We know that Agnes Fletcher Bain was Mrs. Harry Raver from a *New York Times* article dated 7 December 1914. The article recounts the episode in which Mrs. Raver shot herself, apparently in a suicide attempt, after putting on her most precious jewels. When asked why she did it, she reportedly said, "I did it, but I won't tell why." "Dons Costly Gems, Then Shoots Herself," *New York Times,* 7 December 1914, 1. Davide Turconi, in his brief article on the 1919 Maciste serial *The Liberator,* notes that the crediting of Bain as screenwriter links the two films. Davide Turconi, "Stuzzichini: Maciste Liberatore," *Immagine* (Associazione Italiana per le ricerche di storia del cinema) 3 (Summer 1986): 27–29.

35. In the recirculation of *Cabiria* after the film's initial run in 1914, Maciste often displaced D'Annunzio as top biller. "Maciste, the Strongman, the Hero in 'Cabiria' at Dittman's Tonight," *Brownsville (TX) Herald,* 4 March 1916, 6.

36. *Petersburg (VA) Daily Progress,* 25 October 1917, 7; and *Marion (OH) Daily Star,* 21 June 1918, 2.

37. *Middletown (NY) Times Press,* 12 December 1917, 8; *Daily Independent* (Monesenn, Pennsylvania), 22 May 1916, 2; and *Fitchburg (MA) Daily Sentinel,* 21 January 1917, 9, respectively. Another advertisement stated: "The most remarkable thing about this very unusual film is that it is both comedy and tense exciting drama. There is an element of mystery which holds and the action moves with a speed that will create a furore [*sic*] of laughter and excitement." *Piqua (OH) Leader Dispatch,* 17 March 1917, 8.

38. "Giant Actor Stars in Program at Casino," unspecified newspaper review, 24 April 1916, n.p. From the Bartolomeo Pagano/Maciste clippings file in the Billy Rose Theatre Division, New York Public Library of the Performing Arts, hereafter abbreviated as Pagano/Maciste – BRTD-NYPLPA.

39. Richard Koszarski, *An Evening's Entertainment: The Age of the Silent Feature Picture, 1915–1928* (Berkeley: University of California Press, 1990), 259–261; DeCordova, *Picture Personalities,* 72–73; Eve Golden, *Vernon and Irene Castle's Ragtime Revolution* (Lexington: University of Kentucky Press, 2007), 134–139; Lon Davis and Debra Davis, *King of the Movies: Francis X. Bushman* (Albany, GA: BearManor Media, 2009), 27.

40. "News and Flashes from the Cinema's Rays," *New York Sun,* 29 July 1917, 3.

41. *Moving Picture World* (8 January 1916): 317; and *Petersburg (VA) Daily Progress*, 27 October 1917, 7.

42. The quotation appears in an advertisement for *Marvelous Maciste* in the *Oil City (PA) Derrick*, 16 June 1916, 13.

43. As Susan Courtney has written, "The miscegenation fantasies of *Birth* [*of a Nation*] and *The Cheat*, especially, directly transpose their anxieties regarding the political and economic threats posed by men of color into images of those men as sexual threats to white women, displacements that in turn prompt virulent punishment of the former and dramatic containment of the latter through their victimization and rescue." Susan Courtney, *Hollywood Fantasies of Miscegenation: Spectacular Narratives of Gender and Race, 1903–1967* (Princeton, NJ: Princeton University Press, 2005), 62–63. See also Jane Gaines, *Fire & Desire: Mixed-Race Movies in the Silent Era* (Chicago: University of Chicago Press, 2001), 1–23.

44. "Numidian Slave in *Cabiria* Once a Dock Hand in Genoa," *Atlanta Constitution*, 8 August 1914, 4; "*Cabiria*," *Kokomo (IN) Tribune*, 5 April 1915, 6.

45. "Today's Best Photo Play Stories," *Chicago Daily Tribune*, 18 June 1914, 11.

46. "Large Crowds See 'Cabiria' Films," *Trenton (NJ) Evening Times*, 27 August 1914, 2.

47. "Black Wore Off, but He Didn't Die, Brudder Maciste," *Chicago Daily Tribune*, 4 January 1918, 14; and "He Is Not An African!" *Lancaster (OH) Daily Eagle*, 23 April 1918, 2.

48. *La Crosse (WI) Tribune*, 28 October 1916, 9.

49. *Nevada State Journal* (Reno), 12 October 1917, 3.

50. "Answers to Movie Fans," *Sunday Oregonian*, 13 February 1916, 7.

51. "Maciste Won Place in Movies Easily," *Newark (NJ) Eagle*, 21 February 1918, n.p., Pagano/Maciste – BRTD-NYPLPA. Such geographically distant newspapers as the *Daily Leader* of Grand Rapids, Wisconsin, and the *Brownsville Herald* in Texas also picked up the identical story: "Maciste Popular in Home Country," *Daily Leader*, 22 February 1918, 1, and "Stevedore Becomes Hereo [*sic*] in Movies thru Accident," *Brownsville Daily Herald*, 23 February 1918, 6.

52. The *Fort Wayne (IN) Journal-Gazette* reported that in search of "a giant of Herculean strength" to play Maciste, "men were sent out to scour all of Italy to find the required type. After many weeks they came upon some farmers pitching hay and among them was a man of almost unknown size." "Famous Giant of *Cabiria* at Jefferson," *Fort Wayne Journal-Gazette*, 12 September 1916, 10.

53. For more on these subjects, see Jacqueline Reich, "'The World's Most Perfectly Developed Man': Charles Atlas, Physical Culture, and the Inscription of American Masculinity," *Men and Masculinities* 12, no. 2 (2010): 444–461.

54. "More Thrills by Maciste: New Movie Play around the Slave in 'Cabiria,'" *New York Times*, 20 March 1916, 9.

55. *Petersburg (VA) Daily Progress,* 25 October 1917, 7.

56. *Kokomo (IN) Tribune,* 6 June 1916, 9.

57. Michael Kimmel, "Consuming Manhood: The Feminization of American Culture and the Recreation of the American Male Body, 1832–1920," *Michigan Quarterly Review* 33, no. 1 (1994): 7–36.

58. "Maciste Not Dead: Harry Raver Denies the Report," *Billboard,* 6 October 1917, 6. For the background on Florence Turner and Carl Laemmle, see DeCordova, *Picture Personalities,* 58–64.

59. *New York Dramatic Mirror,* 6 October 1917, n.p., Pagano/Maciste – BRTD-NYPLPA.

60. "Pagani in a Class by Himself in a Comedy of War," *Cleveland (OH) Plain Dealer,* 19 January 1918, n.p., Pagano/Maciste – BRTD-NYPLPA.

61. "Death of Maciste Denied," *Philadelphia Inquirer,* 10 March 1918, 18. The article begins: "The death of Maciste, the famous giant of *Cabiria,* which was reported here a few days ago, is officially denied, and he is still with the Italian army doing his bit. He was wounded and as a result of that it became reported that he died. Maciste, who appears in 'The Warrior' at the Colonial this week, is the biggest and strongest man in Italy. He is over seven feet in height and weighs close to three hundred pounds. In spite of his enormous size he has a handsome face and is always in good humor."

62. "Maciste, Giant of 'Cabiria,' in Last Success, 'The Warrior,'" *San Jose Mercury Herald,* 3 April 1918, 10.

63. *Fort Wayne (IN) News and Sentinel,* 15 January 1918, 6.

64. J. F. "Photoplays," *Indianapolis Star,* 25 March 1918, 8.

65. Isenberg, *War on Film,* 204–214.

66. Gen. Armando Diaz had replaced the increasingly unpopular Luigi Cadorna and expanded the shock troops (the *arditi*), raised food rations, and restored much needed trust and morale to those fighting on the front. Mark Thompson, *The White War: Life and Death on the Italian Front, 1915–1919* (New York: Basic Books, 2008), 223–224, 328–368.

67. "The Warrior," *Photoplay* (November 1917), n.p., Pagano/Maciste – BRTD-NYPLP.

68. *Photoplay* (September 1917), n.p., Pagano/Maciste – BRTD-NYPLPA.

69. "Maciste seen as Mighty Warrior," *Los Angeles Examiner,* 12 January 1918, n.p., Pagano/Maciste – BRTD-NYPLPA.

70. "'The Warrior' Starring Maciste One Entire Week at the Owl," *Lowell (MA) Sun,* 12 January 1918, 20.

71. "Maciste in 'The Warrior' Returns to the Owl Theatre," *Lowell (MA) Sun,* 16 February 1918, 4. Lowell also had a large Italian immigrant working-class community that could have contributed to the film's success. See Mario Aste, "They Came in Hope: Pictorial and Oral History of Lowell's Italian Americans," online at http://ecommunity.uml.edu/Italian/they_came_in_hope.pdf.

72. Bowser, *Transformation of Cinema,* 49–52.

73. *Daily Kennebec (ME) Journal,* 20 May 1918, 4.

74. Morris L. Ernst and Pare Lorentz, *Censored: The Private Life of the Movie* (New York: Cornwall Press, 1930), 14–16, 103–114; Lee Grieveson, *Policing Cinema: Movies and Censorship in Early Twentieth-Century America* (Berkeley: University of California Press, 2004), 4–7; Richard Koszarski, *Evening's Entertainment*, 198–208. See also Kevin Brownlow, *Behind the Mask of Innocence* (Berkeley: University of California Press, 1990), 26–93. On female audiences, see Janet Staiger, *Bad Women: Regulating Sexuality in Early American Cinema* (Minneapolis: University of Minnesota Press, 1995), 54–85; and Stamp, *Movie-Struck Girls*, 3–40.

75. Midkiff DeBauche, *Reel Patriotism*, 41–44.

76. Advertisement, *Tyrone (PA) Daily Herald*, 31 July 1920, 2; "Maciste Shows How the Italians Are Fighting," *Indianapolis Examiner*, 25 June 1918, n.p., Pagano/Maciste – BRTD-NYPLPA; "News and Flashes from the Cinema's Rays," *New York Sun*, 29 July 1917, 3. In one case *The Warrior* was on the same bill as official U.S. war pictures "showing as they did the intimate workings of our torpedo boats." *Boston Post*, 26 February 1918, n.p., Pagano/Maciste – BRTD-NYPLPA.

77. "Amusements," *Daily Kennebec (ME) Journal*, 23 August 1918, 8.

78. "'The Warrior' at the Hippodrome Today," *Dallas Morning News*, 6 January 1918, 5.

79. Isenberg, *War on Film*, 146.

80. Review of *The Warrior, Detroit Free Press*, 1 April 1918, n.p., Pagano/Maciste – BRTD-NYPLPA.

81. "Maciste's Final Film," *Boston Transcript*, 19 October 1917, n.p., Pagano/Maciste – BRTD-NYPLPA. The film would not open in Boston until January 1918 at the Boston Theatre, and a review in the *Boston Post* noted its lighter side as well: "It is a powerful drama of love, comedy and war." *Boston Post*, 8 January 1918, n.p., Pagano/Maciste – BRTD-NYPLPA.

82. *Detroit News*, 19 March 1918 and 1 April 1918, n.p., Pagano/Maciste – BRTD-NYPLPA. See also *Morning Herald* (Hagerstown, MD), 23 April 1918, 3, and *Connellsville (PA) Daily Courier*, 2 May 1918, 3.

83. "Mirroring Maciste," *Boston Transcript*, 11 January 1918, n.p., Pagano/Maciste – BRTD-NYPLPA.

84. "'The Warrior' Film Vivid and Thrilling," *New York Times*, 17 July 1917, 7.

85. Ibid.

86. "The Warrior," *Photoplay* (November 1917): n.p., and *Minneapolis Tribune*, 10 March 1918, n.p., Pagano/Maciste – BRTD-NYPLPA.

87. Anthony Anderson, "'The Warrior.' Superfairbanksereno: Maciste in Farcical Bit against the Germans," *Los Angeles Times*, 11 June 1918, 113. On a similar note, one 1922 advertisement for *La trilogia di Maciste*, discussed in the next chapter, termed Fairbanks "il Maciste americano" for its subsequent showing of his film *Un'avventura marocchina* (most likely referring to *Bound in Morocco*, Allan Dwan, 1918).

88. Scott Curtis outlines four distinct aspects to Fairbanks's film star persona, all of which were seamlessly blended to obliterate the distinction

between private actor and public character: youthfulness, despite the fact that he was already thirty-two years old when he started making films; athleticism and physical vigor; optimism; and a democratic spirit. Curtis, "Douglas Fairbanks," 220–221. At the same time, as Gaylyn Studlar has written, Fairbanks becomes a mediating body between many of the tensions of nineteenth-century traditionalism and twentieth-century modernity: exaltation of the Western wilderness versus the feminizing trappings of urbanization, social control versus childlike exuberance, and primitivism versus capitalism. Studlar, *This Mad Masquerade*, 10–89.

89. Gail Bederman, *Manliness and Civilization: A Cultural History of Gender and Race in the United States, 1880–1917* (Chicago: University of Chicago Press, 1995); and Clifford Putney, *Muscular Christianity: Manhood and Sports in Protestant America, 1880–1920* (Cambridge, MA: Harvard University Press, 2001).

90. For more on Macfadden's role in physical culture in relation to Hollywood, see Mark Adams, *Mr. America: How Muscular Millionaire Bernarr Macfadden Transformed the Nation through Sex, Salad, and the Ultimate Starvation Diet* (New York: HarperCollins, 2009), 99–100; and Jacqueline Reich, "Rudolph Valentino, uomo forte," in *Intorno a Rodolfo Valentino: Cinema, Cultura, Società tra Italia e USA negli Anni Venti*, ed. Silvio Alovisio and Giulia Carluccio (Turin: Università di Torino-Kaplan, 2012), 308–324.

91. Douglas Fairbanks, *Laugh and Live* (New York: Britton Publishing Co., 1917), 42, 47; emphasis in original. For more detailed analyses of Fairbanks's writings, see Curtis, "Douglas Fairbanks," 234–235; Studlar, *This Mad Masquerade*, 45–48; and Jeffrey Vance (with Tony Maietta), *Douglas Fairbanks* (Berkeley: University of California Press, 2008), 41–44.

92. On girlhood in relation to Mary Pickford, see Gaylyn Studlar, *Precocious Charms: Stars Performing Girlhood in Classical Hollywood Cinema* (Berkeley: University of California Press, 2013), 19–50.

93. Upcoming announcements for the three films appeared in *La Vita Cinematografica* as early as January 1918, calling it an "extraordinary subject in three episodes," in which "Maciste outdoes Maciste." *La Vita Cinematografica* 9, no. 1–2 (1918): 10; *La Vita Cinematografica* 9, no. 9–10 (1918): 12, 37. Only the documents pertaining to the official government approval of the film, transcribed descriptions of their plots and list of intertitles, remain from the film, housed in the MNC archives. There is also correspondence that points to their distribution in South America (Panama, Venezuela, and Colombia). Based on these documents, Denis Lotti considers the film a serial, due to its shared cast and plot, even though it lacks an overarching title. He gives it the title of "*trittico*" (triptych), in order to distinguish it from the 1920 *La trilogia di Maciste* discussed in chapter 5. Denis Lotti, PhD thesis, "Il divismo maschile nel cinema muto italiano. Protagonisti, film, stereotipi, 1910–1929," Tesi di Dot-

torato di Ricerca, Università degli Studi di Padova, 2011.

94. Two American accounts describe the serial's plot. The first comes from the *New York Dramatic Mirror,* February 1919: "Count Richard Morosini is murdered by his nephew, Stevani, who hopes to inherit the Morosini fortune, only to find that it goes to the Count's grandson. The Count's son has been killed in battle and his wife and child are finally recognized by the choleric Count. Stevani is made guardian of the child. Maciste, an intelligence agent, befriends the wife and child, and when the former is accused of the Count's murder, proves, with the aid of his assistant, Seymour Knott, a comedic detective of the Holmes school, that Stevani is the criminal. The capture of Stevani ends the first episode. The second story shows how Maciste and Knott take up the trail of the kidnapped baby heir to the Morosini millions. The third episode depicts one Dr. Alvarez, a half-crazed scientist, who has a black power over Donna Alvarez. Maciste and Knott, of course, put the doctor where he can do no harm and curb the wicked Donna Alvarez. The baby heir to the fortune is found, and, with his mother, presumably lives happily ever after (880)." The second account is from *Current Opinion* 66, no. 1 (1919): 31. "Maciste, the giant slave of 'Cabiria,' pronounced to be the best motion-picture actor ever made, is here shown in the role of an attaché of the police department, who sets out to solve the mystery of a missing girl – a baby. The child has been kidnapped and its mother has become demented. This task leads Maciste through all sorts of weird and exciting adventures."

95. Turconi, "Stuzzichini: Maciste Liberatore," 28–29. An advertisement for the Morosini mystery appears in the *New Castle (PA) News,* 24 May 1919, 9, as well as in the Chicago *Suburbanite Economist,* 30 May 1919, 6. Denis Lotti confirms Turconi's thesis and expands upon it, matching the narrative of the "*trittico*" with the titles of *The Liberator's* individual episodes.

96. "Harry Raver Announces Serial Starring 'Maciste,'" *Moving Picture World* (30 November 1918): 975.

97. "The Liberator," *Moving Picture World* (7 December 1918): 1116.

98. Unattributed quotations cited at the end of *New York Dramatic Mirror* review, February 1919, 880.

99. The first quotation is from the actual *New York Dramatic Mirror* review; the second, another unattributed quotation at its end.

100. Advertisement in *Suburbanite Economist,* 30 May 1919, 6.

101. Ibid.

102. "Harry Raver Announces Serial Starring 'Maciste,'" 975.

103. *Kingsport (TN) Times,* 10 June 1919, 4.

104. *Moving Picture World* (7 December 1918): 1014–1015.

105. Advertisement for *The Liberator* in the *Kingsport (TN) Times,* 10 June 1919, 4, and *Moving Picture World* (22 February 1919): 987, which termed him "The Italian Douglas Fairbanks."

106. "The 'Selling Value' of 'Maciste,'" *Moving Picture World* (18 January 1919): 303.

107. "I Am Maciste," *Moving Picture World* (8 February 1919): 718.

108. Pierluigi Ercole, "'Little Italy on the Brink': The Italian Diaspora and the Distribution of War Films in London, 1914–1918," in *Cinema, Audiences, and Modernity: New Perspectives on European Cinema History*, ed. Daniel Biltereyst, Richard Maltby, and Philippe Meers (London: Routledge, 2011), 162–163.

109. *La Cinematografia Italiana ed Estera* 11, no. 3 (1917): 39.

110. Cited in Bertellini, *Italy in Early American Cinema*, 250. The basis for his total is Aldo Bernardini, ed., *Archivio del cinema muto italiano* (Rome: ANICA, 1991).

111. Bertellini, *Italy in Early American Cinema*, 249–258. Bertellini has argued that the relationship between cinema and Italian Americans living in the United States, who came predominantly from southern Italy, was more complex than as a means of assimilation. See as well his essays "Epica spettacolare e splendore del vero: L'influenza del cinema storico italiano in America (1908–1915)," in Brunetta, *Storia del cinema mondiale*, 2: 227–265; and "Italian Imageries, Historical Feature Films, and the Fabrication of Italy's Spectators in Early 1900s New York," in *American Movie Audiences: From the Turn of the Century to the Early Sound Era*, ed. Richard Maltby and Melvyn Stokes (London: BFI Publishing), 29–45.

112. *La Follia di New York*, 7 June 1914, 2, as cited in Bertellini, *Italy in Early Italian Cinema*, 253. Advertisements were for the English-language exhibition of the films at the Knickerbocker.

113. The review appears in the *New York Dramatic Mirror*, 22 December 1917, 32.

114. Bertellini, *Italy and Early American Cinema*, 257–258; Campbell, *Reel America and World War I*, 20–21, 57, 92. Campbell also notes the "ever popular features starring Maciste" (21), as well as the existence of two America feature films that portrayed Italian Americans as assimilated into the war effort: *Tony America* (Thomas Heffron, 1918) and *One More American* (William C. deMille, 1918), starring George Beban, the American actor known for his sympathetic characterizations of Italians. For more on Beban and characterizations of Italians, see Bertellini, *Italy and Early American Cinema*, 205–235; and Bertellini, "George Beban: Character of the Picturesque," in Bean, *Flickers of Desire*, 155–173.

115. *Il Progresso Italo-Americano*, 10 August 1917, 5. The advertisement states that the film was comprised of three films: *Le gesta eroiche sull'Adamello*, *La gloriosa presa di Gorizia*, and *Guerra sul mare e nel cielo*. Most likely they were compilations of various documentary films from the army's film agency.

116. Advertisements for *Maciste* appear in *Il Progresso Italo-Americano*, 3 August 1917, 4, and 10 August 1917, 10.

117. "Teatri e Vaudevilles," *Il Progresso Italo-Americano*, 5 August 1917, 3.

118. "Maciste Il Guerriero," *Il Telegrafo*, 13 July 1917, 3.

119. "Un'altra film di D'Annunzio," *Il Telegrafo*, 11 July 1917, 5.

120. *The Hero of the Circus* was predominantly marketed as a circus film, distributed not by Raver but under

the arm of Universal Thrill Picture, a distribution company, and shown on Saturday matinees for younger audiences. "Bring the Kids to this big circus picture, they will be tickled to see it." *Hamburg (IA) Reporter,* 14 February 1929, 10. There are a few advertisements as well for a 1923 film titled *The Unconquered* starring Maciste. "Maciste, the Italian Giant, Is in 'The Unconquered,'" *Baltimore Sun,* 11 February 1923, SM6.

5. Love, Labor, and Leadership

1. H. James Burgwyn, *The Legend of the Mutilated Victory: Italy, the Great War, and the Paris Peace Conference, 1915–1919* (Westport, CT: Greenwood Press, 1993), 200–201 (his translation). The original appears in Gabriele D'Annunzio, *Prose di ricerca,* vol. 1 (Milan: Mondadori, 2005), 953–959.

2. Vanda Wilcox, "From Heroic Defeat to Mutilated Victory: The Myth of Caporetto in Fascist Italy," in *Defeat and Memory: Cultural Histories of Military Defeat in the Modern Era,* ed. Jenny Macleod (New York: Palgrave Macmillan, 2008), 45–61; Martin Clark, *Modern Italy: 1871 to the Present,* 3rd ed. (Harlow, UK: Pearson/Longman, 2008), 249–250.

3. According to Giovanna Procacci, workers' revolts began during World War I as a result of "greater cohesion among the workers and a renewed relationship between trade union organizations" in both city and countryside. War increasingly revealed growing rifts between the classes rather than the ideological cohesion it had hoped for. Giovanna Procacci, "A 'Latecomer' in War: The Case of Italy," in *Authority,*

Identity, and the Social History of the Great War, ed. Frans Coetzee and Marilyn Shevin-Coetzee (Providence, RI: Berghahn, 1995), 3–28, here 23–24. For more on the film and its relationship to the uprisings, see Monica Dall'Asta, *Un cinéma musclé. Le surhomme dans le cinéma muet italien (1913–1926).* (Crisnée: Yellow Now, 1992), 79–80.

4. Daniel L. Horowitz, *The Italian Labor Movement* (Cambridge, MA: Harvard University Press, 1963), 70–86, 120–126.

5. Jonathan Dunnage, *Twentieth-Century Italy: A Social History* (London: Pearson, 2002), 48–51; and Giuseppe Fiori, *Antonio Gramsci: Life of a Revolutionary* (New York: E. P. Dutton, 1971), 138–141.

6. Clark, *Modern Italy,* 244–275; Dunnage, *Twentieth-Century Italy,* 38–71. For more specific details on Italy's economic and financial crisis during the period, see Douglas J. Forsyth, *The Crisis of Liberal Italy: Monetary and Financial Policy, 1914–1922* (Cambridge: Cambridge University Press, 1993), 193–235.

7. Similarly, the image of the war wounded abounds, both directly and indirectly, in German painting after the war, as evidenced in the Metropolitan Museum of Art Exhibit "Glitter and Doom: German Portraits from the 1920s," 14 November 2006–19 February 2007. See the catalogue *Glitter and Doom: German Portraits from the 1920s,* ed. Sabine Rewarld, Ian Buruma, and Mattias Eberle (New Haven, CT: Yale University Press, 2006).

8. Maurizia Boscagli, *Eye on the Flesh: Fashions of Masculinity in the*

Early Twentieth Century (Boulder, CO: Westview Press, 1996), 10.

9. According to Gentile, *combattentismo* was initially more a state of mind than a political movement, led by young intellectuals and returning veterans who were bent on upending the established political and social order and creating a new one based on the ideals learned and experienced in the trenches. Emilio Gentile, *The Origins of Fascist Ideology* (New York: Enigma, 2005), 53–54. On the experience of returning soldiers both in and out of the political sphere, see Giovanni Sabbatucci, *I combattenti nel primo dopoguerra* (Rome-Bari: Laterza, 1974), 3–24; and Andreas Wirsching, "Political Violence in France and Italy after 1918," *Journal of Modern European History* 1, no. 1 (2003): 60–79.

10. This tension between the modern and the antimodern reaches fruition in the construction of masculinity in the Fascist period. See Sandro Bellassai, "The Masculine Mystique: Antimodernism and Virility in Fascist Italy," *Journal of Modern Italian Studies* 10, no. 3 (2005): 314–335.

11. Modernity has increasingly become part of the vocabulary for scholars of early cinema and the silent period. Drawing on the writings of the Frankfurt School, especially those of Walter Benjamin and Siegfried Kracauer, the modernity thesis, as it has come to be known, states that the urban environment of capitalism at the turn of the century, particularly between 1880 and 1920 (the temporal conscription of modernity), as well as changes in technology and culture, brought about

transformation in modes of human perception and new ways about thinking about time and space. The works of Tom Gunning, Miriam Hansen, Vanessa Schwartz, Leo Charney, Stephen Kern, and Ben Singer most cogently articulate this thesis. See, among other works, Walter Benjamin, "The Work of Art in the Age of Mechanical Reproduction," in *Illuminations: Essays and Reflections,* ed. Hannah Arendt, trans. Harry Zohn (New York: Schocken, 1968); *Cinema and the Invention of Modern Life,* ed. Leo Charney and Vanessa R. Schwartz (Berkeley: University of California Press, 1995); Tom Gunning, "The Cinema of Attractions: Early Film, Its Spectator, and the Avant-garde," *Wide Angle* 8, no. 3/4 (1986): 63–70, "An Aesthetics of Astonishment: Early Film and the (In)credulous Spectator," *Art and Text* 34 (Spring 1989): 31–45, "The Whole Town's Gawking: Early Cinema and the Visual Experience of Modernity," *Yale Journal of Criticism* 7, no. 2 (1994): 189–201, and "Tracing the Individual Body: Photography, Detectives, and Early Cinema," in Charney and Schwartz, *Cinema and the Invention of Modern Life,* 15–45; Miriam Hansen, "Decentric Perspectives: Kracauer's Early Writings on Film and Mass Culture," *New German Critique* 54 (Fall 1991): 47–76, "Fallen Women, Rising Stars, New Horizons: Shanghai Silent Film as Vernacular Modernism," *Film Quarterly* 54, no. 1 (2000): 10–22, and "America, Paris, the Alps: Kracauer (and Benjamin) on Cinema and Modernity," in Charney and Schwartz, *Cinema and the Invention of Modern Life,* 362–402; Stephen Kern, *The Culture of Time* and Space, 1880–1918, 2nd ed. (Cambridge, MA: Harvard University Press, 2003); and Ben Singer, Melodrama and Modernity: Early Sensational Cinema and Its Contexts (New York: Columbia University Press, 2001), 101–130. For critiques of the modernity thesis, see David Bordwell, On the History of Film Style (Cambridge, MA: Harvard University Press, 1997), 139–146; and Giorgio Bertellini, Italy in Early Italian Cinema: Race, Landscape, and the Picturesque (Bloomington: Indiana University Press, 2010), 288–291.

12. Rob King, The Fun Factory: The Keystone Film Company and the Emergence of Mass Culture (Berkeley: University of California Press, 2009), 209. For more on the role of mass culture and early American cinema, see Lary May, Screening Out the Past: The Birth of Mass Culture and the Motion Picture Industry, with a new preface (Chicago: University of Chicago Press, 1983).

13. Although there are no clear visual references to the city itself, the association that both Maciste and Itala Film had with that city was clear from the intertitles that appeared against the backdrop of the studio's signature card, which read "ITALA FILM – TORINO."

14. For more on the UCI, see Roberto Chiti and Mario Quarignolo, "La malinconica storia dell'UCI," Bianco & Nero 18, no. 7 (1957): 21–35. The studios incorporated were Caesar Film, Film d'Arte Italiana, Itala Film, Incit, Pasquali e C, Cines, Celio Film, Palatino Film, Tiber Film, Impresa, C.I.T.O.-Cinema, Chimera Film, Medusa Film, Photo Drama, and other smaller studios.

15. Marcia Landy, Italian Film (Cambridge: Cambridge University Press, 1998), 49; Gian Piero Brunetta, Storia del cinema italiano, vol. 1, Il cinema muto, 1895–1929 (Rome: Riuniti, 1993), 238–259; and Riccardo Redi, Cinema muto italiano (1896–1930) (Rome: Biblioteca di Bianco & Nero, 1999), 163–164. Redi's study provides an interesting perspective along with the more canonical and historical Brunetta works. Redi examines contemporary periodicals, such as Cine-Fono, La Rivista Cinematografica, and La Vita Cinematografica to trace the industry's goals, development, reach and failures.

16. Redi, Cinema muto italiano, 175.

17. Brunetta Storia del cinema italiano, 1: 245–52; Landy, Italian Film, 49. Genina's quote is cited in Redi, Cinema muto italiano, 197.

18. For a more detailed examination of Italian cinema in the 1920s, see my "Italian Cinema of the 1920s," in Italian Silent Cinema: A Reader, ed. Giorgio Bertellini (New Barnet, UK: John Libbey, 2013), 135–142.

19. C. B. Bonzi, "Luigi Borgnetto Romano," La Vita Cinematografica 10, no. 23–24 (1919): 77–80. Borgnetto's names appeared in press and on screen in various order, sometimes as Romano Luigi Borgnetto or Luigi Romano Borgnetto.

20. The scene is viewable at http://www.museocinema.it/collezioni/maciste/main.html, Maciste Sequenza #8.

21. The scene is viewable at http://www.museocinema.it/collezioni/maciste/main.html, Maciste Sequenza #9.

22. Boscagli, Eye on the Flesh, 147.

23. The scene is viewable at http://
www.museocinema.it/collezioni
/maciste/main.html, *Maciste
Sequenza #7.*

24. Part 2 of the appendix discusses
how this scene was restored based on
the collation of two different prints.

25. Virtually no archival documentation exists for this film, except for
copies of its script in four languages:
English, Italian, Portuguese, and
French. Correspondence reveals that
the film was intended for distribution in
both England and Australia. MNC Archives, *Maciste innamorato,* A197/1 (sch.
inf.4142).

26. *La Vita Cinematografica* 10, no.
1–2 (1919): 10–11.

27. *La Vita Cinematografica* 10, no.
13–14 (1919): 5–6; and *La Vita Cinematografica* 10, no. 17–18 (1919): 5–6.

28. Tito Alacci, "*Maciste innamorato*
dell''Itala Film,'" *Film* 4, no. 12 (1919):
7. Similarly, the above-cited profile
on Borgnetto stated, "The film made
noise and pleased audiences. Even if
critics hid behind many reservations
and doubts, they still acknowledged its
success." Bonzi, "Luigi Borgnetto Romano," 79.

29. Bertoldo, "La nostra critica:
Maciste innamorato," *La Vita Cinematografica* 10, no. 17–18 (1919): 147–149.

30. Like *Maciste innamorato, La
trilogia di Maciste* was restored in a
collaborative effort of the MNC and
the Cineteca di Bologna in 2010 from a
colored nitrate print with French intertitles, housed at the Archives Françaises
du Film in Bois d'Arcy, destined for
French release. The three episodes were
combined into one full-length feature

film. See the section in part 2 of the appendix that is dedicated to the formal
reconstruction of the film's episodic
structure.

31. Robert Jackson, *Sovereignty:
Evolution of an Idea* (Cambridge, UK:
Polity Press, 2007), 14.

32. Monica Dall'Asta, "Il serial," in
Storia del cinema mondiale, vol. 2, *Gli
Stati Uniti,* ed. Gian Piero Brunetta
(Turin: Einaudi, 1999), 307–312; Richard Koszarski, *An Evening's Entertainment: The Age of the Silent Feature
Picture, 1915–1928* (Berkeley: University
of California Press, 1990), 164–166,
271–273; Kalton C. Lahue, *Continued
Next Week: A History of the Moving
Picture Serial* (Norman: University of
Oklahoma Press, 1964); Buck Rainey,
*Serials and Series: A World Filmography,
1912–1956* (Jefferson, NC: McFarland,
1999), 1–6; and Raymond W. Steadman, *The Serials: Suspense and Drama
by Installment* (Norman: University
of Oklahoma Press, 1977), 50–60. For
Houdini's films in relation to the serial
and sensational melodrama, see Matthew Solomon, *Disappearing Tricks:
Silent Film, Houdini, and the New Magic
of the Twentieth Century* (Urbana: University of Illinois Press, 2010), 108–122.

33. Lahue, *Continued Next Week,*
91–105.

34. Correspondence dated 19 October 1919 to the UCI from an unsigned
Itala executive involved in the production. MNC Archives related to the
three episodes, 1919–1923, A183/1. The
issue did not appear to be resolved until
May 1920 and most likely delayed the
opening of the film. *Il testamento di
Maciste's* intertitles carry the number

377bis, while those of *Il viaggio di Ma-ciste* read 377, signaling the division of the second film into two.

35. "La trilogia di Maciste," *La Vita Cinematografica* XI, numero speciale (December 1920): 324–326.

36. Amma, "La trilogia di Maciste," *La Rivista Cinematografica*," 1, no. 5 (1920): 7–8. The reviewer attended an advanced screening for critics and se-lect invitees.

37. Correspondence dated 4 Janu-ary 1921 from the UCI in Rome titled "'Trilogia di Maciste' Speciale Inglese," MNC Archives relative to the three epi-sodes, 1919–1923, A183/1.

38. Anon., *Bioscope,* London, 16 Sep-tember 1920. Reprinted in *Gli uomini forti,* ed. Alberto Farassino and Tatti Sanguineti (Milan: Mazzotta, 1983), 131.

39. Brochures, MNC online ar-chives, *La trilogia di Maciste,* "Materiali pubblicitari," P41716.

40. Manifesto del Cinema Risorgi-mento *Maciste!,* 13–17 February 1922, MNC online archives, *La trilogia di Maciste,* "Materiali pubblicitari," P00679.

41. Giordano, *Giganti buoni,* 12.

42. This racial discourse returns in the 1920s Maciste films set in Africa, discussed in chapter 6.

43. F. T. Marinetti, "The Foundation and Manifesto of Futurism," originally published in *Poesia* 5, no. 1–2 (1909), reprinted and translated in Günter Berghaus, ed., *F. T. Marinetti: Critical Writings,* new ed., trans. Doug Thomp-son (New York: Farrar, Straus & Gir-oux, 2006), 11–17.

44. Christine Poggi, *Inventing Futur-ism: The Art and Politics of Artificial*

Optimism (Princeton, NJ: Princeton University Press, 2009), 65–149.

45. Marinetti, "Foundation and Manifesto of Futurism," 13.

46. "Extended Man and the King-dom of the Machine," in Berghaus, *F. T. Marinetti,* 85–88, here 86.

47. Christopher E. Forth, *Masculin-ity in the Modern West: Gender, Civiliza-tion, and the Body* (New York: Palgrave Macmillan, 2008), 169. See Boscagli, *Eye on the Flesh,* here as well, in particu-lar chapter 4.

48. Federico Paolini, *Storia sociale dell'automobile in Italia* (Rome: Caroc-ci, 2007), 15–16.

49. Giancarlo Amari, *Torino come Detroit (capitale dell'automobile, 1895–1940)* (Bologna: Cappelli, 1980), 19–20. See also Gianni Rondolino, *Torino come Hollywood* (Bologna: Cappelli, 1980), 23; republished as *I giorni di Cabiria* (Torino: Lindau, 1993).

50. Daniele Marchesini, *L'Italia a quattro ruote. Storia dell'utilitaria* (Bo-logna: Il Mulino, 2012), 15–20; Amari, *Torino come Detroit,* 51. One noble at-tempt was FIAT's 501, but that was still at a cost of 31,000 lire, far out of range for the average Italian. Alberto Bellucci, *L'automobile italiana, 1918–1943* (Bari: Laterza, 1984), 5–6.

51. Many scholars have devotedly ex-plored the interrelations between early cinema and transportation. See Lynne Kirby, *Parallel Tracks: The Railroad and Silent Cinema* (Durham, NC: Duke University Press, 1997); King, *Fun Fac-tory,* 188; Charlie Musser, "Moving To-wards Fictional Narratives: Story Films Become the Dominant Product, 1903–4," in *The Silent Cinema Reader,* ed. Lee

Grieveson and Peter Krämer (London: Routledge, 2004), 87–102, here 92–93; Singer, *Melodrama and Modernity*, 62–90; Kristen Whissel, *Picturing American Modernity: Traffic Technology, and the Silent Cinema* (Durham, NC: Duke University Press, 2008), 1–19; and Whissel, "Transportation," in *Encyclopedia of Early Cinema*, ed. Richard Abel (New York: Routledge, 2005), 925–927. Another interesting convergence between the auto industry and cinema was the series of films produced by the Ford Motor Company in the 1910s and 1920s that "worked to elaborate – at the level of content, form, and circulation – a visual pedagogy for instructing audiences in the new ways of mass production and the corresponding political economy of advanced capitalism." Lee Grieveson, "The Work of Film in the Age of Fordist Mechanization," *Cinema Journal* 51, no. 3 (2012): 25–51, here 26.

52. Gian Piero Brunetta, "Il clown cinematografico tra salotto liberty e frontiera del West," *Griffithiana* 7, no. 24–25 (1985): 11–20, here 17.

53. Singer, *Melodrama and Modernity*, 11; Boscagli, *Eye on the Flesh*, 130.

54. Ricciotto Canudo, "Trionfo del cinematografo," *Nuovo giornale*, 25 novembre 1908, republished in *Filmcritica* 28, no. 278 (1977): 296–302, here 298.

55. Motor, "L'automobilisme et la culture physique," *La Culture Physique* 1 (February 1904), 10, as cited in Forth, *Masculinity in the Modern West*, 178.

56. Forth, *Masculinity in the Modern West*, 177–179.

57. The 2008 restoration, at the L'Immagine Ritrovata laboratory in Bologna, of *Maciste in vacanza* was

undertaken jointly by the Cineteca del Comune di Bologna, the Cineteca Nazionale–Centro Sperimentale di Cinematografia in Rome, and the Museo Nazionale del Cinema in Turin. From an archival point of view, an exploration of this film presents a unique opportunity, for it, among all the Maciste films, has the most available documentation, which covers preproduction, production, and postproduction via internal memos between Itala Film and the UCI; correspondence during the production itself between the studio and the director; and a copious paper trail regarding the film's publicity campaign and worldwide distribution. The archive is housed in the MNC, A184/7.

58. "Cabiria," *La Rivista Cinematografica* 11, no. 7 (1921): 31. The advertisement appears in the same issue on pages 50–51.

59. Silvio Alovisio, *Voci del silenzio. La sceneggiatura nel cinema muto italiano* (Turin: Museo Nazionale del Cinema, 2005), 152. De Stefani participated in the Società Autori Cinematografici (SAC), based in Genoa, which was more along the lines of a labor organization than an agency. De Stefani saw the society as an important step in recognizing the fundamental artistic, commercial, and industrial role that the screenwriter played in the film industry. See Alovisio, *Voci del silenzio*, 211–212.

60. *La Rivista Cinematografica* 1, no. 23–24 (1920): 240.

61. Correspondence housed in the MNC archive, A184/7. Most advertisements did prominently credit De Stefani, with an immediate "below-the-title" billing of "Commedia in 4 parti

di ALESSANDRO DE STEFANI." *La Rivista Cinematografica* 1, no. 22 (1920): 2; *Lux* 11, no. 10 (1920): 19.

62. "Film: Maciste in vacanza," letter dated 1 November 1920 between Itala Film and the UCI, MNC Archives A184/7.

63. The scene is viewable at http://www.museocinema.it/collezioni/maciste/main.html, *Maciste* Sequenza #10.

64. *Torino come Detroit*, 39, 65–66. See also the Diatto company's website at http://www.diatto.it/EN/pagine/compzany2.html.

65. The correspondence between Itala Film and Diatto dates from 13 December 1920 through 19 July 1921. It appears that Itala Film had originally attempted to procure a car from FIAT, but the company refused, declaring in a letter dated 16 December 1920 that they were unable to lend a vehicle to the production. The studio also had corresponded with another car manufacturer, Temperino, which had agreed in principle, in letters dated 17 and 19 November 1920, to supply a car for the production for 1,000 lire, provided its logo would be clearly visible. MNC Archives A184/7.

66. MNC Archives A184/7.

67. Ibid.

68. For more on *Mafarka the Futurist*, see Barbara Spackman, *Fascist Virilities: Rhetoric, Ideology, and Social Fantasy in Italy* (Minneapolis: University of Minnesota Press, 1996), 49–76.

69. It was in fact the Castello di Montalto on the outskirts of Turin, owned by the Baroness Maria Teresa Geisser Celesia di Veliasco, who loaned her property to Itala Film for location shooting.

70. Bonard played an active role in managing her career. Documentation, including correspondence between UCI and Itala Film, reveals the way she monitored her billing in the Maciste films. She was unhappy when she was not promoted as the principal actress in the films or when her name appeared on posters and advertisements in type that was too small to befit her starring role. MNC Archives, A184/7.

71. Stella Dagna, "All'ombra del gigante. Le comprimarie della serie Maciste," in *Non solo dive. Pioniere del cinema italiano*, ed. Monica Dall'Asta (Bologna: Cineteca di Bologna, 2008), 297–303, here 299.

72. Ruth Ben-Ghiat, *Fascist Modernities: Italy, 1922–1945* (Berkeley: University of California Press, 2001). As Stanley Payne has argued: "The country experienced a spurt of industrialization, first in the late nineteenth century and then in the decade before World War I, but this achievement only accentuated the contradictions of a modernization still far from complete. By the era of World War I Italy had achieved a unique, still contradictory, status as the most advanced of the still primarily agricultural countries of Europe, at the same time that it could be considered one of the weakest of those states that had developed a minimal level of modern industrialization." Stanley G. Payne, introduction to Emilio Gentile, *The Struggle for Modernity: Nationalism, Futurism, and Fascism* (Westport, CT: Praeger, 2003), ix–x.

73. Turin's population, known as the proletarian city, increased from 427,000 to 518,000 after the war, with one-third of all jobs being industrial. Clark, *Modern Italy*, 229–233.

74. Anthologized in Mostra internazionale del nuovo cinema, *Tra una film e l'altra. Materiali sul cinema muto italiano, 1907–1920* (Venezia: Marsilio, 1980), 389–399.

75. "Ciò che si fa all'estero," *La Vita Cinematografica* 12, no. 35–36 (1921): 66.

76. Alfred Gehri, "Un'intervista col signor Jacob Karol," *La Vita Cinematografica* 13, no. 39–40 (1921): 74–75.

77. See part 3 of the appendix for details on these films. Lotti has the most extensive documentation of these films in his thesis. An advertisement for *Maciste umanitario,* promoting it as the first of a series of great films starring Maciste, appears in *La Vita Cinematografica* 14, no. 1 (1923): 1. A brief review of *La figlia del re dell'argento* in March 1923 states, "Maciste performs many acts of bravery in this comic adventure mix, and shows himself to be very likeable.... The film is richly filmed and well-photographed." *La Vita Cinematografica* 14, no. 5 (1923): 51.

78. This phenomenon was not limited to actors; the directors Augusto Genina and Carmine Gallone made several films there as well. The idea was to then re-export the stars to their home countries and elsewhere as potential moneymakers. The most copious documentation on the phenomenon is in Vittorio Martinelli, "I Gastarbeiter fra le due guerre," *Bianco & Nero* 39, no. 3 (1978): 3–93.

79. Sabine Hake, *German National Cinema* (London: Routledge, 2002), 7–25. On German serials, see Rudmer Canjels, *Distributing Silent Film Serials: Local Practices, Changing Forms, Cultural Transformations* (London: Routledge, 2011), 24–26. For more on the *Sensationfilm,* see Philipp Stiasny, "Humanity Unleashed: Anti-Bolshevism as Popular Culture in Early Weimar Cinema," in *The Many Faces of Weimar Cinema: Rediscovering Germany's Legacy,* ed. Christian Rogowski (Rochester, NY: Camden House, 2010), 67–83, here 60. Fritz Lang's two-part *Dr. Mabuse, the Gambler* is also considered an example of the *Sensationfilm.* See Sara Hall, "Trading Places: Dr. Mabuse and the Pleasure of Role Play," *German Quarterly* 76, no. 4 (2003): 381–397. For Joe May and the serial/blockbuster, see Christian Rogowski, "Movies, Money, and Mystique: Joe May's Early Weimar Blockbuster, *The Indian Tomb* (1921)," in *Weimar Cinema: An Essential Guide to Classic Films of the Era,* ed. Noah Isenberg (New York: Columbia University Press, 2009), 55–78.

80. Bellucci, *L'automobile italiana,* 20–21.

6. Muscling the Nation

1. For more on violence in Fascism, see Federico Finchelstein, *Transatlantic Fascism: Ideology, Violence, and the Sacred in Argentina and Italy, 1919–1945* (Durham, NC: Duke University Press, 2010), 20–22; and R.J.B. Bosworth, *Mussolini's Italy: Life under the Fascist Dictatorship, 1915–1945* (New York: Penguin, 2005), in particular 121–149. For

the phenomenon of Fascist violence, see Mimmo Franzinelli, *Squadristi. Protagonisti e techniche della violenza fascista, 1919–1922* (Milan: Mondadori, 2003); and Roberta Suzzi Valli, "The Myth of Squadrismo in the Fascist Regime," *Journal of Contemporary History* 35, no. 2 (2000): 131–150. For the use of castor oil in particular, see Alexander J. de Grand, *Italian Fascism: Its Origins and Developments*, 3rd ed. (Lincoln: University of Nebraska Press, 1989), 31–32.

2. "Un'intervista con Maciste," *Films Pittaluga* (15 February 1924), 45–46; and "'Maciste, il gigante buono.' Intervista con Bartolomeo Pagano," *Al Cinemà* 3, no. 11 (1924): 8–10.

3. R.J.B. Bosworth, *Mussolini* (London: Arnold, 2002); Renzo De Felice, *Mussolini il fascista*, vol. 1, *La conquista del potere, 1921–1925* (Turin: Einaudi, 1966); and Denis Mack Smith, *Mussolini: A Biography* (New York: Vintage, 1982). In terms of his speeches and discourses, I have consulted Edoardo and Duilio Susmel, eds., *Opera Omnia di Benito Mussolini*, 35 vols. (Florence: La Fenice, 1951–1962).

4. Marcia Landy, *Stardom, Italian Style: Screen Performance and Personality in Italian Cinema* (Bloomington: Indiana University Press, 2008), 14.

5. Renzo Renzi, *Il fascismo involontario e altri scritti* (Bologna: Cappelli, 1975), 131–181, here 139–140.

6. An August 1923 cover of *La Vita Cinematografica* promotes the film, but the film was distributed in the first months of 1924. *La Vita Cinematografica* 14, no. 15–16 (1923); Vittorio

Martinelli, *L'eterna invasione. Il cinema americano degli anni Venti e la critica italiana* (Gemona: La Cineteca del Friuli, 2002), 505.

7. For more on these revisions of the cinema of the Fascist period, see Mino Argentieri, *L'occhio del regime. Informazione e propaganda nel cinema del fascismo* (Florence: Vallecchi, 1979); Mino Argentieri, ed., *Risate di regime. La commedia italiana, 1930–1944* (Venice: Marsilio, 1991); Ruth Ben-Ghiat, "Envisioning Modernity: Desire and Discipline in the Italian Fascist Film," *Critical Inquiry* 23, no. 1 (1996): 109–144; Gian Piero Brunetta, *Cinema italiano tra le due guerre* (Milan: Mursia, 1975); Philip V. Cannistraro, *La fabbrica del consenso. Fascismo e mass media* (Roma: Laterza, 1975), 273–322; Claudio Carabba, *Il cinema del ventennio nero* (Firenze: Vallecchi, 1974); Gianfranco Casadio, *Il grigio e il nero. Spettacolo e propaganda nel cinema italiano degli anni trenta, 1931–1943* (Longo: Ravenna, 1992); Jean Gili, *Stato fascista e cinematografia. Repressione e promozione* (Roma: Bulzoni, 1981); James Hay, *Popular Film Culture in Fascist Italy: The Passing of the Rex* (Bloomington: Indiana University Press, 1987); Elaine Mancini, *Struggles of the Italian Film Industry during Fascism, 1930–1935* (Ann Arbor: UMI Research Press, 1985); Marcia Landy, *Fascism in Film: The Italian Commercial Cinema, 1930–1944* (Princeton, NJ: Princeton University Press, 1986), and *The Folklore of Consensus: Theatricality in Italian Cinema, 1930–1943* (Albany: State University of New York Press, 1998); Geoffrey

Nowell-Smith, "The Italian Cinema under Fascism," in *Rethinking Italian Fascism*, ed. David Forgacs (London: Lawrence and Wishart, 1986), 142–161; Lorenzo Quaglietti, *Storia economico-politica del cinema italiano dal 1945 al 1980* (Roma: Riuniti, 1980), 13–33; Riccardo Redi, ed., *Cinema italiano sotto il fascismo* (Venice: Marsilio, 1979); Jacqueline Reich and Piero Garofalo, eds., *Re-Viewing Fascism: Italian Cinema, 1922–1943;* and Steven Ricci, *Cinema & Fascism: Italian Film and Society, 1922–1943* (Berkeley: University of California Press, 2008).

8. Alberto Farassino, "Anatomia del cinema muscolare," in *Gli uomini forti*, ed. Alberto Farassino and Tatti Sanguineti (Milan: Mazzotta, 1983), 48; Monica Dall'Asta, *Un cinéma muscle. Le surhomme dans le cinéma muet italien (1913–1926)* (Crisnée: Yellow Now, 1992), 95, 174–176; Gian Piero Brunetta, *Storia del cinema italiano*, vol. 1, *Il cinema muto, 1895–1929* (Rome: Riuniti, 1993), 277–278; Massimo Cardillo, *Il duce in moviola. Politica e divismo nei cinegiornali e documentari "Luce"* (Bari: Dedalo, 1983), 14; and Hay, *Popular Film Culture in Fascist Italy*, 226–228. Other scholars have looked back at the Maciste films as proto-Fascist in their ideology and proto-dictatorial in their representation of authority and, in particular, violence. Steven Ricci also sees a strong connection between the Maciste films and the cinematic productions of the post-silent Fascist period. Ricci, *Cinema & Fascism*, 81–98.

9. P. David Marshall, *Celebrity and Power: Fame in Contemporary Culture*

(Minneapolis: University of Minnesota Press, 1997), 251n6.

10. The Duce's aural presence coincides his visual ubiquity. See Gianni Isola, *L'ha scritto la radio. Storia e testi durante il fascismo (1924–1944)* (Milan: Mondadori, 1998).

11. Renzo De Felice, *Mussolini il fascista*, vol. 1, *La conquista del potere 1921–1925* (op.cit.) and *Mussolini il fascista*, vol. 2, *L'organizzazione dello stato fascista* (Turin: Einaudi, 1968).

12. "Maciste all'inferno," *La Vita Cinematografica* 16, no. 3–4 (1925): 13–14. Also reproduced under the same title, but with different illustrations, in *Al Cinemà* 4, no. 13 (1925): 5–7.

13. My analysis of *Il gigante delle Dolomiti*, as the last film in the Maciste series, is the subject of this study's conclusion.

14. "The emergence of the celebrity is connected to both the emergence of the modern mass as a threatening entity and the strategies employed by various institutions to contain the threat and irrationality of the masses." Marshall, *Celebrity and Power*, 37.

15. Forzano went on to direct one of the most famous propaganda feature films during the Fascist period: *Camicia nera* (Black Shirt, 1933), which depicted the March on Rome. For more on his work, see C.E.J. Griffiths, *The Theatrical Works of Giovacchino Forzano: Drama for Mussolini's Italy* (Lewiston: Edwin Mellen, 2000), and "Italian Cinema in the Thirties: *Camicia nera* and other films by Giovacchino Forzano," *Italianist* 15 (1995): 299–321.

16. Pittaluga remained a major player in the industry and was instrumental

in its reawakening in the 1930s. In 1929 he acquired the Cines studio and officially reopened it the following year, producing several films, including Italy's first sound film, Gennaro Righelli's *La canzone dell'amore* (The Song of Love, 1930) and reopening several Cines movie theaters. On FERT, the historical recuperation by Alberto Friedemann has been invaluable. See his *Fert. Storia di un nome, due società e di tre stabilimenti* (Turin: Associazione F.E.R.T., 2008), 9–31, and *Le case di vetro. Stabilimenti cinematografici e teatri di posa a Torino* (Turin: Associazione F.E.R.T., 2002), 97–116. The website dedicated to FERT has many important sources of information as well: http://fertstorica.it/index2.html. For more on Pittaluga, see Brunetta, *Storia del cinema italiano*, 1: 266–268; and Riccardo Redi, *Cinema muto italiano (1896–1930)* (Rome: Biblioteca di Bianco & Nero, 1999), 167–174. For more on the transition to sound, as well as its relationship to silent cinema, see Giorgio Bertellini, "Dubbing L'Arte Muta: Poetic Layerings around Italian Cinema's Transition to Sound," in Reich and Garofalo, *Re-Viewing Fascism*, 30–82; and Paola Valentini, *Presenze sonore. Il passaggio al sonoro in Italia tra cinema e radio* (Florence: Le lettere, 2007).

17. Silvio Alovisio, "Le riviste del cinema muto: una fonte per la ricerca tecnologica?" *Bianco & Nero* 549 (2004): 31–44.

18. As reprinted in "Gli artisti della 'Pittaluga-Fert' in America," *Films Pittaluga* 1, no. 5–6 (1923): 2.

19. Vittorio Martinelli, *Il cinema muto italiano. I film degli anni ven-ti/1923–1931, Bianco & Nero* 42, no. 4–6 (1981): 171.

20. *La Vita Cinematografica* reports this information in its "Notizie varie" section. *La Vita Cinematografica* 14, no. 20 (1923): 64. Advertisements for the film promoting the ship and its parent company appear in that same issue (6) as well as the December 1923 special edition (24–25).

21. Identical summaries of the film's narrative appear in *Al Cinemà* 3, no. 21 (1924): 8–9, and *Films Pittaluga* 2, no. 11 (1924): 60. Some critics praised the film, especially its urban cinematography as well as the oceanic landscape. See Angelo Cipollini, "Da Pisa," in *La Rivista Cinematografica* 5, no. 11–12 (1924): 79. Others appreciated the characters more than the plot. See Gulliver, "Il nipote d'America," *La Rivista Cinematografica* 7 (April 1924): 22.

22. *Bollettino di Informazioni* 1 (July 1924): 22.

23. Dall'Asta stresses the Italian success of Fairbanks's films as an influence on the shift toward these "superfilms." *Un cinéma musclé*, 155–156.

24. Jacqueline Reich, "Mussolini at the Movies: Fascism, Film, and Culture," in Reich and Garofalo, *Re-Viewing Fascism*, 3–29. Scholars who have studied feature film production during the Fascist period, including myself, have traditionally neglected the silent production of the era, which in Italy lasted through 1930, and for good reason: the films themselves, or rather those that are available for study in archives and *cinématèques,* are of poor quality and little artistic or technical merit, paling in comparison to their

innovative American, German, and Soviet counterparts. Only a minuscule portion of them had any lasting effect on Italian film production. In terms of their ideological positioning, the films revealed little about the relationship between propaganda and artistic production, as Fascist ideology had not taken its firm, totalitarian grasp on Italian culture. One exception to this dearth of study would be *Cinema & Fascism,* by Steven Ricci, who devotes a large swath of his work to the 1920s.

25. Redi, *Cinema muto italiano,* 163–164.

26. Redi uses the term sporadic (*Cinema muto italiano,* 184), and Ricci recalls the state's "unevenly deployed mercantilist approach" between 1922 and 1931 (*Cinema & Fascism,* 58).

27. In the 1910s moral decency became a public preoccupation, with specific guidelines for films of subjects that would warrant intervention on the part of the industry's watchdogs. These issues were of a lesser importance as the crisis in production became the industry's primary concern. Landy, *Italian Film,* 29, and Mancini, *Struggles of the Italian Film Industry,* 26–27.

28. Redi, *Cinema muto italiano,* 184–194.

29. Brunetta, *Storia del cinema italiano,* 1: 272.

30. Some titles with Risorgimento themes: *La cavalcata ardente* (The Fervid Cavalcade, 1925); *Anita o il romanzo d'amore dell'eroe dei due mondi* (Anita, or a Love Story from the Hero of Two Worlds, 1926); *Garibaldi e i suoi tempi* (Garibaldi and His Times, 1926); *I

martiri d'Italia (Italy's Martyrs, 1927); *Un balilla del ''48* (A Ballila from 1848, 1927); *Brigata Firenze* (The Florentine Brigade, 1928); and *Rendenzione d'anime* (Redemption of Souls, 1928). For more on this subject, see Gianfranco Gori, *Patria diva. La storia d'Italia nei film del ventennio* (Florence: La casa Usher, 1989), 43–57.

31. Gian Piero Brunetta, *The History of Italian Cinema: A Guide to Italian Film from Its Origins to the Twenty-first Century,* trans. Jeremy Parzen (Princeton, NJ: Princeton University Press, 2009), 61.

32. Brunetta, *Storia del cinema italiano,* 1: 278.

33. Pierluigi Erbaggio, "Istituto Nazionale Luce: A National Company with an International Reach," in Giorgio Bertellini, ed., *Italian Silent Cinema: A Reader* (New Baret, UK: John Libbey, 2013), 221–231. See also Argentieri, *L'occhio del regime;* Giampaolo Bernagozzi, *Il cinema allo specchio. Appunti per una storia del documentario* (Bologna: Patron, 1985); Marco Bertozzi, *Storia del documentario italiano. Immagini e culture dell'altro cinema* (Venice: Marsilio, 2008); Brunetta, *Cinema italiano tra le due guerre;* and Cannistraro, *La fabbrica del consenso.*

34. Emilio Gentile, "Mussolini's Charisma," *Modern Italy* 3, no. 2 (1998): 219–235. Gentile bases his definition of charisma on Max Weber, as he cites: charisma "applies to a certain quality of an individual personality by virtue of which he is set apart from ordinary men and treated as endowed with supernatural, superhuman, or at least

specifically exceptional powers" (220). On Mussolini's oratory before and during his ascent to power, see Bosworth, *Mussolini*, 97–98.

35. Stephen Gundle, "Film Stars and Society in Fascist Italy," in Reich and Garofalo, *Re-Viewing Fascism*, 315–339, here 320. See also Stephen Gundle, *Mussolini's Dream Factory: Film Stardom in Fascist Italy* (Providence, RI: Berghahn Books, 2013).

36. Stephen Gundle and Lucy Riall, introduction to the Special Issue on Charisma, *Modern Italy* 3, no. 2 (1998): 153–157.

37. Simonetta Falasca-Zamponi, *Fascist Spectacle: The Aesthetics of Power in Mussolini's Italy* (Berkeley: University of California Press, 1997), 42–88.

38. Here I am referring to the brilliant work done in Great Britain, funded by the British Arts and Humanities Research Council, by Stephen Gundle, Christopher Duggan, and Giuliana Pieri on "The Cult of the Duce: Mussolini and the Italians, 1918–1925." The work resulted in a 2010 art exhibit at the Estorick Collection of Modern Italian Art in London titled "Against Mussolini: Art and the Fall of a Dictatorship"; as well as a DVD titled "Mussolini: The Story of a Personality Cult" (University of Warwick/ARHC, 2011); and an edited volume from Stephen Gundle, Christopher Duggan, and Giuliana Pieri, eds., *The Cult of the Duce: Mussolini and the Italians* (Manchester, UK: Manchester University Press, 2013). On the posthumous manifestations of the cult, see Sergio Luzzatto, *The Body of the Duce: Mussolini's Corpse and the For-*

tunes of Italy (New York: Metropolitan Books, 2005).

39. Bosworth, *Mussolini*, 211.

40. Luisa Passerini, *Mussolini immaginario. Storia di una biografia, 1915–1939* (Rome: Laterza, 1991).

41. Enrico Sturani, "Analysing Mussolini's Postcards," *Modern Italy* 12, no. 2 (2013): 141–156. See also his *Otto milioni di cartoline per il Duce* (Turin: Centro Scietifico Editore, 1995), and *Le cartoline del Duce* (Turin: Edizioni del Capricorno, 2003).

42. Francesco Pitassio, "I cinegiornali Luce e la creazione del 'divo' Mussolini," in *Storia del cinema italiano*, vol. 4, *1924–1933*, ed. Leonardo Quaresima (Venice: Marsilio, forthcoming).

43. Landy, *Stardom, Italian Style*, 7.

44. Hay, *Popular Film Culture in Fascist Italy*, 226; Farassino, "Anatomia del cinema muscolare," 48. While Hay does single out Maciste, he also makes appropriate connections to the other Italian screen strongmen, whose "mythological names" were "part of the divistic luminosity in Italian popular culture" (226). For more on Mussolini and aviation, see Bosworth, *Mussolini*, 142–144.

45. "In his many poses, Mussolini provided a basis for the performative acts of an Ideal Fascist citizen. He also appropriated monarchical stances as part of his long-standing campaign to replace the king. In other words, the body of the Duce managed to slip between its positions as the single figurehead of the state and as the every body of daily life under the fascist regime." Karen Pinkus, *Bodily Regimes: Italian Advertising under Fascism* (Minneapolis: University of Minnesota

Press, 1995), 18. For Sergio Luzzatto, these metamorphoses were also part of "Italians' collective fantasies." Luzzatto, *Body of the Duce*, 16–17.

46. Nicola Mazzanti e Gian Luca Farinelli, "Lo spazio scenico del balcone," in *Il cinema dei dittatori. Mussolini, Stalin, Hitler*, ed. Renzo Renzi (Bologna: Gradis, 1992), 97–101. Cardillo, citing an interview with Nino Naldini, notes how "I filmati Luci sono un lungo 'piano-sequenza' della realtà di quell'epoca." Cardillo, *Il duce in moviola*, 36.

47. "[Mussolini's] gestures, while they may have invoked the histrionics of artistic heroes such as D'Annunzio or Marinetti, were more consonant with the acting style of the heroes of silent film," Hay, *Popular Film Culture in Fascist Italy*, 226. See also Cardillo, *Il duce in moviola*, 73–92; Francesco Pitassio, "Famous Actors, Famous Actresses: Notes on Silent Acting Style in Italian Silent Films," in Bertellini, *Italian Silent Cinema*, 255–262, as well as Pitassio's longer study, *Ombre silenziose. Teoria dell'attore cinematografico negli anni venti* (Udine: Campanotto, 2002), and the more theoretical *Attore/divo* (Milan: Il Castoro, 2003).

48. "Mussolini e Farinacci al saggio ginnico organizzato dalla Milizia Volontaria della Sicurezza Nazionale. Gare ginnastiche degli ufficiali della M.V.S.N. al poligono della Farnesina," Istituto Luce, 1925. This and other films are available at http://www.archivio luce.com/archivio. The pose of hands on hips crosses over into fashion photography as well, with many models, both male and female, assuming that

position as they showcase the latest fashions. *Fashion at the Time of Fascism: Italian Modernist Lifestyle, 1922–1943*, ed. Mario Lupano and Alessandra Vaccari (Bologna: Damiani, 2009), 118.

49. See chapter 2. "During his first appearance in *Cabiria*, at the center of the frame, Maciste's weight is distributed on both legs, which are set apart from each other. This posture evokes one of Mussolini's favorite photographic poses: viewers do not see the object of Maciste's glance to the left of the frame. They can only look at Maciste looking. Maciste's muscles, then, are the spectacle that engages the viewer. . . . The body alone signifies the heroic status of this character in the narrative." Angela Dalle Vacche, *The Body in the Mirror: Shapes of History in Italian Cinema* (Princeton, NJ: Princeton University Press, 1993), 46. Later she notes how "The flesh of Pastrone's Maciste turns into the marble of Gallone's Scipio" (49), referring to the 1937 Mussolini-supervised production of Carmine Gallone's historical epic *Scipione l'Africano*.

50. Mazzanti and Farinelli ("Lo spazio scenico del balcone," 100) argue that this ability to act out multiple roles at once sets him apart from Hitler and Stalin, who remained surprisingly consistent in their representations, and for the purposes of this study aligns him with Maciste.

51. "The enormous attention the regime gave to the fashion of its fascist members expressed a radical programme of intervention in the body politic that envisaged an almost apocalyptic disappearance of 'real' natural

bodies." Simonetta Falasca-Zamponi, "Peeking Under the Black Shirt: Italian Fascism's Disembodied Bodies," in *Fashioning the Body Politic: Dress, Gender, Citizenship,* ed. Wendy Parkins (Oxford: Berg, 2002), 145–166, here 146.

52. On Mussolini's personal fashion penchants, see Cardillo, *Il duce in moviola,* 53, 74–76, 91; on the Luce films, see Pitassio, "I cinegiornali Luce." With specific reference to *A Noi!,* see Gian Piero Brunetta, "Divismo, misticismo e spettacolo della politica," in *Storia del cinema mondiale,* vol. 1, *L'Europa. Miti, luoghi, divi* (Turin: Einaudi, 2000), 527–559.

53. Pinkus, *Bodily Regimes,* 16.

54. Patrizia Dogliani, "Sport and Fascism," *Journal of Modern Italian Studies* 5, no. 3 (2000): 326–348, here 326–327.

55. George L. Mosse, *Nationalism and Sexuality: Middle-Class Morality and Sexual Norms in Modern Europe* (Madison: University of Wisconsin Press, 1985), 128.

56. Simon Martin, *Football and Fascism: The National Game under Mussolini* (Oxford, UK: Berg, 2004), 15.

57. Patrick McCarthy, "Summary," special feature on Sports and Society in Italy Today, *Journal of Modern Italian Studies* 5, no. 3 (2000): 322.

58. Gigliola Gori, "Model of Masculinity: Mussolini, the 'New Italian' of the Fascist Era," *International Journal of the History of Sport* 16, no. 4 (1999): 27–61, especially 39–45; on Mussolini's poor health and athletic skills, see Gigliola Gori, "Supermanism and the Culture of the Body in Italy: The Case of Futurism," *International Journal of the History of Sport* 16, no. 1 (1999): 159–165.

A 1934 Luce sound newsreel of this phenomenon is *Le attività sportive del Duce,* Giornale Luce B0570 10/1934, archived online at http://www.youtube.com /watch?v=O1T1y1LP6BA. The film shows him, "during his rare hours of rest," on horseback, fencing, skiing, flying, and swimming, all within the span of a little over one minute. Ricci argues that much of the imagery employed to represent Mussolini the athlete harks back to the strongman cycle of films. Ricci, *Cinema & Fascism,* 79–81.

59. *A Roma Mussolini visita la caserma della Guardia di Finanza,* Giornale Luce A0217 11/28, available online at http://www.youtube.com/watch?v =6fZfXmkoR-g.

60. Lupano and Vaccari, *Fashion at the Time of Fascism,* 244. For examples, see Sergio Luzzatto, *L'immagine del duce. Mussolini nelle fotografie dell'Istituto Luce* (Rome: Riuniti, 2001); and Renzo de Felice and Luigi Goglia, *Mussolini il mito* (Bari: Laterza, 1983). The online archive of the Istituto Luce also has thousands of images: www. archivioluce.com/archivio.

61. Sturani, "Analysing Mussolini's Postcards," 143.

62. *Maciste imperatore,* jointly restored by the Cineteca di Bologna and the MNC and executed at the L'Immagine Ritrovata Laboratory in 2007, is based on the only surviving nitrate copy from Amsterdam's Filmmuseum. The reconstruction of the film and intertitles reflects the archival documents preserved at the MNC. For more detailed information, see part 3 of the appendix.

63. Denis Mack Smith, *Italy and Its Monarchy* (New Haven, CT: Yale University Press, 1989). For more on the relationship between Fascism and the monarchy, see Adrian Lyttelton, *The Seizure of Power: Fascism in Italy 1919–1929*, rev. ed. (London: Routledge, 2004), 90–93. Lotti also notes the film's possible gesture to the extra-cinematic political tension. See Denis Lotti, *Il divismo maschile nel cinema muto italiano. Protagonisti, film, stereotipi, 1910–1929*, Tesi di Dottorato di Ricerca, Università degli Studi di Padova (2011).

64. Antonio Sonnessa, "The 1922 Turin Massacre (*Strage di Torino*): Working-Class Resistance and Conflicts within Fascism," *Modern Italy* 10, no. 2 (2005): 187–205.

65. Jackie Coogan was among the first of the many American stars Mussolini would personally encounter. On his visit to Italy in 1924, Coogan also met the pope. Gian Piero Brunetta, *Il ruggito del Leone. Hollywood alla conquista dell'impero dei sogni nell'Italia di Mussolini* (Venice: Marsilio, 2013), 68.

66. Gambino got his break in the film industry while watching a scene being filmed in which an actor had to fall off a carriage but was reluctant to do so. Gambino volunteered to substitute and thus began his career both in front of and behind the camera (he directed himself in many of the Saetta films). Vittorio Martinelli and Mario Quargnolo, *Maciste & Co. I giganti buoni del muto italiano* (Gemona del Friuli: Cinepopolare Edizioni, 1981), 32–36, Farassino, "Anatomia del cinema muscolare," 30. For a contemporary portrait, see Anonymous, "Saetta: Do-

menico Gambino," *Al Cinemà* 7, no. 49 (1923): 10–11.

67. I found no evidence of advertisements utilizing the longer title.

68. For Dall'Asta, Saetta and Maciste represent two antithetical archetypes: Saetta is the more modern, futurist acrobat, full of dynamism and movement, while Maciste is the more traditional, old-fashioned strongman. *Un cinéma musclé*, 110–113.

69. Sangro was also one of Gabriele D'Annunzio's lovers. Giulio Cattaneo, "La bella Elena," *La Repubblica*, 4 December 1988, 30, available online at http://ricerca.repubblica.it/repubblica /archivio/repubblica/1988/12/04 /la-bella-elena.html.

70. The legacy of Rome, for Emilio Gentile, "was an arsenal from which to draw myths of mobilization and legitimization for political action.... The cult of Romanness, in this sense, was celebrated modernistically as a myth of action for the future." Gentile, *Struggle for Modernity*, 60.

71. Joshua Arthurs, *Excavating Modernity: The Roman Past in Fascist Italy* (Ithaca, NY: Cornell University Press, 2012), 3–4. See also Jan Nelis, "Constructing Fascist Identity: Benito Mussolini and the Myth of Romanità," *Classical World* 100, no. 4 (2007), 391–415; Marla Stone, "A Flexible Rome: Fascism and the Cult of Romanità," in *Roman Presences: Receptions of Rome in European Culture*, ed. Catherine Edwards (Cambridge, UK: Cambridge University Press, 2007), 205–220; and Romke Visser, "Fascist Doctrine and the Cult of Romanità," *Journal of Contemporary History* 27, no. 1 (1922): 5–22.

72. "Masculine corporeality had been structured to signify strength and energy in the very period when these qualities were being appropriated by machines – hence the modernist desire to signify the body as a mechanical apparatus, to not simply emulate and challenge technology but instead identify with it." Maurizia Boscagli, *Eye on the Flesh: Fashions of Masculinity in the Early Twentieth Century* (Boulder, CO: Westview Press, 1996), 129.

73. Aldo Ciatti, "Croquis: Maciste," *Al Cinemà* 4, no. 7 (1925): 7.

74. "Un'intervista con Maciste," *Films Pittaluga* (15 February 1924): 45.

75. *A Roma Mussolini a cavallo*, Giornale Luce A0053 02/1928, available online at http://www.youtube.com /watch?v=WWOneyH7kjs.

76. Reprinted in Cardillo, *Il duce in moviola*, 108–112. Bosworth cites several other contemporary sources that corroborate this article. Bosworth, *Mussolini*, 211.

77. "Mussolini a cavallo lungo la via Appia," Giornale Luce A0226, 11/1928, available online at http://www.youtube .com/watch?v=SkorksarwTQ.

78. Gundle, "The Death (and Rebirth) of the Hero: Charisma and Manufactured Charisma in Modern Italy," *Modern Italy* 3, no. 2 (1998): 173–189, here 181–182. Garibaldi in turn iconically referenced Napoleon, whose myth continued to circulate in the late nineteenth century. See Lucy Riall, *Garibaldi: Invention of a Hero* (New Haven, CT: Yale University Press, 2007), 131–134.

79. Christopher E. Forth, *Masculinity in the Modern West: Gender, Civiliza-* tion, and the Body (New York: Palgrave Macmillan, 2008), 117–138.

80. Il Rondone, "*Maciste imperatore*," *La Vita Cinematografica* 20–21 (30 October–15 November 1924): 54; and "Gulliver, "*Maciste imperatore*," *La Rivista Cinematografica* 5, no. 23 (1924): 27.

81. The restoration of *Maciste all'inferno* was carried out in 2009 by the Cineteca di Bologna and the Museo Nazionale del Cinema. It is based on a duplicate negative of the 1993 restoration done by the Cineteca di Bologna, and it integrates new intertitles based on archival documents preserved at the MNC. The 1993 restoration is documented in several essays in the anthology *A nuova luce. Cinema muto italiano. I/Italian Silent Cinema. Atti di convegno internazionale*, Bologna 12–3 November 1998, ed. Michele Canosa (Bologna: CLUEB, 2000), in particular Gian Luca Farinelli and Nicola Mazzanti, "Maciste torna all'inferno," 293–295.

82. Raffaelle De Berti, "Milano Films: The Exemplary History of a Film Company in the 1910s," in Bertellini, *Italian Silent Cinema*, 113–122; John P. Welle, "Dante in the Cinematic Mode: An Historical Survey of Dante Movies," in *Dante's Inferno: The Indiana Critical Edition*, trans. and ed. Mark Musa (Bloomington: Indiana University Press, 1995), 381–395, and "Dante's *Inferno* of 1911 and the Origins of Italian Film Culture," in *Dante, Cinema, and Television*, ed. Amilcare Iannucci (Toronto: University of Toronto Press, 2004), 21–50; and *Cinegrafie* 20 (2007), which features several articles that discuss the film. Both earlier films drew

inspiration from Gustave Dorè's well-regarded illustrations for the *Inferno*, first published in France in 1861 to great acclaim. Reproductions of the illustrations, with accompanying copy, appear at the University of Virginia's World of Dante project at http://www.worldof dante.org/gallery_dore.html.

83. The film recirculated with added sound in the 1940s, when the 1938 Alfieri laws restricted the major American studio imports into Italy. Riccardo Freda remade the film as part of the peplum genre in 1962. Antonio Costa, "Da Caligari a Mussolini. Il viaggio di *Maciste all'inferno*," in Canosa, *A nuova luce*, 285–292, esp. 286–287.

84. Athos, "La parola del critico: *Maciste all'inferno*," *La Vita Cinematografica* 16, no. 5–6 (1924): 38–39.

85. A 1926 review appears in *La Rivista Cinematografica* 7, no. 9 (1926): 27–28. For more on the film's distribution history, see Friedemann, *Fert: Storia di un nome*, 27.

86. Bosworth, *Mussolini*, 53.

87. Andrea Cicarelli, "Dante and Italian Culture from the Risorgimento to World War I," *Dante Studies, with the Annual Report of the Dante Society* 119 (2001): 125–154; and Gentile, *Sacralization of Politics*, 30.

88. Susan J. Noakes, "Medieval Texts and National Identities: Dante in Red, White, Green: Then Black," *Journal of the Midwest Modern Language Association* 40, no. 1 (2007): 11–24; and Harvey Sachs, *Music in Fascist Italy* (New York: W. W. Norton, 1987), 210. Noakes uses the translations of the lyrics by Herman Finer as they appeared in his

monograph *Mussolini's Italy* (New York: Henry Holt, 1965), 410–411.

89. Thomas Schumacher, *The Danteum. A Study in the Architecture of Literature* (Princeton, NJ: Princeton Architectural Press, 1985).

90. For more on the restoration of the film's intertitles, see part 2 of the appendix.

91. It should be noted that this film precedes F. W. Murnau's *Faust* in its production by one year, even though both films were exhibited in 1926.

92. Dall'Asta, *Un cinema musclé*, 169.

93. Costa, "Da Caligari a Mussolini," 289.

94. Dall'Asta, *Un cinema musclé*, 169–174.

95. Costa, "Da Caligari a Mussolini," 290.

96. Lotti reads this scene as a political allegory, with Pluto as the weak king Vittorio Emanuele III, and even though Maciste serves the interests of the king, it is he who emerges with the people's support. Massimo Cardillo interprets it as a class struggle between the poor, exploited souls, who, like the working class, want their revenge. Massimo Cardillo, "Fregoli e il suo doppio ovvero lo specchio in camicia nera e le spire di celluloide," in Renzo Renzi, ed., *Il cinema dei dittatori. Mussolini, Stalin, Hitler,* with Gian Luca Farinelli and Nicola Mazzanti (Bologna: Grafis, 1992), 70–96, here 70–71.

97. Cardillo, "Fregoli e il suo doppio," 71.

98. *Al Cinemà* 4, no. 13 (1925): 5.

99. The 2009 restoration of *Maciste contro lo sceicco* by the Cineteca di Bologna and the Museo Nazionale del

Cinema in Turin was completed from a duplicate negative of Cineteca's 1992 restoration in conjunction with the Cineteca Nazionale in Milan and the Centro Sperimentale di Cinematografia in Rome. The new intertitles draw from production and archival documents at the museum. The 2007 restoration of *Maciste nella gabbia dei leoni,* carried out by the Cineteca del Comune in Bologna and the Museo Nazionale del Cinema, was based on the two tinted nitrate copies from the Fundação Cinemateca Brasiliera in São Paulo and now preserved in Bologna. The film's and the intertitles' reconstruction owes to the story line and intertitle list housed at the Museo Nazionale in Turin.

100. Richard Dyer, *White* (London: Routledge, 1997), 147.

101. Irmbert Schenk makes an important connection between film genre and colonial aspirations: heroes like Maciste, placed in African or Asian locales, rewrite the failures of Italy's previous colonial enterprises, creating new mythologies in which their strength and power always triumph and never disappoint. Imbert Schenk, "Il 'peplum' italiano. Perché il film storico-monumentale fu 'inventato' in Italia, ovvero: Da *Cabiria* a Mussolini," *Fotogenia* 4/5 (1997/1998): 59–72. See also Irmbert Schenk, "The Cinematic Support to Nationalist(ic) Mythology: The Italian Peplum, 1910–1930," in *Globalization, Cultural Identities, and Media Representations,* ed. Natascha Gentz and Stefan Kramer (Albany: State University of New York Press: 2006), 153–168.

102. Ruth Ben-Ghiat, *Italian Fascism's Empire Cinema* (Bloomington: Indiana University Press, 2015).

103. Vittorio Martinelli, ed. *Il cinema muto italiano. I film degli anni venti / 1921–1922, Bianco & Nero* 42, no. 1–3: 125–126, 151, and 338–339; Martinelli, ed., *Il cinema muto italiano. I film degli anni venti / 1923–1931, Bianco & Nero* 42, no. 4–6 (1981): 24–25. For more on the pirate film as genre, see Michael High, "Positioning the Cinematic Pirate Vilains, Heroes, and Temps," 56 (2014), available at http://www.ejumpcut.org /trialsite/HighPirates/index.html.

104. Marcia Landy, "Mario Camerini," *Encyclopedia of Italian Literary Studies,* ed. Gaetana Marrone (New York: Routledge, 2007), 351–353, as well as Landy's *Fascism in Film,* 241–245 and 258–269, and *The Folklore of Consensus,* 85–106; and Sergio Grmek Germani, *Mario Camerini* (Florence: La Nuova Italia, 1980). On *Rotaie,* see Piero Garofalo, "Seeing Red: The Soviet Influence on Italian Cinema in the Thirties," in Reich and Garofalo, *Re-Viewing Fascism,* 238–240; Hay, *Popular Film Culture in Fascist Italy,* 41–45; Mancini, *Struggles of the Italian Film Industry during Fascism,* 40–43; and Ricci, *Cinema & Fascism,* 107–113. Camerini is perhaps best remembered for what critics have called his *pentologia piccolo-borghese,* a series of five sentimental comedies featuring either or both Vittorio De Sica and Assia Noris: *Gli uomini che mascalzoni* (Men, What Scoundrels, 1932), *Darò un milione* (I'd Give a Million, 1935), *Ma non è una cosa seria* (It's Not Serious, 1936), *Il signor Max* (1937), and *Grandi magazzini* (Department

Store, 1939). For more on these films and Camerini's contribution to the 1930s and the lasting impact of that work, see Carlo Celli, "The Legacy of Mario Camerini in Vittorio de Sica's *The Bicycle Thief* (1948)," *Cinema Journal* 40, no. 4 (2001): 3–17; Jacqueline Reich, "Consuming Ideologies: Fascism, Commodification, and Female Subjectivity in Mario Camerini's *Grandi Magazzini*," *Annali d'Italianistica* 16 (1998): 195–212; and Barbara Spackman, "Shopping for Autarchy: Fascism and Reproductive Fantasy in Mario Camerini's *Grandi Magazzini*," in Reich and Garofalo, *Re-Viewing Fascism*, 276–292.

105. Camerini would later go on to make many films that centered on a conversion narrative, in such later ideologically loaded films as *Il grande appello* (The Great Call, 1936).

106. Ricci, *Cinema & Fascism*, 82–84.

107. See part 2 of the appendix on the difficulties in restoring this scene from 16mm and 35 mm prints.

108. Bertellini, "Duce/Divo: Masculinity, Racial Identity, and Politics among Italian Americans in 1920s New York City," *Journal of Urban History* 31, no. 5 (2005): 685–726; and Jacqueline Reich, "Rodolfo Valentino, 'uomo forte,'" in Silvio Alovisio and Giulia Carluccio, eds., *Rodolfo Valentino. Cinema, cultura, società tra Italia e Stati Uniti* (Turin: Kaplan, 2010), 308–322.

109. Lotti notes how he bears a marked resemblance to Lucifer.

110. Falasca-Zamponi, *Fascist Spectacle*, 79–80. For an image of the *Time* magazine cover of 12 July 1926, see http://www.time.com/time/covers/0,16641,19260712,00.html.

111. See Robin Pickering-Iazzi, "Ways of Looking in Black and White: Female Spectatorship and the Miscege-national Body in *Sotto la croce del sud*," in Reich and Garofalo, *Re-Viewing Fascism*, 194–221, and Ben-Ghiat, *Italian Fascism's Empire Cinema*.

112. Dall'Asta, in her discussion of the film, notes how the lions are symbols of savagery and alterity, and that Africans, like Seida, reject their alterity and conform to the ideals of Western civilization, implying uniformity, standardization, and exclusion of the other. Dall'Asta, *Un cinema musclé*, 161–162.

113. Vittorio Martinelli, "I Gastarbeiter fra le due guerre," *Bianco & Nero* 39, no. 3 (1978): 3–93, here 54; Stella Dagna, "All'ombra del gigante. Le comprimarie della serie Maciste," in *Non solo dive. Pioniere del cinema italiano*, ed. Monica Dall'Asta (Bologna: Cineteca di Bologna, 2008), 297–303, here 303.

114. See part 2 of the appendix on the insertion of intertitles in this sequence.

115. Società Anonima Stefano Pittaluga, *Rassegna di Programmazioni* 5–6 (March-June 1926): 77.

116. Brochure from the Gambrinus Theatre announces the imminent exhibition of the film. MNC online archives, *Maciste contro lo sceicco*, "Materiali pubblicitari," P41734.

117. *Cine-Gazzettino* 2, no. 15 (1927): 1.

118. Martinelli, "I film degli anni venti," 274. Contemporary advertisements note its exhibition in the United States in 1929.

119. "*Maciste all'inferno*," *La Vita Cinematografica* 16, no. 3–4 (1925): 13–14. Also reproduced under the same title

but with different illustrations in *Al Cinemà* 4, no. 13 (1925): 5–7.

120. As quoted in Athos, "La parola del critico. *Maciste all'Inferno*," *La Vita Cinematografica* 16, no. 5–6 (1925): 38–39.

121. Gaetano G. Amendola, "*Maciste contro lo sceicco*," *La Vita Cinematografica* 17, no. 1–2 (1926): 32.

Appendix Part 1

This essay has been written jointly by the authors. Stella Dagna wrote sections 1, 3, 5, 7, and 9 and Claudia Gianetto sections 2, 4, 6, and 8. In the "In Focus" section (part 2) Stella Dagna wrote the text dedicated to *Maciste, Maciste innamorato, Maciste imperatore, Maciste nella gabbia dei leoni,* and *Maciste all'inferno*; Claudia Gianetto wrote those for *Maciste alpino, La trilogia di Maciste, Maciste in vacanza,* and *Maciste contro lo sceicco*. The authors would like to thank all of their colleagues of the Museo Nazionale del Cinema in Turin (MNC), the Cineteca del Comune di Bologna (CB, now the Fondazione Cineteca di Bologna), and the laboratory L'Immagine Ritrovata (IR), which over the years have collaborated on the restoration of Maciste films. A special thanks in particular goes to the film archives that have their own prints available to us and to Giorgio Bertellini, Ivo Blom, Paolo Caneppele, Gianna Chiapello, and Denis Lotti.

1. Excerpt from the manuscript (pp. 26–27) of judgment No. 911 of 7 July 1923 by the Court of Appeals of Turin in the case of the Società Anonima Itala against Bartolomeo Pagano decreed on 27 November 1923. The document is preserved in the State Archives of Turin, United Chambers, Civil and Criminal Court of Turin, Civil Sections, Civil Judgments Volume 1923, Court of Appeal of Turin.

2. Even in the unlikely event of retrieving a film from the past in its complete, integral form, the object's material characteristics will always be different from those of the era to which the film belongs. The films produced in the first half of the twentieth century, for example, were printed on nitrate film with a very different emulsion sensitivity than today's films. Magnetic sound, to take another example, is now converted into optical or digital, with a different result from the original. Film digitization, moreover, changes the nature of the film image to an even greater degree.

3. The sections devoted to *Maciste all'inferno* and *La trilogia di Maciste* in part 2 of this appendix elaborate on these details.

4. Documenting the restoration is crucial, according to one of the basic principles identified by the great theorist Cesare Brandi: "The restoration must be reversible." See Cesare Brandi, *Teoria del restauro* (Turin: Einaudi, 1977). In the case of film this principle translates into the preservation of the originals and, indeed, in the documentation of the materials used and the choices made during the work so that in the future it is possible to identify and amend any eventual mistakes.

5. Many specialists have voiced this need for collaboration and communication: "It is very eloquent that, for instance, the new problems which

the restoration of contemporary art has raised have resulted in considerable academic debate. In film restoration this is very rare, although several archivists also have positions at universities. It is also surprising that the problems of film restoration or the history of film technology have barely been incorporated in academic film studies. This would be useful not just for archives alone, but also for film studies, as the study of original nitrate prints in recent years has already demonstrated that several aspects of film history will need vision." Paul Read and Mark-Paul Meyer, *Restoration of Motion Picture Film* (London: Butterworth-Heinemann, 2000), 76.

6. On the occasion of the restoration of *Cabiria*, Silvio Alovisio and Alberto Barbera edited an entire volume dedicated to the film, *Cabiria & Cabiria* (Turin: Museo Nazionale del Cinema, 2006). Two essays in the volume are devoted specifically to the restoration: Silvio Alovisio, "Il film che visse due volte. *Cabiria* tra antichi segreti e nuove ricerche," 15–44, and Joao De Oliveira, "*Cabiria,* una nuova sfida per il restauro," 54–61. See also Stella Dagna, "Il restauro di *Cabiria*," in *Strategie e Programmazione della Conservazione e Trasmissibilità del Patrimonio Culturale,* ed. Aleksandra Filipović and Troiano Williams (Rome: Issue scientific Fidei Signa, 2013), 394–403. For a commentary on the restoration project, see Paolo Cherchi Usai, "*Cabiria* salvata dalle fiamme," in *Segnocinema* 139 (May 2006): 72–73.

7. *Cabiria* had already been restored in 1995. The need to return to work on the film came from the discov-

ery of the film's production documents, which revealed important differences between the 1914 silent version and the 1931 sound version. With the help of these documents we were able to restore both versions.

8. The restored silent version was presented on 20 March 2006 at the Teatro Regio in Turin, accompanied by the original score of Ildebrando Pizzetti and Manlio Mazza and performed live by "900 Philharmonic Orchestra, conducted by Timothy Brock; a sound print was screened for the first time the next day at Turin's Cinema Massimo.

9. The restored print of *Maciste* was presented to the public on 2 July 2006 at the twentieth annual Festival del Cinema Ritrovato in Bologna, Italy.

10. Until the 1950s films were printed on cellulose nitrate, a highly flammable and explosive material. Given the dangers and tragic accidents caused by fire in the projection booth, after World War II the material base of film became cellulose triacetate. Since then, in many countries the screening of nitrate film has been banned and its transport and storage has been strictly regulated. The danger increases with chemical deterioration, during which the film emits a gas that accelerates its decomposition. In the final stages of colliquation, the reels become glutinous masses that are in turn impossible to unwind. They subsequently calcify, resulting in the film's total loss.

11. This kind of "serial restoration" does not have many precedents of similar duration and continuity. It is not a systematic preservation of a part of a film archive collection (as is the case

of the preservation of the Desmet collection carried out by Nederland Filmmuseum). Instead, it is a work of the discovery, availability, and restoration of a group of films whose existence and location were unknown at first.

12. See *Gli uomini forti*, ed. Alberto Farassino and Tatti Sanguineti (Milan: Mazzotta, 1983); and Monica Dall'Asta, *Un cinéma musclé. Le surhomme dans le cinéma muet italien (1913–1926)* (Crisnée: Yellow Now, 1992).

13. *Maciste contro lo sceicco* and *Maciste all'inferno* were restored in the 1990s by the Cineteca of Bologna. In 2009, under the auspices of this project, the original intertitles for both films were reintegrated into the prints, as were additional sequences found in another print of *Maciste contro lo sceicco* (see the section dedicated to these films in part 2 of the appendix). *Maciste alpino* was restored by the Museo Nazionale del Cinema in 2000, with newly discovered footage added in 2014.

14. The two exceptions are the aforementioned *Maciste alpino* and *Il gigante delle Dolomiti*, restored in 2002 by the Fondazione Cineteca Italiana in Milan.

15. This 20 percent figure of available films, first put forth by Paolo Cherchi Usai, is a commonly adopted total among film archivists. Cherchi Usai specifies, however, that this amount cannot be applied across the board to all national cinemas and directors. A much higher percentage of American films have been preserved, for example, as compared to that of Indian films. See Paolo Cherchi Usai, "La cineteca di Babele," in *Storia del cinema mondiale, v. 5. Teorie, strumenti, memorie,* ed. Gian

Piero Brunetta (Turin: Einaudi, 2001), 965–1067.

16. The issue is broad and complex. Here we just wish to highlight that the digital formats are subject to a process of rapid obsolescence and that the transfer from one medium to another, proposed as a solution to the problem, is an expensive process, almost impossible to sustain for film archives that conserve thousands upon thousands of titles.

17. Paolo Cherchi Usai, *The Death of Cinema: History, Cultural Memory, and the Digital Dark Age* (London: British Film Institute, 2001).

18. "Film restoration is different from all restoration in other fields, where a tradition is already established. Whereas those traditions typically imply work on an original artefact, film restoration implies duplication and/or reconstruction." Vittorio Boarini and Vladimir Opiela, "Charter of Film Restoration," Article II in *Journal of Film Preservation* (November 2010): 38.

19. One of the main advocates of this critical position is Cherchi Usai, who terms "reductionist" the notion that philology is the theoretical base for film reconstruction. FIAF's Code of Ethics recognizes as legitimate the practice of film reconstruction, with some specifications: "1.5 When restoring material, archives will endeavour only to complete what is incomplete and to remove the accretions of time, wear and misinformation. They will not seek to change or distort the nature of the original material or the intentions of its creators" (http://www.fiafnet.org/uk/members /ethics.html).

20. Paragraph 1.7 of FIAF's Code of Ethics: "The nature and rationale of any debatable decision relating to restoration or presentation of archive materials will be recorded and made available to any audience or researcher" (http://www.fiafnet.org/uk/members/ethics.html).

21. The AMIA (http://www.amianet.org) was founded in the 1960s by a group of film archivists with the goal of intellectual and professional exchange. At first it was called Film and Television Archives Advisory Committee (F/TAAC), but the group changed its name in 1990. Today it has hundreds of members and organizes multiple events connected to the film archive world, including an annual conference and the Archive Film Festival. It is located in Los Angeles, California.

22. The FIAF (http://fiaf.chadwyck.com/marketing/about.jsp) was founded in 1938 by the British Film Institute, the Museum of Modern Art in New York, the Cinémathèque Française, and the Reichsfilmarchiv. It is the leading international organization to coordinate film archives. It promotes publications, meetings, and initiatives to support the film practice of restoration and preservation. Its internal three committees focus on technique, cataloging and documentation, and access to collections.

23. Treasures from the Film Archives contains the data of more than forty-eight thousand silent films provided by the film archive members. Members of FIAF and cultural institutions can access the database after registering.

24. Here is a framework of the printing process, which can vary according to the initial materials. In the analog process we first print a duplicate positive (black-and-white)/inter-positive (color) from a negative, which will then be used to produce the duplicate negative or inter-negative and the positive prints. Technical *découpage* is a document that describes the intended form the restored print of the film will take at the end of the restoration work and contains all the relevant information for the task. Each shot is described in the established order of editing, and the origin, length, and color are signaled along with text, graphics, intertitles, intertitle position, and any other relevant information to the restoration.

25. The *truka* (or *truca* or *truke*) is a type of high-resolution optical printer used to create titles, special effects, and reduction in the format of the film, among other tasks. Now out of fashion, the truka was used to print intertitles at the time of the Maciste series.

26. This copious catalogue is online at the MNC, in the "Documenti del cinema muto torinese" section, along with the digitalization of the extra-cinematic materials: www.museocinema.it.

27. See Claudia Gianetto, "I restauri del Museo Nazionale del Cinema. Da *La guerra e il sogno di Momi* a *Gli ultimi giorni di Pompei*," in Carla Ceresa and Donata Pesenti Campagnoni, *Tracce. Documenti del cinema muto torinese nelle collezioni del Museo del Cinema* (Turin: Museo Nazionale del Cinema, 2007), 82–93; Claudia Gianetto, "La pratica del restauro nel cinema muto italiano. Un caso di ricostruzione," in *Introduzione*

al cinema muto italiano, ed. Silvio Alovisio e Giulia Carluccio (Turin: UTET, 2013), 359–389.

28. *Maciste innamorato,* Museo Nazionale del Cinema, A179/1.

29. *Maciste e il nipote d'America,* list of intertitles, s.d., A240/11.

30. For Il Cinema Ritrovato in Bologna, see http://www.cinetecadibologna.it/cinemaritrovato2014; for Le Giornate del Cinema Muto in Pordenone, see http://www.cinetecadelfriuli.org/gcm.

31. MNC Bibliomediateca, http://www.museocinema.it/bibliomediateca.php.

32. Stella Dagna and Claudia Gianetto, eds., *Maciste. L'uomo forte* (2009), DVD and book (Bologna: Edizioni Cineteca di Bologna and Museo Nazionale del Cinema).

33. Stefano Benni, *Il bar sotto il mare* (Milan: Feltrinelli, 1989), 121.

Bibliography

PERIODICALS CONSULTED

Al cinemà
L'Ambrosiano
Atlanta Constitution
L'Avanti
Baltimore Sun
Billboard
Billings (MT) Gazette
Bioscope
Boston Post
Boston Transcript
Brownsville (TX) Daily Herald
Chicago Daily Tribune
La Cine-Fono
Cine-Gazzettino
La Cinematografia Italiana ed Estera
Cleveland (OH) Plain Dealer
Connellsville (PA) Daily Courier
Il Corriere d'America
Corriere della Sera
Current Opinion
Daily Independent (OH)
Daily Independent (PA)
Daily Kennebec (ME) Journal
Daily Leader (WI)
Dallas Morning News
Detroit Free Press
Detroit News

Evening Telegram (NY)
Film
Films Pittaluga
Fitchburg (MA) Daily Sentinel
Fort Wayne (IN) Journal-Gazette
Fort Wayne (IN) News and Sentinel
Hamburg (IA) Reporter
L'Illustrazione Cinematografica
Indianapolis Examiner
Indianapolis Star
Kinematograph and Lantern Weekly
Kingsport (TN) Times
Kokomo (IN) Tribune
La Crosse (WI) Tribune
Lancaster (OH) Daily Eagle
Los Angeles Examiner
Los Angeles Times
Lowell (MA) Sun
Il Maggese Cinematografico
Marion (OH) Daily Star
Middletown (NY) Times Press
Minneapolis Tribune
Moving Picture World
La Nazione
Nevada State Journal (Reno)
Newark (NJ) Eagle
New Castle (PA) News
New York Dramatic Mirror
New York Sun

New York Times
Oil City (PA) Derrick
Petersburg (VA) Daily Progress
Philadelphia Inquirer
Photoplay
Piqua (OH) Leader Dispatch
Il Progresso Italo-Americano
La Rivista Cinematografica
San Jose Mercury Herald
Sandusky (OH) Star Journal
Il Secolo
Suburanite Economist (Chicago)
Sunday Oregonian (OR)
Il Telegrafo
Trenton (NJ) Evening Times
Tyrone (PA) Daily Herald
Variety
La Vita Cinematografica

SECONDARY SOURCES

Abel, Richard. *Americanizing the Mov-
ies and "Movie-Mad" Audiences,
1910–1914.* Berkeley: University of
California Press, 2006.
——. *The Ciné Goes to Town: French
Cinema, 1896–1914.* Updated and exp.
ed. Berkeley: University of California
Press, 1998.
——. "G. M. Anderson: 'Broncho Billy'
among the Early 'Picture Person-
alities.'" In Bean, *Flickers of Desire,*
22–42.
Abel, Richard, Giorgio Bertellini, and
Rob King. Introduction to *Early
Cinema and the "National,"* edited by
Richard Abel, Giorgio Bertellini, and
Rob King, 1–8. Eastleigh, UK: John
Libbey, 2008.
Abruzzese, Alberto. "Gli uomini forti e
le maestre pedani." In Farassino and
Sanguineti, *Gli uomini forti,* 56–66.

Adams, Mark. *Mr. America: How Mus-
cular Millionaire Bernarr Macfadden
Transformed the Nation through Sex,
Salad, and the Ultimate Starvation
Diet.* New York: HarperCollins,
2009.
Adamson, Walter L. *Avant-Garde
Florence: From Modernism to Fascism.*
Cambridge, MA: Harvard University
Press, 1993.
——. "Fascism and Culture: Avant-
Gardes and Secular Religion in the
Italian Case." *Journal of Contempo-
rary History* 24, no. 3 (1989): 411–435.
——. "The Impact of World War I on
Italian Political Culture." In *Euro-
pean Culture in the Great War: The
Arts, Entertainment, and Propaganda,
1914–1918,* edited by Aviel Roshwald
and Richard Stites, 308–329. Cam-
bridge: Cambridge University Press,
1999.
——. "Modernism and Fascism: The
Politics of Culture in Italy, 1903–
1922." *American Historical Review* 95,
no. 2 (1990): 359–390.
Agnew, John. "The Impossible Capital:
Monumental Rome under Liberal
and Fascist Regimes, 1870–1943."
Geografiska Annaler 80B (1998):
229–240.
Alonge, Giaime. *Cinema e guerra.* Turin: UTET, 2001.
——. "Giocando con i soldatini. *La
guerra e il sogno di Momi* tra propaganda e mercato." *Nuovo spettatore* 1,
no. 1 (1997): 167–178.
——. Il desegno armato. *Cinema
d'animazione e propaganda bellica in
Nord America e Gran Bretagna (1914–
1945).* Bologna: CLUEB, 2000.

——. "La guerra come orizzonte e come rappresentazione." Torino D@ams Review (2006). http://www .turindamsreview.unito.it/sezione .php?idart=83.

Alovisio, Silvio. "Il cinema italiano: dalle origini all'avvento del sonoro." In *Attraverso lo schermo. Cinema e cultura cattolica in Italia*. Vol. 1, *Dalle origini agli anni Venti*, edited by Ruggero Eugeni and Dario E. Viganò, 61–95. Rome: Ente dello Spettacolo, 2006.

——. "Il film che visse due volte. *Cabiria* tra antichi segreti e nuove ricerche." In Alovisio and Barbera, *Cabiria & Cabiria*, 26.

——. "Le riviste del cinema muto: una fonte per la ricerca tecnologica?" *Bianco & Nero* 549 (2004): 31–44.

——. *Voci del silenzio. La sceneggiatura nel cinema muto italiano*. Milan: Il Castoro, 2005.

Alovisio, Silvio, and Alberto Barbera, eds. *Cabiria & Cabiria*. Turin: Museo Nazionale del Cinema, 2006.

Amari, Giancarlo. *Torino come Detroit (capitale dell'automobile, 1895–1940)*. Bologna: Cappelli, 1980.

Argentieri, Mino. *L'occhio del regime. Informazione e propaganda nel cinema del fascismo*. Florence: Vallecchi, 1979.

——, ed. *Risate di regime. La commedia italiana, 1930–1944*. Venice: Marsilio, 1991.

Armiero, Marco. *A Rugged Nation: Mountains and the Making of Modern Italy*. Cambridge, UK: White Horse Press, 2011.

Arthurs, Joshua. *Excavating Modernity: The Roman Past in Fascist Italy*. Ithaca, NY: Cornell University Press, 2012.

Aste, Mario. "They Came in Hope: Pictorial and Oral History of Lowell's Italian Americans." http:// ecommunity.uml.edu/italian/they _came_in_hope.pdf.

Atkinson, David, and Denis Cosgrove. "Urban Rhetoric and Embodied Identities: City, Nation, and Empire at the Vittorio Emanuele II Monument in Rome, 1870–1945." *Annals of the Association of American Geographers* 88, no. 1 (1998): 28–49.

Baravelli, Andrea. "L'immagine virile dell'Italia." Paper delivered at the Convegno Sissco, Lecce, 25–27 September 2003.

Barthes, Roland. *Mythologies*. New York: Hill and Wang, 1972.

Bean, Jennifer. *Flickers of Desire: Movie Stars of the 1910s*. New Brunswick, NJ: Rutgers University Press, 2011.

——. "Technologies of Early Stardom and the Extraordinary Body." In Bean and Negra, *Feminist Reader*, 404–443.

Bean, Jennifer, and Diane Negra, eds. *A Feminist Reader in Early Cinema*, Durham, NC: Duke University Press, 2002.

Becker, Jared M. *Nationalism and Culture: Gabriele D'Annunzio and Italy after the Risorgimento*. New York: Peter Lang, 1994.

Bederman, Gail. *Manliness and Civilization: A Cultural History of Gender and Race in the United States, 1880–1917*. Chicago: University of Chicago Press, 1995.

Bellassai, Sandro. "The Masculine Mystique: Antimodernism and Virility in

Fascist Italy." *Journal of Modern Italian Studies* 10, no. 3 (2005): 314–335.

Bellucci, Alberto. *L'automobile italiana, 1918–1943.* Bari: Laterza, 1984.

Ben-Ghiat, Ruth. "Envisioning Modernity: Desire and Discipline in the Italian Fascist Film." *Critical Inquiry* 23, no. 1 (1996): 109–144.

——. *Fascist Modernities: Italy, 1922–1945.* Berkeley: University of California Press, 2001.

——. *Italian Fascism's Empire Cinema.* Bloomington: Indiana University Press, 2015.

Ben-Ghiat, Ruth, and Mia Fuller, eds. *Italian Colonialism.* New York: Palgrave Macmillan, 2005.

Benjamin, Walter. "The Work of Art in the Age of Mechanical Reproduction." In *Illuminations: Essays and Reflections,* edited by Hannah Arendt; translated by Harry Zohn, 217–251. New York: Schocken, 1968.

Berghaus, Günter. *F. T. Marinetti: Critical Writings,* new ed. Edited by Günter Berghaus. Translated by Doug Thompson. New York: Farrar, Straus & Giroux, 2006.

——. *Futurism and Politics: Between Anarchist Rebellion and Fascist Reaction, 1909–1944.* Providence, RI: Berghahn, 1996.

Bernagozzi, Giampaolo. *Il cinema allo specchio. Appunti per una storia del documentario.* Bologna: Pàtron, 1985.

Bernardini, Aldo. "Appunti sul cinema comico muto italiano." *Griffithiana* 7, no. 24–25 (1985): 21–35.

——, ed. *Archivio del cinema italiano.* Vol. 1, *Il cinema muto, 1905–1931.* Rome: Anica, 1991.

——. "Les catholiques et l'avènement du cinema en Italie: promotion et contrôle." In *Une invention du diable? Cinéma des premiers temps et religion,* edited by Roland Cosandey, André Gaudreault, and Tom Gunning, 3–11. Lausanne: Editions Payot, 1992.

——. *Cinema delle origini in Italia. I film "dal vero" di produzione estera.* Gemona: La Cineteca del Friuli, 2008.

——. *Cinema italiano delle origini. Gli ambulanti.* Gemona: La Cineteca di Friuli, 2001.

——. *Cinema muto italiano.* Vol. 3, *Arte, divismo e mercato, 1910–1914.* Rome: Laterza, 1982.

Berruti Sila, and Luca Mazzei. "'Il giornale mi lascia freddo.' I film 'dal vero' dalla Libia (1911–12) e il pubblico italiano." *Immagine. Note di Storia del Cinema* no. 3 (2011): 53–103.

Bertellini, Giorgio. "The Atlantic Valentino: The 'Inimitable Lover' as Racialized and Gendered Italian." In *Intimacy and Italian Migration: Gender and Domestic Lives in a Mobile World,* edited by Loretta Baldassar and Donna Gabaccia, 37–48. New York: Fordham University Press, 2011.

——. "Black Hands and White Hearts: Italian Immigrants as 'Urban Racial Types' in Early American Film Culture." *Urban History* 31, no. 3 (2004): 375–399.

——. "Colonial Autism: Whitened Heroes, Auditory Rhetoric, and National Identity in Interwar Italian Cinema." In *A Place in the Sun: Africa in Italian Colonial Culture from Post-Unification to the Present,* edited by Patrizia Palumbo, 255–278. Berkeley: University of California Press, 2003.

——. "Dubbing L'Arte Muta: Poetic Layerings around Italian Cinema's Transition to Sound." In Reich and Garofalo, *Re-Viewing Fascism*, 30–82.

——. "Duce/Divo: Masculinity, Racial Identity, and Politics among Italian Americans in 1920s New York City." *Journal of Urban History* 31, no. 5 (2005): 685–726.

——. "The Earth Still Trembles: On Landscape Views in Contemporary Italian Cinema." *Italian Culture* 30, no. 1 (2012): 38–50.

——. "Epica spettacolare e splendore del vero: L'influenza del cinema storico italiano in America (1908–1915)." In Brunetta, *Storia del cinema mondiale*, 2: 227–265.

——. "George Beban: Character of the Picturesque." In Bean, *Flickers of Desire*, 155–173.

——. "Italian Imageries, Historical Feature Films, and the Fabrication of Italy's Spectators in Early 1900s New York." In *American Movie Audiences: From the Turn of the Century to the Early Sound Era*, edited by Richard Maltby and Melvyn Stokes, 29–45. London: BFI Publishing, 1999.

——, ed. *Italian Silent Cinema: A Reader*, edited by Giorgio Bertellini. New Baret, UK: John Libbey, 2013.

——. *Italy in Early American Cinema: Race, Landscape, and the Picturesque.* Bloomington: Indiana University Press, 2010.

——. "Resuscitare la storia: *Cabiria* e gli Stati Uniti." In Alovisio and Barbera, *Cabiria & Cabiria*, 174–180.

Bernardini, Aldo, ed. *Archivio del cinema muto. Vol. 1, Il cinema muto, 1905–1931.* Rome: ANICA, 1991.

Bertetto, Paolo, and Gianni Rondolino, eds. *Cabiria e il suo tempo.* Turin: Museo Nazionale del Cinema, 1998.

Bertozzi, Marco. *Storia del documentario italiano. Immagini e culture dell'altro cinema.* Venice: Marsilio, 2008.

Blizek, William L., ed. *The Continuum Companion to Religion and Film.* London: Continuum, 2009.

Bondanella, Peter. *The Eternal City: Roman Images in the Modern World.* Chapel Hill: University of North Carolina Press, 1987.

——. *A History of Italian Cinema.* New York: Continuum, 2009.

Boni, Federico. "Sport, mascolinità e media." In dell'Agnese and Ruspini, *Mascolinità all'italiana*, 79–102.

Bordwell, David. *On the History of Film Style.* Cambridge, MA: Harvard University Press, 1997.

Boscagli, Maurizia. *Eye on the Flesh: Fashions of Masculinity in the Early Twentieth Century.* Boulder, CO: Westview Press, 1996.

Bosworth, R.J.B. *Mussolini.* London: Arnold, 2002.

——. *Mussolini's Italy: Life under the Fascist Dictatorship, 1915–1945.* New York: Penguin, 2005.

Bottomore, Stephen. "Il cinema appare nelle guerre balcaniche e boere, dal 1895 al 1914." In Renzi et al., *Il cinematografo al campo*, 32–39.

Bowser, Eileen. *The Transformation of Cinema, 1907–1915.* Berkeley: University of California Press, 1990.

Boylan, Amy. "Masculinity and Commemoration of the Great War: Gabriele D'Annunzio's *La beffa di Buccari* and Eugenio Baroni's *Monumento al*

Fante." *Italian Culture* 29, no. 1 (2011): 3–17.

———. "Maternal Images in Song, Bronze, and Rhetoric: Mercantini's 'Inno a Garibaldi,' Baroni's *Monumento ai Mille,* and D'Annunzio's *Orazione per la sagra dei Mille.*" *Italian Studies* 66, no. 1 (2011): 40–58.

Braccesi, Lorenzo. "Salgari e l'antico." *Studi Storici* 46, no. 4 (2005): 955–965.

Bracco, Davide, Stefano Della Casa, Paolo Manera, and Franco Prono, eds. *Torino città del cinema.* Milan: Il Castoro, 2001.

Braun, Emily. "Futurist Fashion: Three Manifestoes." *Art Journal* 54, no. 1 (1995): 34–41.

Brownlow, Kevin. *Behind the Mask of Innocence.* Berkeley: University of California Press, 1990.

———. *The War, the West, and the Wilderness.* New York: Alfred A. Knopf, 1979.

Brunetta, Gian Piero. *Buio in sala. Cent'anni di passione dello spettatore cinematografico.* Venice: Marsilio, 1989.

———. *Cent'anni di cinema italiano.* Bari: Laterza, 1991.

———. "Cinema e prima guerra mondiale." In Brunetta, *Storia del cinema mondiale.* 1: 252–275.

———. *Cinema italiano tra le due guerre. Fascismo e politica cinematografica.* Milan: Mursia, 1975.

———. "Il clown cinematografico tra salotto liberty e frontiera del West." *Griffithiana* 7, no. 24–25 (1985): 11–20.

———. "Divismo, misticismo e spettacolo della politica." In Brunetta, *Storia del cinema mondiale.* 1: 527–559.

———. *The History of Italian Cinema: A Guide to Italian Film from its Origins to the Twenty-first Century.* Translated by Jeremy Parzen. Princeton, NJ: Princeton University Press, 2009.

———. "Introduzione." In *Metamorfosi del mito classico nel cinema,* edited by Gian Piero Brunetta, 9–30. Bologna: Il Mulino, 2011.

———. "'Over There.' La guerra lontana." In Brunetta, *Storia del cinema mondiale.* 2: 267–288. Turin: Einaudi, 1999.

———. *Il ruggito del Leone. Hollywood alla conquista dell'impero dei sogni nell'Italia di Mussolini.* Venice: Marsilio, 2013.

———. *Storia del cinema italiano.* Vol. 1, *Il cinema muto, 1895–1929.* Rome: Riuniti, 1993.

———, ed. *Storia del cinema mondiale.* Vol. 1, *L'Europa. Miti, luoghi, divi.* Turin: Einaudi, 2000.

———, ed. *Storia del cinema mondiale.* Vol. 2, *Gli Stati Uniti.* Turin: Einaudi, 1999.

Bultrini, Nicola, and Antonio Tentori. *Il cinema della Grande Guerra.* Chiari: Nordpress, 2008.

Burgwyn, H. James. *The Legend of the Mutilated Victory: Italy, the Great War, and the Paris Peace Conference, 1915–1919.* Westport, CT: Greenwood Press, 1993.

Butters, Gerald. *Black Manhood on the Silent Screen.* Lawrence: University of Kansas Press, 2002.

Caburlotto, Filippo. "D'Annunzio, la Latinità del Mediterraneo e il mito della riconquista." *California Journal of Italian Studies* 1, no. 1 (2010). http://escholarship.org/uc/item/7gx5g2n9.

Calendoli, Giovanni. *Materiali per una storia del cinema italiano*. Parma: Maccari Editore, 1967.

Campbell, Craig W. *Reel America and World War I: A Comprehensive Filmography and History of Motion Pictures in the United States, 1914–1920*. Jefferson, NC: McFarland, 1985.

Canjels, Rudmer. *Distributing Silent Film Serials: Local Practices, Changing Forms, Cultural Transformations*. London: Routledge, 2011.

Cannistraro, Philip V. *La fabbrica del consenso. Fascismo e mass media*. Rome: Laterza, 1975.

Canosa, Michele, ed. *1905: La presa di Roma. Alle origini del cinema italiano – Beginnings of Italian Cinema*. Bologna: Le Mani/Cineteca di Bologna, 2006.

——, ed. *A nuova luce. Cinema muto italiano. I/Italian Silent Cinema I*. Atti di convegno internazionale. Bologna 12–3 November 1998. Bologna: CLUEB, 2000.

Canudo, Ricciotto. "Trionfo del cinematografo." *Nuovo giornale*, 25 novembre 1908. Republished in *Filmcritica* 28, no. 278 (1977): 296–302.

Carabba, Claudio. *Il cinema del ventennio nero*. Florence: Vallecchi, 1974.

Caranti, Chiara. "*Cabiria* 1914 & 1931: la distribuzione in Italia e nel mondo." In Alovisio and Barbera, *Cabiria & Cabiria*, 148–173.

——. "Disordered Traffic: Film Distribution in Italy (1905–1930)." In Bertellini, *Italian Silent Cinema*, 285–294.

Carden-Coyne, Ana. "Classical Heroism and Modern Life: Bodybuilding and Masculinity in Early Twentieth

Century." *Journal of Australian Studies* 63 (2000): 138–149.

Cardillo, Massimo. *Il duce in moviola. Politica e divismo nei cinegiornali e documentari "Luce."* Bari: Dedalo, 1983.

——. "Fregoli e il suo doppio ovvero lo specchio in camicia nera e le spire di celluloide." In Renzi et al., *Il cinema dei dittatori*, 70–96.

Casadio, Gianfranco. *Il grigio e il nero. Spettacolo e propaganda nel cinema italiano degli anni trenta, 1931–1943*. Ravenna: Longo, 1992.

Castello, Giulio Cesare. *Il divismo. Mitologia del cinema*. Turin: Edizioni Radio Italiana, 1957.

Castonguay, James. "The Spanish-American War in United States Media Culture." In Slocum, *Hollywood and War*, 97–108.

Celli, Carlo. "The Legacy of Mario Camerini in Vittorio de Sica's *The Bicycle Thief* (1948)." *Cinema Journal* 40, no. 4 (2001): 3–17.

Celli, Carlo, and Margo Cottino-Jones. *A New Guide to Italian Cinema*. New York: Palgrave Macmillan, 2007.

Ceresa, Carla, and Donata Pesenti Campagnoni, eds. *Tracce. Documenti del cinema muto torinese nelle collezioni del Museo del Cinema*. Turin: Museo Nazionale del Cinema, 2007.

Charney, Leo, and Vanessa R. Schwartz, eds. *Cinema and the Invention of Modern Life*. Berkeley: University of California Press, 1995.

Chenoune, Farid. *A History of Men's Fashion*. Translated by Deke Dusinberre. Paris: Flammarion, 1983.

Cherchi Usai, Paolo. *Giovanni Pastrone*. Florence: La Nuova Italia, 1985.

——, ed. *Giovanni Pastrone. Gli anni d'oro del cinema a Torino.* Turin: UTET, 1986.

——. "Italy: Spectacle and Melodrama." In *The Oxford History of World Cinema,* edited by Geoffrey Nowell-Smith, 123–130. Oxford: Oxford University Press, 1996.

——. *Silent Cinema: An Introduction.* 2nd ed. London: BFI, 2008.

Chiti, Roberto. "Bartolomeo Pagano, un uomo chiamato Maciste." In *Maciste, Omaggio a Bartolomeo Pagano,* 1–6. Turin: Tepotecnica Ernani, 1985.

Chiti, Roberto, and Mario Quarignolo. "La malinconica storia dell'UCI." *Bianco & Nero* 18, no. 7 (1957): 21–35.

Cicarelli, Andrea. "Dante and Italian Culture from the Risorgimento to World War I." *Dante Studies,* with the Annual Report of the Dante Society 119 (2001): 125–154.

Clark, Martin. *Modern Italy: 1871 to the Present.* 3rd ed. Harlow, UK: Pearson/Longman, 2008.

Colette. "Maciste alpin." *Le Film,* 18 June 1917, 26. Anthologized in Colette, *Colette at the Movies: Criticism and Screenplays,* edited by Alain and Odette Virmaux; translated by Sarah W. R. Smith, 28–29. New York: Frederick Ungar, 1980.

Collins, Sue. "Bonding with the Crowd: Silent Film Stars, Liveness, and the Public Sphere." In *Convergence Media History,* edited by Janet Staiger and Sabine Hake, 117–126. New York: Routledge, 2009.

Collins, Suzanne W. "Calling All Stars: Emerging Political Authority and Cultural Policy in the Propaganda Campaign of World War I." PhD diss., New York University, 2008.

Connell, R. W. *Masculinities.* Berkeley: University of California Press, 1995.

Cooper, Mark Garrett. "Pearl White and Grace Cunard: The Serial Queen's Volatile Present." In Bean, *Flickers of Desire,* 174–195.

Coriell, Vernell. "Elmo the Mighty" (1968). Reprinted in *My Father, Elmo Lincoln: The Original Tarzan,* by Marci'a Lincoln Rudolph, 27–43. N.p.:Empire Publication Services, 1999.

Cornelius, Michael G., ed. *Of Muscles and Men: Essays on the Sword and Sandal Film.* Jefferson, NC: McFarland, 2011.

Corner, Paul. "State and Society, 1901–1922." In *Liberal and Fascist Italy, 1900–1945,* edited by Adrian Lyttelton, 17–43. Oxford: Oxford University Press, 2002.

Cosandey, Roland, André Gaudreault, and Tom Gunning, eds. *Une invention du diable? Cinéma des premiers temps et religion.* Lausanne: Editions Payot, 1992.

Costa, Antonio. "Da Caligari a Mussolini. Il viaggio di *Maciste all'inferno.*" In Canosa, *A nuova luce,* 285–292.

Cottino, Luca. "La novità di *Maciste alpino.*" *Italian Culture* 27, no. 1 (2009): 43–59.

Courtney, Susan. *Hollywood Fantasies of Miscegenation: Spectacular Narratives of Gender and Race, 1903–1967.* Princeton, NJ: Princeton University Press, 2005.

Cunsolo, Ronald S. *Italian Nationalism: From Its Origins to World War II.* Malabar, FL: Robert E. Krieger, 1990.

Curreri, Luciano. "Il Fuoco, i Libri, la Storia: Saggio su *Cartagine in fiamme* (1906) di Emilio Salgari." In *Cartagine in fiamme. Romanzo,* by Emilio Salgari, edited by Luciano Curreri, 315–403. Rome: Quiritta, 2001.

——. "Il mito culturale di Cartagine nel primo Novecento tra letterature e cinema." In Alovisio and Barbera, *Cabiria & Cabiria,* 299–307.

Curry, Ramona. "How Early German Film Stars Helped Sell the War(es)." In *Film and the First World War,* edited by Karel Dibbets and Bert Hogenkamp, 139–148. Amsterdam: Amsterdam University Press, 1995.

Curtis, Scott. "Douglas Fairbanks: Icon of Americanism." In Bean, *Flickers of Desire,* 218–241.

D'Amelio Maria Elena. *Ercole, il divo.* San Marino: AIEP, 2012.

D'Annunzio, Gabriele. "Del cinematografo considerato come uno strumento di liberazione e come arte di trasfigurazione." *Corriere della Sera* (18 February 1914). Reprinted in *Giovanni Pastrone: Gli anni d'oro del cinema a Torino,* edited by Paolo Cherchi Usai, 115–122. Turin: UTET, 1986. Reprinted in English as "On the Cinematograph as an Instrument of Liberation and an Art of Transfiguration [1914]," in *Early Cinema,* edited by Richard Abel; translated by Rhiannon Noel Welch, with Giorgio Bertellini, vol. 4, 267–272. New York: Routledge, 2013.

——. "Orazione per la sagra dei Mille. V maggio MDCCCLX–V maggio MCMXV." In *Per la più grande Italia. Orazioni e messaggi di Gabriele D'Annunzio,* edited by Sergio Fu-mich, 29–30. Brembio: Andreani, 2012.

——. *Prose di ricerca.* Vol. 1. Milan: Mondadori, 2005.

Dagna, Stella. "All'ombra del gigante. Le comprimarie della serie Maciste." In *Non solo dive. Pioniere del cinema italiano,* edited by Monica Dall'Asta, 297–303. Bologna: Cineteca di Bologna, 2008.

Dall'Asta, Monica. *Un cinéma musclé. Le surhomme dans le cinéma muet italien (1913–1926).* Crisnée: Yellow Now, 1992.

——. "La diffusione del film a episodi in Europa." In Brunetta, *Storia del cinema mondiale,* 1: 277–323.

——, ed. *Fantômas. La vita plurale di un antieroe.* Pozzuolo del Friuli: Il principe costante Edizioni, 2004.

——. "Italian Film Serials and (Inter) National-Popular Culture." In Bertellini, *Italian Silent Cinema,* 195–202.

——. "Il serial." In Brunetta, *Storia del cinema mondiale,* 2: 289–336.

Dalle Vacche, Angela. *The Body in the Mirror: Shapes of History in Italian Cinema.* Princeton, NJ: Princeton University Press, 1993.

——. *Diva: Defiance and Passion in Early Italian Cinema.* Austin: University of Texas Press, 2008.

Davis, Lon, and Debra Davis. *King of the Movies: Francis X. Bushman.* Albany, GA: BearManor Media, 2009.

De Berti, Raffaele. *Dallo schermo alla carta. Romanzi, fotoromanzi, rotocalchi cinematografici: il film e i suoi paratesti.* Milan: Vita e Pensiero, 2000.

——. "Il film d'avventura italiano tra Salgari e *Captain Blood.*" In *Schermi di regime. Cinema italiano degli anni trenta: la produzione e i generi*, edited by Alessandro Faccioli, 128–139. Venice: Marsilio, 2010.

——. "Milano Films: The Exemplary History of a Film Company in the 1910s." In Bertellini, *Italian Silent Cinema*, 113–122.

De Berti, Raffaele, and Marina Rossi. "Cinema e cultura popolare: i rotocalchi illustrati." In *Il cinema a Milano fra le due guerre*, edited by Francesco Casetti and Raffaele De Berti, special issue of *Comunicazioni Sociali* 10, no. 3–4 (1988): 222–54.

De Felice, Renzo. *Antologia sul fascismo*. Bari: Laterza, 1976.

——. *Fascism: An Informal Introduction to Its Theory and Practice*. Edited by Michael Ledeen. New Brunswick, NJ: Transaction Books, 1976.

——. *Mussolini il fascista*. 4 vols. Turin: Einaudi, 1965–1997.

De Felice, Renzo, and Luigi Goglia. *Mussolini il mito*. Bari: Laterza, 1983.

de Grand, Alexander. *Italian Fascism: Its Origins and Development*, 3rd ed. Lincoln: University of Nebraska Press, 2000.

de Grazia, Victoria. *The Culture of Consent: Mass Organization of Leisure in Fascist Italy*. Cambridge: Cambridge University Press, 1981.

——. *How Fascism Ruled Women, 1922–1943*. Berkeley: University of California Press, 1991.

DeBauche, Leslie Midkiff. *Reel Patriotism: The Movies and World War I*. Madison: University of Wisconsin Press, 1997.

——. "The United States' Film Industry and World War I." In Paris, *First World War and Popular Cinema*, 138–161.

deCordova, Richard. *Picture Personalities: The Emergence of the Star System in America*. Urbana: University of Illinois Press, 1990.

dell'Agnese, Elena. "Tu vuo' fa l'Americano: la costruzione della mascolinità nella geopolitica popolare italiana." In dell'Agnese and Ruspini, *Mascolinità all'italiana*, 3–34.

dell'Agnese, Elena, and Elisabetta Ruspini, eds. *Mascolinità all'italiana. Construzioni, narrazioni, mutamenti*. Turin: UTET, 2007.

Della Casa, Stefano. "Una postilla sul genere mitologico." In *Sull'industria cinematografica italiana*, edited by Enrico Magrelli, 171–179. Venice: Marsilio, 1986.

Della Colletta, Cristina. *World's Fairs Italian Style: The Great Exhibitions in Turin and Their Narratives, 1860–1915*. Toronto: University of Toronto Press, 2006.

Dickie, John. *Darkest Italy: The Nation and Stereotypes of the Mezzogiorno, 1860–1900*. New York: Palgrave Macmillan, 1999.

——. "La macchina da scrivere: The Victor Emmanuel Monument in Rome and Italian Nationalism." *Italianist* 13 (1994): 261–285.

Dogliani, Patrizia. "Sport and Fascism." *Journal of Modern Italian Studies* 5, no. 3 (2000): 326–348.

Doumanis, Nicholas. *Italy*. London: Arnold, 2001.

Dunnage, Jonathan. *Twentieth-Century Italy: A Social History*. London: Routledge, 2002.

Dwyer, Rachel. *Filming the Gods: Religion and Indian Cinema*. London: Routledge, 2006.

Dyer, Richard. *Heavenly Bodies: Film Stars and Society*. New York: St. Martin's, 1986.

———. *Stars*. 1979; rev. ed. London: BFI, 1998.

———. *White*. London: Routledge, 1997.

Eberwein, Robert. *Armed Forces: Masculinity and Sexuality in the American War Film*. New Brunswick, NJ: Rutgers University Press, 2007.

———, ed. *The War Film*. New Brunswick, NJ: Rutgers University Press, 2005.

Eksteins, Modris. *Rites of Spring: The Great War and the Birth of the Modern Age*. Boston: Houghton Mifflin, 1989.

Eley, Geoff. "Culture, Nation, Gender." In *Gendered Nations: Nationalisms and Gender Order in the Long Nineteenth Century*, edited by Ida Blom et al., 27–40. Oxford: Berg, 2000.

Erbaggio, Pierluigi. "Istituto Nazionale Luce: A National Company with an International Reach." In Bertellini, *Italian Silent Cinema*, 221–231.

Ercole, Pierluigi. "'Little Italy on the Brink': The Italian Diaspora and the Distribution of War Films in London, 1914–1918." In *Cinema, Audiences, and Modernity: New Perspectives on European Cinema History*, edited by Daniel Biltereyst, Richard Maltby, and Philippe Meers, 154–165. London: Routledge, 2011.

Ernst, Morris L., and Pare Lorentz. *Censored: The Private Life of the Movie*. New York: Cornwall Press, 1930.

Eugeni, Ruggero, and Dario E. Viganò, eds. *Attraverso lo schermo. Cinema e cultura cattolica in Italia*. Vol. 1, *Dalle origini agli anni Venti*. Rome: Ente dello Spettacolo, 2006.

Ezra, Elizabeth, and Terry Rowden. "General Introduction: What Is Transnational Cinema?" In *Transnational Cinema: The Film Reader*, edited by Elizabeth Ezra and Terry Rowden, 1–12. London: Routledge, 2006.

Fairbanks, Douglas. *Laugh and Live*. New York: Britton, 1917.

Falasca-Zamponi, Simonetta. *Fascist Spectacle: The Aesthetics of Power in Mussolini's Italy*. Berkeley: University of California Press, 1997.

———. "Peeking under the Black Shirt: Italian Fascism's Disembodied Bodies." In *Fashioning the Body Politic: Dress, Gender, Citizenship*, edited by Wendy Parkins, 145–166. Oxford: Berg, 2002.

Farassino, Alberto. "Anatomia del cinema muscolare." In Farassino and Sanguineti, *Gli uomini forti*, 29–51.

———. "Maciste e il paradigma divistico." In Bertetto and Rondolino, *Cabiria e il suo tempo*, 223–232.

Farassino, Alberto, and Tatti Sanguineti, eds. *Gli uomini forti*. Milan: Mazzotta, 1983.

Farinelli, Gian Luca, and Nicola Mazzanti. "Maciste torna all'inferno." In Canosa, *A nuova luce*, 293–295.

Fellini, Federico. "Amarcord Maciste." In Farassino and Sanguineti, *Gli uomini forti*, 182.

Finchelstein, Federico. *Transatlantic Fascism: Ideology, Violence, and the Sacred in Argentina and Italy, 1919–1945*. Durham, NC: Duke University Press, 2010.

Finer, Herman. *Mussolini's Italy.* New York: Henry Holt, 1965.

Finocchiaro Chimirri, Giovanna. *D'Annunzio e il cinema Cabiria.* Catania: CUECM, 1986.

Fiori, Giuseppe. *Antonio Gramsci: Life of a Revolutionary.* New York: E. P. Dutton, 1971.

Forgacs, David, ed. *Rethinking Italian Fascism: Capitalism, Populism, and Culture.* London: Lawrence and Wishart, 1986.

Forsyth, Douglas J. *The Crisis of Liberal Italy: Monetary and Financial Policy, 1914–1922.* Cambridge: Cambridge University Press, 1993.

Forth, Christopher E. *Masculinity in the Modern West: Gender, Civilization, and the Body.* New York: Palgrave Macmillan, 2008.

Franzina, Emilio. "Il tempo libero dalla guerra. Case del soldato e postriboli militari." In Leoni and Zadra, *La grande guerra,* 161–230.

Franzinelli, Mimmo. *Squadristi. Protagonisti e techniche della violenza fascista, 1919–1922.* Milan: Mondadori, 2003.

Friedemann, Alberto. *Le case di vetro. Stabilimenti cinematografici e teatri di posa a Torino.* Turin: Associazione F.E.R.T. 2002.

———. *Fert. Storia di un nome, due società e di tre stabilimenti.* Turin: Associazione F.E.R.T., 2008.

Gabbard, Glen, and Krin Gabbard. *Psychiatry and the Cinema,* 2nd ed. Washington, DC: American Psychiatric Press, 1999.

Gaines, Jane M. *Fire and Desire: Mixed-Race Movies in the Silent Era.* Chicago: University of Chicago Press, 2001.

Galt, Rosalind. "Italy's Landscapes of Loss: Historical Mourning and the Dialectical Image of *Cinema Paradiso, Mediterraneo,* and *Il Postino.*" *Screen* 43, no. 2 (2002): 158–173.

Garofalo, Piero. "Seeing Red: The Soviet Influence on Italian Cinema in the Thirties." In Reich and Garofalo, *Re-Viewing Fascism,* 223–249.

Gentile, Emilio. "Conflicting Modernisms: *La Voce* against Futurism." In Gentile, *Struggle for Modernity,* 27–40.

———. *La Grande Italia: The Rise and Fall of the Myth of the Nation in the Twentieth Century.* Translated by Suzanne Dingee and Jennifer Pudney. Madison: University of Wisconsin Press, 2008.

———. "Mussolini's Charisma." *Modern Italy* 3, no. 2 (1998): 219–235.

———. *The Origins of Fascist Ideology, 1918–1925.* New York: Enigma, 2005.

———. *Politics as Religion.* Translated by George Staunton. Princeton, NJ: Princeton University Press, 2006.

———. *The Sacralization of Politics in Fascist Italy.* Translated by Keith Botsford. Cambridge: Harvard University Press, 1996.

———. *The Struggle for Modernity: Nationalism, Futurism, and Fascism.* Westport, CT: Praeger, 2003.

Germani, Sergio Grmek. *Mario Camerini.* Florence: La Nuova Italia, 1980.

Gibelli, Antonio. *Il popolo bambino. Infanzia e nazione nella Grande Guerra a Salò.* Turin: Einaudi, 2005.

Gibson, Mary. *Born to Crime: Cesare Lombroso and the Origins of Biological*

Criminality. Westport, CT: Praeger, 2002.

Gili, Jean A. *André Deed. Boireau, Cretinetti, Gribouille, Toribio, Foolshead, Lehman.* Genoa: Edizioni Le Mani, 2005.

———. *Stato fascista e cinematografia. Repressione e promozione.* Rome: Bulzoni, 1981.

Ginex, Giovanna, ed. *Metlicovich, Dudovich. Grandi cartellonisti triestini. Manifesti dalla Raccolta "Achille Bertarelli" del Castello Sforzesco di Milano.* Milan: Skira, 2001.

Giordano, Michele. *Giganti buoni. Da Ercole a Piedone (e oltre) il mito dell'uomo forte nel cinema italiano.* Rome: Gremese, 1998.

Giuliani Caponetto, Rosetta. "'Going Out of Stock': Mulattoes and Levantines in Italian Literature and Cinema of the Fascist Period." PhD diss., University of Connecticut, 2008.

Gledhill, Christine, ed. *Stardom: Industry of Desire.* London: Routledge, 1991.

Golden, Eve. *Vernon and Irene Castle's Ragtime Revolution.* Lexington: University of Kentucky Press, 2007.

Gori, Gianfranco. *Patria diva. La storia d'Italia nei film del ventennio.* Florence: La casa Usher, 1989.

Gori, Gigliola. "Model of Masculinity: Mussolini, the 'New Italian' of the Fascist Era." *International Journal of the History of Sport* 16, no. 4 (1999): 27–61.

———. "Supermanism and the Culture of the Body in Italy: The Case of Futurism." *International Journal of the History of Sport* 16, no. 1 (1999): 159–165.

Grace, Pamela. *The Religious Film: Christianity and the Hagiopic.* Oxford: Wiley-Blackwell, 2009.

Greene, Shelleen. *Equivocal Subjects: Between Italy and Africa – Constructions of Racial and National Identity in the Italian Cinema.* New York: Continuum, 2012.

Grieveson, Lee. "Fighting Films: Race, Morality, and the Governing of Cinema, 1912–1915." *Cinema Journal* 38, no. 1 (1998): 40–72.

———. *Policing Cinema: Movies and Censorship in Early Twentieth-Century America.* Berkeley: University of California Press, 2004.

———. "The Work of Film in the Age of Fordist Mechanization." *Cinema Journal* 51, no. 3 (2012): 25–51.

Griffiths, C.E.J. "Italian Cinema in the Thirties: *Camicia nera* and Other Films by Giovacchino Forzano." *Italianist* 15 (1995): 299–321.

———. *The Theatrical Works of Giovacchino Forzano: Drama for Mussolini's Italy.* Lewiston, NY: Edwin Mellen, 2000.

Grifo, Marco. "Alla ricerca del cast perduto: la troupe di *Cabiria.*" In Aloviso and Barbera, *Cabiria & Cabiria,* 110–126.

———, ed. *Il Maggese Cinematografico.* Turin: Biblioteca FERT, 2005.

Gundle, Stephen. "The Death (and Rebirth) of the Hero: Charisma and Manufactured Charisma in Modern Italy." *Modern Italy* 3, no. 2 (1998): 173–189.

———. "Fame, Fashion, and Style: The Italian Star System." In *Italian Cultural Studies: An Introduction,* edited by David Forgacs and Robert Lumley, 309–326. Oxford: Oxford University Press, 1986.

———. "Film Stars and Society in Fascist Italy." In Reich and Garofalo, *Re-Viewing Fascism,* 315–339.

———. *Mussolini's Dream Factory: Film Stardom in Fascist Italy.* Providence, RI: Berghahn Books, 2013.

———. "Sophia Loren, Italian Icon." *Historical Journal of Film and Television* 15, no. 3 (1995): 367–385.

Gundle, Stephen, Christopher Duggan, and Giuliana Pieri, eds. *The Cult of the Duce: Mussolini and the Italians.* Manchester, UK: Manchester University Press, 2013.

Gundle, Stephen, and Lucy Riall. Introduction to the special issue on Charisma, *Modern Italy* 3, no. 2 (1998): 153–157.

Gunning, Tom. "An Aesthetics of Astonishment: Early Film and the (In)credulous Spectator." *Art & Text* 34 (Spring 1989): 31–45.

———. "The Cinema of Attractions: Early Film, Its Spectator, and the Avant-Garde." *Wide Angle* 8, no. 3–4 (1986): 63–70.

———. "Early Cinema as Global Cinema: The Encyclopedic Ambition." In Abel et al., *Early Cinema and the "National,"* 11–16.

———. "Tracing the Individual Body: Photography, Detectives, and Early Cinema." In Charney and Schwartz, *Cinema and the Invention of Modern Life,* 15–45.

———. "The Whole Town's Gawking: Early Cinema and the Visual Experience of Modernity." *Yale Journal of Criticism* 7, no. 2 (1994): 189–201.

Günsberg, Maggie. *Italian Cinema: Gender and Genre.* New York: Palgrave Macmillan, 2005.

Hake, Sabine. *German National Cinema.* London: Routledge, 2002.

Hall, Sara. "Trading Places: Dr. Mabuse and the Pleasure of Role Play." *German Quarterly* 76, no. 4 (2003): 381–397.

Hansen, Bernard. "D. W. Griffith, Some Sources." *Art Bulletin* 54, no. 4 (1972): 493–515.

Hansen, Miriam. "America, Paris, the Alps: Kracauer (and Benjamin) on Cinema and Modernity." In Charney and Schwartz, *Cinema and the Invention of Modern Life,* 362–402.

———. *Babel & Babylon: Spectatorship in American Silent Cinema.* Cambridge, MA: Harvard University Press, 1991.

———. "Decentric Perspectives: Kracauer's Early Writings on Film and Mass Culture." *New German Critique* 54 (Fall 1991): 47–76.

———. "Fallen Women, Rising Stars, New Horizons: Shanghai Silent Film as Vernacular Modernism." *Film Quarterly* 54, no. 1 (2000): 10–22.

Hay, James. *Popular Film Culture in Fascist Italy: The Passing of the Rex.* Bloomington: Indiana University Press, 1987.

Henke, Robert. *Performance and Literature in the Commedia dell'Arte.* Cambridge: Cambridge University Press, 2002.

High, Michael D. "Pirates without Piracy: Criminality, Rebellion, and Anarcho-Libertarianism in the Pirate Film." *Jump Cut: A Review of Contemporary Media* 56 (2014). http://

www.ejumpcut.org/trialsite/HighPirates/index.html.

Hirschman, Charles. "The Origins and Demise of the Concept of Race." *Population and Development Review* 30, no. 3 (2004): 385–415.

Horowitz, Daniel L. *The Italian Labor Movement.* Cambridge, MA: Harvard University Press, 1963.

Hudson, Dale. "'Just play yourself, "Maggie Cheung"': Irma Vep, Rethinking Transnational Stardom and Unthinking National Cinemas." *Screen* 47, no. 2 (2006): 213–232.

I grandi artisti del cinema: Maciste (Bartolomeo Pagano). Milan: Gloriosa Casa Editrice, 1926.

Iarlori, Stefania. "Immagini d'America. Rappresentazioni di Buffalo Bill e Cervo Bianco nella cultura italiana del primo '900." BA diss., University of Genova, 9 July 2008.

Isenberg, Michael T. *War on Film: The American Cinema and World War I, 1914–1941.* London: Associated University Presses, 1981.

Isnenghi, Mario. *La grande guerra.* 1993; Florence: Giunti Editore, 2000.

———. *Il mito della grande guerra.* Bologna: Il Mulino, 1989.

Jackson, Robert. *Sovereignty: Evolution of an Idea.* Cambridge, UK: Polity Press, 2007.

Jandelli, Cristina. *Breve storia del divismo cinematografico.* Venice: Marsilio, 2007.

———. *Le dive italiane del cinema muto.* Palermo: L'Epos, 2006.

———. "'Per quanto immagini, sono riusciti a farsi amare come persone vere.' Attori, recitazione e personaggi

in *Cabiria.*" In Alovisio and Barbera, *Cabiria & Cabiria,* 127–137.

Johnston, Robert K. *Reel Spirituality: Theology and Film in Dialogue,* 2nd ed. Grand Rapids, MI: Baker Academic, 2006.

Kasson, Joy S. *Buffalo Bill's Wild West: Celebrity, Memory, and Popular History.* New York: Hill & Wang, 2000.

Keegan, John. *The First World War.* New York: Alfred A. Knopf, 1999.

Keil, Charlie, and Ben Singer, eds. *American Cinema of the 1910s: Themes and Variations.* New Brunswick, NJ: Rutgers University Press, 2009.

Kelly, Andrew. *Cinema and the Great War.* London: Routledge, 1997.

Kern, Stephen. *The Culture of Time and Space, 1880–1918,* 2nd ed. Cambridge, MA: Harvard University Press, 2003.

Kerr, Catherine E. "Incorporating the Star: The Intersection of Business and Aesthetic Strategies in Early American Film." *Business History Review* 64, no. 3 (1990): 383–410.

Kimmel, Michael. "Consuming Manhood: The Feminization of American Culture and the Recreation of the American Male Body, 1832–1920." *Michigan Quarterly Review* 33, no. 1 (1994): 7–36.

King, Rob. *The Fun Factory: The Keystone Film Company and the Emergence of Mass Culture.* Berkeley: University of California Press, 2009.

Kirby, Lynne. *Parallel Tracks: The Railroad and Silent Cinema.* Durham, NC: Duke University Press, 1997.

Koon, Tracy H. *Believe, Obey, Fight: Political Socialization of Youth in Fascist Italy, 1922–1943.* Chapel Hill: University of North Carolina Press, 1985.

Koszarski, Richard. *An Evening's Entertainment: The Age of the Silent Feature Picture, 1915–1928*. Berkeley: University of California Press, 1990.

Lagny, Michèle. "Popular Taste. The Peplum." In *Popular European Cinema*, edited by Richard Dyer and Ginette Vincendeau, 163–180. London: Routledge, 1992.

Lahue, Kalton C. *Continued Next Week: A History of the Moving Picture Serial*. Norman: University of Oklahoma Press, 1964.

Landy, Marcia. *The Folklore of Consensus: Theatricality in Italian Cinema, 1930–1943*. Albany: State University of New York Press, 1998.

———. *Fascism in Film: The Italian Commercial Cinema, 1930–1944*. Princeton, NJ: Princeton University Press, 1986.

———. *Italian Film*. Cambridge: Cambridge University Press, 2000.

———. "Mario Camerini." *Encyclopedia of Italian Literary Studies*, edited by Gaetana Marrone, 351–353. New York: Routledge, 2007.

———. *Stardom Italian Style: Screen Performance and Personality in Italian Cinema*. Bloomington: Indiana University Press, 2008.

Lasi, Giovanni. "Italy's First Film Star: Asta Nielsen, 'Polaris.'" In *Importing Asta Nielsen: The International Film Star in the Making, 1910–1914*, edited by Martin Loiperdinger and Uli Jung, 234–246. New Barnet, UK: John Libbey, 2013.

———. "La ripresa di Roma/Recapturing Rome." In *1905. La presa di Roma. Alle origini del cinema italiano/Beginnings of Italian Cinema*, edited by Michele

Canosa, 41–114, 157–232. Recco, Genoa: Le Mani, 2006.

———. "Viva Tripoli italiana! Viva l'Italia! La propaganda bellica nei film a soggetto realizzati in Italia durante il conflitto italo-turco (1911–12)." *Immagine. Note di Storia del Cinema* no. 3 (2011): 104–119.

Lawner, Lynne. *Harlequin on the Moon: Commedia dell'Arte and the Visual Arts*. New York: Harry N. Abrams, 1998.

Leab, Daniel J. "Total War On-Screen: The Hun in U.S. Films, 1914–1920." In *"Huns" vs. "Corned Beef": Representations of the Other in American and German Literature and Film on World War I*, edited by Thomas F. Schneider and Hans Wagener, 153–184. Göttingen: V & R Unipress, 2007

Leoni, Diego, and Camillo Zadra, eds. *La grande guerra. Esperienza, memoria, immagini*. Bologna: Il Mulino, 1986.

Locatelli, Ludovico. "Come ai tempi di *Cabiria*." *La Fiera del Cinema* 2, no. 2 (1960): 12–15.

Loiperdinger, Martin, and Uli Jung, eds. *Importing Asta Nielsen: The International Film Star in the Making, 1910–1914*. New Barnet, UK: John Libbey, 2013.

Lombroso, Cesare. *Criminal Man*. Translated by Mary Gibson and Nicole Hahn Rafter. Durham, NC: Duke University Press, 2006.

Lott, Eric. *Love and Theft: Blackface Minstrelsy and the American Working Class*. New York: Oxford University Press, 1993.

Lotti, Denis. "Il divismo maschile nel cinema muto italiano. Protagonisti, film, stereotipi, 1910–1929." Tesi di Dottorato, Università degli Studi di Padova, 2011.

——. *Emilio Ghione, l'ultimo apache. Vita e film di un divo Italiano.* Bologna: Cineteca di Bologna, 2008.

——. "La guerra allusa. L'imperialismo nel cinema di finzione italiano tra propaganda e speranza (1909–12)." *Immagine. Note di Storia del Cinema* no. 3 (2011): 11–52.

Lucanio, Patrick. *With Fire and Sword: Italian Spectacle on American Screens, 1958–1968.* Metuchen, NJ: Scarecrow, 1994.

Lupano, Mario, and Alessandra Vaccari, eds. *Fashion at the Time of Fascism: Italian Modernist Lifestyle, 1922–1943.* Bologna: Damiani, 2009.

Lussu, Emilio. *Un anno sull'altipiano.* Milan: Mondadori, 1971.

Luzzatto, Sergio. *The Body of the Duce: Mussolini's Corpse and the Fortunes of Italy.* New York: Metropolitan Books, 2005.

——. *L'immagine del duce. Mussolini nelle fotografie dell'Istituto Luce.* Rome: Riuniti, 2001.

Lyden, John C. *Film as Religion: Myths, Morals, and Rituals.* New York: New York University Press, 2003.

Lyttelton, Adrian. Introduction to *Liberal and Fascist Italy, 1900–1945,* edited by Adrian Lyttelton, 1–16. Oxford: Oxford University Press, 2002.

——. *The Seizure of Power: Fascism in Italy, 1919–1929.* Rev. ed. London: Routledge, 2004.

Macciocchi, Maria Antonietta. *La donna nera. Consenso femminile e fascismo.* Milan: Feltrinelli, 1977.

Mack Smith, Denis. *Italy and Its Monarchy.* New Haven, CT: Yale University Press, 1989.

——. *Mussolini.* New York: Vintage, 1982.

Mancini, Elaine. *Struggles of the Italian Film Industry during Fascism, 1930–1935.* Ann Arbor: UMI Research Press, 1985.

Marchesini, Daniele. *L'Italia a quattro ruote. Storia dell'utilitaria.* Bologna: Il Mulino, 2012.

Marinetti, Filippo Tommaso. "Extended Man and the Kingdom of the Machine." In Berghaus, *F. T. Marinetti: Critical Writings,* 85–88.

——. "The Foundation and Manifesto of Futurism." In Berghaus, *F. T. Marinetti: Critical Writings,* 11–17.

——. "Futurism and the Great War." In Berghaus, *F. T. Marinetti: Critical Writings,* 245–246.

Marks, Martin Miller. *Music and the Silent Film: Contexts and Case Studies, 1895–1924.* New York: Oxford University Press, 1997.

Marsh, Clive, and Gaye Ortiz, eds. *Explorations in Theology and Film: Movies and Meaning.* Oxford: Blackwell, 1997.

Marshall, P. David. *Celebrity and Power: Fame in Contemporary Culture.* Minneapolis: University of Minnesota Press, 1997.

Martin, Simon. *Football and Fascism: The National Game under Mussolini.* Oxford, UK: Berg, 2004.

Martinelli, Vittorio. "Il cinema italiano in armi." In *Sperduto nel buio. Il cinema muto italiano e il suo tempo,* edited by Renzo Renzi, 35–42. Bologna: Cappelli, 1990.

——, ed. *Il cinema muto italiano. I film del dopoguerra/1919. Bianco & Nero* 41, no. 1–3 (January–June 1980).

——, ed. *Il cinema muto italiano. I film degli anni venti/1921–2. Bianco & Nero* 42, no. 1–3 (January–June 1981).

——, ed. *Il cinema muto italiano. I film degli anni venti/1923–1931. Bianco & Nero* 42, no. 4–6 (July–December 1981).

——, ed. *Il cinema muto italiano. I film del dopoguerra/1920. Bianco & Nero* 41, no. 4–6 (July–December 1980).

——, ed. *Il cinema muto italiano. I film della grande guerra/1915, prima parte. Bianco & Nero* 52, no. 1–2 (1991).

——, ed. *Il cinema muto italiano. I film della grande Guerra/ 1915, seconda parte. Bianco & Nero* 52 no. 3–4 (1991).

——, ed. *Il cinema muto italiano. I film della grande guerra/1916, prima parte. Bianco & Nero* 51, no. 1–2 (1990).

——, ed. *Il cinema muto italiano. I film della grande guerra/1916, seconda parte. Bianco & Nero* 51, no. 3–4 (1990).

——, ed. *Il cinema muto italiano. I film della grande guerra/1917. Bianco & Nero* 50, no. 3–4 (1989).

——, ed. *Il cinema muto italiano. I film della grande guerra/1918. Bianco & Nero* 50, no. 1–2 (1989).

——. "D'Annunzio." *Griffithiana* 21, no. 64 (1998): 26–49.

——. *Le dive del silenzio.* Bologna: Le Mani, 2001.

——. *L'eterna invasione. Il cinema americano degli anni Venti e la critica italiana.* Gemona: La Cineteca del Friuli, 2002.

——. "I Gastarbeiter fra le due guerre." *Bianco & Nero* 39, no. 3 (1978): 3–93.

——. "Lasciate fare a noi, siamo forti." In Farassino and Sanguineti, *Gli uomini forti,* 9–28.

——. "Nascita del divismo." In Brunetta, *Storia del cinema mondiale,* 1: 221–250.

Martinelli, Vittorio, and Mario Quargnolo. *Maciste & Co. I giganti buoni del muto italiano.* Gemona del Friuli: Cinepopolare Edizioni, 1981.

May, Lary. *Screening Out the Past: The Birth of Mass Culture and the Motion Picture Industry,* with a new preface. Chicago: University of Chicago Press, 1983.

Mazzanti, Nicola, and Gian Luca Farinelli. "Lo spazio scenico del balcone." In R. Renzi et al., *Il cinema dei dittatori,* 97–101.

McCarthy, Patrick. "Summary." Special feature on Sports and Society in Italy Today. *Journal of Modern Italian Studies* 5, no. 3 (2000): 322.

McDonald, Paul. *The Star System: Hollywood's Production of Popular Identities.* London: Wallflower, 2000.

McKernan, Luke. "Lo sport nel cinema muto." *Griffithiana* 64 (October 1998): 80–141.

Mecacci, Luciano. "Psicologia e psicoanalisi." In *La cultura italiana del Novecento,* edited by Corrado Stajano and Franca Angelini, 515–558. Bari: Laterza, 1996.

Menarini, Roy, and Paolo Noto. "Dall'economia di scala all'intertestualità di genere." In *L'arte del risparmio: stile e tecnologia,* edited by Giacomo Manzoli and Guglielmo Pescatore, 19–30. Rome: Carrocci, 2005.

Miller, Monica L. *Slaves to Fashion: Black Dandyism and the Styling of Black Diasporic Identity.* Durham, NC: Duke University Press, 2009.

Miller, Toby. "Stars and Performance." In *Film Theory: An Introduction,* edited by Robert Stam and Toby Miller, 595–602. Malden, MA: Blackwell: 2000.

Minguet Batllori, Joan M. *Segundo de Chomón. El cine de la fascinación.* Barcelona: Generalitat de Catalunya, Istitut Català de les Indústres Culturals, 2010.

Mira, Giovanni, and Luigi Salvatorelli. *Storia d'Italia nel periodo fascista,* 2 vols. Turin: Einaudi, 1970.

Mitchell, Jolyon. "Theology and Film." In *The Modern Theologians: An Introduction to Christian Theology since 1918,* 3rd ed., edited by David F. Ford and Rachel Muers, 736–759. London: Blackwell, 2005.

Miyao, Daisuke. "Sessue Hayakawa: The Mirror, the Racialized Body, and *Photogénie.*" In Bean, *Flickers of Desire,* 91–112.

———. *Sessue Hayakawa: Silent Cinema and Transnational Stardom.* Durham, NC: Duke University Press, 2007.

Monteleone, Renato, and Pino Sarasini. "I monumenti italiani ai caduti della grande guerra." In Leoni and Zadra, *La grande guerra,* 631–662.

Morin, Edgar. *The Stars.* Translated by Richard Howard. 1972; Minneapolis: University of Minnesota Press, 2005.

Mosconi, Elena. *L'impressione del film. Contributi per una storia culturale del cinema italiano, 1895–1945.* Milan: Vita & Pensiero, 2006.

———. "Un potente maestro per le folle. Chiesa e mondo cattolico di fronte al cinema." In *Attraverso lo schermo. Cinema e cultura cattolica in Italia.* Vol. 1, *Dalle origini agli anni Venti,* edited by Ruggero Eugeni and Dario E. Viganò, 145–171. Rome: Ente dello Spettacolo, 2006.

Mosse, George L. *Fallen Soldiers: Reshaping the Memory of the World Wars.* New York: Oxford University Press, 1990.

———. *The Image of Man: The Creation of Modern Masculinity.* New York: Oxford University Press, 1996.

———. *Nationalism and Sexuality: Middle-Class Morality and Sexual Norms in Modern Europe.* Madison: University of Wisconsin Press, 1985.

———. *Nationalism and Sexuality: Respectability and Abnormal Sexuality in Modern Europe.* New York: Howard Fertig, 1985.

———. "The Poet and the Exercise of Political Power: Gabriele D'Annunzio." In *Masses and Man: Nationalist and Fascist Perceptions of Reality,* 87–103. Detroit: Wayne State University Press, 1987.

Mostra internazionale del nuovo cinema. *Tra una film e l'altra. Materiali sul cinema muto italiano, 1907–1920.* Venice: Marsilio, 1980.

Muscio, Giuliana. *Piccole Italie, grandi schermi. Scambi cinematografici tra Italia e Stati Uniti, 1895–1945.* Rome: Bulzoni, 2004.

Musser, Charlie. "Moving Towards Fictional Narratives: Story Films Become the Dominant Product, 1903–4." In *The Silent Cinema Reader,* edited by Lee Grieveson and Peter

Krämer, 87–102. London: Routledge, 2004.

Mussolini, Benito. "Dalla neutralità assoluta alla neutralità attiva ed operante." *Avanti!* 18 (October 1914): 3.

Musumeci, Mario, and Sergio Toffetti, eds. *Da La presa di Roma a Il piccolo garibaldino. Risorgimento, Massoneria e instituzioni:l'immagine della nazione nel cinema muto (1905–1909)*. Rome: Gangemi, 2007.

Neale, Steven. "War Films." In Slocum, *Hollywood and War*, 23–30.

Nelis, Jan. "Constructing Fascist Identity: Benito Mussolini and the Myth of Romanità." *Classical World* 100, no. 4 (2007): 391–415.

Niceforo, Alfredo. *L'Italia barbara contemporanea*. Milan: Remo Sandron, 1898.

Nicoll, Allardyce. *The World of Harlequin: A Critical Study of the Commedia dell'Arte*. Cambridge: Cambridge University Press, 1963.

Nietzsche, Friedrich. *Thus Spoke Zarathustra: A Book for All and None*. Edited by Adrian Del Caro and Robert Pippin. Translated by Adrian del Caro. Cambridge, UK: Cambridge University Press, 2006.

Nisbet, Gideon. *Ancient Greece in Film and Popular Culture*. Exeter, UK: Bristol Phoenix Press, 2008.

Noakes, Susan J. "Medieval Texts and National Identities: Dante in Red, White, Green: Then Black." *Journal of the Midwest Modern Language Association* 40, no. 1 (2007): 11–24.

Nobili Vitelleschi, Giovanni. "The Representation of the Great War in Italian Cinema." In Paris, *First World War and Popular Cinema*, 162–171.

Nolan, Steve. *Film, Lacan, and the Subject of Religion: A Psychoanalytic Approach to Religious Film Analysis*. New York: Continuum, 2009.

Nosenzo, Simona. *Manuale tecnico per visionari. Segundo de Chomón in Italia, 1912–1925*. Turin: Associazione F.E.R.T, 2007.

Nowell-Smith, Goeffrey. "The Italian Cinema under Fascism." In *Rethinking Italian Fascism*, edited by David Forgacs, 142–161. London: Lawrence and Wishart, 1986.

O'Rourke, Chris. "How to Become a Bioscope Model: Transition, Mediation, and the Language of Film Performance." *Early Popular Visual Culture* 9, no. 3 (2011): 191–201.

Ojetti, Ugo. *D'Annunzio amico, maestro, soldato, 1894–1944*. Florence: Sansoni, 1951.

Ostwalt, Conrad. *Secular Steeples: Popular Culture and the Religious Imagination*. Harrisburg, PA: Trinity Press International, 2003.

Pacini, Nicoletta. "La promozione di Cabiria: i manifesti e le brochure." In Alovisio and Barbera, *Cabiria & Cabiria*, 210–223.

Palmer, R. Barton, ed. *Larger than Life: Movie Stars of the 1950s*. New Brunswick, NJ: Rutgers University Press, 2010.

Paolini, Federico. *Storia sociale dell'automobile in Italia*. Rome: Carocci, 2007.

Papini, Giovanni. *Maschilità*. Florence: Libreria della Voce, 1919.

Paris, Michael, ed. *The First World War and Popular Cinema: 1914 to the Present*. New Brunswick, NJ: Rutgers University Press, 2000.

Park, Roberta J. "Muscles, Symmetry, and Action: 'Do You Measure Up?' Defining Masculinity in Britain and America from the 1860s to the Early 1900s." *International Journal of the History of Sport* 22, no. 3 (2005): 365–395.

Passerini, Luisa. *Mussolini immaginario. Storia di una biografia, 1915–1939.* Rome: Laterza, 1991.

Pastore, Alessandro. "La patria, la guerra e la montagna. Identità nazionali e conflitti politici nella rete associativa dell'alpinismo italiano (1913–1927)." In *Alla conquista dell'immaginario. L'alpinismo come proiezione di modelli culturali e sociali borghesi tra Otto e Novecento,* edited by Michael Wedekind and Claudio Ambrosi, 143–167. Treviso: Edizioni Antilia, 2007.

Pastrone, Giovanni. *Cabiria. Visione storica del III secolo a. C. Didascalie di Gabriele D'Annunzio.* Edited by Roberto Radicati and Ruggero Rossi. Introduction by Maria Adriana Prolo. Turin: Museo Nazionale del Cinema, 1977.

Patriarca, Silvana. *Italian Vices: Nation and Character from the Risorgimento to the Republic.* Cambridge: Cambridge University Press, 2010.

Payne, Stanley G. Foreword to Gentile, *Struggle for Modernity,* ix–xix.

Petro, Patrice, ed. *Idols of Modernity: Movie Stars of the 1920s.* New Brunswick, NJ: Rutgers University Press, 2010.

——. *Joyless Streets: Women and Melodramatic Representation in Weimar Germany.* Princeton, NJ: Princeton University Press, 1989.

Pezzetti Tonion, Fabio. "Corpo della visione, corpo della narrazione: Maciste in *Cabiria.*" In Alovisio and Barbera, *Cabiria & Cabiria,* 138–145.

Pickering-Iazzi, Robin. "Ways of Looking in Black and White: Female Spectatorship and the Miscege-national Body in *Sotto la croce del sud.*" In Reich and Garofalo, *Re-Viewing Fascism,* 194–221.

Piga, Francesco. *Il mito del superuomo in Nietzsche e D'Annunzio.* Florence: Nuovedizioni Vallecchi, 1979.

Pinkus, Karen. *Bodily Regimes: Italian Advertising under Fascism.* Minneapolis: University of Minnesota Press, 1995.

Pitassio, Francesco. *Attore/divo.* Milan: Il Castoro, 2003.

——. "I cinegiornali Luce e la creazione del 'divo' Mussolini." In *Storia del cinema italiano,* edited by Leonardo Quaresima. Vol. 4, *1924–1933.* Venice: Marsilio, forthcoming.

——. "Famous Actors, Famous Actresses: Notes on Silent Acting Style in Italian Silent Films." In Bertellini, *Italian Silent Cinema,* 255–262.

——. *Ombre silenziose. Teoria dell'attore cinematografico negli anni venti.* Udine: Campanotto, 2002.

Pitassio, Francesco, and Leonardo Quaresima, eds. *Scrittura e immagine. La didascalia nel cinema muto/Writing and Image: Titles in Silent Cinema.* Udine: Forum, 1998.

Poggi, Christine. "Dreams of Metalized Flesh: Futurism and the Masculine Body." *Modernism/Modernity* 4, no. 3 (1997): 19–43.

——. *Inventing Futurism: The Art and Politics of Artificial Optimism.* Princeton, NJ: Princeton University Press, 2009.

Presner, Todd Samuel. "'Clear Heads, Solid Stomachs, and Hard Muscles': Max Nordau and the Aesthetics of Jewish Regeneration." In *Modernism/Modernity* 10, no. 3 (2003): 269–296.

Procacci, Giovanna. "A 'Latecomer' in War: The Case of Italy." In *Authority, Identity, and the Social History of the Great War*, edited by Frans Coetzee and Marilyn Shevin-Coetzee. Providence, RI: Berghahn, 1995.

Prolo, Maria Adriana. "Francesi nel cinema italiano muto." *Bianco & Nero* 14, no. 8–9 (1953): 69–74.

Putney, Clifford. *Muscular Christianity: Manhood and Sports in Protestant America, 1880–1920*. Cambridge, MA: Harvard University Press, 2001.

Quaglietti, Lorenzo. *Storia economico-politica del cinema italiano, 1945–1980*. Rome: Riuniti, 1980.

Raffaelli, Sergio. *Cinema film regia*. Saggi per una storia linguistica del cinema italiano. Rome: Bulzoni, 1978.

———. *L'italiano nel cinema muto*. Florence: Franco Cesati Editore, 2003.

———. "Quando il cinema era mobile." *La Ricerca Folklorica* 19 (April 1989): 103–112.

Rainey, Buck. *Serials and Series: A World Filmography, 1912–1956*. Jefferson, NC: McFarland, 1999.

Re, Lucia. "Italians and the Invention of Race: The Poetics and Politics of Difference in the Struggle over Libya, 1890–1913." *California Italian Studies Journal* 1, no. 1 (2010): 1–58.

Redi, Riccardo, ed. *Cinema italiano sotto il fascismo*. Venice: Marsilio, 1979.

———. *Cinema muto italiano (1896–1930)*. Rome: Biblioteca di Bianco & Nero, 1999.

———. *Il Christus di Giulio Antamoro e di Enrico Guazzoni*. Rome: Associazione Italiana per le Ricerche di Storia del Cinema, 2002.

———. *Film stranieri sugli schermi italiani*. Vol. 1, *1896–1911*. Naples: Giannini, 2003.

Reich, Jacqueline. *Beyond the Latin Lover: Marcello Mastroianni, Masculinity, and Italian Cinema*. Bloomington: Indiana University Press, 2004.

———. "Consuming Ideologies: Fascism, Commodification, and Female Subjectivity in Mario Camerini's *Grandi Magazzini*." *Annali d'Italianistica* 16 (1998): 195–212.

———. "Italian Cinema of the 1920s." In Bertellini, *Italian Silent Cinema*, 135–142.

———. "Mussolini at the Movies: Fascism, Film, and Culture." In Reich and Garofalo, *Re-Viewing Fascism*, 3–29.

———. "Rudolph Valentino, uomo forte." In *Rodolfo Valentino: Cinema, Cultura, Società tra Italia e USA negli Anni Venti*, edited by Silvio Alovisio and Giulia Carluccio, 308–324. Turin: Università di Torino-Kaplan, 2012.

———. "Slave to Fashion: Masculinity, Suits, and the Maciste Films of Italian Silent Cinema." In *Fashion in Film*, edited by Adrienne Munich, 236–259. Bloomington: Indiana University Press, 2011.

———. "Stardom in Italian Silent Cinema." In *The Companion to Italian Cinema*, edited by Frank Burke. Boston: Wiley-Blackwell, forthcoming.

———. "'The World's Most Perfectly Developed Man: Charles Atlas, Physical Culture, and the Inscription of American Masculinity." *Men & Masculinities* 12, no. 2 (June 2010): 444–461.

Reich Jacqueline, and Piero Garofalo, eds. *Re-Viewing Fascism: Italian Cinema, 1922–1943.* Bloomington: Indiana University Press: 2002.

Reinhartz, Adele. *Jesus of Hollywood.* Oxford: Oxford University Press, 2007.

Renzi, Renzo. "Il detto e il non detto." In *Sperduto nel buio. Il cinema muto italiano e il suo tempo,* edited by Renzo Renzi, 9. Bologna: Cappelli, 1990.

———. *Il fascismo involontario e altri scritti.* Bologna: Cappelli, 1975.

Renzi, Renzo, ed. with Gian Luca Farinelli and Nicola Mazzanti. *Il cinema dei dittatori. Mussolini, Stalin, Hitler.* Bologna: Gradis, 1992.

———. *Il cinematografo al campo. L'arma nuova nel primo conflitto mondiale.* Ancona: Transeuropa, 1993.

Renzi, William A. "Italy's Neutrality and Entrance into the Great War: A Re-examination." *American Historical Review* 73, no. 5 (1968): 1414–1432.

Répaci, Antonino. *Da Sarajevo al "maggio radioso": l'Italia verso la prima guerra mondiale.* Milan: Mursia, 1985.

Rewarld, Sabine, Ian Buruma, and Mattias Eberle, eds. *Glitter and Doom: German Portraits from the 1920s.* New Haven, CT: Yale University Press, 2006.

Riall, Lucy. *Garibaldi: Invention of a Hero.* New Haven, CT: Yale University Press, 2007.

Ricci, Steven. *Cinema & Fascism: Italian Film and Society, 1922–1943.* Berkeley: University of California Press, 2008.

Robinson, Cedric J. *Forgeries of Memory and Meaning: Blacks and Regimes of Race in American Theater & Film before World War II.* Chapel Hill: University of North Carolina Press, 2007.

Rogowski, Christian. "Movies, Money, and Mystique: Joe May's Early Weimar Blockbuster, *The Indian Tomb* (1921)." In *Weimar Cinema: An Essential Guide to Classic Films of the Era,* edited by Noah Isenberg, 55–78. New York: Columbia University Press, 2009.

Rondolino, Gianni. "'Affatica meno e rende di più.' Il cinema muto a Torino." In Bertetto and Rondolino, *Cabiria e il suo tempo,* 19–30.

———. "Il cinema torinese nei primi anni Dieci." In Alovisio and Barbera, *Cabiria & Cabiria,* 274–284.

———. *I giorni di Cabiria.* Turin: Lindau, 1993.

———. "Gli impacchi taumaturgici dei miti di celluloide." In *Gabriele D'Annunzio: Grandezza e delirio nell'industria dello spettacolo.* Atti del Convegno Internazionale Torino, 21–23 marzo 1988, 213–228. Genoa: Costa & Nolan, 1989.

———. *Torino come Hollywood.* Bologna: Cappelli, 1980. Republished as *I giorni di Cabiria.* Turin: Lindau, 1993.

Row, Thomas. "Mobilizing the Nation: Italian Propaganda and the Great War." *Journal of Decorative Propaganda Arts* 24 (2002): 140–169.

Rushing, Robert. "Gentlemen Prefer Hercules: Desire/Identification/

Beefcake." *Camera Obscura* 23, no. 3 (2008): 158–191.

Rydell, Robert W., and Rob Kroes. *Buffalo Bill in Bologna: The Americanization of the World, 1869–1922.* Chicago: University of Chicago Press, 2005.

Sabbatucci, Giovanni. *I combattenti nel primo dopoguerra.* Rome: Laterza, 1974.

Sachs, Harvey. *Music in Fascist Italy.* New York: W. W. Norton, 1987.

Sadoul, George. "A colloquio con Giovanni Pastrone." *Centrofilm* 2, no. 14 (1960): 5–13.

Salotti, Marco. "1957–1964: l'industria cinematografica italiana gonfia i muscoli." In *Sull'industria cinematografica italiana,* edited by Enrico Magrelli, 145–149. Venice: Marsilio, 1986.

———. "Un intervista con il figlio de maciste." In Farassino and Sanguineti, *Gli uomini forti,* 182–184.

Saracinelli, Marisa, and Nilde Totti. *L'Italia del Duce. L'informazione, la scuola, il costume.* Rimini: Panozzo, 1983.

Sarti, Roland, ed. *The Ax Within: Italian Fascism in Action.* New York: New Viewpoints, 1974.

Scaglione, Massimo. "Il cinema a Torino. Pochi divi ma tanti comprimari." In Bracco et al., *Torino città del cinema,* 45–56.

Schenk, Irmbert. "The Cinematic Support to National(istic) Mythology: The Italian Peplum, 1910–1930." In *Globalization, Cultural Identities, and Media Representations,* edited by Natascha Gentz and Stefan Kramer, 153–168. Albany: State University of New York Press, 2006.

———. "Il 'peplum' italiano. Perché il film storico-monumentale fu 'inventato' in Italia, ovvero: Da Cabiria a Mussolini." *Fotogenia* 4/5 (1997/1998): 59–72.

Schrader, Paul. *Transcendental Style in Film: Ozu, Bresson, Dreyer.* Berkeley: University of California Press, 1972.

Schumacher, Thomas. *The Danteum: A Study in the Architecture of Literature.* Princeton, NJ: Princeton Architectural Press, 1985.

Schwarz, Angelo. "Le fotografie e la grande guerra rappresentata." In Leoni and Zadra, *La grande guerra,* 745–764.

Sergi, Giuseppe. *The Mediterranean Race: A Study of the Origin of European Peoples.* New York: Charles Scribner's Sons, 1909.

Singer, Ben. *Melodrama and Modernity: Early Sensational Cinema and Its Contexts.* New York: Columbia University Press, 2001.

———. "Serials." In *Encyclopedia of Early Cinema,* edited by Richard Abel, 582–583. New York: Routledge, 2005.

Slocum, J. David. "General Introduction: Seeing through American War Cinema." In Slocum, *Hollywood and War,* 1–21.

———. *Hollywood and War: The Film Reader,* edited by J. David Slocum. London: Routledge, 2006.

Snowden, Frank M., Jr. *Before Color Prejudice: The Ancient View of Blacks.* Cambridge, MA: Harvard University Press, 1983.

Socci, Stefano. *L'ombra scura della religione.* Fiesole: Cadmo, 2002.

Solomon, Jon. *The Ancient World in Cinema*. Rev. and exp. ed. New Haven, CT: Yale University Press, 2001.

Solomon, Matthew. *Disappearing Tricks: Silent Film, Houdini, and the New Magic of the Twentieth Century*. Urbana: University of Illinois Press, 2010.

Sonnessa, Antonio. "The 1922 Turin Massacre (Strage di Torino): Working-Class Resistance and Conflicts within Fascism." *Modern Italy* 10, no. 2 (2005): 187–205.

Sòrgoni, Barbara. *Parole e corpi. Antropologia, discorso giuridico e politiche sessuali interrazziali nella colonia Eritrea (1890–1941)*. Naples: Liguori Editore, 1998.

Sorlin, Pierre. "1914–1918: la guerra invisibile." In *I limiti della rappresentazione*, edited by Leonardo Quaresima, Alessandra Raengo, and Laura Vichi, 153–162. Udine: Forum, 2000.

———. "Cinema and the Memory of the Great War." In Paris, *First World War and Popular Cinema*, 5–26.

———. *Italian National Cinema, 1896–1996*. London: Routledge, 1996.

Spackman, Barbara. *Fascist Virilities: Rhetoric, Ideology, and Social Fantasy in Italy*. Minneapolis: University of Minnesota Press, 1996.

———. "Shopping for Autarchy: Fascism and Reproductive Fantasy in Mario Camerini's *Grandi magazzini*." In Reich and Garofalo, *Re-Viewing Fascism*, 276–292.

Spinazzola, Vittorio. *Cinema e pubblico: lo spettacolo filmico in Italia, 1945–1965*. Rome: Bulzoni, 1985.

Staiger, Janet. *Bad Women: Regulating Sexuality in Early American Cinema*. Minneapolis: University of Minnesota Press, 1995.

———. *Interpreting Films: Studies in the Historical Reception of American Cinema*. Princeton, NJ: Princeton University Press, 1992.

———. *Perverse Spectators: The Practices of Film Reception*. New York: New York University Press, 2000.

Stamp, Shelley. *Movie-Struck Girls: Women and Motion Picture Culture after the Nickelodeon*. Princeton, NJ: Princeton University Press, 2000.

Steadman, Raymond W. *The Serials: Suspense and Drama by Installment*. Norman: University of Oklahoma Press, 1977.

Steimatsky, Noa. *Italian Locations: Re-inhabiting the Past in Postwar Cinema*. Minneapolis: University of Minnesota Press, 2008.

Sternhell, Zeev. *The Birth of Fascist Ideology: From Cultural Rebellion to Political Revolution*. With Mario Snajder and Maia Asheri. Translated by David Maisel. Princeton, NJ: Princeton University Press, 1994.

Stewart-Steinberg, Suzanne. *The Pinocchio Effect: On Making Italians (1860–1920)*. Chicago: University of Chicago Press, 2007.

Stiasny, Philipp. "Humanity Unleashed: Anti-Bolshevism as Popular Culture in Early Weimar Cinema." In *The Many Faces of Weimar Cinema: Rediscovering Germany's Legacy*, edited by Christian Rogowski, 67–83. Rochester, NY: Camden House, 2010.

Stocking, George. "The Turn-of-the-Century Concept of Race." *Modernism/Modernity* 1, no. 1 (1994): 4–16.

Stone, Marla. "A Flexible Rome: Fascism and the Cult of Romanità." In *Roman Presences: Receptions of Rome in European Culture 1789–1945*, edited by Catherine Edwards, 205–220. Cambridge, UK: Cambridge University Press, 2007.

Strauven, Wanda. "From 'Primitive Cinema' to 'Marvelous.'" In *The Cinema of Attractions Reloaded*, edited by Wanda Strauven, 105–120. Amsterdam: Amsterdam University Press, 1999.

Streible, Dan. *Fight Pictures: A History of Boxing and Early Cinema*. Berkeley: University of California Press, 2008.

Studlar, Gaylyn. *Precocious Charms: Stars Performing Girlhood in Classical Hollywood Cinema*. Berkeley: University of California Press, 2013.

——. "Theda Bara: Orientalism, Sexual Anarchy, and the Jewish Star." In Bean, *Flickers of Desire*, 113–136.

——. *This Mad Masquerade: Stardom and Masculinity in the Jazz Age*. New York: Columbia University Press, 1996.

Sturani, Enrico. "Analysing Mussolini's Postcards." *Modern Italy* 12, no. 2 (2013): 141–156.

——. *Cartoline. L'arte alla prova della cartolina*. Manduria (Taranto): Barbieri Editore, 2010.

——. *Le cartoline del Duce*. Turin: Edizioni del Capricorno, 2003.

——. *Otto milioni di cartoline per il Duce*. Turin: Centro Scientifico Editore, 1995.

Susmel, Edoardo, and Duilio Susmel, eds. *Opera Omnia di Benito Mussolini*. 35 vols. Florence: La Fenice, 1951–1962.

Suzzi Valli, Roberta. "The Myth of Squadrismo in the Fascist Regime." *Journal of Contemporary History* 35, no. 2 (2000): 131–150.

Thompson, Mark. *The White War: Life and Death on the Italian Front, 1915–1919*. New York: Basic Books, 2008.

Torres dos Santos, Danúsia. "L'immigrazione italiana a Rio de Janeiro: tracce storiche." www.emigrazione-notizie.org/download.asp?dl=77.

Toulet, Emmanuelle. "Il cinema muto italiano e la critica francese." In *Cinema italiano in Europa, 1907–1929*, edited by Vittorio Martinelli, 11–36. Rome: Associazione Italiana per le Ricerche di Storia del Cinema, 1992.

Turconi, Davide. "G. P. & D.W.G: Il dare e l'avere." In *Pastrone e Griffith. L'ipotesi di una storia*, edited by Guido Cincotti, 33–39. Rome: Bianco e Nero, 1975.

——. "Stuzzichini: *Maciste Liberatore.*" *Immagine. Note di Storia del Cinema* no. 3 (Summer 1986): 27–29.

Valentini, Paola. *Presenze sonore. Il passaggio al sonoro in Italia tra cinema e radio*. Florence: Le lettere, 2007.

Valperga, Giuseppe. "Mitologie popolari dell'uomo forte." In Farassino and Sanguineti, *Gli uomini forti*, 67–70.

Vance, Jeffrey, and Tony Maietta. *Douglas Fairbanks*. Berkeley: University of California Press, 2008.

Ventrone, Angelo. *La seduzione totalitaria. Guerra, modernità, violenza politica (1914–1918)*. Rome: Donzelli, 2003.

Verdone, Mario. "Il film atletico e acrobatico." *Centrofilm* 17 (1971): 3–36.

Visser, Romke. "Fascist Doctrine and the Cult of Romanità." *Journal of Contemporary History* 27, no. 1 (1922): 5–22.

Ward, Larry Wayne. *The Motion Picture Goes to War: The U.S. Government Film Effort during World War I.* Ann Arbor, MI: UMI Research Press, 1985.

Ward, Pete. *Gods Behaving Badly: Media, Religion, and Celebrity Culture.* Waco, TX: Baylor University Press, 2011.

Waters, Hazel. *Racism on the Victorian Stage: Representation of Slavery and the Black Character.* Cambridge: Cambridge University Press, 2009.

Waugh, Thomas. *Hard to Imagine: Gay Male Eroticism in Photography and Film from Their Beginnings to Stonewall.* New York: Columbia University Press, 1996.

——. "Strength and Stealth: Watching (and Wanting) Turn-of-the-Century Strongmen." *Canadian Journal of Film Studies/Revue Canadienne d'ètudes Cinématographiques* 2, no. 2 (1992): 1–20.

Webb, Barbara L. "The Black Dandyism of George Walker: A Case Study in Genealogical Method." *TDR/The Drama Review* 45, no. 4 (2001): 7–24.

Welle, John P. "The Cinema Arrives in Italy: City, Region, and Nation in Early Film Discourse." In Abel et al., *Early Cinema and the "National,"* 164–171.

——. "Dante in the Cinematic Mode: An Historical Survey of Dante Movies." In *Dante's Inferno: The Indiana Critical Edition,* translated and edited by Mark Musa, 381–395. Bloomington: Indiana University Press, 1995.

——. "Dante's Inferno of 1911 and the Origins of Italian Film Culture." In *Dante, Cinema, and Television,* edited by Amilcare Iannucci, 21–50. Toronto: University of Toronto Press, 2004.

Welsh, James M. "The Great War and the War Film as Genre: *Hearts of the World* and *What Price Glory?*" In *Hollywood's World War I: Motion Picture Images,* edited by Peter C. Rollins and John E. O'Connor, 27–38. Bowling Green, OH: Bowling Green State University Press, 1997.

Whissel, Kristen. *Picturing American Modernity: Traffic, Technology, and the Silent Cinema.* Durham, NC: Duke University Press, 2008.

——. "Transportation." In *Encyclopedia of Early Cinema,* edited by Richard Abel, 925–927. New York: Routledge, 2005.

Wilcox, Vanda. "From Heroic Defeat to Mutilated Victory: The Myth of Caporetto in Fascist Italy." In *Defeat and Memory: Cultural Histories of Military Defeat in the Modern Era,* edited by Jenny Macleod. New York: Palgrave Macmillan, 2008.

Winter, Jay. *Sites of Memory, Sites of Mourning: The Great War in European Cultural History.* Cambridge: Cambridge University Press, 1995.

Wirsching, Andreas. "Political Violence in France and Italy after 1918." *Journal of Modern European History* 1, no. 1 (2003): 60–79.

Wojcik, Pamela Robertson, ed. *New Constellations: Movie Stars of the*

1960s. New Brunswick, NJ: Rutgers University Press, 2012.

Wood, Mary. *Italian Cinema*. London: Berg, 2005.

Wright, Melanie J. *Religion and Film: An Introduction*. London: I. B. Taurus, 2007.

Wyke, Maria. "Herculean Muscle!: The Classicizing Rhethoric of Bodybuilding." *Arion* 4, no. 3 (1997): 51–79.

——. *Projecting the Past: Ancient Rome, Cinema, and History*. London: Routledge, 1997.

Index

JACQUELINE REICH is Professor and Chair of the Department of Communication and Media Studies at Fordham University. She is the author of *Beyond the Latin Lover: Marcello Mastroianni, Masculinity, and Italian Cinema* (Bloomington: Indiana University Press, 2004), and co-editor of *Re-viewing Fascism: Italian Cinema, 1922–1943* (Bloomington: Indiana University Press, 2002). She also curates the book series New Directions in National Cinemas for Indiana University Press.